The Energy
Conservation
Papers

A Report to the Energy Policy Project of the Ford Foundation

The Energy Conservation Papers

Robert H. Williams, Editor
Energy Policy Project

Ballinger Publishing Company ● **Cambridge, Mass.**
A Subsidiary of J.B. Lippincott Company

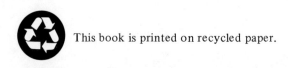 This book is printed on recycled paper.

Published in the United States of America by Ballinger Publishing Company,
Cambridge, Mass.

First Printing, 1975

Library of Congress Catalog Card Number: 74–32304

International Standard Book Number: 0–88410–335–8 HB
0–88410–336–6 PB

Printed in the United States of America

Library of Congress Cataloging in Publication Data

Williams, Robert H 1940–   comp.
  The energy conservation papers.

    CONTENTS: Fels, M.F. and Munson, M.J. Energy thrift in urban transporta-
tion: option for the future.–Hannon, B. et al. Energy, employment, and dollar
impacts of alternative transportation options. [etc.]
    1. Energy conservation–United States. I. Title.
TJ163.4.U6W54   333.7   74–32304
ISBN 0–88410–335–8 H.B.
      0–88410–336–6 Pbk

Table of Contents

List of Figures

List of Tables

Preface

The Energy Policy Project was initiated by the Ford Foundation in 1971 to explore alternative national energy policies. The papers collected in this book are among a series of special studies commissioned by the Project which can, I believe, make a contribution to today's public discussion of energy policies.

At the most, however, each special report deals with only part of the energy puzzle. The Project's own final report, *A Time to Choose: America's Energy Future,* attempts to integrate these parts into a comprehensible whole, setting forth our analysis, conclusions and recommendations for the nation's energy future.

This book, like the others in the series, has been reviewed by scholars and experts in the field not otherwise associated with the Project, in order to be sure that differing points of view were considered. With each book in the series, we offer reviewers the opportunity of having their comments published, but none have chosen to do so.

The Energy Conservation Papers are the authors' reports to the Ford Foundation's Energy Policy Project, and neither the Foundation nor the Project's Advisory Board has assumed the role of endorsing the studies' contents or conclusions. The Energy Policy Project expresses its views in *A Time to Choose* and Robert H. Williams' introduction to this volume.

S. David Freeman
Director
Energy Policy Project

Chapter One

Introduction

Robert H. Williams
Energy Policy Project

In its final report, *A Time to Choose*, the Energy Policy Project (EPP) concludes that the nation's best approach to balancing its energy budget, safeguarding the environment, and protecting the independence of its foreign policy is to cut back growth in energy consumption, through policies that encourage more efficient use of energy. In this volume we bring together several papers on energy conservation stemming from research sponsored by the Project. The papers we include here were especially helpful to the EPP staff in its efforts to formulate a coherent set of energy conservation policies. We believe they provide fresh facts and new insights into their subjects and should be widely available to policy-makers and concerned citizens.

Each chapter in this book deals with a specific aspect of energy conservation. A comprehensive account of the whole subject is presented in the Project's final report, which draws on these papers, other Project studies, and a growing body of outside literature.

In commissioning research on energy conservation, the Project staff kept these considerations in mind: What are the major opportunities for saving energy? What are the institutional obstacles to achieving these savings, and what policies appear most suitable for overcoming them? Are these policies compatible with other important social goals?

The best opportunities for saving energy are to be found where most energy is used—that is, in heating and cooling buildings of all kinds; in transportation, especially in the private automobile; and in the use of industrial process heat, both process steam and direct heat. These areas, which account for about three-quarters of all energy consumption, were the subjects of several of the Project's research efforts.

While the energy-saving potential in buildings and in transportation has been studied a great deal, very little work has been done so far on finding ways to conserve energy in industry, where 40 percent of total energy use takes place. The Project therefore put particular emphasis on industrial energy use, and published two studies on the subject in 1974. *Energy Consumption in Manufacturing* surveyed the six energy-intensive industries that consume nearly four-fifths of all the energy used in manufacturing, and estimated the energy savings that industry is likely to achieve by 1980. The study concluded that in response to rising prices, industry will probably pursue energy conservation measures more purposefully than in the past. Basing its estimate on the price increases anticipated before the Arab oil embargo of October 1973, the study considers it likely that energy use per unit of industrial output will decline by 2 percent per year up until 1980. With the sharp post-embargo prices rises, even greater savings can be expected.

Another Project study published in 1974, *Potential Fuel Effectiveness in Industry*, pursues the possibilities for industrial energy conservation still further. It explores what savings could be achieved with the application of the best available, economically feasible energy conservation technologies for various processes in industry. "Available" technology means that which is already at hand or can be readily developed. The study showed that in six energy-intensive industries (iron and steel, petroleum refining, paper, aluminum, copper, and cement) existing technology could, on the average, cut energy consumption by one-third.

Three of the reports in this volume also shed some light on the industrial use of energy: "Energy Thrift in Urban Transportation," "Energy, Employment and Dollar Impacts of Alternative Transportation Options," and "Energy, Employment and Dollar Impacts of Certain Consumer Options." All of these reports compare the energy it takes to manufacture cars, airplanes, appliances, or other energy-using devices with the energy it takes to run them. A remarkable result in all the studies is that the energy needed to make these devices, averaged over their useful lives, adds up to a small fraction of the energy used in their operation. What this means for energy conservation is that in most cases, it will save considerable energy overall to replace energy-guzzling devices with thrifty ones.

Transportation offers the chance for important energy savings. Indeed, more than one-fifth of the savings which the Project's report, *A Time to Choose*, considers achievable by the year 2000 are in transportation. The chapter entitled "Energy Thrift in Urban Transportation" in this volume shows what opportunities for savings energy lie in a broad range of strategies for design of urban transportation systems. The report compares the energy requirements for present and possible future transportation systems for a medium-sized city. It shows, for example, that among the more commonly discussed options—auto, bus, Personal Rapid Transit (PRT), and Dial-A-Bus—total energy requirements per passenger mile vary as much as fourfold. What is especially noteworthy is that PRT and Dial-A-Bus appear to use even more energy per passenger-mile than today's gas guzzling automobiles. From an energy-saving point of view, improvements in auto fuel efficiency are more promising than these novel modes of transportation.

The chapter entitled "Energy, Employment and Dollar Impacts of Alternative Transportation Options" provides helpful insights into the effects of alternative transportation strategies, not only on total energy use but on employment and consumer costs as well. Total energy costs, as defined in this report, include the energy used for maintenance and disposal, as well as energy requirements in manufacture and operation. For the automobile, indirect energy costs—for auto manufacture, highway construction, insurance, repairs, garages, and so on—add up to as much energy as the gasoline that cars consume. The very extensive life support system for the automobile in this country is as energy-intensive as the automobile itself.

This chapter also points out that while it saves the consumer money and energy to shift over entirely from using a car to using the bus, half measures may not be economical. If the consumer in urban areas keeps his car, while also using the bus, he can lose money, because depreciation and fixed costs for the car will remain whether the car is used or not. The important point here is that energy conservation which narrowly seeks to restrict people from using the cars they already own may be burdensome and ineffective. Energy conservation policies can work if they provide incentives for people to own efficient cars, or if they provide public transit service that is attractive enough so that people might give up their second "commuting car" in favor of public transit.

Besides the more direct opportunities for energy conservation, there are major energy conservation opportunities in "mining" urban and agricultural wastes for energy. Two Project reports on energy recovery from wastes are included in this book—"Potential Energy Conservation from Recycling Metals in Urban Solid Wastes" and "Potential Energy Recovery from Organic Wastes." Recycling urban refuse can save energy in two ways. First, organic wastes in urban refuse can be used as fuel—perhaps as a supplement to coal in fossil-fuel electric generating plans. Recoverable organic waste energy in urban refuse today is equal to at least 6 percent of total coal use. Besides this direct use of organic wastes for fuel, urban refuse offers another possibility for saving substantial amounts of energy, in the recovery and recycling of metals. It takes much less energy to produce metal products from recycled scrap than from virgin ore. Aluminum scrap, for example, requires only 5 percent as much energy to process as metal from ore. The technical feasibility, economics, and policy aspects of metals recycling are covered in one of the chapters in this volume.

The organic wastes study included here not only explores the energy possibilities of urban refuse but also assesses resource recovery from agricultural residues. A surprising finding is that crop residues could eventually furnish three or four times as much useful energy as urban refuse. The study concludes that agricultural wastes could make agriculture a net energy-producing activity. They could yield enough energy to fuel farm machinery, produce fertilizer, meet other farming energy needs, and still have energy left over for activities outside of farming. Crop residues could be converted by anaerobic digestion to methane, or natural gas. This anaerobic digestion process provides an extra benefit: the recovery of nutrients from the residue of the digestion process. These nutrients could then be returned to the soil as fertilizer.

Pointing out the opportunities for saving energy is the first step toward achieving lower growth in energy. Policy-makers also need to explore ways to make it happen. In the matter of energy conservation for buildings, the Project chose to concentrate its research efforts on the legal, financial, social, economic—in short, the institutional problems—of putting new energy-saving technologies into effect. This is the subject of a Project report, published earlier this year, entitled *New Energy Technologies for Building: Institutional Problems and Solutions.* One important point the study makes is that because the building industry has difficulty in raising the capital, builders tend to emphasize low first costs in construction. Thus they tend to bypass techniques which may be more costly initially, but could save energy and money for the occupant over the whole life of the building (that is, life cycle costs—initial costs plus expected operating costs appropriately discounted—are lower). To overcome this obstacle to sound economic planning in the construction industry, policies which would help builders compete on a more equal footing with the rest of the economy for capital should be enacted by the federal government.

The last chapter in this book, "Energy Needs for Pollution Control," has an indirect but important bearing on energy conservation. The objective of this study is to discover how much extra energy it will cost the nation over the next decade to pursue its environmental clean-up goals in dealing with air pollution, water pollution, thermal pollution, and solid waste disposal. This study shows that the total energy requirements for environmental protection are quite small—less than 2 percent of total energy consumption in 1985. An effective campaign to conserve energy does not require relaxation of environmental quality goals; the two are compatible. In some instances, energy conservation and environmental protection are mutually reinforcing. Solid waste management offers an example. When organic wastes are recovered and used as fuel, the result is an energy credit, not a penalty.

It is our hope that the *Energy Conservation Papers* and *A Time to Choose* and the other EPP special reports relating to energy conservation will be useful to policy-makers and citizens generally. Of course, these works do not provide the last word on energy conservation. They represent first steps toward developing both more efficient devices and more effective policy. In the past our research and development efforts, and energy policies in general, have been aimed toward stimulating more supply and promoting greater energy use. These policies are inappropriate today. While additional new supplies are still needed, a much slower rate of energy growth is called for. It is time to turn our efforts to energy conservation because of the important social benefits that slower energy growth offers.

Opportunities for conserving energy are great because our economy has not encouraged energy thrift in the past. But to realize these opportunities will require a firm public commitment and vigorous leadership at all levels of government.

Chapter Two

Energy Thrift in Urban Transportation: Options for the Future

Margaret Fulton Fels
and Michael J. Munson
Princeton University

PREFACE

The purpose of this analysis is to examine some of the many energy consumption patterns for urban passenger transportation which are conceivable for the last quarter of this century. No attempt is made to predict what transportation *will* be like in the future; rather, we lay out a spectrum of possibilities (called options) and estimate the energy consumption which would result from the policies, preferences, and living patterns assumed for each of the options. No option is viewed as more likely than another, and some possibilities—such as telecommunications, whose impact on transportation is totally uncertain—are not included.

It is important for the reader to understand which parts of the analysis are rigorous and which are not. The analysis was carried out in three stages: (1) qualitative development of the options; (2) quantitative evaluation of the energy consumption resulting from each option; and (3) assessment of the results. While we have attempted to be as objective as possible, the set of options chosen here certainly does not exhaust the range of possibilities. Obviously the choice is subject to individual judgment.

The first stage—the construction of the options—is the least rigorous. Even the most sophisticated modeling cannot estimate with certainty how people's travel habits will be affected by fuel price increases, legislative actions, and so on. For each option we discuss how the exact quantities (trip length, fraction of trips by auto, etc.) which define the option might represent people's travel habits in the future. Common sense was often the best tool available to make the quantitative travel estimates consistent with the qualitative assumptions of each option.

The most rigorous part of the analysis is the calculation of the energy results from the travel estimates. Should a skeptical reader wish to construct his own option, the method described here can be used to estimate the resulting energy consumption.

Because as many as 70 travel estimates defined each option, and many or all of these varied from one option to another, no particular energy result can be attributed to any single causal effect, but only to a combination of them. In examining the implications of the results, then, we return to the qualitative approach to assess what changes—societal and institutional—might lead to a reduction in the energy consumed for passenger transportation.

ACKNOWLEDGEMENTS

The authors would like to express appreciation to Professors Paul M. Lion and Alain L. Kornhauser, Directors of the Transportation Program at Princeton, for their invaluable assistance in making available to this effort all the data produced by the Trenton Transit Study. Of particular help in providing these data were Jerome Lutin, Elizabeth English, Linda Hunkins, Richard Oberman, and Edward Lechner. In the Center for Environmental Studies, Professor Robert Socolow provided indispensable guidance during critical phases of this work. In addition, the authors would like to thank the students who participated in this research effort: Joenathan Dean, Russell Barton, Shari Glassman, Elizabeth Garman, and Michael Godnick.

Many people from outside Princeton University were extremely helpful, most of whom have been mentioned in references throughout this report. Additional people who deserve thanks are Steven Hulce of the Motor Vehicle Manufacturers Association and John Davidson of the University of Michigan for useful information, and Katherine Gillman of the Energy Policy Project for her extensive, thoughtful editing of the manuscript.

One of us (MFF) would like to express appreciation to her husband and children for their sustained patience to the completion of this work.

Introduction

We are told now that we are facing a motor-fuel crisis. But it is not a scarcity crisis .... The real crisis before us is a thrift crisis. We must force economies in both production and consumption.

While gasoline was away down in price the majority became wasters, consciously or unconsciously .... Thrift was the last thing to enter our heads.

The net results of gasoline thrift will be more miles to the gallon, more miles to ... every working part of the machine's mechanism .... That is the real crux and crisis of the gasoline situation if you will make a careful analysis of the facts–The Country Gentleman, *May 6, 1916.*

Study Plan and Energy Considerations

The energy resources a person uses to transport himself depend not only on the distance he needs to travel but also on the size and efficiency of his auto (if he has one), and how much he uses other travel modes such as the bus, train, bicycle, or his own feet. Many changes in travel habits could effect an energy reduction: living closer to work or to recreational and shopping facilities; using a smaller auto, carpooling, and more efficient driving habits; or diverting some trips to more energy-thrifty modes.

If an attractive new transportation system is offered in a city, how much can people be expected to use it? The answer depends in part on social attitudes toward transportation changes and in part on the technological nature of the innovation. To what extent will people drive smaller automobiles? Fuel costs, as the buyer perceives them, and style are two important factors here. And, while it is easy to estimate the improved mileage which might come about from a decrease in auto weight, what is the effect of that particular energy-saving on the overall energy consumption for transportation?

Of most interest is the combined energy impact of strategies aimed at energy reduction. Thus, if we hypothesize some changes in people's travel habits and add that to the effect of life style changes which might occur within this century, what, then, is the overall effect on the average energy consumed for urban passenger transportation?

This work attempts to answer these questions by analyzing transportation options for a medium-sized city and its surrounding suburbs. It explores the factors which influence an urbanized area's demand for transportation, and considers how each of the strategies under study might be implemented.

We selected as our working laboratory area the Trenton Standard Metropolitan Statistical Area (SMSA), which is coterminus with Mercer County in New Jersey. After examining the present travel characteristics of the laboratory area's population, we estimated from the aggregated data the weekday travel habits for an average person in that population. These results provided a starting point for the development of several future transportation options. Clearly it is impractical to discuss every plausible combination of the factors which influence energy consumption; instead we chose a set of nine options to cover a reasonable range of possibilities. The results for projected energy consumption are intended to provide a realistic range of energy needs for urban passenger transportation for the years ahead.

Next we describe in detail how the set of options was chosen. They were developed within the confines of three descriptive models of the future: Scenarios A, B, and C. Briefly, Scenario A depicts a continuation of current growth patterns, with energy consumption influenced principally by the average weight of autos. Scenario B includes the effects of innovative technology on people's modes of travel. Scenario C couples the effects of new attitudes or changes in life styles with the innovative technology introduced in Scenario B. The years 1985 and 2000 were selected for the analyses.

Because "continuation of current trends" does not lead to a unique projection, two options are considered for Scenario A: they differ mainly in the size of the average auto used. In A_1 the auto continues to add weight, while in A_2 the weight of the average auto remains approximately the same as it was in 1973.

In Scenario B we examine four viable options: B_1 includes innovative modes of urban passenger transportation to substitute, in part, for automobile travel; in B_2, the use of these novel modes is enhanced by restrictions on the use of autos in the central city. In both these options, B_1 and B_2, we assume the use of the big 1973-size auto of Option A_2. Option B_3 introduces technological changes in the automobile which improve the auto's fuel economy. B_4, the final option in Scenario B, is an optimal combination of B_1, B_2, and B_3, so that the new modes and auto policies introduced in B_1 and B_2 are coupled with the more energy-efficient auto in B_3.

Finally, three options are developed within Scenario C: Option C_1 involves changes in social customs so that people live closer to their work; in C_2, more people live in high-density dwelling units. Both C_1 and C_2 assume the more efficient auto introduced in B_3. Option C_3 hypothesizes a society in which energy consciousness has become part of a different way of life. This last option includes the energy-conserving social characteristics introduced in C_1 and C_2, and, in addition, favors the use of small, extremely efficient autos.

Each option is constructed around several assumptions describing the travel behavior of the population; the size of the typical auto is one such assumption. Important in the analysis are estimates of travel data which show the quantitative effect of each assumption. These data concern trip lengths and the number of trips for various purposes; the fraction of trips by each of the available modes; the energy required for operation and the energy for manufacture; and the average occupancy for each mode. These combined data enable us to determine the per-capita energy consumed for urban personal transportation in each option. (The explicit relationship between the per-capita energy consumption and these travel data is shown in Appendix A.)

Several alternative transportation systems, both traditional—automobile and bus—and innovative—Personal Rapid Transit (PRT), and Dial-A-Ride systems—are included in the study. The private automobile, as the dominant form of transportation in the United States, will inevitably remain a component of any mass transportation system. Because fuel consumption varies greatly among automobiles it is essential to consider autos of several sizes and efficiency levels. The bus is an example of a widely used present-day system which might alleviate today's urban transportation problems.

Personal Rapid Transit is a class of modern, forward-looking systems under serious consideration by urban planners; by virtue of its rider-controlled small vehicles, it offers the advantages of the automobile to an automobile-oriented society. The Dial-A-Ride system consists of a fleet of small bus-like vehicles which, operating on existing highways, offer door-to-door service in the area served.

We examine the automobile and bus as they are now being used in Mercer County. Personal Rapid Transit, Dial-A-Ride, the automobile, and modernized bus systems are treated as they are being contemplated for the future.

For each of these transportation systems, basic energy requirements were calculated.[1] A key measure for each mode is the energy required per vehicle-mile. It is essential to include in this measure not only the fuel the system uses in operation but also the energy that was used in manufacturing the system components (that is, the vehicles and the highway or guideway). For most systems, the energy per vehicle-mile for operation is ten times greater than the energy for manufacture (amortized over the assumed lifetimes of the components). For one of the "systems," walking, the energy required for manufacture of the propulsion system is not included.

Of course, the most meaningful measure is the energy required to transport passengers rather than vehicles. Some knowledge of the average load factor (passengers per vehicle) is needed to estimate, from the energy per vehicle-mile, the energy required to transport one passenger one mile. Average load factors vary with the region being served; special attention will be given to them in our detailed discussion of the options. Another measure, energy per available-seat-mile, provides a comparison of the systems when they are fully loaded and thus operating at maximum efficiency.

Table 2-1 compares energy use for the seven modes included in this study. It also includes figures for rapid rail, which is of interest to larger cities of, say, a million or more. For each mode, three sets of results are shown: the energy consumed per vehicle-mile (with individual contributions from manufacture and operation), the energy consumption for fully occupied vehicles (energy per available-seat-mile), and the energy consumed per passenger-mile for a sample set of load factors.

While the energy per *vehicle-mile* is comparatively large for the bus and the train, they are extremely efficient compared with the other motorized modes (auto, PRT, and Dial-A-Ride) when they are fully loaded. In fact, during rush hour (when they may be more than fully loaded, considering standees) buses and trains are more than ten times as efficient as autos which contain, on the average, 1.4 persons. However, these larger systems do not in general operate at capacity. With a 20 percent occupancy rate, which is more typical, their efficiency advantage over the auto narrows to two-to-one. Under typical load conditions, the bus has little advantage over a 2,000-pound auto; thus the importance of load factors and automobile weight cannot be overemphasized in an energy comparison of modes.

The energy consumed per vehicle-mile is similar for the PRT considered here and a 3,100-pound auto averaging 15 miles per gallon. Thus the PRT vehicle carries people no more efficiently than a 3,100-pound auto, when the number of people per vehicle is the same. When the PRT system* is considered as a whole, its energy efficiency is still lower, because of the inevitable shuttling of empty vehicles to pick up waiting passengers. Similarly, the energy advantage offered by Dial-A-Ride is marginal. Then why do we include these systems in a study concerned with energy thrift? First both PRT and Dial-A-Ride are more efficient than the heavy autos of the present day, and they can be operated with full vehicles during peak hours. Second, intolerable congestion or pollution might make the adoption of some form of mass transportation imperative for cities. One conclusion of this study is that for medium-sized cities, systems such as PRT and Dial-A-Ride which offer the

---

*The operational energy for PRT represents the total energy resources required to generate the electricity which propels the system. It turns out that the net energy of operation *per pound* of vehicle is identical for the 3,600-pound auto, the 3,000-pound PRT vehicle shown here, and the 6,500-pound vehicle for an entirely different PRT system.

Table 2-1. Total Energy Consumption for Several Urban Transportation Modes[a] (in Thousand Btu)

Mode	Auto[b]		City Bus[c]	Rapid Rail[d]	PRT[e]	Dial-A-Bus[f]	Bicycle	Motorcycle	Walk
	Present Average	2,000 Pounds							
Individual contributions									
Operation Vehicle	10.9[g]	5.56	29.6[h]	52.9[i]	9.56[i]	18.4	0.14	2.05	0.22
manufacture	1.32	0.72	0.96	1.37	0.65	1.84	0.14	0.17	–
Guideway manufacture	0.10	0.10	0.27	2.39	0.14	0.17	0.05	0.10	–
Total energy per Vehicle-mile	12.3	6.38	30.8	56.7	10.4	20.4	0.33	2.32	0.22
Energy per available seat-mile	2.05	1.60	0.77	0.79	1.73	2.04	0.33	1.16	0.22
Energy per passenger-mile for "typical" operating conditions[j]	8.9	4.6	3.8	2.6	9.6	10.2	0.33	2.1	0.22

[a] The details of these energy calculations are contained in reference 1; results are shown to at most three significant figures.

[b] These figures shown are for 3,600-pound and 2,000-pound 1973 autos with conventional internal combustion engine (ICE). Estimates for ICE's of other weights or for autos with other engines are contained in Appendix C.

[c] These figures correspond to a 35-foot bus with 40 seats, typically used for urban transportation.

[d] These results are based on the specifications of the BART System in California.

[e] The PRT vehicle corresponds roughly to the six-passenger vehicle designed for Monocab's overhead monorail system manufactured by Rohr Industries, while the guideway energy is taken as the average between two systems: Monocab, and Transportation Technology, Inc. (The latter uses a heavier vehicle more appropriate for 10 to 12 passengers.)

[f] The Dial-A-Bus system studied here is modeled after the system in use in Ann Arbor, Michigan. The 5,000 pound, 10-passenger vehicle is a Ford Econoline Van modified for Dial-A-Bus requirements.

[g] Energy equivalence of gasoline was taken to be 133.8 thousand Btu (TBtu) per gallon, which includes the energy consumed in the crude oil-refining process.

[h] Energy equivalence of diesel fuel was taken to be 147.8 TBtu per gallon; this also includes the refining energy.

[i] The energy shown includes a 30.5 percent efficiency factor for electricity generation and thus represents energy resources. An estimate of the minimum amount of energy required to air-condition and heat the stations was added to the energy of propulsion to obtain the result shown.

[j] The assumed "typical" load factors are: 1.4 persons per auto, 20 percent occupancy for bus, 30 percent for rail, 1.1 passengers (i.e., 20 percent less than auto) per PRT-vehicle, 2.0 passengers for Dial-A-Ride, and 1.1 persons per motorcycle.

"personal" amenities of the auto are the public modes most likely to supplement or replace auto travel.

This has been a general discussion of considerations which might be a part of any urban transportation study. We now pause for a look at the particular urban area on whose transportation characteristics this study has been based.

The Laboratory Area in the Early Seventies

Mercer County, the Trenton SMSA and laboratory area for this research, is located on the western edge of New Jersey and surrounds a single city—Trenton, which has long been the primary city in the county. This primacy is reflected in the area's major roadways, which, like many other cities' roadways, form a stellar pattern with Trenton at the center and the roads radiating off toward the surrounding boroughs and beyond. Current highway plans propose to put an expressway ring around the city and add several expressway radial penetrators into the center of town.[2]

As the map shows in Figure 2-1, the county includes, in addition to Trenton, eight townships and four incorporated boroughs. In the county can be found a complete range of living conditions, from high-density urban to suburban to rural. Affluence and poverty are both well represented.

An examination of the sociodemographic characteristics of the SMSA's population of 304,000 people leads to a convenient division of the county into three regions. The city of Trenton, where 105,000 (35 percent) of the people in the county live, has a high population density of 14,000 people per square mile; as we shall see, this is typical of much larger cities. Another 43 percent of the total county population live in an inner ring of older suburbs where the population density is only one-eighth that of the central city. The remaining 22 percent of the population live in the outlying portion of the county consisting of nine municipalities. Here the average density is extremely low, only 450 people per square mile, and much of the land is undeveloped. In subsequent discussion, the city of Trenton will be designated as Region I, the three townships in the inner ring, comprising the older suburbs, as Region II, and the outlying suburbs as Region III (see Figure 2-1).

Travel data such as the number of trips a person takes each day, the average trip length, or whether he travels by auto or bus depend, in part, on his income level and the population density where he lives. Other elements—whether city people are moving to the suburbs, where jobs are located, the mobility of the people who remain—are also critical to transportation planning for the future. It is even possible that foresighted transportation planning can revitalize a "decaying urban core" and help to reverse the present decentralization trend for people and jobs. Thus a population study must go hand-in-hand with a transportation study. Let us take a look at some of the relevant population

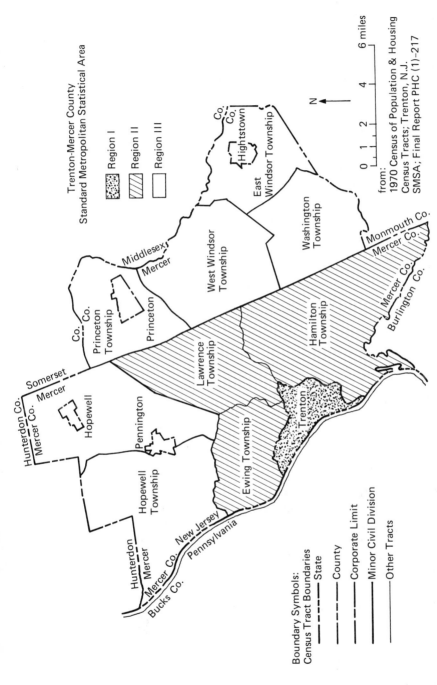

Figure 2-1. A Map of the Trenton SMSA, Representing Study Area, and the Delineation of the Three Regions Comprising the Study Area

characteristics of the Trenton SMSA and also examine how they relate to other cities.

Like many metropolitan areas in the U.S., the Trenton SMSA is characterized by a decaying central city (as measured by its population decline and the slow but steady decline in retail sales) and rapidly developing suburbs. In the last two decades, there was a substantial increase in the county's population, most of it concentrated in the outlying areas. Some of the suburban growth comes from city dwellers moving from city to suburb, leading to the decentralization pattern so common among U.S. cities. One-third of the population increase of the inner townships (Region II) was due to migration out of the city (Region I). Very few of the Trenton residents who moved between 1965 and 1970 went beyond Region I or II. While the inner suburbs are thus strongly tied to the central city, the outlying area (Region III) appears to be somewhat independent of the other two regions, and owes most of its growth to immigration from outside the county. The net result between 1960 and 1970 was an 8 percent decrease in the population of Trenton itself, accompanied by an increase of 25 percent in Region II, and a substantial one of 44 percent in Region III. The overall increase in the county's population was 14 percent.

The decentralization of employment in many urban areas seems to parallel the decentralization of residences. In particular for Trenton, that portion of the county's jobs located within the central city decreased from 58 percent in 1950 to 32 percent in 1970, while the proportion of the jobs in the inner suburbs (Region II) increased substantially. Some of this increase was due to migration of jobs away from the city. In addition, a large share of the new jobs in the county was located in Region II.

On the whole, three-quarters of the people who live in Mercer County also work in Mercer County,* so that, for the most part, the transportation needs of the county are self-contained. In fact, most of the jobs located in the central city or the inner townships are held by people who live in these two regions. Within the county, the three regions are related in their employment patterns as they were for decentralization, i.e., Regions I and II are strongly connected while Region III is relatively autonomous.

Where is the decentralization characterizing many older U.S. cities heading? Will people continue to leave their cities for the suburbs, or at some time will there be a trend back to the city? In this analysis, we chose to consider three decentralization patterns among all those that might conceivably occur.

Briefly, the three patterns are as follows: in the first, the decentralization of population follows a familiar pattern: those who can afford to move do so, and those who can't afford to, stay. In the second, a similar decentralization of jobs and people is assumed to continue until about 1985 at

---

*A number of the residents in Region III work outside the county, and typically commute by train to Philadelphia or New York. Such travel patterns have been omitted from this study whose main interest is travel *within* a metropolitan area.

which time the land values in the central area have deteriorated to a point where massive private redevelopment is economically feasible. In a third pattern, a reversal of the decentralization trend is hypothesized after 1985 due to the decreased property values in the central area and increased accessibility of the outlying area. The three patterns result in central city populations which, respectively, decrease, stay constant, or increase over the time period of the study.

Each of the nine transportation options was analyzed in terms of these three population distribution. Lest the reader despair that the analysis is becoming too complex, all these decentralized patterns, on analysis, turned out to show marked similarities. For the period until the end of the century they all showed a continuation of very high population density, with relatively low income levels, in the central city. None of them showed much increase in Region III's extremely low population density. Travel data, and the resulting energy consumption, vary less among the decentralization patterns than among the nine transportation options. For the purpose of simplification, one decentralization pattern, namely, the reversal trend, was selected for our analysis and discussion of results. Appendix B contains a detailed discussion concerning the effects of decentralization on the nine options and on transportation energy in general, and the salient conclusions will appear in the section "Energy Results and Conclusions."

One reason for choosing the Trenton SMSA as the laboratory area for this study is that certain of its population characteristics are representative of both medium-sized and large urban areas. Table 2-2 shows a comparison of population density and population decline due to net migration out of the city, for selected cities. Cities other than Trenton are shown in three groups: four cities which, like Trenton, have shown a significant population migration to the surrounding SMSA over the past two decades (despite a net population increase in the SMSA's over the same periods); two cities whose total population is very

Table 2-2. A Comparison of Selected Population Characteristics for Trenton and Several Other Cities

City	1970 Population (Thousands)	Population per Square Mile	Population Change 1960-70	Population Change 1950-60
Trenton	105	13,952	−8%	−11%
Chicago	3,367	15,126	−5%	−2%
Washington, D.C.	757	12,321	−1%	−5%
Providence	179	9,901	−16%	−17%
New Haven	138	7,484	−9%	−8%
Stamford, Conn.	109	2,856	+17%	+25%
San Bernardino, Calif.	104	2,348	+13%	+46%
Manhattan	1,539	67,808	−9%	−13%
Los Angeles	2,816	6,073	+14%	+26%

close to Trenton's (which ranks 143rd in the U.S.); and for comparison only, the pair of cities which probably show the greatest contrast of any two U.S. cities, namely, Los Angeles and New York. Some trends are evident from Table 2–2; the same trends are borne out by an examination of additional cities.

First, Trenton's population density is significantly larger than for other cities its size. It resembles that of much larger cities such as Chicago. A look at SMSA's rather than central cities indicates the same trend: while there were 98 SMSA's with larger populations than Mercer County's in 1960, the population density of only 15 of them exceeded Mercer County's 1,169 persons per square mile; the population density of SMSA's the size of Mercer County was more typically 300 persons per square mile. The population decline shown by central Trenton is most characteristic of the larger, older, eastern and midwestern cities; cities of Trenton's size have usually shared in the great surge of population growth of the last two decades.

The similarity between Chicago and Trenton as implied in these data is striking, and this similarity carries over into the regions surrounding these two cities. While the population of the Chicago SMSA is over twenty times that of Mercer County, its population density is only 40 percent higher. In addition, both areas gained population (12 percent for the Chicago SMSA and 14 percent for Mercer County) in contrast to the net out-migration from their central cities.

Trenton has shown a growing disparity in income between the central city and the surrounding suburbs in recent decades. Since 1950, the median income for the city's residents has steadily declined relative to the balance of the county, as is evident in Table 2–3.

A similar disparity is seen in the Chicago SMSA, where the ratio of city income to SMSA income decreased from 0.96 in 1950 to 0.81 in 1970. In general this trend is typical of the bulk of northeastern and midwestern SMSA's.[3]

As Trenton's share of the county's income has declined, its proportion of non-white residents has increased, in contrast to the surrounding suburbs. Again, as in many older urban areas, the racial composition of the central city has shifted rapidly, with whites moving out. Nearly all of the county's black population (93 percent) live in Regions I and II, while the net increase in the whole county's population has been predominantly white. The

Table 2–3. Median Incomes for Trenton and Mercer County

	Median Household Income		
Area	*1950*	*1960*	*1970*
Trenton city	$3,204	$4,779	$6,516
Remainder of county	3,276	6,580	10,051
Ratio of Trenton's income to the rest of county	.96	.73	.65

city also contains a disproportionate fraction of the county's elderly residents. Many of Trenton's jobs are held by people who commute from outside the city limits, so that fewer are available to center city residents.

An overriding determinant of how much people travel and what modes they are likely to use is auto ownership. Recent surveys[4] indicate that 87 percent of the people who ride the Mercer County buses are captive riders, without access to automobiles. Trenton itself, whose bus ridership is substantial, has only 0.8 autos per household, while the average for Regions II and III is 1.4 autos per household (very similar to the national average of 1.45[5]). The county's average is 1.2 autos per household. Nearly three-quarters of the county's autoless households are inside Trenton. Thus it appears that Trenton contains a large number of workers who have no available transportation other than the bus. In fact, of all the people in the county who ride the bus to work, 65 percent live in Trenton; nearly all the rest live in Region II. This disparity in the auto ownership between city and suburb goes hand in hand with the income disparity already discussed.

All of these data reinforce the expectation that Trenton (Region I) contains a large portion of the population which is unlikely to drive or travel very much, and that the surrounding areas, Regions II and III, are now, and are likely to remain, extremely dependent on the automobile. In general, it seems reasonable to expect far less accessibility to the automobile, and less mobility in general, in the central cities than in their suburbs. We anticipate a wide variation in the transportation energy consumption in the three regions: I) perhaps lowest in the central city, where walking and use of public transit modes is feasible by virtue of high-density living and necessary for people without autos; II) higher in the inner suburbs where the automobile is a prevalent way of life, but where interaction with the central city and medium population density make reliance on other modes a possibility; and III) perhaps even higher in the autonomous outlying area, where sprawling development virtually necessitates long, frequent trips by automobile.

From the considerations described above, we conclude that Trenton's transportation needs, both for the present with its relatively high density and the future with its decentralizing population and growing disparity between city and suburb, resemble much more the needs of considerably larger, eastern and midwestern cities, than of cities of comparable size. This work amounts to three independent studies of three very different regions. The central city houses a disproportionate share of the old and the poor. The inner suburbs might be described as "middle America," and the outlying areas are, in the main, affluent suburbia. These regions, markedly different, at varying levels of urbanization, are tied together by travel for employment and enjoyment. We believe that the conclusions drawn here can say something about the potential to lower energy consumption for passenger transportation in similar areas in the U.S.

TRANSPORTATION OPTIONS FOR THE FUTURE

Before conjecturing about transportation in the years 1985 and 2000, it is important to describe the quantitative trip characteristics of the Trenton SMSA in the early 1970s. This data base will serve as the starting point for the development of the nine future options we have selected for study. In particular, a comparison of how much people travel now in the three regions, and for what purpose, will help us make reasonable projections for expected future travel. A careful look at present bus ridership will allow us to estimate how many people in each of the three regions can be expected to take the bus, in the various options.

We turn now to the results of this examination.* They are presented in detail in order to demonstrate a sample set of travel data for the study area. For each of the future options, presentation of the detailed data will be deferred to Appendix A. We shall simply mention important trends resulting from the assumptions within the option. The energy results will be briefly stated after the discussion of each option, but we shall present all nine of the options before comparing them for the purpose of drawing major conclusions.

The Early Seventies

Our assessment of travel within the study area indicates that, on the average, people in the inner suburbs (Region II) travel nearly twice as many miles per day as do the residents of the city (Region I); those in the outlying suburbs (Region III) travel another 50 percent more. (In this analysis, trips are tallied by the residence of the tripmaker. Thus if a resident of Trenton works in Region II, this trip is counted as a work trip for Region I.) Both the average number of trips per day and the average distance for each trip show the same trend, increasing as we proceed from Region I to II to III; these data are shown in Table 2–4. This disparity among regions is rooted in nonwork trips. (In this analysis, trips are categorized according to whether they are for work or for nonwork purposes, e.g., shopping, medical visits, recreation, etc.) People in Region III, over the course of an average work day, travel four times as far for nonwork trips as those in Region I; the corresponding ratio for work trips is only one and a half times. Thus the residents of the more affluent suburbs tend to

---

*Estimates of the travel data were determined from three types of source material: (1) U.S. Census data[6]; (2) studies of the relationship between trip data and population characteristics (residential density, auto ownership, etc.)[7]; and, most important, (3) surveys conducted within the Trenton Transit Study of the Transportation Program, Princeton University. Of these, two involved extensive home interviews: Trenton Urban Area Travel Survey (conducted in 1972 with a 15 percent sample and analyzed by Lutin),[8] and a verbal Survey of Attitudes. The third survey, the 1973 On-Board Bus Survey, represents a 100 percent survey of all riders of the countywide Mercer Metro bus system during a typical work day. (The questionnaire, filled out by over 76 percent of all riders, and up to 90 percent for some bus routes, produced detailed origin-destination data, as well as information indicating whether the rider owned or had access to an automobile.)

Table 2-4.   Travel Data for Mercer County in the Early Seventies

	Region I		Region II		Region III	
	Work	*Other*	*Work*	*Other*	*Work*	*Other*
Trips per person						
(number per day)	0.77	0.83	0.85	1.45	0.83	1.77
Trip length (miles)	5.0	2.7	6.9	3.8	7.6	5.8
Portion of trips						
by auto	0.74	0.59	0.92	0.88	0.84	0.61
by bus	0.13	0.05	0.04	0.01	0.02	0.00
by walking	0.13	0.36	0.04	0.11	0.14	0.39

travel more for perhaps less-than-essential reasons, such as driving far to a favorite shopping center, or visiting friends who live a considerable distance away.

The extra travel in the suburbs is an expected result of the larger number of cars per household and the lower residential density. People in the suburbs also tend to use the automobile for a considerably higher portion of their trips than city residents do. In Trenton, one-quarter of trips to and from work are non-auto. They are evenly split between walking and the bus. By our estimates, this is the only situation where the bus assumes a significant portion (13 percent) of trips. For nonwork trips in the city, the portion drops to 5 percent. In the suburbs, the bus accounts for a small fraction of work trips and virtually none of the nonwork trips.

The average occupancy for all Mercer Metro buses is estimated at only 6.7 passengers per bus. This is because the bus routes extend to the sparsely populated outer edge of the county. The occupancy level *within* the Trenton Central Business District is over twice the county average. Urban buses are particularly well suited for use on densely traveled corridors along which great numbers of people work or live. The low average occupancy, which is typical of most intraurban buses, is probably an inevitable consequence of buses trying to meet the needs of suburban as well as city residents. However, the service provided to city residents who work in the outlying areas can be essential to their livelihood.

The average automobile used in the early 1970s was assumed to weigh 3,600 pounds[9] and to average 12.3 miles per gallon (mpg).* A recent survey[12] which was conducted as a part of this effort indicates that the average occupancy of automobiles driven in Mercer County is approximately 1.4

---

*Estimates for automobile gasoline consumptions are based on data obtained from the testing of automobiles driven on the Federal Emissions Urban Driving Cycle at Environmental Protection Agency Laboratories.[10] This cycle, which corresponds to the early morning commuter run in Los Angeles, is a reasonable approximation for the fuel consumption in a medium-sized urban area such as Trenton. It is reasonable that the national average of 13.7 mpg[11] is higher than the estimate of 12.3 mpg used here for urban driving.

passengers; this represents a combination of 1.2 passengers per auto for work trips and 1.6 for other trips. (This is lower than the national average of 1.9 persons per auto[13] principally because of a large difference in the average occupancy for nonwork trips.)

The resulting transportation energy a Mercer County resident consumes today during an average weekday is 74.1 thousand British thermal units (Btu), or TBtu. By contrast, the residents of the city are energy-thrifty: their per-capita energy consumption is only 38.6 TBtu. The average for Region II is well over twice this amount (89.1 TBtu per person). As expected, it is even greater in Region III (99.7 TBtu).

It is interesting to note that the automobile is responsible for nearly all the transportation energy consumed in all regions of the SMSA. In Trenton, for example, 93 percent of the energy is attributable to the automobile, which is responsible for only 66 percent of the trips. The reasons are twofold: on a passenger-mile basis, the bus uses less than half the energy consumed by the 3,600-pound auto; and walking is essentially "free" in terms of energy costs. Thus at the outset it would seem more profitable to concentrate on measures which might divert trips from the auto to the bus or walking, or make the auto itself more energy-thrifty, than on measures which simply increase the bus load factor without decreasing auto trips.** With this first glimpse of where energy savings might be accomplished, let us proceed to our discussion of the options for the future.

SCENARIO A: CONTINUATION OF CURRENT TRENDS

Scenario A depicts a continuation of present trends through the next three decades. Any changes in the transportation picture would occur without deliberate intervention from public agencies. The basic characteristic of the scenario is the continued domination of the automobile, including an eventual goal of two large gasoline-powered automobiles for every household. Ownership of large, luxury automobiles in the Cadillac-Imperial-Continental class would be common, though many people would own smaller autos out of economic necessity. The average weight of autos directly affects the overall energy consumption for transportation, and the number of two-car households by 1985 and 2000 will influence the per-capita number of trips and the percent of trips by auto.

Another factor affecting miles to be traveled and fuel to be used is highway development. Present plans call for a ring road combined with radials

---

**The portion of the total energy attributable to the bus is so small that measures aimed simply at improving the bus efficiency (e.g., re-routing away from sparsely populated areas) without diverting auto riders have relatively little impact on the overall energy consumption.

around the City of Trenton to provide an automobile link between high density Trenton and the remainder of the county. Urban renewal also has transportation effects. An auto-free shopping mall in downtown Trenton,[14] already underway, is expected to refurbish shopping and recreational facilities in the mall area and stimulate center city economic growth. (This mall, which was opened in the summer of 1973, closes six blocks of Trenton's main street to all vehicular traffic, with the traffic on neighboring parallel streets forming a one-way circle around the mall.[15]) "Continuation of current trends" thus does not necessarily imply a totally bleak outlook for cities. Certainly the reversal of decentralization to be assumed throughout the options in this study is consistent with an optimistic outlook. Efforts to revitalize the central city will undoubtedly take place, and the Trenton mall is an example. Some use of bus expressways and marginal improvements in bus routes, and in buses themselves, are also planned for the near future.

With the private automobile continuing its supremacy, the bus will be used principally by people without access to automobiles. The On-Board Bus Survey, wherein 87 percent of the riders were found to be "transit captives" (that is, with no access to autos), demonstrated that this is the case today. Similarly, the Survey of Attitudes indicates that planned bus improvements are capable of diverting only a few automobile trips to bus trips.*

When society relies almost entirely on the automobile for transportation, the average auto weight is the single most important factor, not only in the fuel consumption of the automobile itself[16] but also in the overall energy consumed for transportation. Thus it is important to consider recent trends in automobile weight.

The average empty weight of U.S. automobiles purchased in 1972 and early 1973 was approximately 3,600 pounds. A careful study of available statistics indicates no downward trend in weight. It is certainly true that the percentage of smaller-than-standard cars produced and sold in the U.S. has been increasing for several years, with the result that dealer inventories on June 1, 1973, had a shortage of small cars and a surplus of larger ones.[17] However, the average weight within size classes has increased several hundred pounds between 1964 and 1972, so that the average (empty) weight over this eight-year period remained nearly constant, within 50 pounds of 3,600 pounds.[18] Compact cars increased from an average curb weight (which includes fuel and thus is estimated here to be about 200 pounds heavier than empty weight) of 3,040 pounds in 1964 to 3,310 in 1972; the intermediate auto increased over 500 pounds. "Smaller than standard" classes today include cars over 4,000 pounds. It is only because sales of cars in smaller classes were increasing that the overall average curb weight did not rise between 1964 and 1973.

---

*These surveys were carried out within the Trenton Transit Study of the Transportation Program, Princeton University; see footnote on p. 20.

The same trends are also evident in statistics supplied by the New Jersey Department of Motor Vehicles, where registration fees are based on auto weights. Despite a gradual increase in registrations of small cars (less than 2,700 pounds) from 6.9 percent in 1964 to 20.5 percent in 1972, registrations of large autos (greater than 3,800 pounds) increased substantially, from 20.5 percent in 1964 to 31.0 percent in 1972.[19]

Much of the weight increase within size classes may be attributed to an effort to construct safer autos,[20] and while the popularity of small cars is increasing, the tendency to add weight to automobiles for safety's sake continues. A 4,300-pound auto has been stated as the target weight for a U.S. Department of Transportation Safety Vehicle, and many automobiles heavier than this were sold in volume in 1973.

It is not yet clear whether cars will continue to get heavier, but it seems reasonable to expect that, without outside intervention, they will not get lighter. Current trends are too complicated to lead to a unique prediction for the average weight of automobiles in 1985 and 2000. The surge in concern for fuel economy precipitated by the Arab oil embargo in October of 1973 indicates how unpredictable the situation is. Thus we have selected two options to represent realistic upper and lower bounds for the future energy consumption resulting from current trends continued through the year 2000. The two options, A_1 and A_2, differ primarily in the size of the average auto assumed, which in turn is influenced by expected fuel costs and by the owner's expectation of fuel availability in the near future.

Option A_1: Everybody Wants a Luxury Car

A projection of the weights of autos in the standard and intermediate classes shows them approaching 5,000 pounds by 1985, with compacts nearing 4,000 pounds. Only an enormous increase in U.S. sales of subcompacts or small imports will temper this weight increase. It seems conceivable that the average weight of automobiles will increase to, or even beyond, the "safety-target" weight of 4,300 pounds. For example, if the low gasoline prices of the 1960s and early seventies were to return, fuel costs would be no deterrent to a decision to buy a large expensive car. The intent of Option A_1 is to provide an estimate of a realistic maximum for personal urban transportation energy consumption. In it we assume that the safety-target "super-big car" represents the maximum average weight for U.S. autos in 1985 or 2000; that small imported cars (amounting to 15 percent of all cars on the road) will increase in average weight to 2,600 pounds; and that the "composite" average auto of Option A_1 weighs 4,050 pounds. The resulting average fuel consumption is expected to be 10.3 mpg, after the imposition of post-1973 standards.*

---

*It has been estimated that a 3 percent penalty will accompany the internal combustion engine's meeting of the 1975 emissions standards.[21] Because so little is known about the fuel penalty associated with the 1976 standards, and faced with the possibility

How are some of the other travel data expected to change over the next 30 years? As incomes continue to rise, increased automobile ownership, particularly in Region I, will generate more and longer trips by the year 1985, and even more in 2000. Although people are expected to live somewhat further from their jobs, most of the increased travel will be for recreational and other nonwork purposes. By far the major portion of all trips will be made by automobile, although that proportion will be less in the center city (Region I) than in the suburbs. In the early 1970s a surprisingly high portion (over 25 percent) of the trips in Regions I and III** were by foot; we assume that this fraction gradually levels off to not more than 10 percent for all three regions by the year 2000. The percentage of trips by bus remains fairly constant: as increased auto ownership in Region I diverts trips from bus to auto, improvements in bus service attract some noncaptive ridership. A slight increase in the occupancy level will result from improved bus routes.

The next result for Mercer County is an increase in daily per-capita energy consumption from 74.1 to 114.3 TBtu in 1985 and 141.3 TBtu in 2000. Thus a near doubling of per-capita energy consumption for transportation is a possibility by the year 2000 under this option. The doubling pattern is fairly uniform among the three regions; per-capita energy consumption increases by a factor of 2.6 as we progress from the central city to the outlying suburbs. The fact that the substantial population increase predicted for Mercer County takes place predominantly in the outer suburbs, where the energy consumption is highest, contributes to the enormous increase in Option A_1.

To test whether the result of this option is a realistic upper limit for expected transportation energy consumption, we cross-check with another calculation which depicts an "energy maximum" situation. In Option A_1, a county resident in the year 2000 is expected to travel 8 miles per day, if he lives in the city; up to 20 miles per day if he lives in the outlying suburbs. If everyone relies exclusively on the super-big car for all trips, the average county resident would consume 153.6 TBtu per day. This is not very different from the result in Option A_1, which assumes the use of other modes, including walking, on occasion. Thus the domination of the automobile in this first option, as constructed, appears close to an upper limit.

Option A_2: Response to Fuel Price Increase

A long-term increase in fuel prices, possibly aggravated by a short-term fear of gasoline scarcity, could make fuel economy a more important

---

that these standards will be relaxed, we shall use the estimates given in the references in Note 10 at the end of the chapter, along with a 3 percent fuel penalty for the internal combustion engine (ICE), to estimate energy consumption in 1985 and 2000.

**In Region III, this is due in part to Princeton, where the high dependence on walking and the low auto ownership are out of scale with the neighboring communities. A reasonable assumption is that the presently anomalous travel behavior of the students and faculty will be less dominant as the non-University population of Princeton increases.

consideration in people's choice of new automobiles. There might be a new balance between those who can afford large cars and the fuel to operate them, and those who make more economical choices. We assume in Option A_2 that the average weight of the auto remains at the 1973 level of 3,600 pounds. Assuming that small imported cars averaging 2,200 pounds amount to 15 percent of all cars on the road, the "composite" automobile weighs 3,400 pounds, with fuel consumption estimated at 12.9 mpg.

Another response to fuel price increases might be a moderate reduction in automobile travel, especially for recreational purposes, compared with Option A_1. Instead of driving a few miles for a loaf of bread, people are likely to economize on the number of trips they make. For Region II, we postulate that the average daily number of nonwork trips, which was substantial in the early 1970s, tapers off. In all three regions, the increase in travel over the next 30 years is less here than in Option A_1. Another difference is that the auto will replace fewer walking trips.

Per-capita energy consumption for daily personal travel in the county will increase in this option from 74.1 TBtu at present to 86.0 TBtu per person in 1985 and 96.3 TBtu per person in 2000. This is an increase of 36 percent over the next 30 years, compared with the 90 percent increase in Option A_1. For the year 2000, the assumptions in A_2 lead to 28 percent less transportation energy use per capita than in A_1. Since the energy per vehicle-mile of the big car here is 20 percent lower than for the super-big car in Option A_1, it is clear that changes in travel behavior which might result from fuel price increases could contribute to a significant energy reduction.

SCENARIO B: INTERVENTION WITH TRANSPORTATION TECHNOLOGIES

Scenario B involves an attempt to satisfy present life style and travel demands with innovative transportation technologies with energy-saving potential. Barring some major changes in society's values, Scenario A depicts the population, location, and trip-making characteristics of current life styles projected into the future. Scenario B differs from Scenario A only in the energy characteristics of the kinds of transportation systems available, and in the relative use of transportation alternatives when more than one is available. In contrast to Scenario A, Scenario B includes externally imposed incentives to stimulate the use of new transportation modes or to reduce fuel consumption. It is assumed, however, that such public interventions will have no significant effect on travel behavior, beyond affecting the choice among alternative travel modes.*

*For the sake of logistics, any new technology to be included in Scenario C will be introduced in Scenario B. In the event that a change in life style or attitude is required for this technology to have a significant impact on travel patterns or on energy consumption, the impact from this technology change will be minimal in Scenario B.

The technological interventions of Scenario B are basically three: (1) innovative transportation modes to replace the automobile as the dominant form of travel; (2) restrictions on the use of automobiles in the central, congested parts of the city; and (3) modifications on automobiles to reduce fuel consumption per vehicle-mile. The options within Scenario B will consider these interventions serparately where practicable, and in combination.

Option B$_1$: Replacement of Automobile
Travel by Innovative Modes

Recent surveys in the study area agree that with dependence on the automobile so strong, a public transit system cannot expect to compete unless it is similar to the auto. Transit captives ride conventional systems such as the bus, but, in general, auto owners will not. We therefore focus our attention on novel modes which offer some of the personal advantages of the automobile: short travel times, door-to-door service, or privacy, to mention a few.

A Dial-A-Ride system serving Ann Arbor, Michigan, reports that over half the riders had access to an automobile, but for reasons of convenience, such as parking difficulty, they chose to use Dial-A-Ride.[22] Thus, the Dial-A-Ride system is one mode which appears capable of diverting riders from private vehicles to public transit. Another such mode is Personal Rapid Transit which offers the "personal" amenities of the private automobile. These two innovative systems are particularly well suited to a city of Trenton's size and population density. They are introduced in Option B$_1$. Improvements in the present bus systems are also included to supplement the new modes, either permanently or at least for the period of planning and construction.

Personal Rapid Transit (PRT) is a demand-responsive system of automobile-sized vehicles which are operated automatically on their own guideway system; PRT thus represents a compromise between fixed-rail mass transit and the private automobile. The idea is that these small vehicles are available on call to a large number of stations.

A person uses the system much as he does an elevator: at a station, he presses a button for his destination, and the computerized system decides which vehicle and which route can take him there in the least time. The fixed guideway on which these vehicles move is a more-or-less uniform grid of closely spaced lines throughout the service area. The system is intended to provide the privacy, security, and flexibility of the automobile, and the efficiency, capacity, and speed of mass transit. It does not require the high residential densities usually associated with mass transit.

There is no question that PRT would be expensive, but unlike the highway and conventional rapid rail, land acquisitions for it are minimal. Elevated structures could be built above existing roadways. In contrast to limited access freeways with infrequent entrances, people living near a guideway would benefit from its proximity. (Optimally a station is constructed between every pair of intersections.)

For the study area we envision a PRT system of six-seat vehicles*
operating on small, and, in most cases, elevated guideways throughout the city
and the surrounding, densely-populated suburbs (Regions I and II). The
components might resemble the Monocab system,[23] which is shown in Figure
2–2. A network of guideway-lines spaced approximately half a mile apart, with
stations at mid-points between intersections, places every residence and activity
center in Region I or II within a quarter-mile walk of a station. Recent
estimates[24] indicate that such a system might have an operating cost of 3.4
cents per passenger-mile, and a break-even fare of 7.8 cents per mile, assuming
two-thirds federal funding of the guideway cost, at $1.5 million per one-way
mile. Figure 2–3 shows the preliminary network on which these estimates were
based.

If PRT is to offer the same personal amenities as the automobile, a
user would not have to ride with a stranger. We therefore assume that the
average number of passengers per occupied PRT vehicle is the same as the
average auto occupancy. An important energy consideration is that if some (say,
20 to 25 percent) of the PRT vehicles are being shuttled around empty, the
effective occupancy will be considerably lower.

The automobile would serve as a feeder from the outlying areas to
the PRT systems, and ample parking facilities at the PRT area's perimeter would
provide the essential link between the auto and PRT. An innovative parking
structure which minimizes land use is a ferris-wheel arrangement manufactured
by Park Mobile,[25] a picture of which appears in Figure 2-2. Professed
advantages of Park Mobile modules are: parking for 22 cars in 500 square feet of
land (vs. 250 square feet per car in ground-level parking), probable security for
the parked automobiles, and average retrieval time of 45 seconds; in addition,
the modules can be grouped together to provide increased parking, they can be
covered for aesthetic purposes, and the structure can be relocated in the event of
a shift of demand from one PRT station to another.

The other chief alternative to private automobiles that we consider is
the Dial-A-Ride system which is also demand-responsive, but compared with
PRT, requires considerably less innovative technology. A fleet of conventional
small buses or vans, with 10 to 20 passenger seats, is used on regular city streets,
and is dispatched by a computer algorithm which minimizes the waiting and
riding time. (If the trip density is less than 225 requests per hour, manual
dispatching is recommended.[26]) The system resembles a taxi service: the user
telephones his or her request to the Dial-A-Ride headquarters; a bus, already

---

*Two sizes of vehicles are currently receiving much development attention:
Four-to-six passenger units (e.g., Monocab of Rohr Industries) and units holding ten to
twelve or even sixteen passengers. (The large Transportation Technology, Inc. vehicles can
hold either six or ten passengers, while the StaRRcar system of Alden Self-Transit Systems,
as designed for Morgantown, West Virginia, uses vehicles designed for eight seated passengers
and thirteen standees). Since we are considering PRT as a potential replacement for the
automobile, the vehicles for the system imagined here will be of the smaller type, weighing
approximately 3,000 pounds.

Figure 2–2. Monocab PRT System Used As a Prototype in This Study, and Park Mobile, a Possible Parking Structure for Use As a Link Between Auto and PRT

carrying other passengers to other destinations, is chosen to pick up the new rider. There are two basic modes for operating Dial-A-Ride: "many-to-many," in which the rider is picked up and delivered at the exact locations he or she requested; and the "many-to-few," in which a person is picked up at any address and delivered to a specified location, such as a shopping center, train station, or place of employment. The return trip is just the opposite. (A conventional bus system is a few-to-few mode.) The many-to-many mode offers the greatest competition to the private automobile, as the success of the Ann Arbor system indicates; but the many-to-few mode has obvious economic advantages as well as the potential of serving more people faster. A combination of the two modes is perhaps most feasible: for example, many-to-few during the morning peak hours, few-to-many at the evening peak, and many-to-many at other times of the day.

Experience with an experimental system in Haddonfield, New Jersey,[27] suggests that serving only a part of a metropolitan area may be uneconomical, because not all destinations in the service area are covered. The Ann Arbor project[28] indicates that economies of scale will accrue if the system serves all rather than a small part of the metropolitan area.

For Option B_1 we envision a Dial-A-Ride system serving the entire

POSSIBLE PERSONAL RAPID TRANSIT NETWORK FOR TRENTON
TRENTON CBD MOBILITY STUDY
GUIDEWAY STATION POSSIBLE EXTENSIONS
30 MILES
62 STATIONS

Figure 2-3. An Heuristic Design of a PRT Network for Trenton Area

builtup region of the study area. Small, ten-seat van-type vehicles, such as those used in Ann Arbor,* would be appropriate (see Figure 2–4). They are sufficient, except perhaps for peak hours when many routine trips are scheduled.

Indications are that Dial-A-Ride cannot hope to break even from rider fares alone; the operating loss for both the Ann Arbor and Haddonfield systems has been greater than $1.00 per passenger. This is aggravated by the fact that the vehicles sometimes carry only one or two passengers; at these times the advantages of Dial-A-Ride are social, not energy-saving. Thus Dial-A-Ride is similar to conventional nonprivate modes; for public service reasons, both may

---

*Larger vehicles, holding 16 to 20 passengers, are used in Haddonfield. The result is a lower average percent of occupancy than seemed apparent in Ann Arbor and a higher operating loss per passenger.

Figure 2-4. Vehicle for Ann Arbor Dial-a-Ride System Used As a Prototype for This Study

have to be funded in part from public funds. In Ann Arbor, the city recently passed a property tax assessment to fund the system on an expanded citywide basis.

Dial-A-Ride can be implemented somewhat faster than PRT so that it may be feasible in the fairly near future, before 1985. Establishing a PRT system within the next 15 to 20 years would be difficult because of the time required for institutional decision-making, capital acquisition, and construction, to say nothing of further research and development.

Option B_1 includes the replacement of some automobile trips by these two new modes. The average automobile in Option B_1 resembles the big car considered in A_1. Prior to 1985 a combination of Dial-A-Ride, conventional but revitalized bus systems, and, of course, the automobile are assumed to serve the transportation needs of the Trenton SMSA. Dial-A-Ride would provide a link, especially for "captives," between home and bus stop, and bus service would be improved to provide incentives for noncaptives to be riders. Improvements include express bus lanes on heavily traveled routes, and attractive, pollution-free air-conditioned buses.

Some time after 1985 an extensive PRT network would be implemented, at which time large conventional buses would be phased out,*

---

*Option B_1 is not inflexibly tied to the assumption concerning phase-out of large buses. As it turns out, trips by Dial-A-Ride are responsible for less than 10 percent of the total per-capita energy consumption, so that the assumed fraction of trips by Dial-A-Bus could include trips by large buses without causing a significant change in the overall results.

since central areas now served by the buses would be served better by PRT, and outlying areas by Dial-A-Ride. Implicit in Option B_1 is *planned* coordination among all available modes. Automobiles and Dial-A-Ride would be used in conjunction with the PRT system. Fare collection schemes for all the public systems could eventually be brought into line with automobile costs as riders perceive them. New fare collection techniques might include replacement of most cash sales by credit card sales.

The introduction of a new mode does not by itself influence the distance people travel. What is expected to change is the proportion the various modes handle: by 1985 Dial-A-Ride could divert many trips from the automobile, and by 2000 PRT could divert still more travelers from automobiles, and absorb the former bus riders besides. These effects are assumed to be more pronounced for work trips than for nonwork trips, and in Trenton more than in the suburbs. For work trips inside the city, PRT is assumed to take on nearly half (45 percent) of the work trips, in contrast to Region III where the impact of these new systems is minimal, except for work trips into the city.

In studying this option, we have attempted to ascertain whether any public transit modes can lure people out of their automobiles. If everyone should abandon his auto and use the bus for all his trips, an enormous energy reduction would result, but this "option" is totally unrealistic. We have instead confined our attention to personal-type transit systems which can compete with the automobile. The introduction of new modes, in the absence of other interventions, is not expected to temper the trend to increasing travel. Calculating the energy consumption resulting from this option, then, we estimate that the average county resident under these conditions would consume 91.8 TBtu per day for transportation in 1985 and 99.7 TBtu in 2000, about 35 percent more than at present. The per-capita energy consumption for Option B_1 is not substantially different from the increase seen for Option A_2.

Option B_2: Restricted Automobile Use

What happens now if the use of the alternate modes, introduced in Option B_1, is stimulated by restricting the use of the automobile in the central city? Let us consider a group of feasible interventions without emphasizing any single strategy. One of these is high-cost limited parking, to curb automobile traffic in certain areas. A second is tolls on vehicles entering the central city. The simplest toll is a fixed fee (e.g., $1.00 or $2.00) per automobile, but a toll based on unused passenger capacity would provide an incentive for carpooling. With a base fee of 50¢ per automobile plus 25¢ for each empty seat, a person driving alone in a large auto would pay $1.75, while a full carpool in a small car would be 12.5¢ per passenger. Ordinarily, the use of tolls means establishing toll stations on all roads entering the restricted area. This is quite impracticable for Trenton, which, like most cities, has a large number of entry roads. One could restrict certain areas to cars bearing fee-paid stickers, such as some university campuses use.

A more drastic intervention is the limitation of auto movement between some zones within the city, as Gothenburg, Sweden, has successfully done.[29] This relatively low-cost scheme requires only painted lines and curbs to define the zones. Within each zone, vehicular movement is permitted without restriction, but the line between zones may be crossed only by public transport vehicles. The effect in Gothenburg was a 50 percent reduction of vehicle volume on several main streets.

Similar success is reported in the London "Oxford Street Experiment"[30] where the closing of its largest shopping street to private autos has permitted previously clogged bus and taxi traffic to flow smoothly. An added bonus is an enormous decrease in carbon monoxide emissions and smoke pollution.

The New Jersey Environmental Protection Agency has recently set up the requirement that automobile traffic in the congested portions of the state be reduced by as much as two-thirds, for the purpose of meeting the ambient air quality standards mandated by the 1970 Clean Air Act.[31] Environmental concerns would most likely be responsible for putting into effect the restrictions described above. However, if such restrictions are simply imposed, with no other action taken, the likely result is a drastic decrease in the use of the central area, which may be inconsistent with the hoped-for revitalization. The provision of alternative modes of transportation along with restrictions on autos in central areas adds up to an attractive strategy. Option B_2 includes this combination of interventions.

It is probable that this option would be effective in diverting trips to alternate modes and in decreasing traffic congestion and pollution. Compared with Option B_1, there should be considerable change in travel patterns, less automobile travel, and more use of the alternative systems. The proportion of trips by bus is expected to increase in Regions I and II but remain unchanged in Region III where it is minimal to start with. This increased ridership is assumed to cause a slight increase in the countywide average occupancy for buses. The restrictions should accelerate a shift to the innovative systems, so that by 1985 Dial-A-Ride would take a greater portion of the trips, and, like the buses, operate with increased average occupancy. The PRT system (coming into operation after 1985) would also increase its ridership due to the auto restrictions. For example, we assume for Region I that PRT takes over 60 percent of work trips and 30 percent of nonwork trips. As in the previous option, a phase-out of the bus system is anticipated by the year 2000, when PRT is operational. Decreased congestion should enable the Dial-A-Ride system to operate more efficiently: shorter waiting times influence more people to call on Dial-A-Ride so that average occupancy increases, and the fuel economy improves, from 7.5 mpg to 9.0 mpg.

It is not expected that restrictions on private auto use will affect the proportion of trips made on foot, or the size of the average auto used.

Therefore, the "big car" of Option B_1 is also part of Option B_2. By 1985, incentives for carpooling should bring about higher average occupancy for autos, the countywide average increasing from 1.4 to 1.7 people per automobile.* This could occur if half the workers in the center city of Trenton travel to work in carpools averaging four persons per car; or, as is more likely, if one-fourth of the commuters in Regions I and II use somewhat smaller carpools.

In this fourth option, some stabilization in energy use begins to emerge. The present level is at 74.1 TBtu daily per person. The effect of restricted auto use in the city keeps the increase to only 3 percent, or 76.5 TBtu per capita, in 1985. However, a significant increase to 85.7 TBtu is indicated by the year 2000, when increased reliance on nonautomotive modes ceases to offset the trend to more travel.

Option B_3: Technological Modifications in the Automobile

The third intervention, modifications in the present automobile to improve fuel economy, can be accomplished in two independent ways: by increasing the efficiency of the gasoline-powered internal combustion engine, or by decreasing the average weight of the vehicles. It may be that one of these measures alone will not yield the anticipated fuel reduction: for example, increased use of accessories could undo much improvement in efficiency. Therefore, in Option B_3 we consider the two measures separately, as independent alternatives for fuel reduction.

Before considering the effect of technological improvements for greater fuel efficiency in the gasoline-powered internal combustion engine (hereafter designated "ICE") we shall examine several potential substitutes for the ICE. Some of these substitutes are particularly adaptable to small cars. If they prove popular, they may provide a boost to the small car population. Examples are the stratified-charge engine, the electric car, and the Wankel (or rotary) engine. Others, such as the diesel-powered engine and the diesel-Wankel, offer a substantial fuel savings when compared with an ICE of similar weight. Some of these substitutes offer the added attraction that they may be able to meet the 1976 emission standards established by the 1970 Clean Air Amendments. The National Academy of Sciences (NAS), in an extensive emissions study carried out for the U.S. Senate,[32] reports that "the system most likely to be available in 1976 in the greatest numbers, the dual catalyst system, is the most disadvantageous with respect to first cost, fuel economy, maintainability and durability."

---

*Throughout this work, a change in the automobile average occupancy implies a proportionate change in the average occupancy for PRT vehicles. Because of the shuttling of empty vehicles, the load factor for PRT is uniformly taken to be 23 percent less than the load factor for the automobile.

Let us briefly examine five ICE substitutes in terms of fuel economy, the 1976 emissions standards,* and the time scale required for production.

Again quoting the NAS report, the stratified-charge engine "bids fair to meet the 1976 standards. . . . The Committee believes that this engine will be certifiable for 1976, at least in small sizes." It is the only engine thus far to have withstood durability emissions testing; and its expected annual incremental cost to meet the 1976 standards is $200 less than that of the dual catalyst system. EPA data[33] show several different stratified-charge engines straddling the fuel economy curve for the 1973 ICE. (The Ford Proco falls above and the Honda CVCC and Texaco engines fall below.) Taking the average, we assume in Scenario B that the fuel economy of a stratified-charge engine is 10 percent better than for a 1973 ICE of the same weight.** A recent study[34] found that by 1980 stratified-charge engines could account for 10 percent of all new auto production, so that by our first target date of 1985 this engine could be a reasonable alternative to the conventional ICE.

The second ICE substitute, the electric car, is attractive from the emissions standpoint because the polluting source is diverted from the overly polluted urban area to the location of the power plan. Present battery technology is sufficiently advanced to power a small 2,000-pound automobile, with performance comparable to a 1,500-pound automobile equipped with ICE. For such a vehicle, with conventional lead-acid batteries, the range of driving between recharges is 50 miles. The overall energy economy*** of such a vehicle is approximately 5 percent better than for a 1,500-pound 1973 ICE.[36] Development of a battery for a much larger vehicle, or with larger range,[37, 38] is likely to take 15 years or more.

The diesel-powered automobile certainly has the best fuel economy of any automotive engine under serious consideration. EPA data[39] show a 3,500-pound diesel with fuel economy 90 percent better than the average 1973

---

*Here we use "1976 standards" to mean those established in 1970, in spite of the fact that imposition of the standards has been postponed. The specified standards are as follows:

Emissions (Grams Per Mile)

	Hydrocarbons	Carbon Monoxide	Nitrogen Oxides
1973	3.0	28.0	3.1
1975	0.41	3.4	3.1
1976	0.41	3.4	0.4

It is the final drastic reduction in nitrogen oxides which is causing the major technological difficulty.

**All comparisons throughout this section are made with the 1973 ICE; where data were derived from comparisons with the 1970 ICE, the 1973 ICE is assumed to consume 10 percent more fuel than its 1970 counterpart.[35]

***Here the electrical energy consumption is traced back to the original fuel sources required to generate the electricity.

ICE of the same weight; slightly smaller diesels show at least 50 percent advantage. In this study we assume a 50 percent advantage for small cars and 90 percent for autos larger than 3,500 pounds.

An additional advantage is that the diesel auto produces considerably less carbon monoxide and hydrocarbon emissions than does the gasoline-powered ICE,[40] although its nitrogen-oxide emissions are comparatively high. There is a notable lack of effort on the part of the U.S. manufacturers to develop small diesel-engine technology and the pollution control devices that must go along with it. Much of the smoke and odor associated with larger diesel engines, such as buses, can be controlled by improved driving practices (minimized idling, for instance) and good matching of the engine and load.[41]

The automotive diesel engine is often in ill-repute because it "does not provide the flexibility, silence and performance for its size that is more easily obtained with the gasoline engine."[42] However, Federal Driving Cycle tests showed it to follow speed-time requirements without lagging behind.[43] Enthusiastic reports by owners of diesel-powered automobiles offer still better testimony to adequacy of performance. Although fewer than 1 percent of the vehicles currently registered in the U.S. are diesel-powered, a production changeover to diesel is possible by 1985.[44] However, a large increase in the portion of diesel produced from a barrel of crude oil would require major changes in the refining industries, and this portion may have an upper limit. With this in mind, we assume that diesel-powered automobiles comprise no more than 20 percent of the total automobile population in Scenario B.

The Wankel engine, along with the stratified-charge, shows promise of withstanding durability tests for emissions.[45] This small engine allows room for elaborate pollution-control equipment (possibly a thermal reactor and catalytic system with exhaust sensor and feedback control), with unknown sacrifice in fuel economy. Present Wankel engines in the U.S. show fuel consumption 20 percent higher than in the 1973 ICE of similar weight. (A fuel penalty of 30 percent is reported in the EPA data, where the comparison is with a pre-1973 ICE.) On the other hand, a Wankel engine being developed by Curtiss-Wright in the U.S. claims a fuel economy slightly better than the ICE of comparable weight at higher speeds, and no worse at medium speeds.[46] Throughout the options in this study, we assume the fuel economy of the Wankel to be 10 percent lower than the 1973 ICE. Since the Wankel is now used in a popular small-sized auto (with fuel economy certainly superior to a large ICE), and since General Motors Corporation is already developing its own Wankel engine, it is plausible to include in Scenario B Wankel-powered autos for 1985.

In standard Wankel engines, it is difficult to achieve high compression ratios, and thus it is not easily operated as a diesel. The final ICE substitute considered here is a hybrid of the diesel and the Wankel engines, which combines a high-compression rotor with a larger low-compression chamber. This results in a smaller engine than the regular diesel. Because it is still in the developmental stage, details of fuel consumption and emissions characteristics are unknown. We assume in this work a fuel economy between the ICE and diesel engines, so that the diesel Wankel averages 20 percent higher mpg than a comparable 1973 ICE.

Appendix C contains a summary of the energy characteristics (including miles per gallon as a function of weight, and manufacture energy) for these five ICE substitutes, in comparison with the 1973 ICE.

Let us now explore improvements in the efficiency of conventional automobiles. Apparently, fuel consumption for an average ICE can be improved by 25 to 30 percent[47] if the following three measures are taken: (1) drag reduction by change of design, for a 5 percent improvement in fuel consumption; (2) reduction in rolling resistance with the use of radial tires, for an improvement of 10 percent; and (3) improvement in the basic engine design, either by optimization of the load-to-engine match or by combining a small engine sufficient for cruising with a "boost" or turbocharger to aid in accelerating. In addition, the replacement of some steel parts with approximately the same volume of aluminum[48] would reduce the weight of the automobile. This causes an increase in the energy of manufacture, but as we shall see, the resulting decrease in fuel consumption generously overcompensates for this over the life of the vehicle.

Even though all these measures for increased fuel economy are technologically available, we must consider whether they will actually appear on the market, and to what extent people will buy and use them. Possible interventions fall into two categories: those which seek to modify the decisions of the manufacturers, and those which seek to modify the decisions of the buyers. Manufacturers produce automobiles in large lots, and save on costs by avoiding custom-manufacture for certain areas. This suggests that the most effective level for intervention would be the federal government.

Some such efforts are currently being considered in several pieces of federal legislation. In May of 1973, Senator Hollings introduced a bill in the U.S. Senate[49] to impose on manufacturers a set of fuel efficiency standards as measured by miles per gallon. This bill proposes detailed standards which would improve by 13 percent the average fuel economy of all vehicles sold between 1973 and 1977, and make an additional improvement of 12 percent in the following two years. These would be mandatory standards, analogous to the emissions standards of the 1970 Clean Air Act. Assuming that a fuel economy improvement of 25 percent is feasible (which it appears to be, especially if a decrease in the average weight takes place) Senator Hollings' bill could be an effective means of reducing energy consumption in automobiles.

Another bill, introduced in the House of Representatives by Congressman Vanik,[50] calls for an elaborate per-vehicle tax program based on an official federal rating of the fuel economy of all new automobiles.* Schedules of tax rates, based on miles per gallon, are proposed for 1976 and 1981. In the 1981 schedule, no tax is imposed on new autos averaging over 20 mpg, while a maximum tax of $768 is imposed when the fuel consumption rate is less than 7 mpg.** In addition to imposing the tax, the bill would require that the fuel economy rating be displayed on window stickers in new cars. The effectiveness of this kind of law depends upon how much of the tax manufacturers would have to absorb, and how much they could pass along to buyers. This, in turn, depends on the price elasticity of the demand for automobiles of different sizes and with different engines, and on the availability of alternatives to new automobiles. Compounding all of these factors is the effect of increased incomes among buyers, a factor which might counter the price effect. This is a complex and speculative area, but it seems a fair assumption that the net result would be a shift in favor of producing small and more efficient automobiles.

Improvement of fuel efficiency of automobile engines might be greatly aided by the passage of a third bill,[51] introduced at the end of 1973 by Congressman George Brown. This bill provides for the National Aeronautics and Space Administration to conduct research and development for ground propulsion systems which are "energy conserving, have clean emission characteristics, and are capable of being produced in large numbers at a reasonable mass production per unit cost." Thus a competent agency would develop the technology necessary to meet new criteria for fuel economy.

We construct transportation Option B_3 to include new technology offering a combination of possible substitutes for the conventional ICE as well as improved efficiency in the present one. Although a significant weight reduction is technologically feasible by 1985, we judge that such a change requires an attitude change, and thus defer this case to Scenario C. Throughout Scenario B the average vehicle weight is assumed not to decrease much below 3,000 pounds. The following two hypothetical situations can, with careful design, provide equivalent alternatives from an energy standpoint:

The first, which is directed more at the manufacturer than at the car buyer, is the application of the improved efficiency measures to the big (3,400 pound) auto of Option A_2. By 1985, a 25 percent increase in fuel economy would yield an average of 16.1 mpg. If we take into account that in 1985 many cars on the road will still be pre-1980, and that urban driving uses more fuel per mile than the national average, then this 16 mpg figure is consistent with the

---

*Since fuel economy varies so widely among vehicles of the same weight, this plan seems preferable to taxation based on vehicle weight alone. Actually, such a system has existed in New Jersey since 1956, when registration fees for automobiles were based on three weight classes. However, the difference in fees among the classes is not in itself sufficient inducement to buy smaller cars.

**Fuel consumption ratings of the new automobiles are based on a comprehensive testing procedure which includes major optional equipment and an urban driving cycle.

goal to achieve a 20 mpg average in *new* cars by 1980.* By the year 2000, an average of 20 mpg for urban driving could be attained by a moderate weight reduction, if the 25 percent improvement in efficiency remained. For example, the substitution of 285 pounds of aluminum for 710 pounds of steel is a feasible way to produce lighter but not smaller cars, which average 20 mpg in urban driving. (The resulting 12 percent increase in the manufacture energy will be more than compensated for by decreased fuel consumption, due to the 12.5 percent reduction in the average weight.) Or, if smaller cars become more popular, in response to incentives for fuel economy, an average auto weight of 3,000 pounds could yield fuel efficiency of 19.4 mpg. The goal of 20 mpg by the year 2000 could be realized if, for example, 3,000-pound diesel-powered autos (at 27 mpg) comprise 8 percent of the automobile population.

The second measure concerns the car buyer. It hypothesizes that consumer infatuation with novel engines could stimulate the small-car market, effecting an average of 20 mpg by the year 2000 even without a 25 percent improvement in efficiency. To accomplish the goals of Option B_3 through this route, we postulate the following: due to incentives for owning small cars, the average weight decreases to 3,100 by 1985, but ICE's remain predominant. The result is an average of 14.9 mpg. By 2000 the auto population consists of the following mixture of 20 mpg autos with overall average weight of 2,700 pounds:

50 percent ICE's averaging 2,475 pounds
10 percent diesels averaging 4,200 pounds
10 percent diesel-Wankels averaging 2,900 pounds
10 percent stratified-charge averaging 2,750 pounds
10 percent electric cars averaging 2,600 pounds
10 percent Wankels averaging 2,200 pounds

Note that if we consider only ICE's, a 20 mpg average implies a reduction of the average weight to 2,400 pounds, which we consider too low for Scenario B.

When compared with the average 3,600-pound ICE currently in use, either of these hypothetical auto populations leads to an almost 20 percent reduction in the energy consumed per automobile-mile** by the year 1985. Another reduction of about 20 percent would occur by 2000. The alternate approaches leading to these energy reductions are summarized in Table 2–5. The variety of available measures provides convincing evidence that the auto's

---

*The national average[52] is 11 percent higher than the value used here for urban driving: see footnote on p. 22. Thus a 20 mpg rating for a new car might correspond to 18 mpg in urban driving; taking the age distribution for automobiles from a recent national survey,[53] the average auto in use in 1985 would average 16 mpg for urban driving.
**It is the total energy consumed per vehicle-mile that is used in the calculation here. Thus the weight and fuel economy enter only implicitly, and the various combinations discussed here will lead to the same result for per-capita energy consumption.

Table 2-5.   Hypotheses for Medium Car of Option B$_3$

Year	Average Weight (in pounds)	Average mpg	Possible Measures	Total Energy Consumed per Vehicle-Mile
1985	3,400 3,100	16 15	25% improved efficiency weight reduction	10.2 TBtu
	2,975	20	25% improved efficiency aluminum substitution	
2000	3,000	20	25% improved efficiency weight reduction 8% of autos diesel powered	8.19 TBtu
	2,700	20	variety of engine types each averaging 20 mpg	

average fuel consumption per mile could realistically decrease over the next thirty years.

In order to examine separately the energy consequences from using more efficient autos, Option B$_3$ adopts the travel patterns of Option A$_2$, which did not include innovative modes. The only major changes are in the auto's average energy consumption; the smaller and/or more efficient automobiles described above are used for the same set of trips. By virtue of greater efficiency in autos alone, per-capita transportation energy consumed daily in 1985 would (at 75.4 TBtu) be 12 percent less than it would otherwise be in Option A$_2$; in 2000 it could (at 67.6 TBtu) be 30 percent less. These reduced figures correspond directly to the automobile energy reduction. This is essentially because in Options A$_2$ and B$_3$, the automobile accounts for nearly all (99 percent) of the energy consumed for transportation, even though only 75 to 90 percent (depending on the region) of the trips are by automobile.

Compared with the present level, the per-capita energy consumption would stay constant through 1985; a similar result was seen in Option B$_2$. This is the first of the options considered in which the average energy consumed per person would actually decrease from the present level by the year 2000. In the event that a 20 mpg *average* in urban driving could be realized by 1985 (instead of the year 2000, as assumed in this option), the present per-capita consumption rate would decline nearly 20 percent by 1985.

Option B$_4$: Combined Interventions

In the fourth option within Scenario B, the imposition of all of the technological interventions previously discussed are considered in combination. We include the new modes introduced in Option B$_1$ together with restrictions on the use of automobiles in the central city, considered in Option B$_2$; where the auto is used, the medium-sized, fuel-thrifty auto of Option B_3 is assumed to represent the average. Essentially, this option adopts the trip characteristics of Option B_2 and the automobile fuel economy characteristics of Option B_3.

The result is a marked decrease in transportation energy consumption between the early 1970s and 1985, to 67.9 TBtu per person per day. The decrease does not continue, and the consumption rate levels off to 68.9 TBtu per person in the year 2000. The new modes, encouraged by restrictions on auto use, combined with fuel-thrifty autos, bring about a more drastic reduction than the use of more efficient cars alone. But as the automobile becomes more efficient, it approaches the energy economy of other modes. By 2000, therefore, the two options, B_3 and B_4, yield nearly identical energy consumption rates.

SCENARIO C: MODIFICATIONS OF LIFE STYLES AND ATTITUDES

Scenarios A and B have been developed in the light of our best understanding of current living patterns and life styles. They include assumptions based on the continuation of those life styles. The technological modifications introduced are intended to help satisfy the travel needs of those life styles in the most efficient manner practicable. However, the behavior patterns embodied in current life styles are only one set of possibilities. Life styles may change. This final scenario includes the impact of three specific attitude changes on travel behavior. They are considered here individually, although they are not necessarily mutually exclusive. Throughout Scenario C, all of the technological interventions included in Option B_4 are adopted, so that Option B_4 is used here as a baseline.

The first new attitude change, embodied in Option C_1, is that people desire to live much closer to their place of work. We assume that this attitude arises from considerations beyond the cost of travel to and from work. One motive might be a wish to integrate work life and home life more closely. The distinctions between private and work activities might become less rigid; work hours might become more flexible; or working at home part of the time might be more feasible. Thus many people would place a premium on being able to locate their homes and work places close together.

The second basic attitude change, included in Option C_2, focuses on how close to their neighbors people wish to live. It is assumed in this option that a majority of people choose to live in close proximity to other people, so that the metropolitan area would be characterized by high-density residential clusters. This attitude toward living near neighbors can be quite independent of the attitude toward living near work as assumed in the previous option.

For the final option, C_3, we hypothesize that people become extremely aware of the amount of energy they use, and that energy consumption will be an important criterion for many decisions. We call this phenomenon "energy consciousness." We do not postulate that people would change their lives for the sake of saving energy per se. But the change might be spurred by a fear of irreparable environmental damage, or concerns about depletion of energy resources if exponential growth in demand for energy were not tempered. It is credible that the decline in the birth rate in this country has been due in part to fears of long-range consequences of overpopulation. And the analogy can be carried further: it is possible that a felt necessity to save energy will produce short-term changes in life styles which people will eventually adopt as preferable to the old ones, just as many people now view smaller families as enhancing the quality of life. Is it conceivable that society will look askance at energy spendthrifts, as it now tends to frown on families with many children?

We do not attempt to predict, but only conjecture about a change in attitude favoring energy consciousness. A shift from current economic practices might well accompany such a change. Emphasis would shift away from materialistic values, where luxury cars and big houses are desired, toward closer human relations and "simpler" (or, at least, less expensive) pleasures of life. People might choose a combination of living near work, to spend more time with family, and living near neighbors whose company they enjoy. Bicycling on paths in a wooded park near home might become more popular than driving miles to find a picnic area. In general, we assume in Option C_3 that walking, bicycling and motorcycling will become much more prevalent, and where automobiles are used they will be smaller and need relatively little fuel.

In order to make bicycling feasible, it is assumed for Scenario C that special bikeways will be available, not only for the sake of safety (one out of three bicycle accidents involves an automobile)[54] but also to provide an inexpensive incentive for increased bicycling. For example, abandoned railroad beds are easily converted to bikeways; in addition, Federal Highway Trust Funds may be used for constructing bicycle paths if the construction is in conjunction with a Federal Aid Highway project.[54] We have also included motorcycling among the available modes, in view of its high energy efficiency of over 70 passenger-miles per gallon of gasoline (based on an average mileage of 65 mpg and an occupancy rate of 1.1 people per motorcycle[55]). But the physical dangers of motorcycles may counteract the energy advantages. Recent data show that in the event of an accident, the rate of death or injury for motorcycles (estimated at 80 percent) is far greater than it is for automobiles (where the rate is 10 percent).[56] The fatality rate for motorcycles is three times that for autos.[57] This assumes that the motorcyclist shares the automobile roadway, which seems reasonable for vehicles which travel as fast as autos. This study does not include externally imposed incentives for motorcycling, but assumes that this mode will take on a maximum of 5 percent of all trips in Secnario C.

Interventions, such as those included in Scenario B, can promote the use of energy-thrifty travel modes, but attitude changes in a free society reflect many diverse elements; they are not shaped by government action alone. In Scenario C, citizen-action groups might play an important role in promoting the desirability of living near work, or of high-density living, perhaps in the central city. An example is the Greater Cleveland Growth Association's ad captioned "How would you like to spend more time at home than getting there?" shown in Figure 2–5. Auto advertisers might strive to create for small efficient cars the same aura of excitement that belonged exclusively to large luxury cars in the 1960s. Indeed, such advertising began to appear in response to the Arab oil embargo, as shown in Figure 2–5. With the aid of such ads, people's preferences might shift to autos that get better gasoline mileage.

Option C_1: Desire to Live Near Work

A steadily shortening work week, and relaxation and variability in working hours could be a factor in changing attitudes so that people choose to live closer to their work. Higher prices for gasoline or lower auto insurance rates for policyholders who report short work trips might add to the incentives. Increasing automation of manufacturing processes, and a concomitant shift to jobs in service industries might be another factor. Probably the most important motive would be a desire to integrate home life and work life, towards a more unified style of productive and satisfying living.

Whatever the causes, the basic changes in this option, compared with the baseline of Option B_4, will be in the density and pattern of development. One assumption is that the present pattern of large employers or clusterings of employers in a small number of centers would continue. In this case, the development pattern would probably emerge as a small number of large, dense

How would you like to spend more time at home than getting there?

Sex, power, prestige and 25 MPG.

Toyota Celica GT 5-speed.

Figure 2–5. Advertisements Reflecting Attitude Changes Toward Living Near Work and Driving Efficient Automobiles

centers, located either in the existing center city or in the surrounding built-up townships (Regions I or II). This differs from the typical nineteenth-century industrial city, with its extreme degree of centralization of jobs and dwelling places. Instead we envision a continued decline of the central city for a time while outlying centers are developing. When redevelopment of the inner city becomes feasible, it would then emerge as a new center among the rest. In this case, the current decentralization trend would undergo a reversal, probably sometime after 1985. The result would be somewhat higher residential densities and considerably shorter (and perhaps fewer) work trips. The same could hold true for shopping trips, and even recreational trips where places of employment offer social activities, or workers socialize mainly with fellow workers.

However, the other nonwork trips are likely to be trips between one center and another; these could be fairly long. Overall, we assume shorter trips than those of Scenario B for 1985 and 2000. The trip lengths of Option C_1 for the year 2000 are only moderately longer than today's. A shift from auto to walking, bicycling or motorcycling, for both work and nonwork trips, might go along with shorter trips. (In Region III this change would be apparent for nonwork trips only by 1985, but would show up for all trips in 2000.) The medium-sized auto of Options B_3 and B_4 is adopted in this option. The overall efficiency of the auto would improve with higher average occupancy, due to the feasibility of carpooling.* We assume here that occupancy increases to 2.0 people per auto by the year 2000.

A somewhat different development pattern could emerge if employment by small employers, or disaggregated large employers, becomes more common. In this case, jobs would probably follow the employees. Assuming that people still prefer to live at relatively low density in their own houses on their own lots, the resulting pattern could be a loose pattern of many small villages throughout the area, with small shopping or employment centers. Assuming continued decentralization into the 1980s, the central area might decline until it too consisted of one or more of these villages.** Work and shopping trips would be shorter, in which case walking and cycling would be more common. It is quite likely that trips for other purposes, particularly recreation and social, would become longer.

---

*Many employers have effectively organized carpools for their employees,[58] and the Auto Occupancy Survey, carried out within this project, finds indications that in the Trenton area many employees would be interested in an organized carpooling effort.[59]

**In the beginning of this chapter, we mentioned that a reversal in the present decentralization trend would be assumed throughout the main development of the options, and that a discussion of the effect of two other decentralization patterns would be deferred to Appendix B. We make an exception in the case of Option C_1, where the decentralization trend and the development pattern leading to home-work proximity are interdependent. The two very different development patterns which might emerge from this attitude change are consistent with two different decentralization trends. Subsequent references to Option C_1 will imply the large-center hypothesis which is consistent with the reversal decentralization pattern.

The main difference in travel patterns between the previous case of a few large centers and this case of many small villages is that here the average distance traveled for nonwork purposes is longer, reflecting the need to travel to other centers for facilities that some village centers lack. It is principally for this reason that per-capita energy consumption turns out to be 20 percent higher for the many-village case than when the development pattern results in a few large centers. Hereafter Option C_1 will refer to the large-center case.

The development and density patterns described in Option C_1 require major changes from the existing situation. There is already extensive investment in the present development which is quite inconsistent with the new patterns contemplated here. This capital investment is heaviest in current housing stock, although commercial and industrial facilities are also important. The point is not that the patterns described would be impossible, but that they would take time to achieve. Zoning changes would be needed to allow for somewhat higher residential densities, and for mixing residential and commercial job-producing land uses. These changes could be made more readily if land-use control were on a larger scale than at the present level of municipalities. At any rate, although considerable progress could be made in the next decade or so, it is quite doubtful that the development patterns of this option could be fully realized much before the year 2000.

Following the assumptions made in this option, an attitude shift toward wanting to live near work would have a significant impact on energy consumption. Results show that a county resident in 1985 would consume 55.3 TBtu per day, 25 percent lower than the present level; by 2000 the decrease is still greater, to 32.1 TBtu per person per day. This value is even below the present per-capita energy consumption of Trenton residents, whose travel patterns are already energy-thrifty.

Option C_2: Desire To Live Near Neighbors

Where in Scenarios A and B we assumed that people aspire to own houses on large private lots and view high-density housing as a last resort, in this option we posit a shift in preferences to favor high-density residential living. Living in luxurious high-rise apartments overlooking a park might become fashionable. People might own their own apartment and also a small parcel of land not far away to be used, say, for gardening. Thus the suburban population which in the early seventies lived in individual houses, each on a private plot of land, might be distributed in clusters, each consisting of 1,000 or 2,000 families. Each cluster would be self-sufficient to some degree in social, recreational, and shopping needs.*

The basic impact of this attitude change would be a decrease in distances people need to travel for nonwork purposes. Whereas a visit to a friend

*(This assumption presupposes the revitalization of the central city, and thus is consistent only with the reversal decentralization trend.)

in the previous options might have entailed a drive across town, here it could be simply a walk next door, and thus not even constitute a trip. The number of nonwork trips per person is expected to be lower here than in Option C_1. Higher residential densities would probably attract commercial facilities, so that shopping trips, too, would be shortened. Vast plots of land would become available for recreational facilities, such as public parks or private clubs.

However, the impact on work trips might be quite different. If relatively large and location-fixed employers continue to be the rule, a pattern of several job centers throughout the area, not contiguous with the high-density residential areas, might well evolve. People would choose their residential location in order to be near their friends, rather than near their work. The proximity of home and work postulated in the previous option is not a part of Option C_2; in fact, we assume the opposite, that one effect of high-density living is to lengthen the average work trip.

If high-density living is to be attractive, it must offer, through innovative architecture, the same privacy that individual plots of land provide. Building codes might ensure privacy by requiring visual and acoustical isolation from adjacent units. This could be expensive; except for the affluent, federally subsidized low-interest loans might be required. Since multifamily structures are apt to result in more efficient heating systems and lower unit cost, for installing phone and other utility lines, some of the increased capital costs might be offset by lower charges for utilities and services.

Because of rigidities in the present patterns of capital investment, major changes in development patterns would be much less apparent in 1985 than in 2000. Current zoning ordinances against high-density development in the suburbs would have to be removed before any effect could be seen. But even before high-density dwellings are built in the suburbs, favorable new attitudes toward high-density living would probably stimulate the revitalization of the central city.

This attitude change would not, in itself, strongly affect how much people use the automobile, but the resulting change in development and density patterns would be more conducive to walking and cycling, and might make policies which encourage the use of other modes more effective. The chance of living near a fellow worker is enhanced in high-density living; thus the average occupancy for autos is assumed to increase to 2.0 people per car by the year 2000.

This development pattern is expected to have the least impact on the travel patterns in the outlying suburbs (Region III), except that people who would have otherwise used Region III as a "bedroom community" for commuting to, say, New York or Philadelphia, would now choose to live in higher-density areas nearer work. Thus, for Option C_2, the population in these suburbs is assumed to be 30 percent lower in 2000 than in the previous options.

Although the development patterns assumed in this option and the previous one are very different and affect very different aspects of people's lives, the energy savings estimated from the two options are surprisingly similar. The high-density residential pattern produces a result for 1985, 55.0 TBtu per person per day, which is almost exactly the same as in Option C_1; for 2000, the result, 45.1 TBtu is quite a bit higher. The energy reduction for the next 30 years from either of these two development patterns is so substantial that we ascribe little significance to the fact that one result is higher than the other. Keeping in mind that our results are closely tied to the assumptions, we do, however, feel confident in concluding that either attitude change—in favor of living near work or in favor of living near neighbors—would result in very large energy savings.

Option C_3: Energy Consciousness

In the final option, we assume an energy-aware population which would live near work, in clusters of many people living close together. Energy consciousness would go beyond living patterns; it would also favor the most energy-thrifty modes, and perhaps even less travel altogether, other than for work or necessary shopping. People would travel shorter distances for recreation, or they would use some mode other than the private automobile. Thus this final option represents an optimal combination of the energy-saving trends in the previous options.

Almost all of the interventions from Scenario B are emphasized here. The net effect is to amplify the results described in Option B_4 with the added effects of the shorter work trips and higher residential densities of Options C_1 and C_2. Trips are fewer and shorter, cars purchased are fewer and smaller, alternative modes are used more frequently, and attitudes that favor limiting the use of automobiles are prevalent.

It is likely that the impact on travel behavior would begin to show up immediately, especially in an increase in walking and cycling. Changes in the overall development pattern would occur more slowly due to rigidities in the stock of urban buildings, roads, and facilities. The impact would probably be strongest in the inner suburbs (Region II) which would begin to take on the trip characteristics of the city (Region I), as higher-density, self-sufficient clusters of employment centers and residences emerge. For workers living in Region II, reliance on public modes would be almost as great as in Region I, and the work trips would not be much longer. Throughout all regions, the individual modes (walking, bicycling, and motorcycling) are assumed to absorb a large portion of trips, with the effect that very few work trips in the inner regions would be by automobile. For the county as a whole, carpooling in the small, four-passenger vehicles used by most car-owners would become the rule rather than the exception; the average of three persons per automobile is assumed here as the maximum attainable by the year 2000. PRT and Dial-A-Ride occupancy rates also increase.

How small and efficient can autos become by 1985 and 2000? In Option B_3 we considered two measures separately: an efficiency improvement *or* a weight reduction. In Option C_3 both measures are implemented simultaneously. Using a procedure and technology similar to that of Option B_3, we explore three possibilities: a reduction in weight; reduced weight with moderate improvements in efficiency; and reduced weight with the maximum feasible efficiency improvements.

In order of increasing energy reduction, the specific possibilities are:

a. Through 1985 the ICE continues to dominate the auto population, but average auto weight decreases to 2,500 pounds, and fuel efficiency improves to an average of 19 mpg. By 2000, other types of small cars have entered the auto population, to yield the following distribution:

> 30 percent ICE's averaging 2,000 pounds
> 20 percent electric cars averaging 1,500 pounds
> 20 percent stratified-charge averaging 1,500 pounds
> 10 percent Wankel averaging 2,000 pounds
> 10 percent diesel-Wankel averaging 2,000 pounds
> 10 percent diesels averaging 2,000 pounds.

The resulting average auto weighs 1,800 pounds, and its mileage is 29 mpg.

b. Weight reduction proceeds as described in the first situation, for both 1985 and 2000, with an added 15 percent increase in fuel economy due to improvements in auto efficiency.

c. Weight reduction proceeds exactly as described in the first situation, but in both 1985 and 2000, improved efficiency yields a 25 percent increase in fuel economy; in addition, the use of aluminum in place of some steel effects a further reduction of 12.5 percent in the average weight to 1,650 pounds.

The energy characteristics of these three hypotheses are summarized in Table 2–6. The first situation is probably the most realistic of the three, while the fuel economy of the third no doubt is optimistic. Compared with the average auto on the road today, the auto in the first hypothesis would be more than twice as efficient (per vehicle-mile) by 2000. It would consume 30 percent less

Table 2–6. Candidates for Small Car in Option C_3

	1985			2000		
Hypothesis	*Average Weight (in pounds)*	*mpg*	*Energy per Vehicle-Mile*	*Average Weight (in Pounds)*	*mpg*	*Energy per Vehicle-Mile*
a	2,500	19	7.9 TBtu	1,800	29	5.5 TBtu
b	2,500	22	7.2 TBtu	1,800	33	4.8 TBtu
c	2,500	24	6.5 TBtu	1,650	36	4.4 TBtu

energy than the medium-sized auto assumed in the four previous options. We adopt the car described in the first hypothesis as the "small auto" of Option C_3.

At this point, we anticipate the reader's concern about the safety characteristics of small autos. It is true that a collision between a 2,000-pound and a 5,000-pound auto is extremely dangerous for the small car at any speed; however, the danger would be less if autos were uniformly smaller. In addition, speed limits on high-speed freeways might be lowered for the sake of safety.* As for a collision with a fixed object, many safety features do not require added weight: air bags, or crunchable, elongated front ends are two examples. These can protect a small light car as well as a large one. In Option C_3, the extreme weight decrease is postulated for the year 2000, which allows time for innovative improvements in the safety features of small autos.

Option C_3 attempts to arrive at an estimated lower limit on the energy that people will use for personal transportation over the next 30 years, while preserving or enhancing a high standard of living. The results show an enormous decline in the per-capita daily energy consumption: to 24.2 TBtu in 1985 and only 14.7 TBtu in 2000. This is approximately one-tenth of the upper limit estimated in Option A_1.

We intended Options A_1 and C_3 to depict the maximum and minimum energy consumption which might reasonably be expected for an average work day's travel in an urbanized area. However, the great disparity in results for these extremes may raise questions. Are some of the assumptions in Option C_3 unreasonable? Let us examine this final option more closely.

One of the possible effects of energy consciousness is to increase the portion of trips made by walking and cycling. To estimate how much of the energy reduction in Option C_3, as well as in C_1 and C_2, is due to this change, we varied the distribution of nonwork trips among available modes, while keeping all other travel data constant. In Option C_3, the decline in auto trips which accompanies an increase of nearly 40 percent in walking and cycling in Region III, causes only a 7 percent drop in per-capita energy consumption. Option C_1 and C_2 show similar trends. Thus it appears that the energy reduction of Option C_3 is not due to an exaggeration of walking and cycling trips.

Neither are the results overly sensitive to the efficiency assumed for the average auto. For example, what would happen if we use the most energy-efficient auto in Table 2-6 (hypothesis "c")? We present this calculation as an effort to depict a feasible "energy-minimum" situation, to accompany the results of the "energy-maximum" situation discussed along with Option A_1. The resulting "minima" are 21.5 TBtu per person per day in 1985 and 13.7 TBtu in 2000—surprisingly close to Option C_3 with its slightly less efficient auto (hypothesis "a" in Table 2–6).

*In early 1974, a byproduct of the lowering of freeway speed limits, which was directed at reducing fuel consumption, was an improvement in safety records on the freeways.[60]

Even a 30 percent reduction in the automobile's energy consumption per passenger-mile (which results from increased occupancy as well as efficiency) causes only a 10 percent reduction in overall per-capita energy consumption for transportation by 2000. Thus the connection between automobile fuel economy and overall transportation energy is not as strong here as it was in the previous options. A very important consequence of Option C_3 is that the automobile no longer dominates, either in trips or in total energy use.

Option A_1 has been compared with an energy-maximum situation and Option C_3 with an energy-minimum situation, in which the assumptions for each option were pushed to extremes. In both cases, the extreme result was similar to the actual result of the option. Thus we conclude with confidence that the nine options span a realistic range of expected energy requirements for urban passenger transportation over the next 30 years.

ENERGY RESULTS AND CONCLUSIONS

Comparison of Countywide Per-Capita Results for Options

At last we are ready to examine the energy implications of all nine options. Let us begin by looking at a figure which shows how the energy a county resident uses to transport himself on weekdays would vary among the options between now and the year 2000 (see Figure 2–6). The picture shows a certain symmetry: by the year 2000 the *decrease* in energy consumption for the small-car, energy-conscious option (C_3) is almost as large as the *increase* which would follow from the luxury car, energy-oblivious option (A_1). The two limiting cases appear as mirror images of each other. Between these extremes, the other options group themselves roughly according to their parent scenarios.

We can examine the energy results for the options from two points of view. First, for the target dates 1985 and 2000, how does the projected energy consumption vary among the options? The answer puts future energy consumption in the perspective of "what might otherwise be." One conclusion of this study is that if society chooses a course of unrestrained energy growth, as in Option A_1, that is indeed a choice and not a necessity. The energy use level of Option A_1 is not inevitable; transportation energy in the future could conceivably be a small fraction of this amount. We have pointed out the enormous discrepancy between the two extreme options, for which the results differ by a factor of 5 in 1985 and a factor of 10 in 2000. As new technology is introduced in Scenario B, modifying Scenario A's continuation of present trends, the potential for a 40 percent drop in 1985 per-capita energy consumption, and 50 percent savings in 2000 becomes apparent. Even more dramatically, as the attitude changes in Scenario C are added to the technological innovations in Scenario B, per-capita energy consumption declines by a factor of 4 in 1985 and factor of 7 in 2000.

A second point of view considers what future energy consumption is

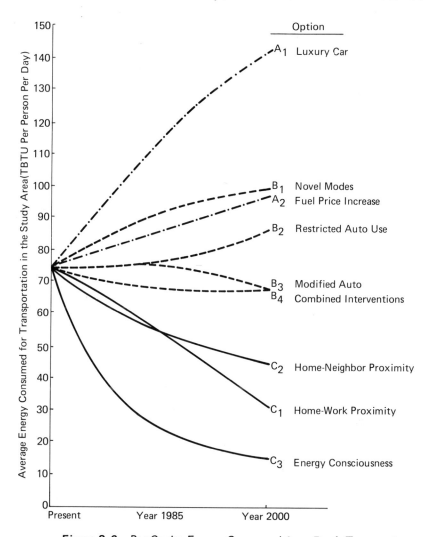

Figure 2-6. Per-Capita Energy Consumed for a Day's Transportation in the Study Area, for the Present and for Each of the Nine Options in 1985 and 2000

likely to be relative to what it is now. In reality, we cannot jump from one option to another in the year 1985 or 2000; rather, we move forward in time from the transportation of the 1970s, possibly to something like one of the options described here. Comparing anticipated future energy use with present consumption, we find that where energy growth is unrestrained (Option A_1), per-capita energy consumption increases by 60 percent by 1985 and 100 percent by 2000. In the other direction it is possible that in an energy-conscious world

(Option C$_3$) per-capita energy consumption would be one-third of its present value by 1985, and one-fifth by 2000.

Total per-capita energy usage is calculated from the energy consumed per passenger-mile for each available travel mode, with each mode weighted according to its use. Before attempting to explain the differences and similarities among modes as shown in Figure 2–6, let us take time out to look at how the energy efficiency varies among modes in the nine options, both for 1985 and 2000 (see Table 2–7).

The measure here for energy efficiency is the average energy consumed per passenger-mile. Energy efficiency can increase as energy consumption per vehicle-mile declines, or as average occupancy rises, or both.* We have concluded that marked improvement of intrinsic energy characteristics is technologically feasible for the automobile but not for other modes. This improvement, combined with increased average occupancy, produces a range of energy efficiencies for the auto which varies by a factor of more than 5 among the options for the year 2000. For the other modes, the variation is not nearly so dramatic—a factor of 2 at the most; our assumption is that improved efficiency in these modes comes principally from increased occupancy. The consequence is that the auto, which in Option A$_1$ is the great energy-consumer, is only 50 percent less efficient than the city bus in 1985 in Option C$_3$. By the year 2000 it is competitive with the motorcycle.

It is interesting that the city bus, even assuming a mediocre 20 percent occupancy level, is on a par, energy-wise, with the efficient autos of Scenario C. We consider a total shift to buses impracticable: hence the need for emphasis on improved auto efficiency, to achieve substantial overall savings in transportation energy.

The importance of occupancy levels in Dial-A-Ride and PRT vehicles is obvious from Table 2–7. In energy terms the gasoline-powered Dial-A-Ride vehicle is on a par with the big auto in Options A$_2$ and B$_1$ for 1985; in 2000, by virtue of increased average occupancy it is comparable to the medium auto of Option B$_4$. (As Table 2–7 shows, Dial-A-Ride is actually the least efficient of all modes in Option B$_1$, 1985; this reflects our assumption of low average occupancy.) For Option C$_3$ in 2000, the assumed Dial-A-Ride and PRT systems are equally efficient as people-movers, but they are still less than half as efficient as the small auto which this option includes. Of course, no motorized modes in any case can compete in energy terms with human propulsion—walking and bicycling.

About half of the tenfold variation in per-capita energy use among modes and options arises from improved efficiency of the auto. In view of the

---

*Specifically, the energy consumed per passenger-mile is calculated from the quotient of these two quantities: the energy consumed per vehicle-mile and the average number of passengers per vehicle. Actual values assigned to these quantities are found, for all the options, in Appendix A.

Table 2-7. Energy (TBtu) Consumed per Passenger-Mile for the Travel Modes Comprising Each Option, for 1985 and 2000

	Auto	Bus	Dial-a-Ride	PRT	Walk	Bicycle	Motorcycle
The Present	8.6	4.6	—	—	0.22	—	—
Option in 1985:							
A₁	10.1	3.9	—	—	0.22 →	—	—
A₂	8.1	3.9	—	—		—	—
B₁	8.1	3.9	13.6	—		—	—
B₂	7.1	3.1	8.1	—		—	—
B₃	7.1	3.9	—	—		—	—
B₄	6.2	3.1	8.1	—		—	—
C₁	7.1	2.6	8.1	—		0.34 →	2.1 →
C₂	6.2	2.6	8.1	—			
C₃	3.9	2.6	6.8	—			
Option in 2000:							
A₁	10.1	3.1	—	—	0.22 →	—	—
A₂	8.1	3.1	—	—		—	—
B₁	8.1	—	8.1	9.2		—	—
B₂	7.1	—	5.0	8.1		—	—
B₃	5.7	3.1	—	—		—	—
B₄	5.0	—	5.0	8.1		—	—
C₁	4.1	—	5.0	6.7		0.34 →	2.1 →
C₂	4.1	—	5.0	6.7			
C₃	1.8	—	4.3	4.5			

complexity of quantities (70 in total) which define each option,* we shall attempt to highlight the salient features of each one. The remaining variation is basically due to changed trip lengths and shifts to travel modes that are more efficient than automobiles.

Figure 2–6 depicts some dramatic changes among the options in per-capita energy consumption. In 2000, energy consumption is 30 percent lower for Option A_2 than for Option A_1. The principal difference is that automobile size shrinks from a super-big to a big car. In terms of energy results, Option B_1 (Novel Modes) differs little from A_2; but B_2 (Restricted Auto Use) shows substantially lower results. The carpooling assumption for Option B_2 causes a significant decrease in the auto's energy consumption per passenger-mile. Without that assumption, the results for B_2 would be difficult to distinguish from those of A_2. It appears that restricted auto use in the city, as envisioned in this study, brings about reduced energy use mainly by virtue of increased auto occupancy. Greater use of alternate modes is in itself of limited value in saving energy, given our assumption that new modes, to attract riders, must be reasonably competitive with cars in comfort and convenience.

The energy consumption of Option B_3 (Modified Auto) parallels the result of B_2 to 1985. The energy characteristics of Option B_3's medium-sized car are significantly different from those of earlier options. As it happens, the big-car-with-carpooling assumption in Option B_2 produces the same energy consumption per passenger-mile as does the medium-car-without-carpooling assumption in Option B_3, for 1985. By 2000, the auto fuel economy of Option B_3 more than compensates for the increased auto occupancy of Option B_2, so that overall energy use drops by 20 percent.

Option B_4 (Combined-Intervention), with the same medium car as in Option B_3, shows a drop in the energy consumption rate by 1985, but the savings level off by 2000. By that time, energy use for transportation in Options B_4 and B_3 is approximately the same. If we omit the carpooling assumption from Option B_4, then energy consumption is about the same as in Option B_3 in 1985, and greater than Option B_3 for 2000. In this case, the chief difference in these two options lies in the use of PRT and Dial-A-Ride; for B_3 they are not available. Our results thus imply that carpooling is more effective in saving energy than Dial-A-Ride and PRT.

As we proceed from Scenario B to Scenario C, the various life style changes cause different, but in all cases, striking reductions in per-capita energy consumption. Option C_1, which assumes that people wish to live much closer to their work than they do at present, would create a major change by 2000, when compared with the already energy-thrifty situation in Option B_3 or B_4.

---

*These quantities described how much people travel, by what modes, and the energy and occupancy characteristics of each mode. Appendix A contains the relationship between the per-capita energy consumption and these quantities, as well as the values assigned to these quantities for each option.

Option C_2, which considers the effects of higher-density dwelling, yields an energy reduction in 1985 comparable to the previous option. By 2000 Option C_1, that of living closer to work, shows up as a somewhat more effective way of saving transportation energy than increasing residential densities.*

If people combine some degree of high-density living with home-work proximity, if they choose to walk on many of their short trips, and, in addition, if they own few, very small autos, this mix (Option C_3) would yield the greatest energy reduction of all. Comparing Option C_3 with the previous option, we find a 30 percent reduction in the auto's energy consumption (per vehicle-mile) by the year 2000, and a drop of nearly 70 percent in the overall per-capita energy consumption. Increased average occupancy of the modes used, as well as a shift to walking and bicycling, is responsible for a large fraction of the change. We conclude from the results of these three options that higher-density living can be one key to energy reduction. Shorter daily work-trips and a generally raised energy consciousness offer an even greater potential for energy savings.

We find, then, a significant drop in the energy consumption pattern whenever the characteristics of the "average" auto are changed, and in addition, when an attitude change strongly affects the travel patterns. Within Scenario B, it is clear that major energy savings arise from the lighter, more efficient, or more fully occupied automobiles.

This study's conclusions suggest that policies which promote effective public transit in a city may also indirectly improve auto efficiency, by encouraging higher occupancy in cars. Restrictions on auto use, which is a policy that fits with greater use of alternate modes, simultaneously promote carpool-ing.** But it must be emphasized that the use of alternate modes such as Dial-A-Ride and PRT, even combined with restrictions on auto use, brings about only a marginal saving of energy, unless the characteristics of cars (i.e., energy per vehicle-mile and average occupancy) also change. This implies that alternate modes per se are of limited value for saving energy, when compared with improving the efficiency (per passenger-mile) of automobiles.

Probably the main reason for this surprising result is that in the forseeable future, the automobile, of all travel modes, offers the greatest flexibility in its energy characteristics. Buses must be large to meet the peak-hour demand. The PRT system, if it is to maintain its personal nature in

---

*Whether to attach great significance to this hierarchy is questionable, especially in view of the fact that the results for C_1 are strongly tied to the assumption concerning the projected decentralization trend; a change in this assumption produced a result for Option C_1 which was closer to the result for Option C_2. Suffice it to say that either of these life style changes would apparently cause a reduction in the energy consumed for transportation.

**It is not reasonable to restrict auto use without providing alternatives, and an obvious way to provide incentives for using the new system would be to place restrictions on the use of its chief competitor, the private auto.

order to compete with the automobile, offers very little energy advantage over a moderate-sized automobile carrying the same number of people; it is even *more* energy-intensive than a small auto.

Clearly alternate modes would become more energy-attractive if their average occupancy were increased. The city bus, fully loaded, is over 10 times as efficient as a 3,600-pound auto with today's average occupancy, per-passenger mile. However, observations made in this project conclude that a significant increase in the load factor of buses is hard to attain. Most of the bus riders at present in Mercer County are "transit captives," without other means of transportation. Even if the proportion of noncaptive riders were to double, overall ridership would increase only 13 percent. Extending bus routes outside the central business district has the unfortunate result of cutting the average load factor in half. A combination of large buses for peak hours with the same number of small Dial-A-Ride buses for off-peak hours is a possible solution. Such a system, however, would be extremely capital-intensive. The energy efficiency of small buses is much lower than that of large buses (energy per seat-mile for small 10 passenger vans is more than double that for large diesel-powered buses), so that the energy advantages of such a system might not warrant the increase in capital cost.

In considering potential solutions to rising energy costs, we do not intend to dismiss as unimportant the role of nonprivate transportation. Almost any public system is more energy-efficient than a large private automobile. Even a large city bus carrying three passengers is thriftier in energy use than a 2,600-pound auto carrying only the driver. But it is economically difficult for public transit to compete with cars. Highway systems are supported to an extent that is considered inconceivable for buses and trains.* For the sake of convenience, the automobile system is extremely inefficient—vehicles are idle much of the time, and passenger loads are low; no public system could tolerate such inefficiences.

It seems reasonable to conclude that the auto is the only transportation system in the U.S. which is capable of operating *without* a subsidy. Continued dominance of the private automobile depends upon continued road building. Curtailment of road construction could act as a boost to mass transit, both by making its use more attractive and by freeing highway funds for subsidies for it.

Throughout this study we assume that fares for public systems— PRT, Dial-A-Ride, or the conventional bus—must be comparable to, or cheaper than, auto expenses, if they are to assume a substantial share of trips. Indications

---

*Present public highway funding for construction and maintenance totals over $20 billion per year from federal, state and local sources,[61] while recent congressional legislation calls for $11.8 billion for a six-year mass transit subsidy,[62] or one-tenth the annual level of highway support.

are that none of these public systems can be self-supporting.* If they are to be successful and provide a needed public service, they will no doubt require *operation* subsidies from public funds. Since an effective system must serve the greater part of a metropolitan area, and thus cross municipal boundaries, funding at the level of the state, and probably the federal, government is called for. (This suggests the establishment of a state authority to coordinate and operate local transit systems. The New Jersey State Department of Transportation to some extent has this authority now, but has often been accused of being concerned less with meeting the transport needs of the people in the cities than getting the most highway for the dollar.)

Even though public transit may not provide the greatest energy-saving solution in medium-sized metropolitan areas, other motives may impel cities to improve public transit in the future. Important among these motives are: reducing pollution, relieving congestion, and providing transportation for autoless citizens. These systems, if well planned and carried out, might prove more attractive and satisfactory than big private cars. Possibly more important, the availability of alternate modes can be a necessary first step for some of the energy-saving policies such as the auto-use restrictions considered in Scenario B, or even high-density development patterns such as those postulated in Scenario C.

Returning now to the attitude changes in Scenario C, the extreme in energy reduction is found in energy-conscious Option C_3. This is due not to one single factor, but rather to a combination: living conditions which lead to shorter trips, higher-density living, and greater use of energy-thrifty modes of travel. The small auto in Option C_3 is indeed 30 percent more efficient than the medium-sized auto in the previous four options, but the disparity in energy use among these options is far greater than 30 percent. For 2000, the per-capita energy consumption for Option C_3 is less than half that of Options C_1 and C_2. It is a small fraction of the transportation energy use in Options B_3 and B_4. Thus we conclude that the great energy savings of Option C_3 are due in part to the use of very efficient automobiles, but even more to life style changes which affect people's living patterns and modify their travel demands.

What is the energy outlook for the future, compared with the present? In our extreme cases, we have seen a potential for cutting per-capita energy consumption for transportation to one-fifth today's level by 2000 (Option C_3). Option A_1 demonstrates the possibility that it may double. Even

*The Mercer County Improvement Authority, which has operated the Mercer Metro bus system since 1968 when it was taken over from bankruptcy by the county, operates at a net loss; even though state and county subsidies provided 22 percent of the operating expenses, farebox receipts in fiscal 1972, covering nearly 70 percent of the expenses, were not sufficient to make up the remainder (reference 3). Even the modern Bay Area Rapid Transit District in northern California, with its technological innovations and unprecedented attractive features, anticipates annual operating deficits on the order of $30 million.

with the assumed effect of fuel price increases in Option A_2, energy consumption would still increase by 30 percent in the next 30 years. Average auto weight remains the same as now in Option A_2, but overall travel increases—an apparent result of the continued trend toward owning more automobiles.

The intermediate options demonstrate that major changes would be required to keep energy consumption at present levels. In Option B_2 where restricted auto use in the city is assumed to stimulate carpooling, there is only a minimal increase in transportation energy use by 1985. By 2000 energy consumption increases again. The medium-sized, more efficient auto of Option B_3 offers for the first time the possibility of an energy reduction, albeit a small one, between the present and 2000. Only when life styles and living patterns are changed do we find very substantial reductions from today's level in the per-capita energy consumption associated with urban transportation (about half the present level in Options C_1 and C_2).

Results for the Three Regions

The breakdown of the study area into three regions makes possible independent observations for three different levels of urbanization. The densely populated city of Trenton (Region I) has transportation problems in common with other U.S. cities experiencing an economic and population decline. The immediate surrounding area, the inner suburbs comprising Region II, has received the population and jobs leaving the city. The affluent suburbs on the outer edge of the metropolitan area (Region III in this case) remain more or less autonomous in that their development and growth do not depend on the inner regions.

We were able to examine programs which are suitable to one region but have little relevance to the others. For example, public transportation systems might provide a reasonable substitute for cars in Region I, while in the time period the study covers the sparsely populated Region III remains almost entirely dependent on the private auto. Table 2–8 shows a breakdown of the per-capita energy consumed for transportation in the three regions, for the early 1970s and for each of the nine options in 1985 and 2000.

Trends in energy reduction follow much the same pattern for each region as for the study area as a whole; but the magnitude of the energy results for each option varies widely among the three regions. For a given option, energy consumption in Region I is generally less than one-half of what it is in Region II; and Region II energy use is generally at least 20 percent lower than in Region III. From the inner to the outer regions, that is, from city to suburbs, accessibility to autos increases, and average trip distances are longer, because of lower residential densities.

To a surprising extent, the per-capita energy results for Region II closely resemble those for the entire area. The similarity becomes more marked as 2000 approaches; at this time the results for Region II and for the whole

Table 2-8. Per Capita Energy Consumption for the Purposes of an Average Weekday's Transportation in the Study Area (TBtu per Person per Day, for the Present and in 1985 and 2000 According to the Options for the Future)

Option:	Scenario A: Continuation of Current Trends		Scenario B: Technological Innovations				Scenario C: Lifestyle Changes		
	A_1	A_2	B_1	B_2	B_3	B_4	C_1	C_2	C_3
	Luxury Car	Fuel Price Increase	Novel Modes	Restricted Auto Use	Modified Auto	Combined Intervention	Home Near Work	Home Near Neighbors	Energy Consciousness
Average auto:[a]	Super-big	Big	Big	Big	Medium	Medium	Medium	Medium	Small
Year 1985									
Early 1970s[b]									
Region I	(38.6)								
Region II	(89.1)								
Region III	(99.7)								
County average	(74.1)								
Region I	59.4	44.4	49.2	39.3	39.3	35.5	28.3	29.7	12.6
Region II	127.0	91.8	96.3	80.2	80.6	71.3	54.6	54.3	21.2
Region III	145.7	117.4	126.6	106.1	102.7	93.9	86.0	86.4	41.0
County average	114.3	86.0	91.8	76.5	75.4	67.9	55.3	55.0	24.2
Year 2000									
Region I	(38.6) 71.0	51.9	57.7	49.5	36.9	45.1	18.4	30.7	8.9
Region II	(89.1) 144.4	95.6	100.0	86.4	67.2	71.7	29.7	44.7	14.7
Region III	(99.7) 187.0	129.7	130.7	111.6	90.8	82.9	46.8	64.5	20.1
County average	(74.1) 141.3	96.3	99.7	85.7	67.6	68.9	32.1	45.1	14.7

[a] Characteristic weights and mileages of these four basic autos were assumed to be:
(present average: 3,600 lb., 12 mpg)
super-big: 4,050 lb., 10 mpg
big: 3,400 lb., 13 mpg
medium: 3,400 lb., 16 mpg in 1985; 3,000 lb., 20 mpg in 2000
small: 2,500 lb., 19 mpg in 1985; 1,800 lb., 29 mpg in 2000.
[b] Present level of energy consumption is given in parentheses, for comparison.

SMSA differ by only 1 or 2 percent for most options. It appears that in some sense the inner suburbs comprising Region II represent an average for the country as a whole. Can we conclude that the transportation needs of the inner suburbs in the Trenton area are representative of nondeclining, medium-sized metropolitan areas in general? It will be remembered that the city of Trenton is similar in many points to older and larger declining cities. Most cities the size of Trenton have a considerably lower population density (2,000 or 3,000 people per square mile, vs. Trenton's 14,000) and are continuing to grow rapidly. (See Table 2–2, where two cities Stamford, Connecticut, and San Bernardino, California show these characteristics.) As residential density is a most important determinant of travel behavior, we suggest that the trends in future energy consumption shown here for the inner suburbs (or for the metropolitan area as a whole) may apply to medium-sized growing cities or to larger metropolitan areas with these cities as their centers.

Only with advanced technological innovations plus major life style changes, as in Option C_1 in the year 2000, does per-capita energy consumption for the study area as a whole come to resemble energy use in the central city of today (see Table 2–8). (The fact that the city's per-capita energy consumption is low is partially due to the high-density residential living in the city, but it is also attributable to Trenton's low income and high unemployment levels, neither of which is a strategy we wish to advocate for the purposes of reducing energy consumption.) In Scenario C, because people live closer to their work or to each other, the shorter trip lengths which today are distinctive to the densely populated central city become characteristic of the outer regions as well. However, at no point do the population densities of the outer regions resemble the city's. Though higher population densities may reduce the demand for energy, inner-city densities throughout urbanized areas are not necessary for an overall reduction in transportation energy.

Effect of Different Decentralization Assumptions

It is clear that energy consumption for passenger transportation varies with population distributions. In order to estimate future population distributions, some assumptions concerning decentralization trends had to be made. We mentioned early in this chapter that we examined the nine transportation options on the basis of three separate decentralization patterns. The results we have so far discussed were based on a reversal-decentralization trend, where decentralization of the central city continues until about 1985, at which point the city's property values have fallen to a low enough level to stimulate growth within the city. The two other patterns were: controlled decentralization, in which the population of the central city stabilizes at some intermediate time; and continued decentralization through the year 2000.

Deferring the detailed results to Appendix B, we remark that the energy variation due to the three different decentralization patterns was only moderate (a few percent), in contrast to the much wider variation among options for any single decentralization pattern. In part, this is because the present enormous differences in population densities of the three regions are assumed to persist through 2000, no matter how the trend may run. Even if the central city goes on losing its population to the suburbs at the present rate, it will still remain at least four times more densely populated than Region II through 2000 (over 10,000 people per square mile). The outlying areas (Region III) will remain sparsely populated, with never many more than 1,000 people per square mile. In general, cities in the U.S. from now until 2000 have long-range transportation problems which will not be solved, and may even be aggravated, by migration away from the central city. If the major conclusions of this study are valid for the case we adopted (reversal-decentralization), they would hold at least as well for any other likely decentralization pattern.

On the whole, per-capita energy use is highest with continued decentralization, declines in the controlled pattern, and is lowest with the reversal trend. In 1985, the differing effects of various decentralization patterns are most pronounced in Region II, to which the population is or is not migrating, depending on the assumptions involved, while the effect in Region III is minimal. By 2000, when the effects of the three decentralization patterns have diverged, the greatest effect is seen in Region I, where the revitalization of the city depends on the extent to which decentralization has continued or reversed. This effect is somewhat masked in the energy results for the entire study area because per-capita energy consumption in Region I is so low compared to the two other regions.

It should be noted that revitalization of the central city, and a reversal (to some degree) of the current decentralization trend, appear to be necessary conditions for Scenario C's life style changes, which affect home and job patterns. If executives stay in the suburbs while the blue-collar workers live in the city, commuting long distances to work will necessarily continue. If rich and poor are separated in the same way, the disparity between city and suburb will widen. The likely event is total dependence on the auto in the suburbs, and diminished support for public transit in the city.

Land use controls traditionally have been the responsibility of local units of government, each of which protects the goals of its own individual municipality by local zoning decisions without regard for other communities. The development patterns considered here, either toward reversing the decay of the central city or the radical change in living patterns in Scenario C, would probably require a degree of centralization for land use and utility decisions in the near future. (A more complete discussion of land-use controls is given in the separate report listed in the third reference of this chapter.) Thus decisions would be shifted from local to the state or county level.

Total Energy Consumption for the County

All of our conclusions thus far have been drawn from per-capita energy results. If a scarcity of petroleum should develop, total energy consumption would become a more relevant figure to examine. Table 2–9 shows the expected total energy consumption for travel on a weekday in the study area, for the early 1970s, and for the nine future options for 1985 and 2000. (Again we return to the assumed reversal-decentralization trend.) The total energy results vary according to the options in much the same way as per-capita results; the conclusions already stated can be applied to total energy consumption as well. The only difference is that because of the increased population in 2000, the trends for total energy use are less dramatic than for per-capita energy consumption.

Under the assumptions this study makes, future energy consumption for the population as a whole is considerably higher than present energy consumption, except for Scenario C. This implies that future energy consumption for transportation in the area studied here, and thus probably in many other metropolitan areas, will increase significantly by 1985 and even more so by 2000, unless some of Scenario C's district changes in life style and energy characteristics of automobiles take place.

CONCLUDING REMARKS

Many of the energy-reducing strategies considered in this analysis focus directly on the automobile. At present, in our study area, the auto is responsible for 98 percent of the total energy consumed for urban transportation. Is this dominance likely to continue? From Table 2–10 we see that the auto's role varies widely among the nine options.

Where the auto is far and away the principal energy-consumer, as in Options A_1, A_2, and B_3, any improvement in its energy efficiency produces a proportionate decrease in the overall energy consumed to transport people. In these cases, an emphasis on fuel-thrifty automobiles is the technological measure which makes the biggest difference. As we progress through other options, the combined use of efficient autos and other energy-thrifty modes dilutes the

Table 2–9. Total Energy Consumed by the Population of the Study Area as a Whole, for the Purposes of an Average Weekday's Transportation (Billion Btu per Day, for the Present and in 1985 and 2000 According to the Options for the Future)

Option	A_1	A_2	B_1	B_2	B_3	B_4	C_1	C_2	C_3
			Early 1970s: 22.5 Billion Btu per Day						
1985	45.1	33.9	36.2	30.1	29.7	26.8	22.4	21.7	9.32
2000	68.6	47.0	48.7	41.7	32.9	33.6	16.1	20.4	6.93

Table 2-10. Extent of Dominance of Automobile in Future Options, for Study Area As a Whole, in the Year 2000

Option	A_1	A_2	B_1	B_2	B_3	B_4	C_1	C_2	C_3
Portion of total energy attributable to auto	1.00	0.99	0.71	0.65	0.99	0.57	0.55	0.49	0.36

dominance of the automobile. By 2000 less than half of total transportation energy consumption will be attributable to the automobile in Option C_3. When the auto's fuel economy reaches a certain level (about 30 mpg), the relation between still better fuel efficiency and further overall energy savings is considerably weakened. In these cases greater savings are apt to flow from shifts in preference toward living nearer work, perhaps in high-density clusters combining residences and employment centers.

Thus we conclude that there is no single strategy that will most effectively temper growth in energy consumption for urban transportation. What works best in a densely populated city may not work at all in the neighboring suburbs. A policy which is effective when the auto dominates is not so effective if living patterns reduce the auto's role. Mass transit in place of the auto usually saves energy; but generalizations about its energy-saving benefits without sufficient regard for other factors, such as future development patterns, can prove false. Even changes in living patterns which help to revitalize the central city do not invariably result in less travel. A more important element is where people live in relation to the facilities they need for employment, shopping, recreation, and society of other people. In general, smaller, more efficient autos carrying more passengers, more effective use of public transportation, and altered living arrangements so that people live closer to their work and to other people, all have the potential of saving energy. The greatest energy reduction will come about through a combination of all these changes, including a change in outlook so that concern for energy thrift becomes part of a different way of life.

Appendix A

Travel Data and Its Relation to Energy Consumption

TRAVEL DATA REQUIRED FOR THE ANALYSIS

In order to estimate energy savings resulting from various transportation strategies, it was necessary to develop formalism which takes us from travel data for the population in question to the total energy consumption resulting from their travel. Ultimately the quantity we want to calculate is the average per capita energy consumed for the purposes of transportation during a typical weekday: call this "e". Clearly this depends on the amount the average person travels, which in turn depends on the average number (η) and average length (L) of the trips he takes. In addition, if β_m represents the percent of passenger-miles which is traveled on mode m, then the product $\beta_m \eta L$ is the average number of miles a person travels each day on the mth travel mode. A measure of the energy efficiency of the available modes is given by the average energy consumed to transport one passenger one mile: letting ϵ_m represent the average energy consumed per vehicle-mile for the mth mode, and λ_m, the load factor or average number of passengers per vehicle for that mode, then the average energy consumed per passenger-mile is given by ϵ_m/λ_m. We can combine these quantities to find the average per capita energy consumption

$$e = \sum_m [(\epsilon_m/\lambda_m)\beta_m] \ \eta L \tag{1}$$

where the summation extends over all available modes.

Ordinarily a transportation planning study yields a distribution of trips rather than passenger-miles, by mode and/or purpose. For example, we might know, for a given purpose "p", the distribution of trips using mode m (i.e., "modal split"), as given by α_{mp} where $\sum_m \alpha_{mp} = 1$, and, in addition, the average number of trips each person takes for purpose p, denoted η_p so that

$\Sigma_p \eta_p = \eta$. Then, of all the trips a person takes during an average weekday, the fraction which are by the mth mode *and* for purpose p is given by

$$\gamma_{mp} = \alpha_{mp}\, \eta_p/\eta \quad \text{where} \quad \sum_{m,p} \gamma_{mp} = 1. \tag{2}$$

If $L_p^{(m)}$ is the average length of the trips by the mth mode for purpose p, then the passenger-mile distribution can be rewritten

$$\beta_m = \sum_p \gamma_{mp}\, L_p^{(m)}/L \tag{3}$$

where the overall average trip length L is given by

$$L = \sum_{m,p} \gamma_{mp}\, L_p^{(m)}.$$

We now set up a minimum set of parameters sufficient for the evaluation of the average energy consumed for a weekday's transportation:

η_p : effective number of trips per person for purpose p

α_{mp} : fraction of trips for purpose p using mode m ("modal split")

$L_p^{(m)}$: average trip length for purpose p (using mode m)

λ_m : persons per vehicle for mode m

ϵ_m : energy consumed per vehicle-mile for mode m

N : total population

We can express the per capita energy consumption e in terms of these parameters. Using Eqs. (1), (2), and (3), the final form for e becomes:

$$e = \sum_m \left[(\epsilon_m/\lambda_m) \sum_p \eta_p\, \alpha_{mp}\, L_p^{(m)} \right]. \tag{4}$$

Here the summation extends over all available modes and all trip purposes. The total energy E consumed by the study area's population consisting of N persons is therefore

$$E = Ne. \tag{5}$$

For the analysis here, seven modes are included: auto, bus, Dial-a-Ride, PRT, walk, bicycle and motorcycle. In addition, trip purpose is broken into two categories: "work" and non-work (which we will denote "other"). In this way, separation into rush-hour, which is dominated by work trips, and non-rush-hour demands is facilitated.

Average trip lengths can generally be estimated for work as distinct from non-work trips, but further disaggregation by mode is not always feasible— hence the partial suppression of the superscript in $L_p^{(m)}$. For the purposes of our analysis here, we assume that, in nearly all cases, for a given purpose, the trip lengths are independent of mode.[a] Thus we can write $L_p^{(m)} = L_p$. The only exceptions are the humanly propelled modes: for walking, we assume an average trip length of one mile and for bicycling, two miles, for both work and other purposes. Thus our trip-length analysis reduces to two estimates: average trip length for work and average trip length for other purposes.

The study area, Mercer County, is considered to consist of three regions possessing three distinct travel patterns. The regions are:

Region I : City of Trenton
Region II : Urbanized area surrounding Trenton
Region III: Remainder of County.

Trips by a resident in I to or within another region will contribute to the travel characteristics of Region I; the same is true for the residents of II and III. Thus we end up with three sets of energy results. Letting $e^{(I)}$ and $E^{(I)}$ denote the per capita and total energy consumption for population $N^{(I)}$ in Region I, and using similar notation for Regions II and III, we can calculate the per capita energy $\bar{e}$ and total energy consumption $\bar{E}$ for the entire study area:

$$\bar{E} = E^{(I)} + E^{(II)} + E^{(III)} \tag{6}$$

and

$$\bar{e} = \bar{E} / \left(N^{(I)} + N^{(II)} + N^{(III)} \right). \tag{7}$$

[a]It is probably reasonable to assume that trip lengths differ more for work and non-work purposes, than they do for two different modes (e.g., auto and bus), between the same origin and destination.

Equations (6) and (7) in combination with Equation (4) were used to calculate the final results presented in Figure 2-6 and Tables 2-8 and 2-9.

Our procedure was to estimate, in addition to the population N, the following travel parameters for *each* of the three regions: average number of trips for work and non-work purposes (η_p), average trip-length by the same two purposes (L_p), and modal split for each purpose (α_{mp}). The same values for the parameters, ϵ_m and λ_m, which measure the energy efficiency of the modes were used for all the three regions; this reflects the considerable travel among the regions, as when a resident of an outlying suburb drives in city traffic, and therefore these values represent an overall county average.[b]

DETERMINATION OF THE TRAVEL DATA FOR THE PRESENT SITUATION IN THE STUDY AREA

Transportation in the early 1970's in Mercer County was used as a foundation for the development of the nine options. In order to indicate how one might estimate the travel parameters described above, we present here a brief discussion of how we arrived at the travel data for the present situation in the three regions in Mercer County. The reader is reminded that these data represent a composite of data from 1970 and results from surveys conducted between 1970 and the summer of 1973.

Population, and therefore density, figures were taken from the 1970 Census.[1] Most of the trip parameters for Region I were estimated with the aid of data supplied by the Trenton Transit Study. Lutin's analysis [2] of the Trenton Urban Area Travel Survey (UATS), a 1972 home interview survey of 15% of Trenton's households, yielded an estimate of 1.60 trips generated per person per day, i.e., using the notation established in Section A, $\eta = 1.60$ for Region I. This analysis attributed 48% of this total to work trips. If we use the subscript "w" to denote "work" trips and "o" to denote "other" trips, then $\eta_w = 0.77$ and $\eta_o = 0.83$.

All of the Trenton Transit Study's data apply to Region I, but not to Region II or III. Two observations were useful in expanding these Region I

---

[b]The use of an overall county average for ϵ_m and λ_m increases the ease with which we can isolate the energy effects of improving automobile mileage, decreasing average vehicle weight, or changing the energy characteristics of any one of the modes, while the travel behavior of the population remains unchanged. For example, let $\bar{e}$ be the per capita energy consumption resulting from ϵ_1, the average automobile energy consumption per vehicle-mile. Consider a change in ϵ_1 to $\epsilon_1 + \Delta\epsilon_1$ while all other "parameters" are held constant. If f_1 is the fraction of $\bar{e}$ attributable to the auto (and this is readily computed from the expression in Eq. (4)), then the revised per capita energy consumption is given by $\bar{e} + \Delta\bar{e}$ where

$$\frac{\Delta\bar{e}}{\bar{e}} = f_1 \frac{\Delta\epsilon_1}{\epsilon_1}$$

results to the remainder of the county. First, this value for η_w is within 1% of the estimate we would have obtained if we had assumed each worker makes two one-way work trips per day, i.e., η_w is well-approximated by twice the number of workers divided by the total population. We used this algorithm to estimate η_w for Region II and III. Second, the total per capita number of trips, η, was in agreement with predictions from the 1961 Pittsburgh Study [3] which estimates η as a function of residential density. By applying residential densities for Regions II and III to the analysis in the Pittsburgh Study, we estimated η for Regions II and III, and from that, $\eta_o = \eta - \eta_w$.

For the average length of trips for work and other purposes, we again relied on the UATS data, which includes average trip times according to purpose. By applying estimated average speeds (18 mph for auto, 14 mph for bus, which were estimated by the Trenton Transit Study's Survey of Trenton traffic; and 3 mph for walking) to the number of trips by mode, we converted the average trip times by purpose (approximately 20 minutes for work and 16 minutes for other) to the average trip lengths by purpose. The results are L_w = 5.0 and L_o = 2.7 miles; the overall average trip length L = 3.8 miles for Region I. To expand the Region I figure to the remainder of the county, ratios were calculated for work trips using Census data on the number of work trips from each municipality to the CBD, the remainder of the central city, the remainder of the county, or outside the county. Estimates were made of average distances between these residential locations and job locations, and average trip lengths were calculated. These estimates gave "as-the-crow-flies" distances which were considerably lower than actual travel distances. However, the ratios between the values for each of the three regions seemed reasonable, and were applied to the previously mentioned trip length estimates for Region I in order to get estimates for L_w and L_o for the remaining regions.

Throughout the analysis, the following indexing convention was used for the available modes:

m	*mode*
1	auto
2	bus
3	Dial-a-Ride
4	PRT
5	walk
6	bicycle
7	motorcycle

To determine the distribution of trips among the various transportation modes available (modal split), the Census data provided good estimates for work trips, for all three regions.[4] Under the assumption used throughout this study, that the train is not used for trips within the county (but, rather, for trips to New

York or Philadelphia), we considered only auto, bus and walk trips to estimate, respectively, α_1^w, α_2^w and α_5^w for the three regions.[c] Estimates for non-work trips relied on the findings of the Trenton Transit Study for Region I, and a combination of these findings and less systematic observations for Regions II and III. Briefly, for Region I the overall distribution of trips by mode, α_m, independent of purpose, was estimated from the UATS data; α_m^o was then calculated from α_m and α_m^w where

$$\alpha_m = \frac{\eta_w \alpha_m^w + \eta_o \alpha_m^o}{\eta}.$$

To estimate α_m^o for Regions II and III, we applied the ratio of walking trips for non-work to walking trips for work, i.e., α_5^o / α_5^w, for Region I to Regions II and III; thus from α_5^w we obtained α_5^o for Regions II and III. As implied by the Pittsburgh Study, a low bus ridership, i.e., a small value for α_2, was assumed for Regions II and III, and α_1^o is then given by $\alpha_1^o = 1 - \alpha_2^o - \alpha_5^o$ for each region. We comment that the bus capturing 8.9% of all trips in Trenton is encouragingly consistent with results obtained by the Trenton Transit Study's On-Board Bus Survey: $\alpha_2 = 0.089$ represents 14,910 trips, while the Survey measured an average of 14,772 bus trips per work day.

Finally, the load factors and energy consumption characteristics of the various modes must be determined. Since more accurate estimates for these parameters are available for the study area as a whole than for the regions individually, and since we are ultimately interested in an analysis of energy consumption of the entire study area, we used an overall average of λ_m and ϵ_m.

The load factors, i.e., number of persons per vehicle, for two modes (in particular, auto and bus; clearly, for walking, $\lambda_5 = 1$.) must be determined for the present situation. Average automobile occupancy, i.e., λ_1, was estimated from data collected in a survey conducted as part of this project during the summer of 1973. The primary purpose of this Auto Occupancy Survey was to measure λ_1^w and λ_1^o, and these data and their analysis are presented in a separate report.[5] Briefly, the results give $\lambda_1^w = 1.24 \pm .02$ and $\lambda_1^o = 1.63 \pm .03$. The average $\lambda_1 = 1.44$ passengers per automobile was used in the analysis. For the bus, λ_2 was determined from data supplied by the On-Board Bus Survey. For each of the ten routes covered by Mercer Metro, the average number of passengers per round trip and the average trip length per passenger were measured. By converting the average trip length (which, averaged over all routes, was 2.3 miles) to the percent of the round trip which a passenger covered on the average, we obtained an average occupancy of $\lambda_2 = 6.7$ passengers per bus.

[c]In order to separate mode from purpose, for clarity we replace the previous notation α_{mp} with α_m^{work} and α_m^{other}, or, abbreviated, α_m^w and α_m^o.

Estimates for the final parameter, ϵ_m, the energy per vehicle-mile for each mode, were summarized in Table 2-1, and discussed in a separate report [6]. Since the energy characteristics of the auto, as given by ϵ_1, received much attention in this study, Appendix C is devoted to the parameter ϵ, and its dependence on weight and engine type.

VALUES FOR THE TRAVEL DATA USED IN THE ANALYSIS

We are now ready to present the actual values assigned to all of the travel and energy parameters used in this analysis. The transportation planner or anyone else interested in these fine details should be cautioned that these values were not generated by rigorous mathematical models, but rather, they represent our best estimates for the values which the various parameters should assume.[d] The following tables contain these estimates, for each of the three regions comprising the study area, for travel in the early 1970's[e] and for each of the nine options considered for the dates 1985 and 2000. In addition, for one the options, C_1, in which the desire to live near work generated two distinct development patterns, two tables are presented.

[d]In terms of precision, these values can probably be estimated to only one significant figure. The last significant figure serves only to indicate relative changes and the direction of change with respect to corresponding values in other options.
[e]Actually Table A-1 duplicates Table 2-4, but is included here to facilitate comparison.

Table A-1.   Travel Parameters for the Study Area in the Early 1970's

Parameter			Region I		Region II		Region III		County Total
Population		N	104,786		132,007		67,323		304,116
Density (person/ sq. mile)			13,972		1,728		474		1,346
trip purpose		(p)	work	other	work	other	work	other	
Trips per person per day		η_p	0.77	0.83	0.85	1.45	0.83	1.77	
Trip length (miles)[a]		L_p	5.0	2.7	6.9	3.8	7.6	5.8	
Modal split	auto	α_{1p}	0.74	0.59	0.92	0.88	0.84	0.61	
	bus	α_{2p}	0.13	0.05	0.04	0.01	0.02	0.00	
	D-a-R	α_{3p}	–	–	–	–	–	–	
	PRT	α_{4p}	–	–	–	–	–	–	
	walk	α_{5p}	0.13	0.36	0.04	0.11	0.14	0.39	
	bicycle	α_{6p}	–	–	–	–	–	–	
	motorcycle	α_{7p}	–	–	–	–	–	–	

Energy (TBtu) per Vehicle-Mile and Load Factor		
auto	$\epsilon_1 = 12.3$	$\lambda_1 = 1.44$
bus	$\epsilon_2 = 30.8$	$\lambda_2 = 6.70$
D-a-R	$\epsilon_3 = \,-$	$\lambda_3 = \,-$
PRT	$\epsilon_4 = \,-$	$\lambda_4 = \,-$
walk	$\epsilon_5 = 0.22$	$\lambda_5 = 1.00$
bicycle	$\epsilon_6 = \,-$	$\lambda_6 = \,-$
motorcycle	$\epsilon_7 = \,-$	$\lambda_7 = \,-$

[a]In this and the following tables, the values shown for L_p apply to the motorized modes; for walking, $L_p = 1$ mile and for bicycling, $L_p = 2$ (all p).

Table A-2. Travel Parameters for Option A_1, in the Years 1985 and 2000 (Everybody Wants a Luxury Car)

		1985							County	2000							County
Parameter		Region I		Region II		Region III			Total	Region I		Region II		Region III			Total
Population	N	106,000		174,800		113,250			394,050	111,500		218,050		156,350			485,900
Density (persons/sq. mile)		14,130		2,290		800			1,740	14,870		2,850		1,100			2,150
trip purpose	(p)	work	other	work	other	work	other			work	other	work	other	work	other		
Trips per person per day	η_p	0.77	0.88	0.85	1.80	0.84	1.85			0.78	0.94	0.85	2.00	0.84	2.16		
Trip length (miles)	L_p	5.7	3.1	7.0	4.2	7.6	5.9			5.9	3.6	7.1	4.5	7.8	6.3		
Modal split — auto	α_{1p}	0.81	0.76	0.93	0.92	0.88	0.80			0.85	0.87	0.94	0.95	0.95	0.90		
bus	α_{2p}	0.12	0.04	0.03	0.00	0.02	0.00			0.10	0.03	0.02	0.00	0.00	0.00		
D-a-R	α_{3p}	–	–	–	–	–	–			–	–	–	–	–	–		
PRT	α_{4p}	–	–	–	–	–	–			–	–	–	–	–	–		
walk	α_{5p}	0.07	0.20	0.04	0.08	0.10	0.20			0.05	0.10	0.04	0.05	0.05	0.10		
bicycle	α_{6p}	–	–	–	–	–	–			–	–	–	–	–	–		
motorcycle	α_{7p}	–	–	–	–	–	–			–	–	–	–	–	–		

Energy (TBtu) per Vehicle-Mile and Load Factor:

	1985	2000
auto	$\epsilon_1 = 14.6$	$\epsilon_1 = 14.6$
bus	$\epsilon_2 = 30.8$	$\epsilon_2 = 30.8$
D-a-R	$\epsilon_3 = $ –	$\epsilon_3 = $ –
PRT	$\epsilon_4 = $ –	$\epsilon_4 = $ –
walk	$\epsilon_5 = 0.22$	$\epsilon_5 = 0.22$
bicycle	$\epsilon_6 = $ –	$\epsilon_6 = $ –
motorcycle	$\epsilon_7 = $ –	$\epsilon_7 = $ –
auto	$\lambda_1 = 1.44$	$\lambda_1 = 1.44$
bus	$\lambda_2 = 8.00$	$\lambda_2 = 10.00$
D-a-R	$\lambda_3 = $ –	$\lambda_3 = $ –
PRT	$\lambda_4 = $ –	$\lambda_4 = $ –
walk	$\lambda_5 = 1.00$	$\lambda_5 = 1.00$
bicycle	$\lambda_6 = $ –	$\lambda_6 = $ –
motorcycle	$\lambda_7 = $ –	$\lambda_7 = $ –

Table A-3. Travel Parameters for Option A_2 in the Years 1985 and 2000 (Fuel Price Increase)

Parameter		1985 Region I		Region II		Region III		County Total	2000 Region I		Region II		Region III		County Total
Population	N	107,000		176,500		110,500		394,000	113,000		221,500		153,500		488,000
Density (persons/sq. mile)		14,270		2,310		780		1,740	15,070		2,900		1,080		2,160
trip purpose	(p)	work	other	work	other	work	other		work	other	work	other	work	other	
Trips per person per day	η_p	0.77	0.75	0.85	1.40	0.84	1.80		0.78	0.78	0.85	1.35	0.84	1.85	
Trip length (miles)	L_p	5.7	3.2	7.0	4.5	7.6	6.3		5.9	3.7	7.1	5.0	7.8	6.4	
Modal split auto	α_{1p}	0.79	0.71	0.93	0.90	0.88	0.77		0.83	0.82	0.93	0.90	0.90	0.85	
bus	α_{2p}	0.12	0.04	0.03	0.00	0.02	0.00		0.10	0.03	0.03	0.00	0.00	0.00	
D-a-R	α_{3p}	–	–	–	–	–	–		–	–	–	–	–	–	
PRT	α_{4p}	–	–	–	–	–	–		–	–	–	–	–	–	
walk	α_{5p}	0.09	0.25	0.04	0.10	0.10	0.23		0.07	0.15	0.04	0.10	0.10	0.15	
bicycle	α_{6p}	–		–		–			–		–		–		
motorcycle	α_{7p}	–		–		–			–		–		–		

Energy (TBtu) per Vehicle-Mile and Load Factor

1985:

auto	$\epsilon_1 = 11.7$		$\lambda_1 = 1.44$
bus	$\epsilon_2 = 30.8$		$\lambda_2 = 8.00$
D-a-R	$\epsilon_3 = $ –		$\lambda_3 = $ –
PRT	$\epsilon_4 = $ –		$\lambda_4 = $ –
walk	$\epsilon_5 = 0.22$		$\lambda_5 = 1.00$
bicycle	$\epsilon_6 = $ –		$\lambda_6 = $ –
motorcycle	$\epsilon_7 = $ –		$\lambda_7 = $ –

2000:

auto	$\epsilon_1 = 11.7$		$\lambda_1 = 1.44$
bus	$\epsilon_2 = 30.8$		$\lambda_2 = 10.00$
D-a-R	$\epsilon_3 = $ –		$\lambda_3 = $ –
PRT	$\epsilon_4 = $ –		$\lambda_4 = $ –
walk	$\epsilon_5 = 0.22$		$\lambda_5 = 1.00$
bicycle	$\epsilon_6 = $ –		$\lambda_6 = $ –
motorcycle	$\epsilon_7 = $ –		$\lambda_7 = $ –

Table A-4. Travel Parameters for Option B_1, in the Years 1985 and 2000 (Novel Modes)

Parameter		1985						County Total	2000						County Total
		Region I		Region II		Region III			Region I		Region II		Region III		
		work	other	work	other	work	other		work	other	work	other	work	other	
Population	N	107,000		176,500		110,500		394,000	113,000		221,500		153,000		487,500
Density (persons/sq. mile)		14,270		2,310		780		1,740	15,070		2,900		1,080		2,160
trip purpose	(p)	work	other	work	other	work	other		work	other	work	other	work	other	
Trips per person per day	η_p	0.77	0.75	0.85	1.40	0.84	1.80		0.78	0.78	0.85	1.35	0.84	1.85	
Trip length (miles)	L_p	5.7	3.2	7.0	4.5	7.6	6.3		5.9	3.7	7.1	5.0	7.8	6.4	
Modal split auto	α_{1p}	0.68	0.66	0.85	0.85	0.78	0.75		0.36	0.58	0.60	0.65	0.70	0.78	
bus	α_{2p}	0.12	0.04	0.03	0.00	0.02	0.00		–		–		–		
D-a-R	α_{3p}	0.12	0.07	0.08	0.05	0.10	0.05		0.12	0.07	0.08	0.05	0.10	0.05	
PRT	α_{4p}	–		–		–			0.45	0.20	0.28	0.20	0.10	0.02	
walk	α_{5p}	0.08	0.23	0.04	0.10	0.10	0.20		0.07	0.15	0.04	0.10	0.10	0.15	
bicycle	α_{6p}	–		–		–			–		–		–		
motorcycle	α_{7p}	–		–		–			–		–		–		

Energy (TBtu) per Vehicle-Mile and Load Factor

1985:

auto	$\epsilon_1 = 11.7$	$\lambda_1 = 1.44$
bus	$\epsilon_2 = 30.8$	$\lambda_2 = 8.00$
D-a-R	$\epsilon_3 = 20.4$	$\lambda_3 = 1.50$
PRT	$\epsilon_4 = $	$\lambda_4 = $
walk	$\epsilon_5 = 0.22$	$\lambda_5 = 1.00$
bicycle	$\epsilon_6 = $	$\lambda_6 = $
motorcycle	$\epsilon_7 = $	$\lambda_7 = $

2000:

auto	$\epsilon_1 = 11.7$	$\lambda_1 = 1.44$
bus	$\epsilon_2 = $	$\lambda_2 = $
D-a-R	$\epsilon_3 = 20.4$	$\lambda_3 = 2.50$
PRT	$\epsilon_4 = 10.4$	$\lambda_4 = 1.12$
walk	$\epsilon_5 = 0.22$	$\lambda_5 = 1.00$
bicycle	$\epsilon_6 = $	$\lambda_6 = $
motorcycle	$\epsilon_7 = $	$\lambda_7 = $

Table A-5. Travel Parameters for Option B_2, in the Years 1985 and 2000 (Restricted Use of Auto)

Parameter		1985 Region I		Region II		Region III		County Total	2000 Region I		Region II		Region III		County Total
Population	N	107,000		176,500		110,500		394,000	113,000		221,500		153,000		487,500
Density (persons/sq. mile)		14,270		2,310		780		1,740	15,070		2,900		1,080		2,160
trip purpose	(p)	work	other	work	other	work	other		work	other	work	other	work	other	
Trips per person per day	η_p	0.77	0.75	0.85	1.40	0.84	1.80		0.78	0.78	0.85	1.35	0.84	1.85	
Trip length (miles)	L_p	5.7	3.2	7.0	4.5	7.6	6.3		5.9	3.7	7.1	5.0	7.8	6.4	
Modal split — auto	α_{1p}	0.59	0.62	0.82	0.83	0.78	0.75		0.16	0.48	0.46	0.60	0.68	0.77	
bus	α_{2p}	0.18	0.05	0.04	0.02	0.02	0.00		—	—	—	—	—	—	
D-a-R	α_{3p}	0.15	0.10	0.10	0.05	0.10	0.05		0.15	0.07	0.10	0.05	0.10	0.05	
PRT	α_{4p}	—	—	—	—	—	—		0.62	0.30	0.40	0.25	0.12	0.03	
walk	α_{5p}	0.08	0.23	0.04	0.10	0.10	0.20		0.07	0.15	0.04	0.10	0.10	0.15	
bicycle	α_{6p}	—	—	—	—	—	—		—	—	—	—	—	—	
motorcycle	α_{7p}	—	—	—	—	—	—		—	—	—	—	—	—	

Energy (TBtu) per Vehicle-Mile and Load Factor — 1985:

	auto	bus	D-a-R	PRT	walk	bicycle	motorcycle
ϵ	$\epsilon_1 = 11.7$	$\epsilon_2 = 30.8$	$\epsilon_3 = 20.4$	$\epsilon_4 =$	$\epsilon_5 = 0.22$	$\epsilon_6 =$	$\epsilon_7 =$
λ	$\lambda_1 = 1.65$	$\lambda_2 = 10.00$	$\lambda_3 = 2.50$	$\lambda_4 =$	$\lambda_5 = 1.00$	$\lambda_6 =$	$\lambda_7 =$

Energy (TBtu) per Vehicle-Mile and Load Factor — 2000:

	auto	bus	D-a-R	PRT	walk	bicycle	motorcycle
ϵ	$\epsilon_1 = 11.7$	$\epsilon_2 =$	$\epsilon_3 = 17.3$	$\epsilon_4 = 10.$	$\epsilon_5 = 2.15$	$\epsilon_6 =$	$\epsilon_7 =$
λ	$\lambda_1 = 1.65$	$\lambda_2 =$	$\lambda_3 = 3.50$	$\lambda_4 = 1.29$	$\lambda_5 = 1.00$	$\lambda_6 =$	$\lambda_7 =$

Table A-6. Travel Parameters for Option B_3, in the Years 1985 and 2000 (Modified Auto)

Parameter		1985 Region I work	other	Region II work	other	Region III work	other	County Total	2000 Region I work	other	Region II work	other	Region III work	other	County Total
Population	N	107,000		176,500		110,500		394,000	113,000		221,500		153,000		487,500
Density (persons/sq. mile)	(p)	14,270		2,310		780		1,740	15,070		2,900		1,080		2,160
trip purpose		work	other	work	other	work	other		work	other	work	other	work	other	
Trips per person per day	η_p	0.77	0.75	0.85	1.40	0.84	1.80		0.78	0.78	0.85	1.35	0.84	1.85	
Trip length (miles)	L_p	5.7	3.2	7.0	4.5	7.6	6.3		5.9	3.7	7.1	5.0	7.8	6.4	
Modal split — auto	α_{1p}	0.79	0.71	0.93	0.90	0.88	0.77		0.83	0.82	0.93	0.90	0.90	0.85	
bus	α_{2p}	0.12	0.04	0.03	0.00	0.02	0.00		0.10	0.03	0.03	0.00	0.00	0.00	
D-a-R	α_{3p}	—	—	—	—	—	—		—	—	—	—	—	—	
PRT	α_{4p}	—	—	—	—	—	—		—	—	—	—	—	—	
walk	α_{5p}	0.09	0.25	0.04	0.10	0.10	0.23		0.07	0.15	0.04	0.10	0.10	0.15	
bicycle	α_{6p}	—	—	—	—	—	—		—	—	—	—	—	—	
motorcycle	α_{7p}	—	—	—	—	—	—		—	—	—	—	—	—	

Energy (TBtu) per Vehicle-Mile and Load Factor

	1985	2000
auto	$\epsilon_1 = 10.2$	$\epsilon_1 = 8.19$
bus	$\epsilon_2 = 30.8$	$\epsilon_2 = 30.8$
D-a-R	$\epsilon_3 = -$	$\epsilon_3 = -$
PRT	$\epsilon_4 = -$	$\epsilon_4 = -$
walk	$\epsilon_5 = 0.22$	$\epsilon_5 = 0.22$
bicycle	$\epsilon_6 = -$	$\epsilon_6 = -$
motorcycle	$\epsilon_7 = -$	$\epsilon_7 = -$
	$\lambda_1 = 1.44$	$\lambda_1 = 1.44$
	$\lambda_2 = 8.00$	$\lambda_2 = 10.00$
	$\lambda_3 = -$	$\lambda_3 = -$
	$\lambda_4 = -$	$\lambda_4 = -$
	$\lambda_5 = 1.00$	$\lambda_5 = 1.00$
	$\lambda_6 = -$	$\lambda_6 = -$
	$\lambda_7 = -$	$\lambda_7 = -$

Table A-7. Travel Parameters for Option B_4, in the Years 1985 and 2000 (Combined Interventions)

Parameter		1985 Region I	Region II	Region III	County Total	2000 Region I	Region II	Region III	County Total
Population	N	107,000	176,500	110,500	394,000	113,000	221,500	153,000	487,500
Density (persons/sq. mile)		14,270	2,310	780	1,740	15,070	2,900	1,080	2,160
trip purpose	(p)	work other	work other	work other		work other	work other	work other	
Trips per person per day	η_p	0.77 0.75	0.85 1.40	0.84 1.80		0.78 0.78	0.85 1.35	0.84 1.85	
Trip length (miles)	L_p	5.7 3.2	7.0 4.5	7.6 6.3		5.9 3.7	7.1 5.0	7.8 6.4	
Modal split auto	α_{1p}	0.59 0.62	0.82 0.83	0.78 0.75		0.16 0.48	0.46 0.60	0.68 0.77	
bus	α_{2p}	0.18 0.05	0.04 0.02	0.02 0.00		– –	– –	– –	
D-a-R	α_{3p}	0.15 0.10	0.10 0.05	0.10 0.05		0.15 0.07	0.10 0.05	0.10 0.05	
PRT	α_{4p}	– –	– –	– –		0.62 0.30	0.40 0.25	0.12 0.03	
walk	α_{5p}	0.08 0.23	0.04 0.10	0.10 0.20		0.07 0.15	0.04 0.10	0.10 0.15	
bicycle	α_{6p}	– –	– –	– –		– –	– –	– –	
motorcycle	α_{7p}	– –	– –	– –		– –	– –	– –	

Energy (TBtu) per Vehicle-Mile and Load Factor:

1985:

$\epsilon_1 = 10.2$ $\lambda_1 = 1.65$
$\epsilon_2 = 30.8$ $\lambda_2 = 10.00$
$\epsilon_3 = 20.4$ $\lambda_3 = 2.50$
$\epsilon_4 = -$ $\lambda_4 = -$
$\epsilon_5 = 0.22$ $\lambda_5 = 1.00$
$\epsilon_6 = -$ $\lambda_6 = -$
$\epsilon_7 = -$ $\lambda_7 = -$

2000:

$\epsilon_1 = 8.19$ $\lambda_1 = 1.65$
$\epsilon_2 = -$ $\lambda_2 = -$
$\epsilon_3 = 17.3$ $\lambda_3 = 3.50$
$\epsilon_4 = 10.4$ $\lambda_4 = 1.29$
$\epsilon_5 = 0.22$ $\lambda_5 = 1.00$
$\epsilon_6 = -$ $\lambda_6 = -$
$\epsilon_7 = -$ $\lambda_7 = -$

Table A-8. Travel Parameters for Option C_1, in the Years 1985 and 2000 (Home Near Work), Where a Few Large Centers Result[a]

Parameter		1985 Region I work	other	1985 Region II work	other	1985 Region III work	other	County Total	2000 Region I work	other	2000 Region II work	other	2000 Region III work	other	County Total
Population	N	115,000		185,000		105,000		405,000	125,000		230,000		150,000		505,000
Density (persons/sq. mile)	(p)	15,330		2,420		740		1,790	16,670		3,010		1,060		2,230
Trips per person per day	η_p	0.76	0.76	0.78	1.22	0.83	1.80		0.74	0.80	0.76	1.15	0.83	1.85	
Trip length (miles)	L_p	4.5	2.5	6.0	3.5	7.0	5.0		3.4	2.2	4.5	3.4	6.0	4.6	
Modal split — auto	α_{1p}	0.55	0.57	0.75	0.76	0.78	0.71		0.10	0.24	0.32	0.51	0.67	0.68	
bus	α_{2p}	0.16	0.04	0.06	0.02	0.02	0.00		–	–	–	–	–	–	
D-a-R	α_{3p}	0.14	0.09	0.09	0.05	0.10	0.04		0.15	0.06	0.08	0.04	0.08	0.04	
PRT	α_{4p}	–		–		–			0.55	0.30	0.40	0.20	0.10	0.03	
walk	α_{5p}	0.10	0.22	0.07	0.10	0.06	0.18		0.12	0.27	0.13	0.15	0.09	0.16	
bicycle	α_{6p}	0.03	0.05	0.02	0.05	0.03	0.06		0.05	0.08	0.05	0.07	0.04	0.07	
motorcycle	α_{7p}	0.02	0.03	0.01	0.02	0.01	0.01		0.03	0.05	0.02	0.03	0.02	0.02	

Energy (TBtu) per Vehicle-Mile and Load Factor:

1985:
$\epsilon_1 = 10.2$, $\epsilon_2 = 30.8$, $\epsilon_3 = 20.4$, $\epsilon_4 = -$, $\epsilon_5 = 0.22$, $\epsilon_6 = 0.34$, $\epsilon_7 = 2.32$

$\lambda_1 = 1.44$, $\lambda_2 = 12.00$, $\lambda_3 = 2.50$, $\lambda_4 = -$, $\lambda_5 = 1.00$, $\lambda_6 = 1.00$, $\lambda_7 = 1.10$

2000:
$\epsilon_1 = 8.19$, $\epsilon_2 = -$, $\epsilon_3 = 17.3$, $\epsilon_4 = 10.4$, $\epsilon_5 = 0.22$, $\epsilon_6 = 0.34$, $\epsilon_7 = 2.32$

$\lambda_1 = 2.00$, $\lambda_2 = -$, $\lambda_3 = 3.50$, $\lambda_4 = 1.56$, $\lambda_5 = 1.00$, $\lambda_6 = 1.00$, $\lambda_7 = 1.10$

[a]This is based on an assumed reversal of the decentralization trend, referred to as Δ_- in Appendix B.

Table A-9. Travel Parameters for Option C_1, in the Years 1985 and 2000 (Home Near Work), Where Many Small Centers Result[a]

Parameter		1985 Region I		Region II		Region III		County Total	2000 Region I		Region II		Region III		County Total
Population	N	105,500		150,000		120,000		375,500	106,500		215,000		165,000		486,500
Density (persons/sq. mile)	(p)	14,070		1,960		840		1,660	14,200		2,810		1,160		2,150
trip purpose		work	other	work	other	work	other		work	other	work	other	work	other	
Trips per person per day	η_p	0.77	0.75	0.80	1.25	0.80	1.70		0.75	0.80	0.79	1.20	0.79	1.65	
Trip length (miles)	L_p	4.5	3.0	6.0	4.0	7.0	6.0		3.4	3.2	4.5	4.2	6.5	6.2	
Modal split — auto	α_{1p}	0.48	0.54	0.71	0.78	0.78	0.71		0.09	0.20	0.20	0.54	0.72	0.68	
bus	α_{2p}	0.20	0.06	0.08	0.02	0.02	0.00		–	–	–	–	–	–	
D-a-R	α_{3p}	0.17	0.10	0.11	0.05	0.10	0.04		0.15	0.08	0.10	0.04	0.08	0.04	
PRT	α_{4p}	–	–	–	–	–	–		0.56	0.32	0.50	0.22	0.05	0.03	
walk	α_{5p}	0.10	0.18	0.07	0.10	0.06	0.18		0.12	0.25	0.13	0.12	0.09	0.16	
bicycle	α_{6p}	0.03	0.08	0.02	0.04	0.03	0.06		0.05	0.10	0.05	0.06	0.04	0.07	
motorcycle	α_{7p}	0.02	0.04	0.01	0.01	0.01	0.01		0.03	0.05	0.02	0.02	0.02	0.02	
Energy (TBtu) per Vehicle-Mile and Load Factor — auto		$\epsilon_1 = 10.2$				$\lambda_1 = 1.44$			$\epsilon_1 = 8.19$				$\lambda_1 = 2.00$		
bus		$\epsilon_2 = 30.8$				$\lambda_2 = 12.00$			$\epsilon_2 = -$				$\lambda_2 = -$		
D-a-R		$\epsilon_3 = 20.4$				$\lambda_3 = 2.50$			$\epsilon_3 = 17.3$				$\lambda_3 = 3.50$		
PRT		$\epsilon_4 = -$				$\lambda_4 = -$			$\epsilon_4 = 10.4$				$\lambda_4 = 1.56$		
walk		$\epsilon_5 = 0.22$				$\lambda_5 = 1.00$			$\epsilon_5 = 0.22$				$\lambda_5 = 1.00$		
bicycle		$\epsilon_6 = 0.34$				$\lambda_6 = 1.00$			$\epsilon_6 = 0.34$				$\lambda_6 = 1.00$		
motorcycle		$\epsilon_7 = 2.32$				$\lambda_7 = 1.10$			$\epsilon_7 = 2.32$				$\lambda_7 = 1.10$		

[a]This is based on an assumed stabilization of the decentralization trend, referred to as Δ_O in Appendix B.

Table A-10. Travel Parameters for Option C_2, in the Years 1985 and 2000 (Home Near Neighbors)

1985

Parameter		Region I		Region II		Region III		County Total
Population	N	115,000		185,000		95,000		395,000
Density (persons/sq. mile)	(p)	15,330		2,420		670		1,750
trip purpose		work	other	work	other	work	other	
Trips per person per day	η_p	0.76	0.64	0.76	1.10	0.83	1.75	
Trip length (miles)	L_p	5.5	2.5	7.5	3.5	8.5	5.5	
Modal split — auto	α_{1p}	0.59	0.57	0.82	0.76	0.78	0.71	
bus	α_{2p}	0.18	0.04	0.04	0.02	0.02	0.00	
D-a-R	α_{3p}	0.15	0.09	0.10	0.05	0.10	0.04	
PRT	α_{4p}	–	–	–	–	–	–	
walk	α_{5p}	0.06	0.22	0.03	0.10	0.06	0.18	
bicycle	α_{6p}	0.01	0.05	0.01	0.05	0.03	0.06	
motorcycle	α_{7p}	0.01	0.03	0.00	0.02	0.01	0.01	

Energy (TBtu) per Vehicle-Mile and Load Factor (1985):

	Energy		Load Factor
auto	$\epsilon_1 = 10.2$		$\lambda_1 = 1.65$
bus	$\epsilon_2 = 30.8$		$\lambda_2 = 12.00$
D-a-R	$\epsilon_3 = 20.4$		$\lambda_3 = 2.50$
PRT	$\epsilon_4 =$ –		$\lambda_4 =$ –
walk	$\epsilon_5 = 0.22$		$\lambda_5 = 1.00$
bicycle	$\epsilon_6 = 0.34$		$\lambda_6 = 1.00$
motorcycle	$\epsilon_7 = 2.32$		$\lambda_7 = 1.10$

2000

Parameter		Region I		Region II		Region III		County Total
Population	N	130,000		220,000		102,000		452,000
Density (persons/sq. mile)	(p)	17,330		2,880		720		2,000
trip purpose		work	other	work	other	work	other	
Trips per person per day	η_p	0.75	0.75	0.75	0.98	0.83	1.75	
Trip length (miles)	L_p	6.0	2.2	8.5	3.4	9.0	6.0	
Modal split — auto	α_{1p}	0.16	0.24	0.46	0.51	0.68	0.69	
bus	α_{2p}	–	–	–	–	–	–	
D-a-R	α_{3p}	0.15	0.06	0.10	0.04	0.10	0.04	
PRT	α_{4p}	0.62	0.30	0.40	0.20	0.12	0.02	
walk	α_{5p}	0.05	0.27	0.02	0.15	0.05	0.16	
bicycle	α_{6p}	0.01	0.08	0.01	0.07	0.03	0.07	
motorcycle	α_{7p}	0.01	0.05	0.01	0.03	0.02	0.02	

Energy (TBtu) per Vehicle-Mile and Load Factor (2000):

	Energy		Load Factor
auto	$\epsilon_1 = 8.19$		$\lambda_1 = 2.00$
bus	$\epsilon_2 =$ –		$\lambda_2 =$ –
D-a-R	$\epsilon_3 = 17.3$		$\lambda_3 = 3.50$
PRT	$\epsilon_4 = 10.4$		$\lambda_4 = 1.56$
walk	$\epsilon_5 = 0.22$		$\lambda_5 = 1.00$
bicycle	$\epsilon_6 = 0.34$		$\lambda_6 = 1.00$
motorcycle	$\epsilon_7 = 2.32$		$\lambda_7 = 1.10$

Table A–11. Travel Parameters for Option C_3, in the Years 1985 and 2000 (Energy Consciousness)

Parameter		1985 Region I		Region II		Region III		County Total	2000 Region I		Region II		Region III		County Total
Population	N	110,250		167,500		107,500		385,250	118,250		217,500		133,500		469,250
Density (persons/sq. mile)		14,700		2,190		760		1,700	15,770		2,850		940		2,080
trip purpose	(p)	work	other	work	other	work	other		work	other	work	other	work	other	
Trips per person per day	η_p	0.74	0.56	0.76	0.90	0.84	1.80		0.71	0.59	0.74	0.87	0.84	1.80	
Trip length (miles)	L_p	3.8	1.8	4.5	2.9	6.5	4.1		3.3	1.7	4.3	2.8	6.4	3.8	
Modal split — auto	α_{1p}	0.35	0.38	0.37	0.69	0.70	0.65		0.10	0.24	0.14	0.45	0.60	0.58	
bus	α_{2p}	0.25	0.07	0.28	0.03	0.02	0.00		–	–	–	–	–	–	
D-a-R	α_{3p}	0.20	0.15	0.20	0.08	0.08	0.05		0.30	0.09	0.35	0.10	0.07	0.05	
PRT	α_{4p}	–	–	–	–	–	–		0.30	0.22	0.26	0.15	0.08	0.02	
walk	α_{5p}	0.10	0.25	0.07	0.10	0.10	0.15		0.18	0.25	0.12	0.15	0.11	0.21	
bicycle	α_{6p}	0.07	0.10	0.05	0.08	0.07	0.12		0.08	0.15	0.09	0.12	0.11	0.10	
motorcycle	α_{7p}	0.03	0.05	0.03	0.02	0.03	0.03		0.04	0.05	0.04	0.03	0.03	0.04	

Energy (TBtu) per Vehicle-Mile and Load Factor

	1985		2000	
auto	$\epsilon_1 = 7.88$	$\lambda_1 = 2.00$	$\epsilon_1 = 5.53$	$\lambda_1 = 3.00$
bus	$\epsilon_2 = 30.8$	$\lambda_2 = 12.00$	$\epsilon_2 = -$	$\lambda_2 = -$
D-a-R	$\epsilon_3 = 20.4$	$\lambda_3 = 3.00$	$\epsilon_3 = 17.3$	$\lambda_3 = 4.00$
PRT	$\epsilon_4 = -$	$\lambda_4 = -$	$\epsilon_4 = 10.4$	$\lambda_4 = 2.33$
walk	$\epsilon_5 = 0.22$	$\lambda_5 = 1.00$	$\epsilon_5 = 0.22$	$\lambda_5 = 1.00$
bicycle	$\epsilon_6 = 0.34$	$\lambda_6 = 1.00$	$\epsilon_6 = 0.34$	$\lambda_6 = 1.00$
motorcycle	$\epsilon_7 = 2.32$	$\lambda_7 = 1.10$	$\epsilon_7 = 2.32$	$\lambda_7 = 1.10$

NOTES

1. *Census Tracts, Trenton, New Jersey SMSA,* Bureau of the Census, U.S. Department of Commerce (Final Report PHC(1)–217).
2. Jerome M. Lutin, "Personal Rapid Transit, Policy and Technology: A Case Study", Unpublished Master's Thesis, 1973, School of Architecture and Urban Planning, Princeton University.
3. Pittsburgh Area Transportation Study, Vol. I, City of Pittsburgh, in cooperation with U.S. Department of Commerce, Bureau of Public Roads, November 1971.
4. Detailed statistics are contained in a separate report prepared within this project in 1973: "Trenton in the 1970s: Profile of a Region in Flux", by Michael J. Munson and Joenathan Dean.
5. This survey is described in a separate report: "Auto Occupancy Survey", by Shari Glassman, Elizabeth Garman and Michael Godnick.
6. Details appear in a separate report of work carried out as a part of this project: "Comparative Energy Costs of Urban Transportation Systems," by Margaret Fulton Fels.

Appendix B

Three Possible Decentralization Patterns, and Their Effect on Energy Consumption

The distribution of population over the entire study area affects the travel pattern for any transportation scheme; and therefore, each of the nine transportation options was studied in terms of three distinct decentralization patterns, covering the range of possibilities which conceivably could occur. Briefly, letting the symbol Δ denote decentralization, we describe these three patterns as follows:

Δ_+ : continuation of current decentralization trends throughout the time period of the study.

Δ_0 : continuation of the decentralization trends until some intermediate time at which point the population of the central city becomes constant.

Δ_- : continuation of the decentralization trend until some intermediate time at which point a reversal takes place and the central city population begins to grow again.

In Δ_+, decentralization of population follows a familiar pattern: those who can afford it move and those who cannot afford it stay; the central city loses population and its median income lags behind that of the remainder of the SMSA.

In Δ_0, the current decentralization of jobs and people is expected to continue until about 1985 at which time the land values in the central area will have deteriorated to a point where massive private redevelopment is economically feasible. After 1985, the number of people and jobs in the central city holds constant, but social characteristics change drastically: The poor are caught between redevelopment demand in the central city and in the expensive outlying areas. There remains a middle ring of high-density housing with poor facilities, where the average income is low. In Δ_0, people live in the central area because of

85

its amenities, rather than primarily for the sake of accessibility; thus there is not necessarily a correlation between residence location and work place. Jobs are distributed throughout the region, with the possibility of much outward commuting.

In the reversal decentralization pattern Δ_-, the current pattern of decentralization continues until 1980 at which time the low property values plus increased accessibility of outlying areas starts a reversal. From 1980 to 1985 the decentralization tapers and beginning in 1985, there is actually a reversal of the trend. Redevelopment will be primarily for residential rather than employment purposes, so that jobs may remain in the outer areas (in which case travel times remain large). The residential density in the central area will be higher in Δ_- than it was in Δ_0, and the poor will again be caught in the squeeze between the central area redevelopment and the high-priced, low-density outlying areas.

It is important to note at this point that, while information concerning population distribution is to some extent contained in Δ_+, Δ_0, and Δ_-, it is the combination of the assumptions in the options with these decentralization patterns that determines the propinquity of home and work. Travel times for work and other purposes clearly depend not only on the locations of various activity and employment centers, but on the correlation of these centers with the workers' residential locations.

Because the assumptions for the main discussion of the options were assumed to be consistent with the reversal decentralization trend (Δ_-), we shall pick up from our discussion in Chapter II, and simply mention, for each option, how the controlled decentralization case Δ_0 and the continued decentralization case Δ_+ differ from Δ_-. We comment here that many of the differences which occur for the three decentralization trends in the first option will hold for the other options; therefore, with the exception of Option A_1, our discussion will be brief.[a]

THE EFFECT OF DECENTRALIZATION ON THE NINE OPTIONS

Option A_1: Everybody Wants a Luxury Car

The impacts of the three different decentralization patterns on Option A_1 deal primarily with the location of the population within the county, and the length of trips, with minimal changes on the number of trips made.

The situation which depicts the reversal of the existing decentralization trends (Δ_-) will obviously result in an increase in the population of Region I after 1985, a continued increase in Region II, and a somewhat diminished increase in Region III. The number of trips generated will be slightly fewer (par-

---

[a]For the sake of brevity, the exact travel data for each option-decentralization combination will not be included here. For Δ_-, the reader is referred to the tables in Appendix A, while data for Δ_0 and Δ_+ are available from the authors.

ticularly non-work) as a result of the population density being slightly higher than for the other decentralization patterns, but trip lengths will be greater in Region I, as will the proportion of auto trips, due to the decentralization of jobs and the need for outward commuting. Since this decentralization pattern antici- pates the revival of the central area as a shopping area (one of several in the county), and since it is expected that the new residential development in the central city will be accompanied by supportive services, non-work trips will probably be somewhat shorter for Region II than in the other decentralization patterns. The effect of this pattern on Region III will be minimal, mainly in a slightly lower population growth than is expected from the other decentraliza- tion patterns. The impact of increased income is expected to be as indicated in the other patterns, with a more pronounced effect on Region I due to the presence of new wealthier residents. Basically, in Region I it is anticipated that the wealthier people will choose to use their private automobile more often than the expected center-city population in the other two patterns, Δ_0 and Δ_+, and there will be a corresponding decrease in the proportion of trips taken by the other modes.

The controlled pattern (Δ_0), with eventual stabilization, will result basically in a change in the distribution of the population throughout the county. It is expected that the central city will stop declining in population by about 1980–1985, and will then hold constant at that level. This will result in some- what fewer people living in Region II at both the 1985 and 2000 data points. The impact on the number of people in Region III will be minimal over the reversal decentralization pattern. Trip length should be slightly, but not mark- edly, shorter in this decentralization pattern. The number of trips taken per person will probably not change from Δ_-, nor will the modal distribution, except that in 2000 Region I is expected to show a slight increase in the number of work trips, and a rather significant increase in walking trips. Again, due to rising incomes, more and longer trips will be generated in 2000 than in 1985.

In the continued decentralization trend (Δ_+), the population of the City of Trenton is expected to continue to decrease through the year 2000, with most of the outmigration from the city locating in the three in-lying townships (Region II). It is expected that the major part of immigration to the county will locate in this region, but there will also be growth in the outlying portions of the county, Region III. With both jobs and residences decentralizing, and a decreased emphasis on the Trenton CBD as a "center," trip length for both work and non-work purposes will increase considerably, even more than was expected in the two previous decentralization cases.

Option A_2: Response to Fuel Price Increase

Option A_2 will show basically the same general patterns of develop- ment as A_1, except that densities will be slightly higher, non-work trips slightly fewer, and trip lengths slightly shorter, all reflecting the increased cost of automobile fuel and the assumption that people will consume less of the more expensive commodity. Essentially the same trends as we go from Δ_- to Δ_0 to Δ_+ are expected in Option A_2 as were seen in A_1. In general, slightly higher densities are expected, with the central city, Region I, not decreasing in population quite as fast as in A_1, and with Region II having a slightly higher density than A_1. Region III will have slightly less growth than that described in Option A_1. This pattern is repeated in the other two decentralization patterns.

Option B_1: Replacement of Auto Travel by Innovative Modes

The decentralization patterns will induce only one minor change other than those trends discussed for Option A_1, and that will be in the modal distribution for Region I. Decentralization pattern Δ_-, calling for revitalization of the central city with relatively wealthy people who commute outwards and tend to own more automobiles, will result in a smaller portion of trips going by bus or Dial-a-Ride. The only exception is for PRT when it is introduced. The wealthier, more sophisticated population is expected to make greater use of this mode than would happen with continued decentralization (Δ_+). This general pattern is true for both work and non-work trips, but again only in the central city.

Option B_2: Restricted Auto Use

For Option B_2, the pattern of change in the travel parameters due to the three decentralization patterns will be as described in Option A_2, with Δ_- showing a slightly decreased density, and, in addition slightly fewer and shorter trips in the outer regions, with the opposite true for Region I.

The development of a Dial-a-Ride system in conjunction with the imposition of restrictions on the use of automobiles in the central area is compatible with the pattern of continued decentralization (Δ_+) if the Dial-a-Ride system operates in the many-to-many mode. One might note, however, that the use of restrictions on the use of automobiles in the central area is a much weaker policy when the decentralization has progressed to the point where the central area is little more concentrated than surrounding areas. The use of Dial-a-Ride in the many-to-few mode is most applicable to the remaining two alternative development patterns.

Option B_3: Technological Modifications in the Auto

Since Option B_3 essentially amounts to the superposition of a more efficient auto on the assumptions in Option A_2, the impact of the three decentralization patterns is the same here as it was in Option A_2.

Option B_4: Combined Interventions

All of the travel data assumed for Option B_4 are the same as in restricted-auto Option B_2. And this similarity holds for all three decentralization patterns. (Energy and load factor data are adopted from Option B_3).

Option C_1: Desire to Live Near Work

One of the concomitants of the current decentralization trend is people moving farther away from their work, within the metropolitan area but (with housing costs highest in the outlying region) as far away from the central city as their income will allow. Therefore, the concept of people wanting to live near their work is not consistent with the continued decentralization trend in Δ_+, and only two decentralization patterns are considered for Option C_1. Because they produced such dissimilar development patterns, namely, small low-density villages as a result of Δ_0 and high-density clusters from Δ_-, both option-decentralization combinations were discussed in Chapter II, and the resulting travel data for Option C_1 for Δ_0 as well as Δ_- are included in the tables in Appendix A.

Option C_2: Desire to Live Near Neighbors

Since a desire for high-density living is probably inconsistent with a desire to move away from the city, we assume that Option C_2 is consistent only with the recentralization pattern Δ_-. Therefore, only the one option-decentralization combination already discussed in Chapter II is considered.

Option C_3: Energy Consciousness

Depending on how strong the desire for higher densities becomes, the final option is consistent with either the decentralization pattern calling for recentralization, Δ_-, or that calling for a population plateau for the center city, Δ_0. The differences will be manifest in different population and density figures, with Δ_- having greater population in Regions I and II than does the Δ_0 variation. Consequently, people are expected to travel less in the higher density, recentralization case Δ_-, with shorter trip lengths and fewer trips especially for non-work purposes. Another assumed effect of recentralization is a slightly greater reliance on private automobiles in Regions I and II for work trips. For non-work trips, greater use of PRT in Region I is assumed.

Thus for Scenario C, when the attitude changes and the decentralization assumptions are combined, many of the logically possible combinations turn out to be internally inconsistent. The pattern of continued decentralization is inconsistent with all of the above attitude changes considered, so that Δ_+ was excluded from this scenario. In addition, Option C_2, which calls for high-density living, is consistent only with the pattern of recentralization, Δ_-. Thus, out of the nine possible combinations, only five were considered.

ENERGY RESULTS

We are now ready to present the complete set of results. For each of the future dates, each option-decentralization combination comprises an entry in the following summary tables. Table B-1 shows the per capita energy results for the study area as a whole, for 1985 and 2000. The rows which show the results for the reversal (Δ_-) pattern correspond to the results derived in Chapter II and presented in Tables 2–8. In Chapter II, we discussed the observation that the energy consumption patterns vary less among the decentralization patterns for a given option than they do among the options; this is clear from Table B-1. In general, the results decrease as we go from Δ_+ to Δ_0, and decrease only slightly or stay about the same as we go from Δ_0 to Δ_-, probably because, as the city becomes more revitalized, the travel pattern in the surrounding area resembles that of city-dwellers who, we have observed, are comparatively energy-thrifty in their travel behavior.

How does decentralization affect the energy consumption patterns within each of the three regions which comprise the study area? The following tables, Tables B-2 through 4, show respectively the per capita energy results for Regions I, II, and III. (Each table is analagous to Table B-1 in the way in which option-decentralization combinations appear.) As might be anticipated, the effect of the decentralization patterns on the individual regions is minimal in Region III, reflecting the outlying suburbs' relative independence with respect to the inner regions. The effects of the decentralization trends are considerably more pronounced in Region II, to which the population is or is not migrating, depending on the assumptions involved. By the year 2000, by which time the three decentralization patterns have diverged, the greatest effect is seen in Region I where the revitalization of the city depends on the extent to which decentralization has continued or reversed itself. Unlike the results for the study area as a whole, the per capita energy consumption within the city (Region I) is, for most options (at least within Scenarios A and B), maximum when recentralization (Δ_-) is assumed. Here, revitalization means that more wealthy people return to the city and the concomitant rise in auto ownership results in an increased rate of energy consumption.[b]

Among the options, the extent of decentralization has the greatest effect on those within Scenario C, i.e., Options C_1 and C_3 (since Option C_2 was consistent only with Δ_-). The attitude changes toward wanting to live nearer work or neighbors are expected to have a direct impact on the future development pattern, which in turn is strongly tied to the trend to, or not to, decentralize. In these cases, the option cannot really be separated from the decentralization assumptions. For Option C_1, two distinctly different develop-

[b]The results for the study area as a whole do not show this maximum for Δ_- because a combination of the least energy consumption and smallest population in the city causes Region I to have the least effect on the overall energy results.

Table B-1. Per Capita Energy Consumption (TBtu) for the Study Area as a Whole for Each Option-Decentralization Combination, in 1985 and 2000

Option:		Scenario A		Scenario B				Scenario C		
		A_1 Luxury Car	A_2 Fuel Price Increase	B_1 Novel Modes	B_2 Restricted Auto Use	B_3 Modified Auto	B_4 Combined Intervention	C_1 Home Near Work	C_2 Home Near Neighbors	C_3 Energy Con- sciousness
Year 1985 Decentraliza- tion Pattern	Δ_+	118.8	88.1	93.9	77.1	76.8	69.3	ϕ	ϕ	ϕ
	Δ_0	115.4	85.7	91.8	75.8	75.1	67.6	61.4	ϕ	27.0
	Δ_-	114.3	86.0	91.8	76.5	75.4	67.9	53.3	55.0	24.2
Year 2000 Decentraliza- tion Pattern	Δ_+	151.2	99.3	102.1	87.4	69.3	69.6	ϕ	ϕ	ϕ
	Δ_0	143.0	96.3	100.3	85.7	67.6	68.6	38.6	ϕ	15.7
	Δ_-	141.3	96.3	99.7	85.7	67.6	68.9	32.1	45.1	14.7

Δ_+ : Continuation of Current Decentralization through 2000
Δ_0 : Stabilization of Central City Population after Some Decentralization
Δ_- : Reversal of Decentralization Trend after Some Decentralization
ϕ : Non-Viable Combination

Table B-2. Per Capita Energy Consumption (TBtu) for Region I for Each Option-Decentralization Combination in 1985 and 2000

	Scenario A		Scenario B				Scenario C		
Option:	A_1 Luxury Car	A_2 Fuel Price Increase	B_1 Novel Modes	B_2 Restricted Auto Use	B_3 Modified Auto	B_4 Combined Intervention	C_1 Home Near Work	C_2 Home Near Neighbors	C_3 Energy Con-sciousness
Year 1985 Decentraliza-tion Pattern									
Δ_+	54.3	40.3	45.7	35.5	35.8	32.4	φ	φ	φ
Δ_0	53.6	39.9	45.1	34.8	35.2	32.1	29.7	φ	13.7
Δ_-	59.4	44.4	49.2	39.3	39.3	35.5	28.3	29.7	12.6
Year 2000 Decentraliza-tion Pattern									
Δ_+	67.2	48.5	54.3	46.1	34.8	42.3	φ	φ	φ
Δ_0	59.4	43.4	52.9	44.7	31.1	41.3	21.5	φ	9.56
Δ_-	71.0	51.9	57.7	49.5	36.9	45.1	18.4	30.7	8.87

Δ_+ : Continuation of Current Decentralization through 2000
Δ_0 : Stabilization of Central City Population after Some Decentralization
Δ_- : Reversal of Decentralization Trend after Some Decentralization
φ : Non-Viable Combination

Table B-3. Per Capita Energy Consumption (TBtu) for Region II for Each Option-Decentralization Combination in 1985 and 2000

Option:	Scenario A		Scenario B				Scenario C		
	A_1 Luxury Car	A_2 Fuel Price Increase	B_1 Novel Modes	B_2 Restricted Auto Use	B_3 Modified Auto	B_4 Combined Intervention	C_1 Home Near Work	C_2 Home Near Neighbors	C_3 Energy Con- sciousness
Year 1985									
Decentralization Pattern Δ_+	132.4	94.9	100.0	81.9	82.9	73.7	φ	φ	φ
Δ_0	130.7	92.8	98.0	81.2	81.2	72.0	59.7	φ	24.2
Δ_-	127.0	91.8	96.3	80.2	80.6	71.3	54.6	54.3	21.2
Year 2000									
Decentralization Pattern Δ_+	154.3	96.9	100.0	86.0	67.2	71.7	φ	φ	φ
Δ_0	148.5	95.9	100.0	86.0	67.2	71.7	36.5	φ	16.0
Δ_-	144.4	95.6	100.0	86.4	67.2	71.7	29.7	44.7	14.7

Δ_+ : Continuation of Current Decentralization through 2000
Δ_0 : Stabilization of Central City Population after Some Decentralization
Δ_- : Reversal of Decentralization Trend after Some Decentralization
φ : Non-Viable Combination

Table B-4. Per Capita Energy Consumption (TBtu) for Region III for Each Option-Decentralization Combination in 1985 and 2000

Option:	Scenario A		Scenario B				Scenario C		
	A_1 Luxury Car	A_2 Fuel Price Increase	B_1 Novel Modes	B_2 Restricted Auto Use	B_3 Modified Auto	B_4 Combined Intervention	C_1 Home Near Work	C_2 Home Near Neighbors	C_3 Energy Consciousness
Year 1985 — Decentralization Pattern									
Δ_+	150.9	118.4	126.6	106.1	102.7	93.9	ϕ	ϕ	ϕ
Δ_0	147.8	117.4	126.6	106.1	102.7	93.9	91.1	ϕ	44.4
Δ_-	145.7	117.4	126.6	106.1	102.7	93.9	86.0	86.4	41.0
Year 2000 — Decentralization Pattern									
Δ_+	192.8	132.4	132.8	113.3	92.5	82.9	ϕ	ϕ	ϕ
Δ_0	190.8	132.4	132.8	113.3	92.5	82.9	51.9	ϕ	20.5
Δ_-	187.0	129.7	130.7	111.6	90.8	82.9	46.8	64.5	20.1

Δ_+ : Continuation of Current Decentralization through 2000
Δ_0 : Stabilization of Central City Population after Some Decentralization
Δ_- : Reversal of Decentralization Trend after Some Decentralization
ϕ : Non-Viable Combination

94

ment patterns emerged from Δ_0 and Δ_-, and the result that the energy consumption is less for Δ_- than for Δ_0 is probably because the desire to live near work in some sense reinforces the recentralization pattern (Δ_-). Similarly, this observation may be carried to the final option, where the minimum energy results are seen, for all regions, when energy-consciousness (Option C_3) is combined with recentralization (Δ_-).

Appendix C

Dependence of Automobile
Energy Consumption on
Weight and Engine Type

The relationship between the energy efficiency of the internal combustion engine (ICE) and the alternatives included in this analysis was discussed in Chapter II for the development of Option B_3. Five ICE substitutes were considered: the rotary (Wankel) engine, stratified charge, diesel, diesel-Wankel and electric. For the total energy consumed per automobile-mile, two contributions must be considered: operation energy, corresponding to the average mileage, and the manufacture energy for the vehicle. (In addition, the contribution from the highway construction must be included, but this is uniform among the alternative autos; the resulting contribution appeared in Table 2-1. The resulting dependence of mileage on vehicle weight for all the alternatives is shown in Figure C-1. Since these alternatives were considered "future" systems, the mileage figures[a] are for engines which meet the post-1976 emissions standards set up by the 1970 Clean Air Amendment. The basis for these results was EPA data for the 1973 ICE [1]; for comparison these results are also shown, and as mentioned in Chapter II, for a post-1976 ICE a 3 percent penalty is associated with meeting the emissions standards. Use of the ratio of the energy equivalence of fuel[b] to the mileage gives the dependence of the operation energy per vehicle-mile on vehicle weight, for the 1973 ICE and any of the alternatives.

For each ICE substitute, the manufacture energy was calculated on the basis of an auto with performance equivalent to a 2000-pound conventional auto (i.e., ICE). These calculations were carried out as a part of this project [2], and were based on a previous analysis of the energy required to manufacture a conventional auto [3]. The results for the five substitutes are shown in Table C-1.

---

[a] Clearly for the electric car, the fuel economy is given by TBtu per vehicle-mile. The energy-equivalence of gasoline is used to convert this to mpg in Figure C-1.

[b] If we include the energy for petroleum refining, the energy equivalent becomes 133.8 TBtu for a gallon of gasoline and 147.8 TBtu for a gallon of diesel fuel.

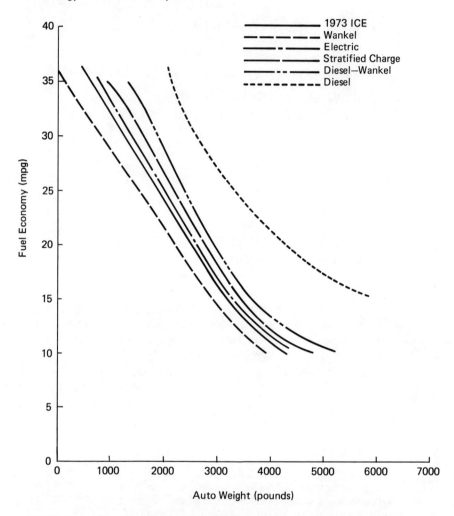

Figure C-1. The Variation of Fuel Economy with Vehicle Weight, for the 1973 ICE and Five Other Engine Types.

Thus if we wish to consider an automobile of a specified weight with one of the above engine types, we can calculate the energy consumption per vehicle-mile in the following way. Let x represent the weight, and $m(x)$ the corresponding mileage as a function of weight for the 1973 ICE, as shown in Figure C-1. If A_i is the ratio of the mileage for the ith alternative to $m(x)$ (i.e., to the 1973 ICE mileage)[c], and if G is the energy equivalence of a gallon of

[c]This ratio (A_i), used in Figure C-1, is assumed to be a constant independent of weight for each alternative.

the relevant fuel (gasoline or diesel), then $G/\left(A_i m(x)\right)$ is the operation energy (TBtu) consumed per vehicle-mile.

In order to include the manufacture energy, we assume a lifetime of 100,000 miles for each vehicle, and divide the results shown in Table C–1 by this lifetime to obtain the energy contribution per vehicle-mile for a 2000-pound auto: call the result "B_i". For a vehicle weighing x pounds, the manufacture contribution to the total energy per vehicle-mile becomes

$$x\, B_i/S$$

where S is the weight of the standard used in the evaluation, i.e., $S = 2000$ lb. here. Finally, we must include the contribution from the highway construction, C, where in this analysis we estimate

$$C = 0.10 \text{ TBtu/vehicle-mile.}$$

Therefore, if $e^{(i)}$ represents the total energy consumed per vehicle-mile for the ith auto-type, we can write

$$e^{(i)} = G/\left(A_i m(x)\right) + x\, B_i/S + C. \tag{1}$$

The actual values used in this analysis for the constants describing the five ICE substitutes as well as the ICE are given in Table C–2. Thus the operation and manufacture contributions, and the total energy consumption per vehicle-mile for the various vehicle-types of any weight may be computed from Eq. (1).

Table C–1. Energy of Manufacture[a] for Five Alternatives to the ICE, with Performance Comparable to a 2,000-Pound ICE

Engine Type	Electric	Stratified Charge	Wankel	Diesel	Wankel-Diesel
Energy of Manufacture	63.8[b]	65.5	59.4	80.2	65.5
(Million TBtu per vehicle)					

[a]Derivation of the results appears in the work done by Russell Barton as a part of this project.[2]

[b]This value represents the average between autos equipped with zinc-air and lead-acid batteries (see Reference 2).

Table C–2.   Quantities Needed for the Evaluation of Energy Consumption $\epsilon^{(i)}$ Per Vehicle-Mile for Several Automobile Types Where $\epsilon^{(i)} = G/\left(A_i m(x)\right) + XB_i/S + C$ (in TBtu)

Type	Electric $i = 1$	Stratified Charge $i = 2$	Wankel $i = 3$	Diesel $i = 4$	Wankel- Diesel $i = 5$	1973 ICE $i = 6$
A_i	1.05	1.1	0.9	1.9[a]	1.2	1.0[b]
B_i	0.64	0.66	0.59	0.80	0.66	0.73

For diesel and Wankel-diesel, $G = 147.8$; otherwise, $G = 133.8$. In addition, $S = 2000$, $C = 0.10$ and $m(x)$ is the mileage value for the 1973 ICE taken from Figure C–1 for a vehicle weighing x pounds.

[a]For diesel autos weighing less than 3500 pounds, $A_4 = 1.5$ is probably a more reasonable estimate.
[b]For post-1976 ICE, $A_6 = 0.97$ should be used.

NOTES

1. "Fuel Economy and Emission Control", U.S. Environmental Protection Agency, November 1972 (Office of Air and Water Programs, Mobile Source Pollution Control Program).
2. Russell Barton, "Energy Requirements for Urban Vehicles", 1973, Report of research carried out as part of this project.
3. R.S. Berry and M.F. Fels, "The Energy Cost of Automobiles", *Bulletin of Atomic Scientists* (Science and Public Affairs), December 1973.

Notes to Chapter Two

The following reports of work conducted within this project are available upon request from Margaret Fulton Fels, Center for Environmental Studies and Transportation Program, Princeton University, Princeton, New Jersey: Margaret Fulton Fels, "Comparative Energy Costs of Urban Transportation Systems"; Michael J. Munson and Joenathan Dean, "Trenton in the 1970's: Profile of a Region in Flux"; Shari Glassman, Elizabeth Garman, and Michael Godnick, "Auto Occupancy Survey"; and Russell Barton, "Energy Requirements for Urban Vehicles."

1. Margaret Fulton Fels, "Comparative Energy Costs of Urban Transportation Systems," Transportation Program Report #74-TR-2, Princeton University, 1974 (To be published in *Transportation Research*).
2. Jerome M. Lutin, "Personal Rapid Transit, Policy and Technology: A Case Study," Unpublished masters thesis, School of Architecture and Urban Planning, Princeton University, 1973.
3. Michael J. Munson and Joenathan Dean, "Trenton in the 1970's: Profile of a Region in Flux," Working paper of the School of Architecture and Urban Planning, Princeton University, 1974.
4. These surveys were carried out under the auspices of the Trenton Transit Study within the Transportation Program, Princeton University.
5. Nationwide Personal Transportation Study, Report #2, "Annual Miles of Automobile Travel," U.S. Department of Transportation, Federal Highway Administration, April 1972.
6. *Census Tracts, Trenton, N.J. SMSA*, Bureau of the Census, U.S. Department of Commerce (Final Report PHC (1)-217).
7. "Pittsburgh Area Transportation Study," Vol. I., City of Pittsburgh, in cooperation with U.S. Department of Commerce, Bureau of Public Roads, November 1961.
8. ———. Lutin, "Personal Rapid Transit."
9. This is substantiated from data of auto specifications in *Automotive News 1973 Almanac* (Detroit, 1973) and *Almanacs* from earlier years.

10. U.S. Environmental Protection Agency, "Fuel Economy and Emission Control" (Office of Air and Water Programs, Mobile Source Pollution Control Program, November 1972); and John J. Brogan, "Alternative Power Plants" (Paper presented at 1973 SAE National Auto Engineering Meeting, Detroit, May 1973).

11. *Highway Statistics 1970*, U.S. Department of Transportation, Federal Highway Administration (USGPO #5001-0025).

12. Shari Glassman, Elizabeth Garman, and Michael Godnick, "Auto Occupancy Survey" (Conducted as part of this project, summer 1973).

13. National Personal Transportation Study, Report #1, *Automobile Occupancy*, U.S. Department of Transportation, Federal Highway Administration, April 1972.

14. *New York Times*, 19 August 1973: and "Trenton: Department of Planning and Development Takes an Activist Approach to Solve Transportation Problems," a City of Trenton report.

15. *Ibid.*

16. U.S. EPA, "Fuel Economy and Emission Control."

17. *New York Times*, 24 June 1973.

18. See Note 9.

19. William Saley, New Jersey Department of Motor Vehicles, private communication.

20. U.S. EPA, "Fuel Economy and Emmission Control."

21. Professor Marc Ross, University of Michigan, private communication.

22. William Drake et al., "Ann Arbor Dial-A-Ride Pilot Project, Final Report," April 1973.

23. This Monocab system of Rohr Industries was demonstrated at TRANSPO 72, Dulles International Airport, June 1972.

24. A. L. Kornhauser and J. L. Dais, "Assessing Area-Wide Personal Rapid Transit" (Paper presented at the International Conference on Transportation Research, Bruges, Belgium, June 1973).

25. Ronald Madsen, Park Mobile, Inc., private communication and unpublished reports.

26. H. Seidman and D. Retzloff, "Evolution of a Rapid Transit System in a Low Density Metropolitan Area," *Proceedings, Ground Transportation Symposium*, Santa Clara, California, June 1973.

27. M. J. Zobrak and D. Medville, "The Haddonfield Dial-A-Ride Experiment: Interim Results" (Paper presented at the International Conference on Transportation Research, Bruges, Belgium, June 1973).

28. Drake et al., "Ann Arbor Dial-A-Ride Pilot Project."

29. Curt M. Elmberg, "The Gothenburg Traffic Restraint Scheme" (Paper presented at International Conference on Transportation Research, Bruges, Belgium).

30. *New York Times*, 29 June 1973.

31. *1970 Clean Air Act*, U.S. Environmental Protection Agency, December 1970.

32. National Academy of Sciences, "Report on Motor Vehicles Emissions," Congressional Record–Senate, 28 February 1973, pp. S3617–3640.

33. U.S. EPA, "Fuel Economy and Emission Control."
34. "Research and Development Opportunities for Improved Transportation Energy Usage," Summary Technical Report of the Transportation Energy R & D Goals Panel, U.S. Department of Transportation, September 1973.
35. Ross, private communication.
36. Russell Barton, "Energy Requirements for Urban Vehicles," Report written as senior independent work, Princeton University; research concerning energy of manufacture and operation of electric cars and other ICE substitutes was carried out as a part of this project.
37. "Research and Development Opportunities," U.S. DOT.
38. D. V. Ragone, "Review of Battery Systems for Electrically Powered Vehicles," SAE Report #680453.
39. U.S. EPA, "Fuel Economy and Emission Control."
40. National Academy of Sciences, "Report on Motor Vehicles Emissions."
41. "Guide to Reduction of Smoke and Odor from Diesel-Powered Vehicles," Southwest Research Institute and Office of Air Programs, EPA, Research Triangle Park, North Carolina, September 1971.
42. Ernest Starkman, "General Motors and Energy Conservation." In *1973 Report on Progress in Areas of Public Concern*, General Motors Corporation, GM Technical Center, Warren, Michigan.
43. U.S. EPA, "Fuel Economy and Emission Control."
44. "Research and Development Opportunities," U.S. DOT.
45. National Academy of Sciences, "Report on Motor Vehicles Emissions."
46. Charles Jones (of Curtiss-Wright Corp,), "A Survey of Curtiss-Wright's 1958–1971 Rotating Combustion Engine Technological Developments," SAE report #720468.
47. "Research and Development Opportunities," U.S. DOT.
48. C. N. Cochran, "Aluminum—Villian or Hero in Energy Crisis?" Alcoa Research Laboratories, Pennsylvania, 1973.
49. U.S. Senate Bill S. 1903, Introduced by Senator Hollings on 30 May 1973 (copy of bill and private communication).
50. U.S. House of Representatives Bill H.R. 7531, Introduced by Congressman Vanik on 3 May 1973 (copy of bill and private communication); in addition, U.S. Senate Bill S. 2036, introduced by Senator Moss on 18 June 1973, proposes similar legislation.
51. U.S. House of Representatives Bill H.R. 11503, Introduced by Congressman George Brown on 15 November 1973.
52. *Highway Statistics 1970.*
53. National Personal Transportation Study, Report #2.
54. "Bicycling for Recreation and Commuting," U.S. Department of the Interior, U.S. GPO-1972-#461–880.
55. "Research and Development Opportunities," U.S. DOT.
56. Lewis Buchanan, "An Overview of the Motorcycle and Bicycle Problem" (Paper presented at the Cycle Safety Conference, Lansing, Michigan, January 1973).
57. Patricia F. Waller, Patricia Z. Barry, and William S. Rouse, "Motorcycles: 1.

Estimated Mileage and Its Parameters," University of North Carolina Highway Safety Research Center, Chapel Hill, North Carolina, 1968.

58. "Pool It," Highway Users Federation, Washington, D.C., 1973.
59. Glassman, Garmen, and Godnick, "Auto Occupancy Survey."
60. *New York Times*, 28 January 1974. p. 19.
61. *1972 Automobile Facts and Figures*, Motor Vehicles Manufacturers Association of the U.S., Detroit, Michigan.
62. *New York Times*, 4 October 1974. p. 1.

Chapter Three

Energy, Employment and Dollar Impacts of Alternative Transportation Options

Bruce Hannon, Robert Herendeen,
F. Puleo, and Anthony Sebald
Center for Advanced Computation
University of Illinois, Urbana

As the demand for energy in this county outruns our ability to increase supply, the concerned public and policy-maker alike are taking a closer look at just how efficiently we provide and use that energy in our modern society.

Transportation and its supporting services and manufacture account for approximately 41.8 percent of the total energy consumed in the United States;[1] thus it offers substantial opportunities for saving energy. There are two complementary approaches to energy conservation in transportation. One is to improve efficiency through technical change (smaller cars, diesel engines, etc.) or through more efficient use of existing transport modes (reduced speed limits, incentives for car pools, etc.). The other approach, which is the subject of this chapter, examines the energy conservation opportunities of switching from one transport mode to another, in the context of today's transportation systems. This report also examines the dollar costs and employment impacts of these transportation mode switches. Specifically, we use input-output analysis[1,2] to calculate the total energy impact of different transportation modes, along with dollar costs (to the consumer) and employment impacts of both intercity and urban transport modes. Intercity transport modes considered are the railroad, the airplane, and the automobile. The bus and the automobile are the urban transport modes considered.

Each travel mode is treated as an entire system of passenger transportation. The costs are evaluated in units of dollars, British thermal units (Btu) and man-years of labor, which are required, both directly and indirectly, to provide each unit of transportation service.

INTERCITY TRANSPORT

Previous studies of energy use in intercity rail and air transportation[3,4,5] have dealt only with the direct energy impact—i.e., fuel for propulsion. A total energy impact assessment should take into account the indirect energy impact as well—for example, the energy required in equipment manufacturing, repair and maintenance, and construction of terminals and airports.

In the analysis we establish the total dollar, energy, and labor (DEL) impacts of rail and air passenger transportation for 1963 and 1971. We also include the DEL impacts of intercity auto transportation from a previous study[6] for comparison with the rail and air figures.*

If the consumer were to save money in switching from one form of transportation to another, the question of what he does with the savings cannot be ignored. Whatever he does with the money he saves will directly or indirectly involve an energy cost. If he should spend the savings on gasoline, the energy savings would be negated. But there are many goods and services which demand much less energy than transportation. If the consumer were to spend his savings there, most of the energy savings from the transportation switch would be preserved. We do not predict how the consumer would spend his savings, but we have provided in Appendix A a list of consumer activities along with their energy intensities (Btu per dollar expended). The interested reader can determine the energy impact of whatever spending pattern he deems likely.

Dollar Impact of Intercity Transportation

Airplane travel in 1963 was almost twice as expensive per passenger mile as rail, with travel essentially equal to rail (see Table 3–1). By 1971 (see Table 3–2), the ranking was still the same, but rail and car travel had increased in cost while the cost of air travel had actually dropped slightly.**

Energy Impacts of Intercity Transportation

Most studies which examine the direct energy costs of intercity transportation rank air transportation as the most energy intensive, in Btu per passenger-mile; cars next; and railroads last, or least energy-intensive. Our study corroborates these results for 1971 (Table 3–2). However, for 1963 (Table 3–1) we find that the energy-intensiveness of railroads was actually greater than that of cars. The drop in direct energy-intensiveness between 1963 and 1971 for rail and air travel may be due to any of several factors: larger, more efficient jets; cancellation of rail runs with very low load factors; and so on. We have not studied the matter enough to be sure of the reasons.

When *total* energy inputs, direct and indirect, are considered, air

---

*It must be noted that the direct energy use is defined here to be all energy directly purchased by the rail line, the airline, or the car owner for purposes of providing transportation. In the case of rail and air, it therefore includes motive fuel as well as lighting and heating of offices, terminals, etc. Thus direct energy use figures used here are not exactly comparable to those of other researchers who define direct energy as motive power fuel only.

**It must be remembered that *all* auto associated expenses are included in the auto cost figures. The 4.7¢ per passenger-mile cost of operating the car in 1971 corresponds to a total cost of 2.9 x 4.7 = 13.6¢ per car-mile.

Table 3-1. DEL Costs of Air, Rail, and Auto Transportation, 1963

	$D(\$/Mile)^a$	$E(Btu/Mile)^a$			$L(10^{-6}\ Man\text{-}Yr/Mile)^a$		
		Direct	Total	Tot/Dir^d	Direct	$Total^d$	Tot/Dir^d
Passenger[b]							
Air	0.060	8,200	11,300	1.4	3.7	6.7	1.8
Rail	0.032	3,400	5,800	1.7	3.2	5.6	1.7
Car[c]	0.036	3,200	6,200	2.0	–	3.8	–
Freight							
Air	0.272	55,800	81,000	1.5	16.1	37	2.3
Rail	0.013	900	1,500	1.7	1.3	2.0	1.5

[a]Results per service mile: for passenger, per passenger mile; for freight, per ton mile.
[b]Passenger load factors: air, 53.1% (see reference 7); rail, 32.7% (see reference 8). car, 2.9 passenger miles per vehicle mile including driver (see reference 9).
[c]Assumed to be a fairly expensive one of the low-priced three (Ford, Chevrolet, Plymouth) getting 14.2 mpg.
[d]Calculated before rounding off the direct and total coefficients.

Table 3-2. DEL Costs of Air, Rail, and Auto Transportation, 1971

	D($/Mile)[a]	E(Btu/Mile)[a]			L(10⁻⁶ Man-Yr/Mile)[a]		
		Direct	Total	Tot/Dir[d]	Direct	Total	Tot/Dir[d]
Passenger[b]							
Air	0.058	7,200	9,800	1.4	2.1	3.8	1.8
Rail	0.044	2,300	4,000	1.7	4.2	7.2	1.7
Car[c]	0.047	3,400	5,900	2.0	—	3.2	—
Freight							
Air	0.205	53,600	80,000	1.5	7.8	20	2.3
Rail	0.016	800	1,600	1.7	.82	1.4	1.5

[a]Results per service mile: for passenger, per passenger mile; for freight, per ton mile.

[b]Passenger load factors: air, 48.5% (see reference 7); rail, 37.1% (see reference 8); car, 2.9 passenger miles per vehicle mile including driver (see reference 9).

[c]Assumed to be a fairly expensive one of the low-priced three (Ford, Chevrolet, Plymouth) getting 13.6 mpg.

[d]Calculated before rounding off the direct and total coefficients.

travel emerges as the most energy-intensive mode and rail travel the least, for both 1963 and 1971 (see Tables 3–1 and 3–2).

The ratios of total energy to direct energy vary substantially from one form of transportation to another. In the case of the car, indirect energy costs are as great as the direct energy costs. Apparently the infrastructure associated with the auto (auto manufacture, highway construction, insurance, repairs, and so on) is relatively more important than that associated with other modes.

It is important to point out that the auto considered for this energy ranking is fairly large and inefficient (getting around 14 mpg). The auto energy-intensiveness would be substantially lower if the car were more efficient or if the car load factor were higher. It is likely that a very large car (getting about 9 mpg) would be *more* energy-intensive than a plane.

Employment Impacts of Intercity Transportation

As Tables 3–1 and 3–2 indicate, our study found that air travel was the most labor-intensive of the three travel modes in 1963 but almost the least labor-intensive in 1971. (We consider our labor figures to be subject to greater error than our energy figures.) The substantial reduction in labor-intensiveness for air travel in this period may be due to the "modernization" of the air transportation industry, which grew very rapidly during this time. At the same time railroad passenger service was declining so that large labor-saving innovations became more difficult to implement.

DEL Costs of Specific Trips

Besides the DEL (Dollar Energy Labor) costs for average transportation conditions (summarized in Tables 3–1 and 3–2) we have also examined the DEL costs of three specific trips, chosen on the basis of their intermediate length (200 to 400 miles) and relatively heavy use (see Tables 3–3 and 3–4). The difference in mileage actually traveled by the different modes has been taken into account.

1. Dollars. The car was generally the least expensive mode. Exceptions were the New York to Washington trip in 1971 and Los Angeles to San Francisco trip in both years. Except for San Francisco-Los Angeles in 1971, air travel was the most expensive. It is interesting to note that while the New York-Boston and New York-Washington air fares increased by over 50 percent in that period, the San Francisco-Los Angeles fare decreased by 4 percent.

2. Energy. The modes in order of increasing energy-intensiveness are train, car, plane, though car and train were sometimes nearly equal. The only exception to this ranking is the San Francisco-Los Angeles trip in 1963, where the rail trip had a small energy disadvantage relative to the car.

Table 3-3. DEL Costs for Three Specific Trips, 1963

		$D(\$)^a$		$E(Million\ Btu)$	$L(10^{-3}\ Man\text{-}Yr)$
		Actual^b	Average^c	Total (Direct plus Indirect)	Total (Direct plus Indirect)
New York–Boston	Air	13.00	11.30	2.1	1.3
	Rail	11.58	7.50	1.4	1.3
	Car	8.84	7.72	1.4	0.83
New York–Washington, D.C.	Air	15.35	12.84	2.4	1.4
	Rail	10.65	7.28	1.3	1.3
	Car	10.55	7.93	1.4	0.85
San Francisco–Los Angeles	Air	16.95	21.04	4.0	2.4
	Rail	11.00	15.65	2.8	2.7
	Car	14.34	14.15	2.5	1.5

^{a}Includes tolls: N.Y.–Boston, $1.47; N.Y.–Wash., $3.45; S.F.–L.A., $0.25. Also see footnotes for Tables 3–1 and 3–2.

^{b}Derived from industry sources for the specific trip.

^{c}Derived by multiplying the average costs per mile (see Table 3–1) by the trip length in miles.

Table 3-4. DEL Costs for Three Specific Trips, 1971

		$D(\$)^a$		$E(Million\ Btu)$	$L(10^{-3}\ Man\text{-}Yr)$
		$Actual^b$	$Average^c$	Total (Direct plus Indirect)	Total (Direct plus Indirect)
New York–Boston	Air	22.22	10.92	1.9	0.72
	Rail	16.00	10.28	0.94	1.7
	Car	11.40	10.29	1.3	0.69
New York–Washington, D.C.	Air	24.07	12.41	2.1	0.81
	Rail	13.00	9.97	0.91	1.6
	Car	13.18	10.57	1.3	0.70
San Francisco–Los Angeles	Air	16.25	20.34	3.5	1.3
	Rail	12.75	21.43	2.0	3.5
	Car	17.84	17.65	2.2	1.2

[a]Includes tolls: N.Y.–Boston, $1.47; N.Y.–Wash., $3.45; S.F.–L.A., $0.25. Also see footnotes for Tables 3–1 and 3–2.
[b]Derived from industry sources for the specific trip.
[c]Derived by multiplying the average costs per mile (see Table 3–1) by the trip length in miles.

3. Labor. In 1963 the automobile trips were significantly less labor-intensive than either rail or air. Due to the large increases in productivity for the airlines mentioned previously, car and air were nearly equally labor-intensive in 1971 and both were less labor-intensive than rail, by a factor of 2 to 3.

URBAN TRANSPORTATION SYSTEMS

Our research on urban transportation attempts to answer the following questions:
- What are the total (direct and indirect) energy and employment costs per passenger for typical United States urban cars and bus sytems?
- What are the dollar costs per passenger for these transportation systems?
- What are the dollar, energy, and employment impacts if an average urban car driver becomes an average urban bus passenger?
- What are the dollar, energy, and employment impacts when an urban car driver decides to become an urban bus passenger in the context of an unchanging system?
- If the dollar cost per passenger rises or falls with the transfer from a car to a bus, what are the energy and employment impacts of this net change in dollar costs?
- If energy conservation is a goal, how can the system be modified to allow voluntary change to the least energy-consumptive system?

Energy Use in Urban Transportation
Fuel consumption by automobiles in urban areas amounts to 7.1 percent of total U.S. energy use. If indirect energy use is also taken into account, this share is increased to 12.3 percent. In contrast, fuel and total consumption by urban buses amounts to only 0.14 and 0.24 percent, respectively, of total U.S. energy use. Clearly the automobile dominates urban passenger transport energy consumption and is a major single consumer (see Table 3–5).

At the same time the urban automobile contributes 99.6 percent of the urban vehicle miles for passenger transportation while carrying 93.4 percent of the passenger trips. The urban bus, by contrast, contributes about 0.3 percent of the urban vehicle miles and carries 4.5 percent of the urban passenger trips (see Table 3–6).

Direct energy consumption per mile of travel for compact automobiles, standard automobiles, and urban buses have been calculated by others (see Table 3–7).

Attributes of Urban Transportation Systems
Bus companies and individual urban cars have the following attributes:

Table 3-5.   Distribution of Direct and Total United States Energy Used by Selected Transportation Categories

Transportation Category		Percent of All Transportation Energy	Percent of All U.S. Energy
	.... Directly	55.3[c]	23.1[b]
Total transportation used (1963)	.... Directly and Indirectly	100	41.8[b]
	.... Directly	28.5	11.9[b]
All U.S. autos used (1963)	.... Directly and indirectly	49.5	20.7[b]
	.... Directly	17.0[d]	7.1
All urban autos used (1971)	.... Directly and indirectly	29.4	12.3[e]
	.... Directly	0.33[d]	0.14
All urban buses[a] used (1971)	.... Directly and indirectly	0.58	0.24[f]

[a]This includes urban, rural, and school buses (not intercity).
[b]See reference 1.
[c]Assumes that transportation and the GNP have similar indirect energy intensities.
[d]See reference 10.
[e]Assumes that urban autos and average autos have similar indirect energy intensities.
[f]Assumes that indirect energy intensities for buses are the same as for average autos.

- Dollar, energy, and labor (DEL) costs for *overhead*, the fixed annual costs for the availability of equipment.
- Dollar, energy, and labor (DEL) costs for *operation*, the annual costs for the use of the equipment and provision of services.
- Dollar, energy, and labor (DEL) costs for *streets*, the annual costs of maintenance and new constructions of bus and automobile rights-of-way.
- Dollar, energy, and labor (DEL) costs for *disposal*, the costs of final recovery and the recycle value of all equipment no longer used.

The first three of these costs contribute additively to the total DEL costs of bus companies and urban cars. The dollar return upon disposal may be likened to the return of a deposit and has to be subtracted from the overhead dollar cost. However, the energy and labor costs which this deposit causes in the recoverable parts and recycling industry is a cost to the system, and has to be added to the overhead energy and labor costs.

Table 3-6.   Energy and Performance Characteristics for the Urban Bus and Automobile

Mode	Percentage of Total U.S. Energy Consumption (1971)	Percentage of Total U.S. Urban Vehicle-Miles for Passenger Transportation (1970)	Percentage of Total Urban Passenger Trips (1970)
Urban auto	12.3[a]	99.62[b]	93.4[d]
Urban bus	0.24[a]	0.31[c]	4.5[e]

[a]See Table 3-5.

[b]Based on 494.5 billion automobile-miles (see reference 11) and 1.88 billion transit vehicle-miles (see reference 12).

[c]Corresponding to 1.41 billion urban bus-miles plus 8 percent (see reference 12 and footnote (d) below).

[d]Average automobile trip length in incorporated places = 8.3 miles (see reference 13). Urban automobile mileage as in footnote (b). Transit passenger trips = 7.33 billion plus 8 percent adjustment factor (see reference 12). Comparison of Federal Highway Statistics and American Transit Association (ATA) data on urban buses reveals that the ATA does not account for approximately 8 percent of the U.S. urban bus fleet.

[e]Urban bus passenger trips = 5.03 billion plus 8 percent (see reference 12 and footnote (d) above).

Table 3-7.   Direct Energy Consumption per Unit of Transportation Service by Urban Bus and Automobile

Mode	Seat-Miles/ Gallon[b]	Passenger-Miles/ Gallon[c]	Btu/ Seat-Mile[b]	Btu/ Passenger-Mile[c]
Compact automobile	120[d]	42[d]	1,300[f]	–
Urban automobile	64[d]	15[d]	2,817[f]	8,100[g]
Urban bus[a]	215[e]	110[d]	1,548[f,h]	3,700[g]
	220[d]	125[e]		

[a]See References 10, 14 and 16 for slight variations in their definition of this mode.

[b]Based on theoretical average seating capacity.

[c]Based on approximation of actual passenger load.

[d]See reference 10.

[e]See reference 14.

[f]See reference 15.

[g]See reference 16.

[h]The figures of reference 15 are not comparable because they have expressed their values in Btu/revenue passenger, not Btu/passenger-mile.

Attribute Measurements

Each attribute is measured in dollar, energy, and labor (DEL) costs. Dollar cost is obtained directly from operations data.

The measurement of each variable was made after an extensive data search involving 140 urban bus companies and urban car operation in 28 major U.S. cities in 1971. The bus data base was made up primarily of larger bus companies; the auto data came from leasing companies. This tends slightly to depress the average bus cost and elevate the average car cost. We also found major variations in bus data from one company to the next; data for the urban car in the 28 cities wermore homogeneous.

The component DEL costs for bus companies (38 company averages) and the urban car (28 city averages) are given in Tables 3–8 and 3–9, respectively, for 1971.

To obtain the DEL cost comparison between the urban car and the urban bus, the average number of passengers and their average trip lengths must be known.

In the case of the urban auto, each car is driven 11, 200 miles per year on the average, each trip averages 8.3 miles, and there are on the average 1.9 passengers per trip.[13] Thus the number of passengers who use a car each year is

$$\frac{(11{,}200 \text{ miles/car year}) \times (1.9 \text{ passengers/trip})}{8.3 \text{ miles/trip}} = 2564$$

On the average, each bus company accumulates 8.37 million bus miles and carries 26.7 million passengers each year.[17] Combining this information with an average load of 12 passengers/bus,[18] we obtain the average bus passenger trip length as

$$\frac{(8.37 \times 10^6 \text{ bus miles/company-year}) \times (12 \text{ passengers/bus})}{26.7 \times 10^6 \text{ passengers / company-year}} = 3.76 \text{ miles}$$

These data are utilized to construct Table 3–10, which shows that on the average, the automobile costs less per passenger mile, but demands far more energy and is less labor-intensive.

Car-Bus Transfer

This study considered two situations in which people might shift from urban cars to buses: one is a nationwide change (or a shift of the average consumer); the other, an individual change. We have made differing assumptions to accord with these two situations; the subsequent effects of each on DEL costs are quite different. The DEL costs of both the nationwide shift and the

Table 3-8.   DEL Costs per Bus Company per Year (1971)

No.	Variable	Dollar (Thousands)	Energy (Billion/ Btu)	Labor (Man-Years)
	Overhead			
1.	Manufacture	625	43.3	47.2
	Operation			
2.	General maintenance	828	17.1	34.9
3.	New tires and tubes	10.4	0.883	0.484
4.	Retread tires and tubes	93.8	2.69	5.48
5.	Repairs	892	66.9	83.8
6.	Station	47.8	2.58	3.23
7.	Transportation	946	22.0	74.3
8.	Drivers	4,140	0.0	0.0
9.	Driver-years	0.0	0.0	407
10.	Fuel volume energy	0.0	257	0.0
11.	Fuel cost to produce	122	21.2	4.26
12.	Fuel cost to transport	8.05	1.30	0.428
13.	Fuel cost to wholesale	75.2	2.21	6.29
14.	Fuel cost to retail	24.6	0.71	11.1
15.	Lub. oil volume energy	0.0	3.28	0.0
16.	Lub. oil cost to produce	6.10	1.06	0.213
17.	Lub. oil cost to transport	0.402	0.065	0.021
18.	Lub. oil cost to wholesale	3.76	0.110	0.314
19.	Lub. oil to retail	1.23	0.036	0.145
20.	Administration	1,670	33.0	88.2
21.	Traffic services	47.6	0.937	2.51
22.	Advertising	31.7	0.856	1.67
23.	Insurance	351.6	7.50	23.5
24.	Licenses	228	15.0	12.8
25.	Rents	37.2	0.573	1.01
	Total Operation	9,570	457	762
	Streets			
26.	Taxes	228	15.1	12.2
27.	Fuel volume tax	186	12.3	10.0
	Total Streets	414	27.4	22.2
	Disposal			
28.	Recoverable value	23.5	1.78	6.76
29.	Recyclable value	2.61	0.606	0.34
	Total Disposal	26.1	2.38	7.10
	Grand Total	10,600	530	839

individual change are calculated for different trip purposes (work, family business, education, recreation) and for a weighted average trip.*

*Note that the average bus trip length is almost half the average car trip length (Table 3-10). This indicates that the urban bus and car now actually serve different urban areas: the bus operates in the predominately urban area and the car operates mainly in the

Table 3–9. DEL Costs per Urban Car per Year (1971)

No.	Variable	Dollar	Energy (Million Btu)	Labor (10^{-3} Man-Years)
	Overhead			
1.	Manufacture	325.	21.1	20.0
2.	Rail transport	4.08	0.242	0.272
3.	Truck transport	4.08	0.279	0.288
4.	Wholesale	8.15	0.251	0.716
5.	Retail	66.0	4.29	8.18
6.	Financing charge	70.6	0.922	3.70
	Total Overhead	478	27.1	33.1
	Operation			
7.	Maintenance	146	4.17	8.51
8.	Repairs	125	3.58	7.30
9.	Fuel volume energy	0.0	118	0.0
10.	Fuel cost to produce	93.7	16.3	3.27
11.	Fuel cost to transport	8.93	1.77	0.466
12.	Fuel cost to wholesale	62.3	1.83	5.22
13.	Fuel cost to retail	42.8	1.24	5.05
14.	Insurance	237	5.07	15.9
15.	Licenses	19.7	1.30	1.11
16.	Local government	25.2	1.56	1.34
	Total Operation	761	155	48.2
	Streets			
17.	Fuel volume tax	94.1	6.24	5.05
18.	New constructions	25.2	1.67	1.35
	Total Streets	119	7.91	6.40
	Disposal			
19.	Recoverable value	4.03	0.31	1.16
20.	Recyclable value	0.403	0.09	0.05
	Total Disposal	4.43	.04	1.21
	Grand Total	1,350	190	88.9

Nationwide change. For the situation in which average consumers, nationwide, shift from car to bus, we have made the assumption that there are no "fixed costs" in the long run. Therefore, the DEL costs per passenger-trip stay the same for the remaining trips by car, while passengers shift from cars to buses. The "average" car will last longer and depreciate less if it is used less; and for this case we assume no style-dependent depreciation. Thus overhead costs are distributed over a longer period of time. We also assume that "fixed costs," such

suburbs. For any car-to-bus transfer, therefore, a bus would have to drive over twice as far for each passenger than at present. If the car-to-bus transfer were such that bus ridership slightly more than doubled, then the data of Table 3–10 would still apply.

Table 3-10. DEL Cost Comparison for Urban Bus and Urban Car, 1971

Urban Bus	Dollar	Energy (Thousand Btu)	Labor (10^-6 Man-Years)
Cost per passenger	0.396	19.8	31.4
Cost per passenger-mile	0.105	5.28	8.35
Urban Car			
Cost per passenger	0.528	74.1	34.7
Cost per passenger-mile	0.069	8.93	4.18

as insurance and licenses, decline with each incremental transfer of passengers, since auto driving as a whole will decrease. The nationwide change model transfers the "average" car passenger to the "average" bus as though the *entire* nation were shifting its mode of urban travel.

The changes in the DEL costs of urban transportation for this nationwide change are given for various trip purposes in Table 3–12, making use of the car trip characteristics given in Table 3–11. On the average, there would be a savings of dollars, energy, and labor accompanying a nationwide shift from car to bus. The greatest savings would occur for work and recreational trips. Using data in Tables 3–11 and 3–12, the reader can estimate DEL costs of a partial national shift from cars to buses in urban areas.

Individual Shift. In this case we consider the situation where the average individual car owner changes his personal and family urban travel from car to bus, while the system as a whole does not change. The annual operating costs of the car decrease; but we make the assumption here that fixed or overhead costs remain essentially the same. Depreciation due to style changes and the custom of turning cars in frequently is assumed to continue unchanged; insurance rates and license fees do not decline. In addition, there will be cost *increases* associated with using the bus. (The cost to the passenger of using the

Table 3-11. Parameters Characterizing Auto Trips

Trip Purpose	Passengers per Trip	Miles per Trip	Fraction of Car-Miles	Passengers per Car-Year
Work	1.4	10.2	0.406	1,540
Family business	1.9	5.6	0.200	3,800
Education	2.6	4.7	0.049	6,200
Recreation	2.5	13.1	0.333	2,140
Weighted average	1.9	8.3	1.000	2,560

Source: See reference 13.

Table 3-12. Total DEL Decrease (+) per Car per Year, Nationwide Transfer, 1971

Trip Purpose	Dollar	Energy (Million Btu)	Labor (10^{-3} Man-Years)
Work	+303	+ 64.8	+16.5
Family business	- 30.2	+ 22.9	- 6.07
Education	- 53.9	+ 3.29	- 5.17
Recreation	+169	+ 49.1	+ 7.28
Weighted average	+339	+139	+ 8.47

bus is estimated on the basis of average DEL costs, derived from data in Table 3–10. These are DEL cost changes to the system, not to the individual.)

For this calculation the amount, type, and purpose of urban travel are assumed to be the same as at present. The shift from car to bus is assumed to occur incrementally by travel purpose in this order: work, recreation, family business, and education.

The DEL cost changes for an individual shifting from a car to the bus are summarized in Table 3–13 for various trip purposes. In this case, where fixed costs remain the same as an individual makes the shift, the dollar cost to the traveler rises, energy consumption falls, and employment increases.

A significant decrease in energy consumption and an increase in employment could occur if the nation were to shift, on the average, to urban buses from passenger cars. But clearly the average person will not readily change from a car to the bus even though such a change would save energy, if it would cost him money to do so. The individual who shifts a portion of his urban travel to buses while keeping his car will indeed have greater dollar costs per mile.

Typically, a person might at first transfer only part of his car needs to the bus; he would discover that this is a dollar costly process. The weighted average in Table 3–13 assumes that the individual has switched entirely to the bus but still keeps his car in operating condition. If he sells the car, the net costs would be as given in the bottom row of Table 3–12. The easiest car to eliminate would be the second car used for work trips. It is worthwhile to note that

Table 3-13. Individual Transfer DEL Cost Decrease (+) per Car-Year, 1971

Trip Purpose	Dollar	Energy (Million Btu)	Labor (10^{-3} Man-Years)
Work	- 14.7	+ 49.7	- 5.43
Family business	-186	+ 15.5	-16.9
Education	- 92.2	+ 1.47	- 7.82
Recreation	- 91.2	+ 36.8	-10.7
Total	-443	+102	-45.6

Table 3-14.   Energy and Labor Intensities for 1971

	Energy (Thousand Btu per Dollar)	Labor (10^{-6} Man-Yrs/$)
Bus company	50.1	79.2
Urban car	140	65.7

approximately 30 percent of metropolitan families owned two or more cars in 1971.[19] Thus an energy conservation policy aimed at upgrading bus service may be especially effective in persuading the commuter to sell his second commuting car in favor of using the bus.

Energy and Employment Impacts in Shifting from Cars to Buses. The ratios of energy and labor costs to dollar costs are measures of the energy- and labor-intensities of bus companies and urban cars. These intensities, shown in Table 3-14, are valid for both the nationwide and the individual modal shift cases. The urban car has a greater energy impact but provides less employment than the bus, per dollar.

Using values given in Table 3-12 and 3-13, we can also calculate the rate of saving which a shift to buses would produce (that is, the energy or labor saved per dollar saved). As shown in Table 3-15, the greatest energy savings rate in the individual transfer case occurs for recreation trips and the least for education trips.

The data in Table 3-15, along with data in Table 3-A1 of Appendix A, can be used to show possible total energy impacts of shifting to the bus, in cases where both energy and dollars are saved. On the average in the nationwide change case, for example, about 411,000 Btu are saved for every dollar that is saved. It is important to know whether the person who saves money by switching to the bus will still be conserving energy when the impact of spending his savings is taken into account. From Table 3-A1 we see that as long as the

Table 3-15.   Energy and Labor Impacts per Dollar Saved for a Nationwide Change and Individual Transfer, 1971 (Decrease is +)

Trip Purpose	Nationwide Change		Individual Transfer	
	Energy (Thousand Btu/Dollar)	Labor (10^{-6} Man-Yrs/$)	Energy (Thousand Btu/Dollar)	Labor (10^{-6} Man-Yrs/$)
Work	+214	+ 54.6	−338	+369
Family business	−759	+201	− 83.1	+ 90.5
Education	− 61.0	+ 95.9	− 15.9	+ 84.8
Recreation	+291	+ 43.1	−403	+117
Weighted average	+411	+ 25.0	−230	+103

Table 3-16. Gasoline Prices Needed to Produce Equal Variable Car and Bus Cost (¢/Gallon), 1971.

Trip Purpose	
Work	42
Family business	154
Education	272
Recreation	72
Weighted average	93

consumer does not spend his savings on fuel or electricity he will still save energy. In the individual transfer case, of course, the consumer spends more dollars on transportation while saving energy. Thus the total energy savings of the shift to bus travel are augmented, because money is diverted from other expenditures. How great the extra energy savings will be depends on what other goods and services the consumer might choose to forego, and how energy-intensive they are.

Modifying the Environment. Two changes in economic conditions could reduce the extra expense which we calculate would occur when an individual shifts to using the bus while still keeping his car. These are higher prices for auto fuel or lower bus fares through the increasing number of riders. We now consider what changes are required to reach the breakeven point for various trip purposes.

1. Changing the Cost of Fuel. The changes in the fuel costs for automobile use needed to nullify the changes in the dollar cost for the individual car/bus transfer are given for various trip purposes in Table 3-16. These fuel prices should be considered relative to the average gasoline price in 1971 of 37.7¢/gallon (which corresponds to a fuel cost of 2.7¢/mile for a car getting 13.96 mpg). We see that in 1971 the price of fuel had to be increased on the average to 93¢/gallon for there to be no dollar cost increase in switching from the car to the bus. However, in the case of work trips, a fuel price of only 42¢/gallon is all that is required to break even.

2. Changing the Number of Passengers Using the Bus. To calculate the number of passengers per bus company per year required to reduce the bus cost so that it becomes equal to the variable costs of owning a car, we assume that the total bus company costs remain the same, while an increase in number of passengers reduces the average fare.

The estimated percentage charges for dollar costs only are given in Table 3-17.

We see that, on the average, bus companies would have to increase by 77 percent their total number of passengers to make the transfer from car to

Table 3-17. **Percent Increase in Bus Passengers to Produce Equal Variable Car and Bus Costs**

Trip Purpose	
Work	6
Family business	163
Education	329
Recreation	48
Weighted average	77

buses produce equal cost to the consumer. But an increase of only 6 percent in ridership for work trips would be enough to make the dollar cost of bus and car equal, for this trip purpose.

CONCLUSIONS

Bus Companies

It cost an average urban bus company about $10.6 million, 530 billion Btu, and 839 man-years of labor to operate an average of 256 buses in 1971. Each bus carried an average of 267,000 revenue passengers in 1971 at a total cost of 39.6¢, 19,800 Btu, and 31.4×10^{-6} man-years of labor per revenue passenger-mile.

Urban Cars

The cost of using one standard American automobile exclusively for an average amount of urban travel in 1971 was $1,350, 190 million Btu, and 88.9×10^{-3} man-years of labor. The American urban automobile was used for an average of 1,350 vehicle trips, and each trip was approximately 8.3 miles long. In travelling this amount, each average urban car provided 2,560 passenger trips at a total cost of 52.8¢, 74,000 Btu and 34.7×10^{-6} man-years of labor per passenger-trip. This is equivalent to 6.9¢, 8,900 Btu and 4.2×10^{-6} man-years of labor per urban passenger-mile. Again, this includes both the fixed and variable costs and the direct and indirect costs of urban car transportation. Home garage costs were not included because of a lack of data.

Comparison

Urban bus travel costs 52 percent more money, uses 42 percent less energy, and is twice as labor-intensive as urban car travel on a per-passenger-mile basis when total actual user costs are compared. While many people habitually make comparisons between different modes of transportation on a per-mile basis, we feel that for urban passenger transportation it is more meaningful to base comparisons on a functional unit rather than an arbitrary mileage basis. For this reason our car-bus transfer model considers shifting people from car to bus for each of four different trip purposes. For the average passenger *trip* urban bus travel costs 25 percent less money, 73 percent less energy, and 9.5 percent less labor than travel by the urban car. These comparisons are based on total costs to the system of transportation. The numerical values may therefore be greater than the direct out-of-pocket expenses.

In making the comparison in this manner, there are, no doubt, statistically significant differences in the number of miles travelled by the car and bus modes for each of the four trip purposes. The extent of the differences remains unknown because of the absence of detailed bus-use data. It is our judgement that in the long run, any present differences in urban car and bus trip lengths for different purposes would be largely mitigated by compensating changes in travel patterns, route design and urban activity location. For this reason we caution against simplistic comparisons of the two modes.

Nationwide Change

If urban car travel transferred to bus travel, there would be a total savings by the system of $339,139 million Btu, and 8.47 x 10^{-3} man-years of labor per car for the year 1971. These estimates are based on a long-term national change in urban travel from cars to buses.

The amount of dollars, energy, and labor that would be saved by a transfer of passengers from urban cars to buses for each of the four major types of travel purposes and for the weighted average travel are indicated in Table 3–12. The largest dollar saving would come from transferring work travel ($303) and recreational travel ($169) to the urban bus. There would be no dollar saving in transferring family business and educational travel from the urban car to urban bus. On the contrary, it would cost $30 and $54 per car per year more, respectively.

The transfer of all categories of urban travel from cars to buses would decrease the amount of energy used. The energy saving per car would be greatest for the transfer of work travel (65 million Btu) followed in order by recreation travel (49 million Btu), family business travel (23 million Btu), and educational travel (3.3 million Btu).

A shift of work and recreational travel from cars to buses would save 16.5 x 10^{-3} and 7.28 x 10^{-3} man-years of labor, respectively, per car. Family business and educational travel would require 6.07 x 10^{-3} and 5.17 x 10^{-3} more man-years of labor, respectively. Overall there would be a small decrease in the amount of labor needed to provide the same amount of urban travel.

The shift to bus saves the consumer money which will be spent and consequently involves a new round of energy and employment. How much energy and employment will be required depends on the consumer choice of where he would spend his newfound dollar savings.

Individual Transfer

The individual urban car user who changes to the bus for all urban travel purposes or for some partial combination thereof, while continuing to own an average car, will experience the DEL changes shown in Table 3–13. Substitution of the bus for the car costs more for each travel purpose from a low of $15/year to a high of $186/year. Substitution of the bus for the car while still keeping the car causes a greater demand for labor and less for energy, for all urban travel purposes.

The weighted average values for DEL for the individual substitution indicate that it would cost $443 more, save 102 million Btu, and require 45.6 x 10^{-3} more jobs per urban car per year for an individual urban car owner to retain ownership of his car but to give up using it for urban travel and use the bus in its place.

These figures go to the heart of the policy problem of inducing people to change from urban auto to buses.

If we make the plausible assumption that, short of a nationwide changeover to bus travel, fixed costs for auto ownership will remain fairly constant, it is simply not economical in a dollar sense for an individual to replace *some* of his auto use by bus. If, for example, a person owns a special auto used only for work trips and he decides to take a bus to work to save energy, he will lose money *unless* he disposes of this auto.

Two steps to remove the dollar disincentive in giving up the auto and taking the bus are: taxing auto fuel and reducing the bus cost. We found that, on the average, the price of gasoline would have to rise from 37 to 93 cents per gallon (1971) or bus ridership would have to increase by 77 percent, before the variable cost of the car and bus cost were equal. But for work trips the price of gasoline need only be 42 cents per gallon or bus ridership must increase only 6 percent for the switch to buses to be economic.

Appendix A

Energy Intensities of Personal Consumption Activities

The U.S. Department of Commerce has published a detailed study of personal consumption. Eighty-three "activities" (e.g., purchased meals and beverages) are broken down into their component expenditures by input-output sector. In this form they are easily converted to energy. Table 3–A1 lists the results, which have been scaled from 1963 to 1971 using published deflators.

The dollar breakdown is a national average, and undoubtedly incorporates many arbitrary assumptions. If you never buy hot dogs when you go to a ball game, your energy-intensity for activity 71, "spectator sports," is probably not average. Nonetheless, Table 3–A1 offers some guidance on how to direct your spending if you desire decreased energy impact.

Note that the average of all personal consumption expenditures in 1971 was 70,000 Btu/$. Only 7 of the 83 activities were more energy-intensive.

Table 3-A1. Energy Intensities of Personal Consumption Activities (Energy Intensity Ranked Sector Table, 1971)

Rank	Title	Energy Intensity (Thousand Btu/$)
1.	Gas	990
2.	Other fuel & ice	630
3.	Electricity	505
4.	Gasoline & oil	480
5.	Airline transportation	131
6.	Water & other sanitary services	79
7.	Cleaning preparations	78
8.	Other intercity transportation	70
9.	Bridge & road tolls	66
10.	Intercity bus transportation	64
11.	Tires, tubes & parts	62
12.	Railway & sleeping car	60
13.	Kitchen & household appliances	59
14.	Toilet articles	58
15.	Taxicab transportation	57
16.	New & used cars	56
17.	Stationery, writing supplies	56
18.	Clothing issued to military	55
19.	Street & local bus transport	54
20.	Drug prep & sundries	52
21.	Semidurable house furnishings	51
22.	China, glassware, tableware	51
23.	Railway (Commuter) transport	49
24.	Durable toys & sport equipment	48
25.	Nondurable toys & sports equipment	45
26.	Other durable house furnishings	45
27.	Food furnished to govt.	45
28.	Food prod. & consump. on farm	44
29.	Radio & TV receivers	43
30.	Magazines & newspapers	42
31.	Food purch. for off-prem. consump.	41
32.	Furniture	37
33.	Shoe cleaning and repair	36
34.	Other household operat. expenditures	35
35.	Private elem. & second. school	35
36.	Private higher education	35
37.	Books and maps	35
38.	Other housing	34
39.	Flowers, seeds, plants	33
40.	Women's & children's clothing	33
41.	Other private education	33
42.	Purchased meals and beverages	32
43.	Jewelry & watches	32
44.	Other prof. medical services	32
45.	Ophthalmic & orthoped. prod.	31
46.	Men's & boy's clothing	31
47.	Other clothing & accessories	31
48.	Laundering in establishment	30
49.	Garment cleaning, repair	30
50.	Radio & TV repair	28

Table 3–A1.   continued

Rank	Title	Energy Intensity (Thousand Btu/$)
51.	Shoes and footwear	28
52.	Clubs and fraternal organizations	28
53.	Relig. & welfare activities	28
54.	Funeral & burial expenses	26
55.	Other personal business	26
56.	Private hospitals	26
57.	Automobile repair & maintenance	24
58.	Automobile insurance	22
59.	Health insurance	22
60.	Life insur. handling expenses	22
61.	Financial intermediaries	22
62.	Other recreational expenses	21
63.	Tobacco products	20
64.	Telephone & telegraph	19
65.	Commercial amusements	19
66.	Legal services	19
67.	Tenant occ. nonfarm dwelling	18
68.	Brokerage charges	18
69	Parimutuel net receipts	18
70.	Foreign travel by US residents	17
71.	Motion picture theaters	16
72.	Spectator sports	15
73.	Theaters and opera	15
74.	Barber, beauty shops	15
75.	Bank service charges	13
76.	Dentists	11
77.	Physicians	10
78.	Owner occ. nonfarm dwelling	8
79.	Rental value of farmhouse	8
80.	Expend abroad by US govt.	5
81.	Domestic service	0
82.	Expend. in US by foreigners	0
83.	Personal remit. to foreigners	0

Notes to Chapter Three

This chapter was based on detailed reports, prepared for the Energy Policy Project, which are available on request from Bruce Hannon, Energy Research Group, Center for Advanced Computation, University of Illinois, Urbana 61801. These reports are: Anthony Sebald and Robert Herendeen, "The Dollar, Energy, and Employment Impacts of Air, Rail, and Automobile Passenger Transportation," Center for Advanced Computation Document No. 96, September 1974; and Bruce Hannon and F. Puleo, "Transferring from Urban Cars to Buses: The Energy and Employment Impacts," Center for Advanced Computation Document No. 98, April 1974.

1. See R. Herendeen,"An Energy Input-Output Matrix for the United States, 1963," Document No. 69, Center for Advanced Computation, University of Illinois, Urbana, March 1963.
2. Hugh Folk, and Bruce Hannon, "An Energy, Pollution and Employment Policy Model," CAC Document No. 68, Center for Advanced Computation, University of Illinois, Urbana.
3. E. Hirst, "Energy Intensiveness of Passenger and Freight Transport Modes 1950–1970," Report EP-44, Oak Ridge National Laboratory, April 1973.
4. R. A. Rice, "Systems Energy as a Factor in Considering Future Transportation" (Paper presented at the American Society of Mechanical Engineers Annual Meeting, December 1970).
5. W. I. Mooz, "The Effect of Fuel Price Increases On Energy Intensiveness of Freight Transport," Report R-804-NSF, Rand Corporation, Santa Monica, California, December 1971.
6. See reference 1 or E. Hirst and R. Herendeen, "Total Energy Demand for Automobiles," Society of Automotive Engineers, New York (Paper presented at International Automotive Engineering Congress, Detroit, January 1973). The figures used here are slightly revised, and differ from those in the above by a few percent.
7. U.S. Civil Aeronautics Board, "Report of Air Carrier Traffic Statistics," December 1963 and December 1972 (1971 data).

8. Obtained form interpolation/extrapolation from data in "Transportation Facts and Trends," Transportation Association of America, Washington, D.C., July 1972.

9. U.S. Department of Transportation, Federal Highway Administration, "Nationwide Personal Transportation Study," Report No. 1, Auto Occupancy, April 1972, Table 1, p. 8. As reported on page 10 of Report No. 8 of the above study, nearly three-fourths of all home to work automobile trips are 10 miles or less. The 2.9 load factor was therefore preferred over the overall 2.2 factor.

10. W. P. Goss, and J. G. McGowan, "Transportation and Energy—A Future Confrontation," *Transportation* 1 (3, 1972: 265–289).

11. U.S. Department of Transportation, Federal Highway Administration. *Highway Statistics 1970* Table VM–1, p. 52.

12. U.S. Bureau of Census, *Statistical Abstract of the United States, 1972* (1973), Section 2, Transportation Land, Table 910.

13. U.S. Department of Transportation, Federal Highway Administration *National Personal Transportation Study* (1972). Reports No. 1, 2, and 3.

14. R. A. Rice, "System Energy as a Factor in Considering Future Transportation," *ASME* Paper No. 70-WA/Ener-8.

15. R. M. Michaels and A. B. Maltz, "Energy Requirements in Urban Transportation, (Paper presented at the First Annual Illinois Energy Conference, 15 June 1973, sponsored by the University of Illinois and the State of Illinois).

16. E. Hirst, "Energy Intensiveness of Passenger and Freight Transport Modes: 1950–1970," ORNL-NSF Environmental Program-44, 1973.

17. American Transit Association, *1971 Transit Operating Report, Revenues, Expenses, Operating Statistics,* 1971, Parts II and IV.

18. U.S. Dept. of Transportation, letter; Alexander French to Bruce Hannon, November 15, 1973.

19. Automobile Manufacturers Association, Inc., *1971 Automobile Facts and Figures,* 1971.

Chapter Four

Energy, Employment, and Dollar Impacts of Certain Consumer Options

Robert Herendeen and
Anthony Sebald
Center for Advanced Computation
University of Illinois, Urbana

Are there consumer products on the market today which provide similar service, comfort, and convenience but which differ significantly in their total energy impact? If so, what would be the costs—first, in dollars to the consumer, and second, in employment—of moving toward the less energy-intensive alternatives? These are the questions we have addressed in our research on consumer products.

We have analyzed nine groups of consumer products for their dollar, energy, and labor (DEL) costs (See Table 4–1). In some instances we analyze pairs of similar products. The dollar cost of a product is what the consumer pays for the item itself plus the cost of all activities connected with its ownership and use. Energy cost is the total primary energy required; labor cost is the total man-years of employment.* Total energy (or dollars or labor) must include indirect costs as well as direct.

Assessing indirect costs involves conceptual problems. For example, does the energy to manufacture home water pipes contribute to the energy impact of the dishwasher? We would say yes, except that the pipes would probably be there anyway—so that the incremental energy impact of the dishwasher would not include the pipes. On questions like this, we have had to decide arbitrarily on where to truncate the search for indirect contributions. Such decisions are noted when made.

METHODOLOGY

Almost all indirect energy and labor impact has been evaluated through use of input-output (I/O) coefficients developed for 1963.[1,2]

The development, applications, and limitations of the coefficients is described in reference 1 (energy) and reference 2 (labor).

*Throughout this report labor costs do *not* include home labor.

Table 4-1. Product Groups Studied

1. Kitchen appliances
2. Mechanical vs. outdoor clothes drying
3. Home laundry vs. laundromat
4. Paper vs. cloth towels
5. Disposable vs. cloth diapers
6. Disposable paper dishes vs. earthenware
7. Mechanical vs. hand dishwashing
8. Fresh, frozen, and canned fruits
9. Wood vs. metal household furniture

The general model for DEL costs adds the impacts of all contributing factors on an annual basis. The total cost is given by:

capital cost + maintenance cost + disposal cost + operating cost

where each is expressed on a per-year basis. (To annualize we have had to obtain lifetimes of devices, or number of uses during the lifetime.) Energy is expressed in British thermal units (Btu) and labor in man-years.

Dollar cost is computed similarly; this means the assumed interest rate is zero. In Appendix A we discuss the reason for this choice, and the potential errors resulting.

The Savings Reinvestment Question

In comparing any pair of alternatives for their energy and labor cost, we must also ask how any money saved would be spent instead. (If it is spent on gasoline, the energy savings probably is negated.)

Because it would be incorrect to assume that the consumer will spend the savings in a predictable manner, we have provided in Appendix A of Chapter 3 a list of consumer activities with their energy intensities (Btu per dollar expended).

The interested reader can determine the energy impact of whatever alternative he might choose for spending any money saved. If he chose an activity lower in energy-intensity than the one he has given up, he would save energy.

Wood Energy Cost

Wood, if not committed to making things, could conceivably be burned productively. We have included this energy as part of the total energy cost of the appropriate items. We have also have done this for oil- or natural gas-based products, such as plastics. On the other hand, we have *not* accounted for potential recovery of energy from productive burning of the final product because today little garbage is burned productively.

What Kinds of Answers are Provided

First, we provide the DEL cost of the consumer products and services, measured in 1971. Second, with adequate qualifications we can predict the DEL consequences of changes in consumption. The qualifications include (a) basic limitations of I/O analysis (see reference 1); (b) a need for a long adjustment period. For example, we have annualized the cost of many large appliances over a 14-year lifetime. Hence the statement that "X amount of energy will be saved by a shift from frost-free to conventional refrigerators by Y people, or A number of jobs will be produced" would be true only after approximately 14 years, and it assumes that technology stays constant.

Most of the choices within a product group are not completely comparable. Often one is less convenient or more time-consuming, and implies some difference in life style. The consumer may weigh this difference against the dollar, energy, and labor costs which we present.

RESULTS

One outstanding conclusion we can draw from our work is that water heating (after space heating and cooling) is an especially important area in which to concentrate energy conservation efforts. We found that water heating energy was by far the dominant factor in several of our product groups.

Second, there is a great spectrum of energy conservation options within product groups. We have tried to simplify this, but often could not because we would have glossed over what seem to be worthwhile options. For example, for washing, assuming an automatic washer to begin with, we still have these options: (1) electric or gas water heat, (2) warm or cool rinse, (3) electric, gas, or no dryer. These choices involve 12 different possibilities. While this complicates our presentation, it seems unavoidable.

Third, we have had to make arbitrary, but we hope reasonable, assumptions on "equivalence" of products. For example, what is the cloth equivalent of one 170-sheet roll of paper towel? We assumed it is 14 hand-sized towels and two rags. In some cases we feel uncertain enough of our choices that we provide information so the reader can use his own equivalence. Unfortunately this requires considerable effort.

Fourth, we have obtained some results which indicate that minimum energy does not always imply minimum environmental impact. For some home washing options, we find that paper towels are *less* energy-intensive than cloth. One must, therefore, weigh the question of total environmental impact.

DEL Costs of Kitchen Appliances

We have obtained the DEL costs of 25 kitchen appliances. From these results one can build up the energy and labor impact of his or her own set of appliances. To illustrate, we have compared three sample kitchens.

We have accounted for the energy and labor to make and maintain appliances as well as to operate them. We found it useful to define a ratio, "Q."

$$Q = \frac{\text{capital energy} + \text{maintenance energy} + \text{disposal energy}^*}{\text{annual operation energy}}$$

All energies are in primary terms. Operation energies used in the home are delivered with these efficiencies (see reference 1):

electricity—25.8 percent

gas—85.5 percent

Data on operational energies and purchase prices come from industry associations [3,4,5] and represent averages for typical use. Here we are not investigating the effect of reducing use of a given appliance; we take an all-or-nothing approach. Manufacturing, sales, and maintenance energy were evaluated using I/O coefficients.[1] Maintenance costs are difficult to obtain, but were estimated as follows: if the appliance cost less than $20, it was assumed to last 8 years and be retired without maintenance. If it cost more than $20, it was assumed to last 14 years and receive a total lifetime maintenance bill equaling one-half the purchase price. The one exception is that water heaters were assumed to fall in the first category.

The annualized total energy cost, e_{tot}, is then

$$e_{tot} = (1 + Q/t)e_{op} \tag{2}$$

where t is the lifetime in years and e_{op} is the yearly operational energy.

The ratio Q/t expresses the importance of the indirect energy requirements. Appliances which provide heating or cooling tend to have low Q's (e.g., $Q = 1$ for a kitchen range), while those which produce only mechanical motion have higher Q's (e.g., $Q = 7$ for an electric mixer). For high Q appliances, e_{tot} is quite sensitive to changes in lifetime; for low Q, it is not. Thus prolonging the lifetime of low Q appliances through increased durability will effect relatively little energy savings.

In Table 4–2 are listed the DEL costs for 25 appliances. An arbitrary kitchen may be constructed from these. As an example, we have looked at three kitchens, from rather Spartan to lavishly equipped, or "full." The results are presented in Table 4–3 and Figure 4–1.

From Table 4–3, we see that the full set (including frostless refrigerator and freezer, washer and dryer, and dishwasher) has a yearly energy impact of about 120 million Btu (gas) and 150 million Btu (electric). This is the equivalent of five or six tons of coal.

The "moderate" kitchen differs from the full in its substitution of conventional freezer and refrigerator for frostless models where possible, and in its

---

*Disposal energy is negligible for appliances. We did not place maintenance energy in the denominator since maintenance is often sporadic; hence often "operational energy" is the only perceived yearly cost.

Table 4-2. DEL Costs of 25 Appliances

	Appliance Complement						Operational[a] Energy (10^5 Btu/Yr)	Q (Years)	t (Years)	Q/t	Total Energy (10^5 Btu/Yr)	Total Dollars (per Yr)	Total Jobs (10^-4 Man-Yr/Yr)
	Spartan		Moderate		Full								
Appliances	G	E	G	E	G	E							
Blender						x	2.0	7.2	14	0.51	3.0	2.6	2.6
Can opener						x	0.66	11	8	1.3	1.5	1.7	1.9
Clothes washer	x		x			x	13	14	14	0.97	27	28.	26
Clothes dryer, gas			x		x		70	2.2	14	0.15	81	28	23
Clothes dryer, electric				x		x	130	0.97	14	0.07	140	39	27
Coffeemaker				x		x	10	0.61	8	0.08	15	4.3	3.2
Dishwasher				x		x	50	3.7	14	0.26	61	31.	26
Garbage disposal						x	4.0	12	14	0.87	7.4	7.1	6.5
Exhaust fan						x	5.7	2.5	14	0.18	6.7	3.2	2.9
Freezer, conv., 15 c.f.				x			160	1.1	14	0.08	170	49.	34
Freezer, frostless, 15 c.f.						x	230	0.73	14	0.05	250	62	39
Frying pan						x	25	0.82	14	0.06	26	7.3	5.3
Hot plate				x		x	12	0.54	8	0.07	13	3.5	2.5
Iron				x		x	19	0.48	8	0.06	20	5.3	3.7
Electric knife						x	1.1	13	14	0.96	2.1	2.4	2.5
Mixer				x		x	1.7	7.5	14	0.53	2.6	2.3	2.4
Range, gas	x		x				120	1.3	14	0.09	130	34	26
Range, electric		x		x		x	160	1.2	14	0.08	170	51	36
Refrig., conv. 12 c.f.	x			x			96	2.2	14	0.16	110	45	35
Refrig. frostless, 12 c.f.						x	160	1.3	14	0.09	180	56	40
Toaster				x		x	5.2	1.9	8	0.23	6.4	3.1	2.9
Vacuum cleaner			x		x		6.1	6.4	14	0.45	8.8	8.0	7.0
Water heater, gas	x			x	x		370	0.15	8	0.02	380	46	22
Water heater, electric		x				x	560	0.11	8	0.01	570	104	50
Waffle iron				x		x	2.9	3.1	8	0.39	4.1	2.6	2.6

Notes: G = gas appliance; E = electrical appliance.
[a] Converted to primary energy terms.

Table 4–3. DEL Costs of Three Sets of Appliances

	Spartan	Moderate	Full
Dollars/Yr.			
Gas	153	252	334
	(.45)[a]	(.75)	(1)
Electric	228	339	424
	(.54)	(.80)	(1)
Energy (10^6 Btu/Yr.)			
Gas	65	95	117
	(.54)	(.80)	(1)
Electric	87	123	148
	(.59)	(.84)	(1)
Labor (10^{-4} Man Yr./Yr.)			
Gas	110	180	250
	(.44)	(.75)	(1)
Electric	150	230	290
	(.51)	(.78)	(1)

[a]Number in parentheses is fraction of total for full appliance set. We have rounded off some figures after calculation. In this and subsequent tables, small discrepancies may therefore be noted.

absence of a dishwasher and many smaller appliances (blender, can opener, garbage disposal, exhaust fan, electric frying pan, hot plate, electric knife, and waffle iron). Its energy impact is about four-fifths that of the full kitchen. Many of the rejected appliances are small energy users.

The Spartan kitchen retains only four basic appliances: range, clotheswasher, water heater,* and refrigerator (not frostless). Here, the energy cost is about 55 percent of the full kitchen. Thus, these four appliances are responsible for over half of the energy required by the full kitchen set of about 20.

As expected, electric options increase energy use and expense. The additional annual energy cost of an all-electric full kitchen is about 31 million Btu, or one ton of coal equivalent, an increase of 26 percent over the all-gas option. The additional yearly cost is $90, an increase of 27 percent over the all-gas option.

In spite of all the attention we have paid to manufacturing and maintenance energy cost, operational energy (in primary terms) accounts for over 90 percent of the total energy impact. Those appliances which have a high Q are not very significant energy consumers overall. They contribute little to the total.

*We have not computed the reduced use of the water heater due to a lack of a dishwasher. Roughly speaking, hand and machine dishwashing require the same amount of hot water.

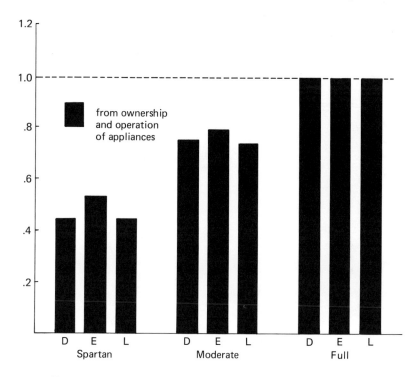

Figure 4-1. DEL Costs of Three Sets of Appliances

DEL Costs of Mechanical and Outdoor Clothes Drying

We compare an electric-pilot gas dryer, or an all-electric, with a clothesline-pole combination. The dryers are assumed to have a lifetime of 4,000 39-minute cycles, and the outdoor equipment to last through four thousand hangings of a similar load.

Table 4–4 shows the total energy and labor impact of the dryer. This is compared with the outdoor drying option in Table 4–5 and Figure 4–2.

Our conclusions, noting again that home labor is not included and we have not accounted for possible spending of money saved, are as follows:

The gas and electric dryers are: 7 and 11 times as expensive, 35 and 71 times as energy-intensive, 8 and 9 times as labor-intensive, respectively, as outdoor drying.

DEL Cost of Home Laundry vs. Laundromat

Two questions arise in this product group. First, are there DEL economies of scale in laundromat operation which overbalance the added DEL costs of constructing, lighting, and space conditioning a building built expressly as a laundromat? Second, how significant is transportation to the laundromat?

Table 4–4. DEL Cost of Drying Clothes Mechanically (One 39-Minute Cycle)

Function	Dryer type	Cost (Cents)	Primary Energy (Btu)	Labor[b] 10^{-6} Man-Yr
Manufacture and sale of dryer	Gas	4.9	3,100	4.5
	Electric	4.1	2,600	3.8
Maintenance	Gas	2.4	680	2.6
	Electric	2.1	580	2.2
Operation	Gas	1.6	15,400 (12,100 direct)[a]	0.59
	Electric	7.1	43,000 (11,100 direct)[a]	3.1
Total	Gas	8.9	19,000	7.7
	Electric	13.3	46,000	9.1
Ratio	(Gas/Electric)	0.7	0.4	0.9

[a]Direct energy actually supplied to unit.
[b]Does not include homeowner's labor.

To obtain the DEL costs of home laundry operation, we had to consider several subproblems, such as the DEL costs of hot water. We found it necessary to keep distinct a large number of home laundry options, depending on presence or absence of a dryer, type (electric or gas) of water heater, etc.

For the laundromat data, on the other hand, we used an actual case study of three local laundromats in Urbana Illinois, in which actual energy bills were obtained. We assumed that the space conditioning and lighting energy of the building was a part of the energy cost of laundromat laundering, whereas for home laundry no correction was needed.

Table 4–5. DEL Costs of Clothesdryer vs. Clothesline (All Quantities per 39-Minute Cycle)

Option	Cost (Cents)	Energy (Btu)	Labor (10^{-6} Man-Years)
Gas dryer electric pilot	8.9 (.67)	19,000 (.42)	7.7 (.85)
Electric dryer	13.3 (1)	46,000 (1)	9.1 (1)
Outdoor drying	1.2 (.09)	600 (.014)	1.0 (.11)

Note: Quantities in parentheses are DEL costs relative to the electric dryer case.

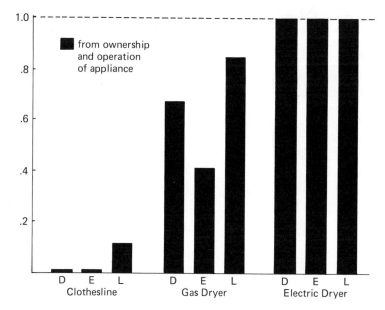

Figure 4-2. Dollar, Energy, and Labor Impact of Three Ways of Drying Clothes

It was necessary to obtain a definition of a "load." A load has not one universally accepted meaning but depends on standards of cleanliness, type of fabric, etc. We did find, however, that for washing, commercial and home machines do handle equivalent loads.[6,7]

A few additional aspects of laundromat laundering should be mentioned. First, laundromats almost always use gas for all their heating needs. Second, a laundromat user often "must" use the dryer, as he has no place to hang the wash. (For our laundromat case studies we could not separate energy used for washing from that used for drying; our laundromat energies represent an empirical average of customer behavior.) Third, while the laundromat machines may be more durable (they have a heavier drive mechanism), they are subjected to harder use. Also, since capital and maintenance energies total only about 10 percent of the total energy cost of home laundering, differences in machine durability would have a very small effect on total energy cost. For the laundromat the additional DEL costs of automobile transportation are based on an average American automobile and include all automobile associated costs. The results are given in Table 4-6 and Figures 4-3, 4-4, and 4-5.

Out conclusions are that for all but the most expensive home options (such as electric water heater and dryer), the laundromat is a more expensive way to wash clothes, even with no driving. If automobile transportation is included, the laundromat expense is still greater.

Table 4-6. DEL Costs of Laundromat Washing[a] (One Load)

Component	Dollar (Cents)	Energy (Btu)	Labor (10^{-6} Man-Years)
Facilities construction and maintenance		1,100	4.8
Washer and dryer	42	1,600	1.8
Gas and electricity:			
Air-conditioned		111,000	3.3
Not air-conditioned		103,000	
Water		2,700	1.6
Maintenance		430	1.7
Detergent	6	5,000	4.4
Total	48	122,000 with A/C[b]	17.5
		114,000 without A/C	

[a]Excluding transportation.

[b]A/C denotes air-conditioned laundromat.

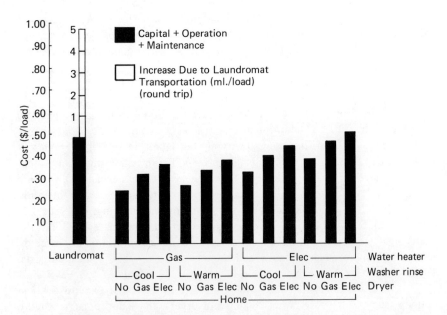

Figure 4-3. Dollar Cost of Washing and Drying a Load of Wash in a Laundromat vs. at Home

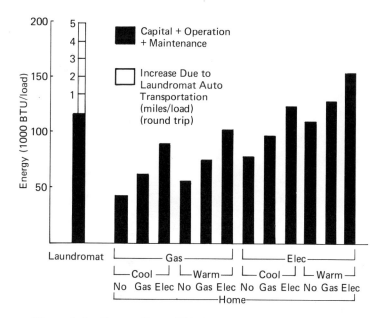

Figure 4-4.   Energy Cost of Washing and Drying a Load of Wash
in a Laundromat vs. at Home

Compared with most of the home laundry options, the laundromat
uses more energy. When auto transportation is considered, there is an energy
advantage of home laundry in virtually all cases.

The laundromat option uses less labor than all but the most spartan
home option, but a few miles of driving increases the labor impact to equality.

Let us compare DEL costs for a specific home option—gas water
heater, warm rinse, electric dryer. (This is the most common arrangement for
households with dryers, which today includes 30 percent of households.[8]). For
this case, the laundromat is about 20 percent more expensive, 15 percent more
energy-intensive, and 50 percent less labor-intensive than home laundering. The
use of auto transportation will increase the energy difference and decrease the
labor difference.

DEL Costs of Paper and Cloth Towels

We found a wide range of opinions on the substitutability of paper
and cloth towels. To allow readers to make their own choices, we compute the
DEL costs for a roll of paper towels (170 sheets) and one clean 15" x 27" towel.
We also make a comparison for a reasonable substitution.

The dominant factor in the energy cost of a cloth towel is the
washing and drying. The towels are assumed to last 300 washings. In all cases an
automatic washer is assumed. The energy content of the paper is included.

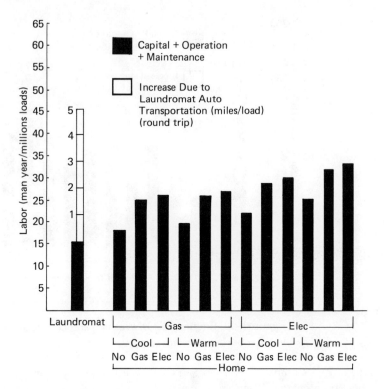

Figure 4-5. Labor Cost of Washing and Drying a Load of Wash in a Laundromat vs. at Home

Table 4–7 lists the DEL costs for a single towel. For comparison readers may multiply this entry times the number of towels they judge adequate to substitute for a roll of paper towels. We assume that a rag for cleaning spills equals one towel.

We chose 14 towels and 2 rags as a reasonable equivalent for a roll of paper towels. In Table 4–8 and Figures 4–6, 4–7, and 4–8 we compare DEL costs.

Our conclusions: cloth towels are less expensive than paper towels. Even if the energy content of the paper is included, the cloth towels are more energy-intensive by a factor of up to 2.3 depending on home washing options. Clcth towels are less labor-intensive than paper. It must be emphasized that these conclusions apply only to the particular choice we made for cloth-paper equivalence.

DEL Costs of Disposable vs. Cloth Diapers

We compare a gauze prefolded (cloth) diaper used with waterproof pants, and a disposable diaper.* Both were selected from the 1963 Sears

*Cloth: Prefolded, 8 larger center, 4 larger edge, 14" x 21". Disposables: 14" x 19" flat.

Table 4-7. DEL Costs of One Cloth Hand Towel[a]

Water Heater	Washer Rinse	Dryer	Cost (Cents)	Primary Energy (Btu)	Labor (10^{-6} Man-Yr.)
Gas	Cool	No	1.3	1,700	.65
Gas	Cool	Gas	1.5	2,300	.87
Gas	Cool	Electric	1.7	3,200	.92
Gas	Warm	No	1.3	2,100	.69
Gas	Warm	Gas	1.6	2,800	.91
Gas	Warm	Electric	1.7	3,700	.95
Electric	Cool	No	1.6	2,900	.79
Electric	Cool	Gas	1.8	3,500	1.0
Electric	Cool	Electric	2.0	4,400	1.1
Electric	Warm	No	1.8	3,900	.88
Electric	Warm	Gas	2.0	4,500	1.1
Electric	Warm	Electric	2.2	5,300	1.2
For comparison:					
One roll of paper towels (including disposal)			39	27,000	26
Energy content of paper towels			—	10,100	—
Total				37,100	

[a]15″ × 27″ approximate weight, 4 oz.

Table 4-8. DEL Costs of "Equivalent" Paper and Cloth Towels

Water Heater	Washer Rinse	Dryer	Cost (Cents)	Primary Energy (Btu)	Labor (10^{-6} Man-Yrs.)
Gas	Cool	No	20.3	27,000	10.4
Gas	Cool	Gas	24.5	37,000	13.9
Gas	Cool	Electric	26.9	51,000	14.7
Gas	Warm	No	21.4	34,000	11.0
Gas	Warm	Gas	25.6	44,000	14.5
Gas	Warm	Electric	27.8	58,000	15.3
Electric	Cool	No	24.8	46,000	12.6
Electric	Cool	Gas	29.0	56,000	16.2
Electric	Cool	Electric	31.4	70,000	17.0
Electric	Warm	No	28.0	62,000	14.2
Electric	Warm	Gas	32.2	72,000	17.8
Electric	Warm	Electric	34.4	85,000	19.0
For comparison, using an electric wringer washer[a]					
Gas	Cool	No	15.0	13,000	6.6
One roll of paper towels, including disposal			39.0	27,000	26
Wood energy			—	10,100	—
Total, paper towels			39.0	37,100	26

[a]Based on a single local case study.

144

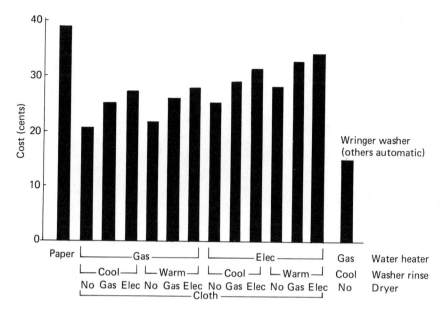

Figure 4-6. Dollar Cost of Paper vs. Cloth Towels (16 Cloth Towels, 1 Roll Paper)

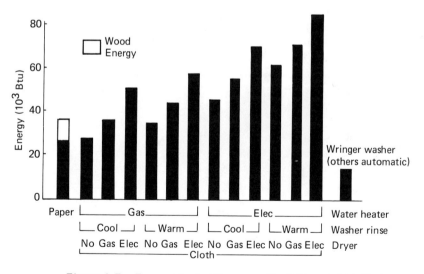

Figure 4-7. Energy Cost of Paper vs. Cloth Towels (16 Cloth Towels, 1 Roll Paper)

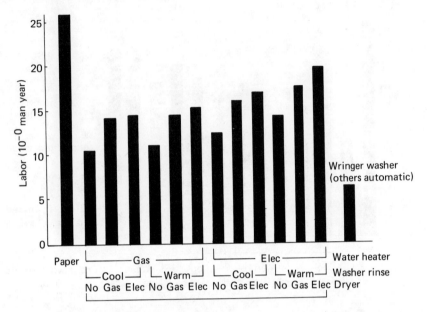

Figure 4-8. Labor Cost of Paper vs. Cloth Towels (16 Cloth
Towels, 1 Roll Paper)

Roebuck and Company catalog. We have assumed that cloth diapers are home
washed in an automatic washer, but that plastic pants (one change of pants to
every two cloth diaper changes) are washed by hand. Table 4–9 and Figures 4–9,
4–10, and 4–11 list the DEL costs.

Our conclusions: disposables are more expensive, by at least a factor
of 2.5. Disposables (including the paper energy content) are more energy-
intensive than half of the cloth diaper options, and less energy-intensive than the
remainder. Disposables are more labor-intensive than any cloth option. (Note
again that this does not include home labor.)

DEL Costs of Disposable Paper
and Earthenware Dishes

We compare the DEL costs of an earthenware cup and plate vs. a
paper cup and plate. "Earthenware" is "inexpensive china"; it is strictly defined
as "low-fired clay, which is slightly porous and opaque and covered with a
non-porous glaze."* We chose a sturdy paper plate and cup: a 9-inch plastic
coated plate and a 7-ounce plastic coated hot cup.

We assumed that china dishes last two years, at two uses per day,
and that a plate and cup constitute 2/50 of a dishwasher load. Due to difficulty

*Compare "china:" "a hand-fired ceramic ware with a dense, vitrified, but
opaque, body."

Table 4-9. DEL Costs of Disposable vs. Cloth Diapers

Water Heater	Washer Rinse	Dryer	Cost (Cents/ Change)	Primary Energy (Btu/Change)	Labor (10⁻⁶ Man-Yr./ Change)
Disposable diapers			4.4	2,700	2.8
Cloth diapers					
Gas	Cool	No	.98	1,600	1.3
Gas	Cool	Gas	1.2	2,100	1.5
Gas	Cool	Electric	1.3	2,900	1.5
Gas	Warm	No	1.0	1,900	1.3
Gas	Warm	Gas	1.3	2,500	1.5
Gas	Warm	Electric	1.4	3,200	1.5
Electric	Cool	No	1.3	2,800	1.7
Electric	Cool	Gas	1.5	3,300	1.9
Electric	Cool	Electric	1.6	4,100	1.9
Electric	Warm	No	1.4	3,700	1.8
Electric	Warm	Gas	1.7	4,200	2.0
Electric	Warm	Electric	1.8	4,900	2.0

Note: The above cloth diaper totals include the following manufacturing and hand plastic pants laundry DEL costs:

Manufacturing (diaper, pins, and plastic pants)			.23	80	.2
Plastic pants laundry (hand option)					
Gas water heater			.09	270	.6
Electric water heater			.16	560	.9

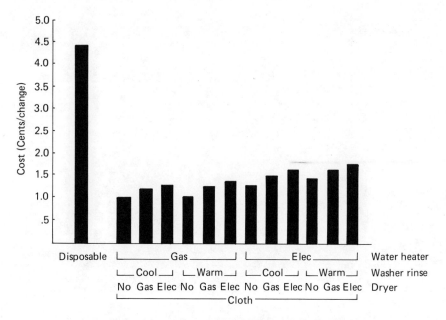

Figure 4-9. Dollar Cost of Disposable vs. Cloth Diapers

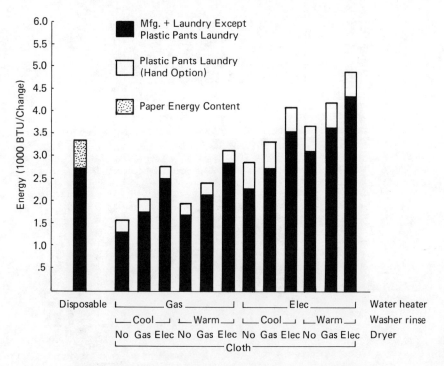

Figure 4-10. Energy Cost of Disposable vs. Cloth Diapers

148

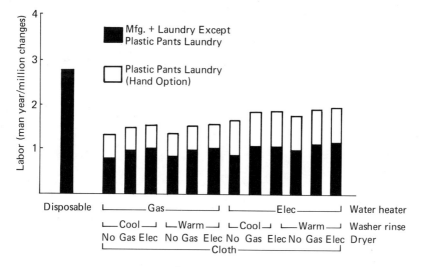

Figure 4–11. Labor Cost of Disposable vs. Cloth Diapers

in determining good average figures for hand dishwashing DEL costs (see the next section), we assumed a mechanical dishwasher. As is generally true for items that are washed often in their lifetimes, the capital energy contribution was relative small, so that the actual choice of lifetime is quite unimportant to the energy conclusions we obtain. Results are shown in Table 4–10.

Conclusions: disposable paper dishes are at least 6 times as expensive as earthen-ware; 3 times as energy-intensive (gas water heater) or 1.7 times (electric water heater) as earthenware; and are at least 7 times as labor-intensive as earthenware. (Home labor is not included.)

Table 4–10. DEL Costs of Paper vs. Earthenware Plates

	Cost (Cents)	Energy (Btu)	Labor (10^{-6} Man-Yr.)
Earthenware			
Manufacturing	.09	50	.10
Washing—gas[a]	.48	1,300	.32
electric[a]	.70	2,300	.44
Total—gas	.57	1,400	.42
electric	.79	2,300	.54
Disposables	4.9	3,400	3.8
Wood energy		600	—
Total	4.9	4,000	3.8

[a]Water heater type.

Table 4-11.   DEL Costs of a Dishwasher Load

Function	Cost (Cents/Load)	Primary Energy (Btu/Load)	Labor (10⁻⁶ Man. Yr./Load)
Capital cost	3.1	1,900	2.8
Maintenance	1.6	440	1.7
Operation			
1. Water (14 gal.)	0.94	770	0.47
2. Water heat			
gas water heater	1.8	19,000	1.4
electric water heater	8.7	42,000	5.2
3. Soap	1.9	1,800	1.6
4. Electricity	1.6	9,900	0.71
Total gas heater	12	34,000	8.6
Total electric heater	17	57,000	11.0

**DEL Costs of Washing Dishes
by Hand and in a Dishwasher**

We have found such a wide variety of hand dishwashing techniques that we can give no definite answer as to relative DEL costs. Readers will have to determine their own habits and compute the energy and labor impact from the information we provide.

A typical automatic dishwasher can handle 10 place settings—the dishes used by a family of four—in one day. The largest contributor to the energy cost is the hot water used (see Table 4–11). The next largest factor is the operational energy; this is relatively large because a dishwasher often contains a heater to heat the input water, and sometimes another to dry the dishes after washing.

We assumed that hand washing has a modest requirement for capital goods (dishpan, rack, brush, clean dish towel, etc.) and that hand and machine washing use the same amount of detergent per article washed. The energy contribution of hot water dominates hand washing as well. We have therefore expressed hand dishwashing results, as a function of hot water used, in Figures 4–12, 4–13, and 4–14. We list the volume of hot water in gallons, or "sinkfuls." A 15" x 14" x 8" sink filled to a depth of 6" requires 5.4 gallons. Thus a sinkful of "hot" water requires 5.4 gallons of hot (140 degree) water; a sinkful of warm water (115 degree) requires 3.9 gallons of hot (140 degree) water. (Cold water has essentially zero DEL cost compared with hot.)

Conclusions: the dishwasher uses 14 gallons of hot water to do a family's dirty dishes, or the equivalent of 2.6 sinkfuls of hot water, assuming that no additional hot water is used for pre-rinsing. It appears that dishwashers are quite efficient in their use of water, and that it would take considerable effort to hand wash these dishes with that little hot water.

If hand washing did use 14 gallons of hot water, we could conclude:

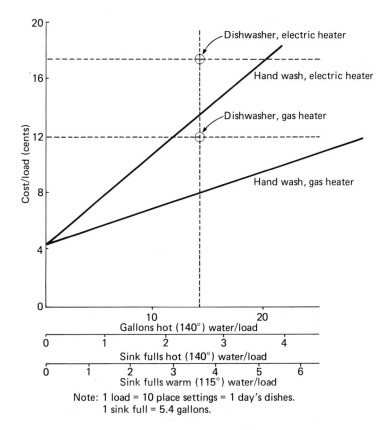

Figure 4-12.   Dollar Cost of Hand vs. Mechanical Dishwashing

hand washing is 20 to 30 percent less expensive; hand washing is 20 to 25 percent less energy-intensive; hand washing is 30 to 40 percent less labor-intensive. (Again: home labor is not included.)

DEL Costs of Fresh, Frozen, and Canned
Fruits and Vegetables, 1963*

We compare the DEL costs of equal servings of a selection of fresh, frozen, and canned fruits and vegetables. Home refrigeration contributes significantly to the energy cost and is included.** We have studied those fruits

---

*Because of relatively rapid price raises we do not feel that the 1963 results can be extended to 1971 with confidence.

**About 45 percent of the average family's food bill is spent for perishables other than baked goods. In 1963 this amounted to about $900/family (*Statistical Abstract of the United States, 1971*, Tables 538, 542). Based on our work, we find the energy impact of this food is approximately $900 x 50,000 Btu's/$ = 45 million Btu. From Table 4-2, we saw that a refrigerator had an energy impact of about 9 million Btu/year, or about one-fifth of that of the food stored within.

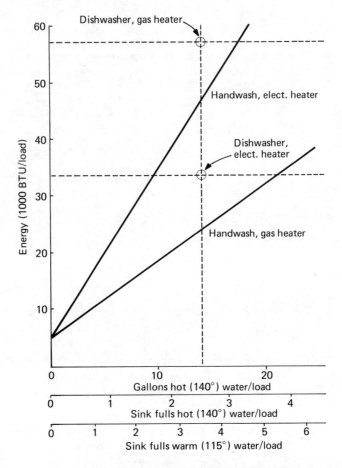

Figure 4–13.   Energy Cost of Hand vs. Mechanical Dishwashing

and vegetables which are available in all three forms; we have not considered the full spectrum of perishables.

Table 4–12 shows that on a per-dollar basis, in producer's prices, canned and frozen fruits and vegetables are about 75 percent more energy-intensive than fresh. When converted to purchaser's (i.e., consumer's) prices, the difference drops to about 30 percent, which is still significant. Price data are thus important in assessing energy impacts. There are two complications with price data: first, the difficulty of normalizing to an equivalent serving;[9] second,

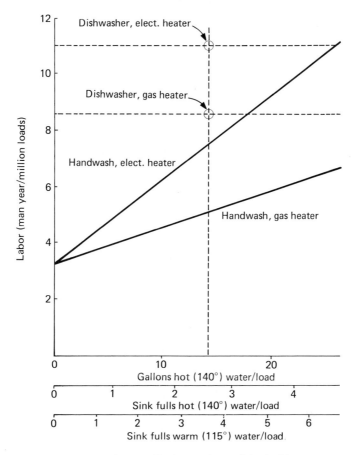

Note: 1 load = 10 place settings = 1 day's dishes.
1 sink full = 5.4 gallons.

Figure 4–14.   Labor Cost of Hand vs. Mechanical Dishwashing

the difficulty of obtaining representative price data, since fresh food prices fluctuate seasonally and locally.

We found only one price source which offered consistent data for the three forms of food—fresh, frozen, and canned—for a spread of products.[10] These data were collected for a 12-month period for four cities—Oakland, Milwaukee, New Orleans, and Philadelphia. The base year was 1959–60, a possible problem, since our I/O results are for 1963, but we used the prices without modification, as listed in Table 4–13.

Given the difficulties mentioned, we feel we can try only to answer

Table 4-12. Energy and Labor Coefficients for Fresh, Frozen, and Canned Foods, 1963

Sector	Energy Coefficients, 1963, Btu/$			Labor Coefficient (10^{-4} Man-Yr./$)	
	Producer's Price	Purchaser's Price	Modified[a]	Producer's Price	Purchaser's Price
Fruit and tree nuts	38,700	40,900	51,900	1.9	1.6
Vegetables, sugar, and miscellaneous crops	40,600	42,100	43,900	1.3	1.4
Frozen fruit and vegetables	68,700	57,800	66,300	1.2	1.3
Canned fruit and vegetables	72,300	61,800	61,800	1.2	1.3

[a]Modified to account for refrigeration required for perishables.

Table 4-13. Comparative Retail Costs for Fresh, Frozen, and Canned Fruits and Vegetables, 1959–60[a]

	Serving (Oz.)	Weighting Factor[b]	Cost/Serving (Cents)			Cost Ratio	
			Fresh	Frozen	Canned	Frozen/Fresh	Canned/Fresh
Vegetables							
Corn, cut	2.9	.68	7.4	5.9	6.2	.80	.84
Peas	2.8	1.13	13.0	6.0	5.0	.46	.38
Spinach	3.4	.20	12.1	7.9	7.0	.65	.58
Lima beans	2.9	.17	12.0	7.1	7.7	.59	.64
Asparagus	2.1	.17	9.5	9.7	8.3	1.02	.87
Beets	3.2	.072	4.4	–	4.4	–	1.00
Green beans	2.3	.45	4.3	5.7	5.4	1.33	1.26
Broccoli spears	3.3	.056	6.1	9.0	–	1.48	–
Brussels sprouts	2.7	.035	7.4	8.1	10.8	1.10	1.40
Carrots	2.8	.02	3.0	5.2	4.3	1.73	1.43
					Average for vegetables	0.76	0.72
Fruit							
Orange juice	4.4	1.59	7.6	3.7	4.1	.49	.54
Peaches, drained	3.7	.40	5.8	13.8	9.3	2.38	1.60
Peaches and liquids	4.4	–	–	10.0	6.3	–	–
Grapefruit, drained	3.4	–	6.2	10.7	7.5	1.73	1.21
Grapefruit and liquids	4.3	–	6.5	7.9	5.6	1.22	.86
Pineapple, drained	3.2	.24	7.1	11.4	8.0	1.61	1.13
Pineapple and liquids	4.2	–	–	8.9	6.8	–	–
Cherries, drained	3.9	.35	17.1	9.6	7.8	.56	.46
Cherries and liquids	4.9	–	–	6.7	6.0	–	–
Strawberries	3.5	.156	12.1	18.3	23.3	1.51	1.93
					Average for fruit	0.93	0.80
					Average without orange juice	1.54	1.17
					Average for all fruits and vegetables	0.83	0.77

[a]From: "Comparative Costs to Consumers of Convenience Foods and Home Prepared Foods," Marketing Research Report No. 609, U.S. Department of Agriculture, June 1963.

[b]Weighting factor: from above document, pp. 8, 12. This is the dollar price for the fresh equivalent of all canned and for frozen product bought per hundred dollars of food expenditures. Thus, for example, the average consumer bought canned and frozen cut corn which would have cost 60 cents if he had bought it fresh, per hundred dollars spent on food. This is not the cost of the fresh product he actually bought.

this question: if one consistently buys only fresh, only frozen, or only canned fruits and vegetables where there is a choice, which policy is least energy-intensive?

Since we do not know what fraction of the average home refrigerator's space (α) is allocated to our selection of fruits and vegetables, we have plotted DEL costs as a function of the fraction in Figures 4–15, 4–16, and 4–17.

From Table 4–13, we see that for the "average" purchase pattern for fruits and vegetables, frozen and canned foods are cheaper than fresh. The cost of frozen foods is 83 percent of that for equivalent fresh produce, and canned foods cost 77 percent as much as fresh. (Note that these ratios do not apply to every type of fruit and vegetable, since several are available in only one form, e.g., lettuce.) While the choice of α depends on personal habit, we feel that less than one-tenth of the typical refrigerator is allocated to fruits and vegetables. (We are concerned here with less than $2.00 worth of food per week, in 1960 prices.)

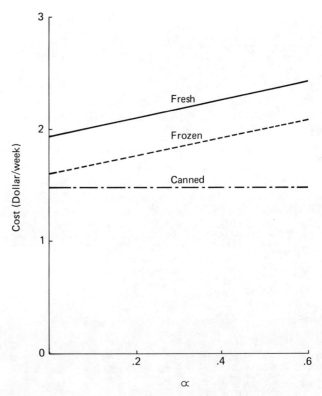

Figure 4–15. Dollar Cost of Fresh, Frozen, and Canned Fruits and Vegetables

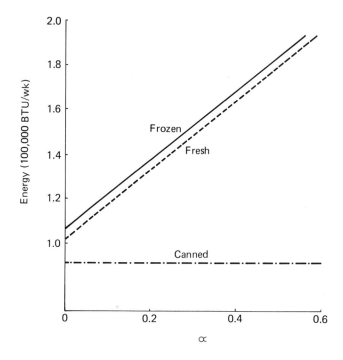

Figure 4-16. Energy Cost of Fresh, Frozen, and Canned Fruits and Vegetables

Conclusions: if we assume $\alpha = 0.1$ and note that differences in costs of less than 10 percent are not statistically significant, we find in increasing order: Dollars: Canned and frozen (equal), fresh; Energy: Canned, frozen and fresh (equal); Labor: Canned and frozen (equal), fresh. It will be noted that fresh food is costliest in all three categories. However, this statement refers to the average American diet of fresh produce, which includes December oranges and February strawberries, even if you live in Minnesota. We feel that *local* fresh produce, in season, is probably an energy saver, assuming you don't drive very far to obtain it.

DEL Cost of Wood and Metal
Household Furniture

Obtaining representative furniture prices is a bit difficult, since some furniture is a low-volume, high-profit product.[11] Again we used the Sears, Roebuck and Company catalog. We made somewhat arbitrary choices of products, and made no attempt to evaluate relative durability. Hence our results will yield only the total energy and labor impacts of the purchase, not the annual impacts. (In most of the other product groups we have taken into

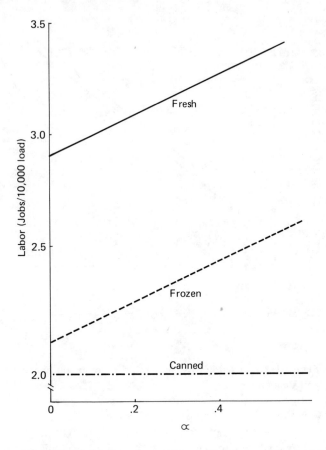

Figure 4–17. Labor Cost of Fresh, Frozen, and Canned Fruits and Vegetables

Table 4–14. DEL Costs Metal Household Furniture Relative to Wood, 1963[a,b]

Product	Dollars	Energy	Labor
Dinette set	.83	1.3 (1.1)[c]	0.75
Playpen	1.0	1.6 (1.2)	0.91
High chair	.95	1.5 (1.2)	0.87
Sink cabinet	.76	1.2 (1.0)	0.70
Wall cabinet	.68	1.1 (0.9)	0.62
Base cabinet	.79	1.3 (1.1)	0.72

[a]In each case the DEL costs are relative to wood, i.e., DEL = 1 for wood.

[b]These figures are for purchase only; no lifetime effects are included.

[c]Figures in parentheses include a correction for the energy content of the wood.

account product lifetimes.) Our results are for 1963. We found little wood furniture available in 1971; the economy was evolving toward metal furniture in this period. This was found to be the more energy-intensive option.

For 1963, the energy-intensity per dollar of metal furniture is 2.0 times that of wood furniture, in producer's prices;[11] when converted to purchaser's prices the ratio is reduced to 1.6 (66,000 Btu/$ to 42,000 Btu/$), still a significant difference. The higher energy-intensity for metal furniture is based in large part on the energy-intensity of metals production[12] Table 4–14 gives the final energy and labor costs.

Conclusions: for the selection of furniture we chose, metal is more expensive, and is usually less so than wood furniture. Because of metal furniture's relatively high energy-intensity per dollar, the metal option has a higher energy cost than the wood for all furniture selected if the energy content of the wood is neglected. Metal is less labor intensive than wood.

Appendix A

The Effect of Interest Rates on Dollar Cost

In this study we have used a zero interest rate in computing dollar costs because of the difficulty of determing (a) how, or whether, the purchase is financed; (b) the maintenance payment schedule. In this Appendix we compute examples of cost increases if we were to include an interest rate.

The question we ask is this: What annual payment p (assumed equal for each year) must we make to be sure all payments (initial cost, maintenance, operation) will be covered as they become due?

Suppose we borrow all the money needed to purchase, operate, and maintain the device. We will seek bank loans of amounts and timing as given by $C(n)$, the payment due in the year n.

At the same time, suppose we are depositing in a trust fund a constant yearly amount p so that at the end of n years (the lifetime of the device), the money in the trust fund is exactly equal to what we owe the bank. We pay the bank, the device has served through it useful life, and we owe no more money.

At the end of this period the value of what we owe the bank is

$$\sum_{n=1}^{N} C(n) (1 + r)^{N-n}, \text{ where r is the interest rate.}$$

At that time the value of what we have in the trust fund is

$$p (1 + r)^{N-1} + p (1 + r)^{N-2} + - - - - + p$$

$$= p \left[\frac{(1 + r)^N - 1}{r} \right]$$

Equating the two expressions yields

$$p = \frac{r}{(1 + r)^N - 1} \sum_{n=1}^{N} C(n) (1 + r)^{N-n} \tag{1}$$

If $r = 0$,

$$p_0 = \frac{1}{N} \sum_{n=1}^{N} C(n) \tag{2}$$

We have used eqn(2) to compute dollar cost. Let us compare p_0 and p for different values of r and different payment schedules.

Case 1: Down payment of value C and yearly cost of value unity.

In this case eqn. (1) can be written

$$p = \frac{r}{(1 + r)^N - 1} C(1 + r)^{N-1} + 1$$

while

$$p_0 = 1 + \frac{C}{N}$$

Thus $p = 1 + \beta \frac{C}{N}$, where $\beta = \dfrac{Nr(1 + r)^{N-1}}{(1 + r)^{N-1}}$

We compute values of β for case 1.*

r =	.06	.18
N = 5	1.12	1.35
10	1.28	1.89
15	1.46	2.49

We see that the effect of the interest rate is to as much as double the effective dollar cost contribution from the original purchase. If $\frac{C}{N}$ is large (it might be of order one for a refrigerator), the ratio p/p_0 could be around 1.5; i.e., a 50 percent error.

---

*6% is the best bank interest rate; 18% is a typical credit card rate. We have assumed that the same rate applies to borrowing or lending.

Case 2: Down payment of value C, yearly cost of value unity, and maintenance cost of value C/4 at one-third and two-thirds of the lifetime.

For this case we expect the effect of the interest rate to be less pronounced.

$p_0 = 1 + \frac{3}{2} \frac{C}{N}$ If we wrote $p = 1 + \beta \frac{3}{2} \frac{C}{N}$, we find, for N = 15,
$\beta = 1.29$ for r = 0.06
$ 1.93$ for r = 0.18

The effect is indeed less, but still of order two, leading to errors of order 50 percent in dollar cost.

These errors are thus implicit in all dollar results in this report, if one believes that the interest rate should be included.

Note that if we include interest effects in dollar cost, there is then the question of *energy* cost of banking, etc., which we have also ignored. It is small, in any case, relative to the energy cost already obtained.

(Note added in proof:) For discussing the broad spectrum of consumer options treated here, we felt comfortable in ignoring the interest rate. For a specific consumption decision involving a large capital cost, especially in comparing two models of the same type of appliance (conventional vs. frost free refrigerator, say), the interest rate should be included.

Energy Intensities of Personal Consumption Activities

The U.S. Department of Commerce has published a detailed study of personal consumption. Eighty-three "activities" (e.g., purchased meals and beverages) are broken down into their component expenditures by input-output sector. In this form they are easily converted to energy. Table 4–B1 lists the results, which have been scaled from 1963 to 1971 using published dollar deflators.

The dollar breakdown is a national average, and undoubtedly incorporates many arbitrary assumptions. If you never buy hot dogs when you go to a ball game, your energy intensity for activity 71, "spectator sports," is probably not average. Nonetheless, Table 4–B1 offers some guidance on how to direct your spending if you desire decreased energy impact.

Note that the average of all personal consumption expenditures in 1971 was 70,000 Btu/$. Only 6 of the 83 activities were more energy intensive than this.

Table 4B-1. Energy Intensities of Personal Consumption Activities (Energy Intensity Ranked Sector Table, 1971)

Rank	Title	Energy Intensity (Thousand Btu/$)
1.	Natural gas	990
2.	Other fuel & ice	630
3.	Electricity	505
4.	Gasoline & oil	480
5.	Airline transportation	131
6.	Water & other sanitary services	79
7.	Cleaning preparations	78
8.	Other intercity transportation	70
9.	Bridge & road tolls	66
10.	Intercity bus transportation	64
11.	Tires, tubes & parts	62
12.	Railway & sleeping car	60
13.	Kitchen & household appliances	59
14.	Toilet articles	58
15.	Taxicab transportation	57
16.	New & used cars	56
17.	Stationery, writing supplies	56
18.	Clothing issued to military	55
19.	Street & local bus transport	54
20.	Drug prep & sundries	52
21.	Semidurable house furnishings	51
22.	China, glassware, tableware	51
23.	Railway (commuter) transport	49
24.	Durable toys & sports equipment	48
25.	Nondurable toys & sports equipment	45
26.	Other durable house furnishings	45
27.	Food furnished to govt.	45
28.	Food prod. & consump. on farm	44
29.	Radio & TV receivers	43
30.	Magazines & newspapers	42
31.	Food purch. for off-prem. consump.	41
32.	Furniture	37
33.	Shoe cleaning and repair	36
34.	Other household operat. expenditures	35
35.	Private elem. & second. school	35
36.	Private higher education	35
37.	Books and maps	35
38.	Other housing	34
39.	Flowers, seeds, plants	33
40.	Women's & children's clothing	33
41.	Other private education	33
42.	Purchased meals and beverages	32
43.	Jewelry & watches	32
44.	Other prof. medical services	32
45.	Ophthalmic & orthoped. prod.	31
46.	Men's & boy's clothing	31
47.	Other clothing & accessories	31
48.	Laundering in establishment	30
49.	Garment cleaning, repair	30
50.	Radio & TV repair	28
51.	Shoes and footwear	28

Table 4B-1 continued

Rank	Title	Energy Intensity (Thousand Btu/$)
52.	Clubs and fraternal organizations	28
53.	Relig. & welfare activities	28
54.	Funeral & burial expenses	26
55.	Other personal business	26
56.	Private hospitals	26
57.	Automobile repair & maintenance	24
58.	Automobile insurance	22
59.	Health insurance	22
60.	Life insur. handling expenses	22
61.	Financial intermediaries	22
62.	Other recreational expenses	21
63.	Tobacco products	20
64.	Telephone & telegraph	19
65.	Commercial amusements	19
66.	Legal services	19
67.	Tenant occ. nonfarm dwelling	18
68.	Brokerage charges	18
69.	Parimutuel net receipts	18
70.	Foreign travel by US residents	17
71.	Motion picture theaters	16
72.	Spectator sports	15
73.	Theaters and opera	15
74.	Barber, beauty shops	15
75.	Bank service charges	13
76.	Dentists	11
77.	Physicians	10
78.	Owner occ. nonfarm dwelling	8
79.	Rental value of farmhouse	8
80.	Expend. abroad by US govt.	5
81.	Domestic service	0
82.	Expend. in US by foreigners	0
83.	Personal remit. to foreigners	0

Notes to Chapter Four

This chapter was based on a detailed report, prepared for the Energy Policy Project, which is available on request from Robert Herendeen, Energy Research Group, Center for Advanced Computation, University of Illinois, Urbana 61801. This report is: Robert Herendeen and Anthony Sebald, "The Dollar, Energy, and Employment Impacts of Certain Consumer Options," Center for Advanced Computation Document No. 97, April 1974.

1. R. A. Herendeen, *An Energy Input-Output Matrix for the United States, 1963: User's Guide*, CAC Document No. 69, Center for Advanced Computation, University of Illinois, Urbana, March, 1973.
2. Hugh Folk and Bruce Hannon, "An Energy, Pollution and Employment Policy Model," CAC Document No. 68, Center for Advanced Computation, University of Illinois, Urbana.
3. "Annual Energy Requirements of Electric Household Appliances," Electric Energy Association, New York, 1971.
4. "Use of Gas by Residential Appliances," American Gas Association, Arlington, Virginia, November, 1972.
5. *Merchandising Week*, New York, 1972 statistical issue.
6. Telephone conversation with Warren Barren of the Whirlpool Corporation, Benton Harbor, Michigan, June 1973.
7. Telephone conversation with James Thayer of the Speedqueen Corporation, Ripon, Wisconsin, July 1973.
8. *Merchandising Week*, 1972.
9. Canned foods contain much water. See "Why Net Weight Spells Nonsense on Canned Food Labels," *Consumer Reports*, October, 1972.
10. "Comparative Costs to Consumers of Convenience Foods and Home-Prepared Foods," Marketing Research Report No. 609, Marketing Economics Division, U.S. Department of Agriculture, June 1963. The data are for 1959–60.

11. M. Rieber, personal communication.
12. Clark Bullard and Robert Herendeen, "Energy Use in the Commercial and Industrial Sectors of the U.S. Economy, 1963," CAC Document No. 105, Center for Advanced Computation, University of Illinois, Urbana.

Chapter Five

Potential Energy Conservation from Recycling Metals in Urban Solid Wastes

William E. Franklin,* David Bendersky,
William R. Park, and Robert G. Hunt*
Midwest Research Institute

Approximately 125 million tons of urban solid wastes are collected and discarded annually in the United States. These discarded wastes contain an estimated 10.6 million tons of ferrous metals, 800,000 tons of aluminum, and 400,000 tons of other nonferrous metals, including copper.

The recovery of ferrous metals, aluminum, and copper-based metals from mixed urban wastes is technologically feasible. Mechanized systems to recover these metals and other resources from mixed urban wastes have been developed, although most have not yet been proven in commercial operations. Source separation (manual) programs have been initiated in many communities, but most are aimed at paper rather than metals. The aluminum industry has a successful program underway to collect aluminum cans for recycling, and recovers about 16 percent of aluminum beverage cans for that purpose.

The *recycling* of ferrous metals, aluminum, and copper recovered from urban wastes appears to be technically feasible. Preliminary indications are that these metal wastes can be used as scrap charges in conventional metal production techniques. However, the quality of these metal wastes has not yet been firmly established, and there has been little experience to date in their actual recycling.

The energy required to recover and recycle ferrous metals, aluminum, and copper from urban wastes is considerably less than the energy requirements to produce these metals from ores. If the metals that are recoverable from urban wastes were recycled, this would amount to 6.9 million tons of ferrous metals, 400,000 tons of aluminum, and 100,000 tons of copper in 1975. The recovery and recycling of these metals would lead to substantial energy conservation compared to the use of metals derived from virgin raw materials. The total energy requirement for producing finished metal from (a) virgin ore and (b) scrap derived from municipal waste is shown in Table 5-1.

These values include the Btu expenditures necessary to remove the

*Now with Franklin Associates, Prairie Village, Ks.

Table 5-1. The Total Energy Requirement for Producing Finished Metal

Metal	*Energy (10^6 Btu) Required To Produce one Ton from*		*Conservation Potential (Percent)*
	Ore	*Urban Scrap*	
Ferrous metal	49	6.75	86
Aluminum	251	9.5	96
Copper	71	6.7	91

ore or scrap from the source body, to transport it, to process it to finished metal form.

The energy savings possible exceeds 86 percent in all cases and is as high as 96 percent for aluminum. Based on the estimate of the amount of metal recoverable from urban waste and the net energy saved by recycling for each metal, a total of 403.1 x 10^{12} Btu could be conserved annually by recycling these three metals from urban waste. This savings is equivalent to the heat content of 3.22 billion gallons of gasoline.

While metals recycling costs may be lowered somewhat under presently available technology, it is usually not economically profitable to separate mechanically only the three metals considered here without also processing the other resources in mixed urban wastes. However, present trends—rising prices for recovered metals, scarcity and high costs of land for solid waste disposal, high energy costs, and other factors—favor the development and installation of recovery processes. Source separation of urban wastes would significantly reduce the costs of recovery; this recovery technique, however, has not yet been proven practical (for metals) on a national scale.

There is market for all three major metals recovered from urban wastes. The extent to which these waste metals are used will depend on their availability, quality, and costs. In any case, however, the metals-producing industries can and will absorb recovered metals at current market prices.

The Federal Resource Recovery Act of 1970 stimulated considerable national activity towards the recovery and recycling of urban solid wastes. Now several states and local governments have initiated significant solid waste management programs with emphasis on recycling. In addition, the trends to scarcity in ores, rising prices, and environmental effects of using virgin materials are tending to bring metal recovery from urban wastes into a more favorable position than has previously been the case.

INTRODUCTION

Large quantities of mixed municipal and industrial solid wastes are generated in this country. Most of these wastes are presently dumped, land-filled, incinerated, or otherwise discarded. These discarded wastes contain a significant quantity of metals. The purpose of this study is to determine the feasibility of recovering and recycling the principal metals (ferrous metals, aluminum, and copper) contained in these wastes and to estimate the resultant savings in energy on a national level.

The recycling of scrap metal is not new. Traditionally, the metal-producing industries have used significant amounts of scrap metal in the manufacture of new metals. However, most of the recycled scrap metal has come from three sources: "home" scrap generated by the primary metal manufacturer, "prompt" scrap generated by the fabricators of metal products, and "obsolete" scrap from discarded products collected by scrap dealers. Almost none of the metal scrap presently recycled comes from mixed municipal and industrial wastes.

Getting rid of solid wastes has become a major problem for U.S. cities. The great numbers of people living in cities and suburbs and their affluent living standards produce large quantities of wastes which must be regularly collected and disposed of. Recent bans on open-dumping and burning practices have forced the cities to use more sophisticated and expensive disposal techniques, such as sanitary landfills. As a consequence, waste collection and disposal have become a major financial burden for many U.S. cities. Although most unsalvaged industrial solid wastes are collected by private haulers, their waste disposal problems are similar to those of the cities' refuse departments.

The recovery and recycling of the resources in mixed municipal and industrial solid wastes are recent concepts in the U.S.A. (although resource recovery from wastes has been practiced in Europe for some years), prompted by the primary metals—ferrous, aluminum, and copper—in mixed urban wastes. Under an Environmental Protection Agency (EPA) grant program, full-scale resource recovery demonstration plants have been constructed or are planned at Franklin, Ohio; St. Louis, Missouri; Baltimore, Maryland; San Diego, California; and Lowell, Massachusetts. It should be pointed out, however, that these are first-generation plants and in most cases are not yet fully developed.

The most common system for recovering the metals from mixed urban wastes is illustrated in Figure 5–1. The mixed waste is first shredded, then sent through an air classifier which separates the metals and other heavy materials from the rest of the waste by density. A magnetic separator separates the ferrous metals from the nonferrous material. The heavy media (sink/float) technique may be used to separate the aluminum from the other nonferrous metals.

All of the systems listed in Table 5–2 use magnetic separators to recover the ferrous metals from the rest of the wastes. The principle of magnetic separators is illustrated in Figure 5–2. The mixed wastes are conveyed on a feed belt to the magnetic separator where the ferrous metals are attracted to the magnet. The nonferrous wastes drop into the first bin while the ferrous metals

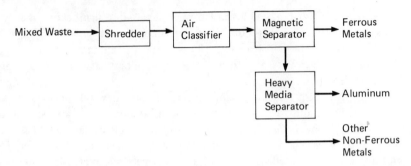

Figure 5-1. Typical Metal Recovery System

are conveyed to the end of the magnet where they drop into a separate bin. Magnetic separators are available commercially.*

The principal method being developed for separating aluminum from mixed solid wastes is the "heavy-media" (sink/float) technique. This separation technique, originally developed for the mineral-processing industry, depends upon the difference in the specific gravities of aluminum and the other materials in the mixed waste. The mixed waste is suspended in a fluid whose specific gravity is intermediate between aluminum and the other materials in the waste. Depending upon the specific gravities of the fluid used, the aluminum will either float to the top or sink to the bottom. In most cases the aluminum is floated off the top, the lighter materials (such as paper and plastics) in the waste having been previously removed by air classification or other separation techniques. In one type of nonferrous metals recovery system, aluminum and glass (heavier materials are previously removed) sink in the heavy media process, and the aluminum is separated from the glass by high voltage electrostatic separators operating on the difference in electrical conductivity of the two materials.[1]

In the case of the Black-Clawson system, which is a wet-shredding (slurry) process, the aluminum is removed by first cycloning the slurry, then drying the heavy fraction, magnetically separating the ferrous metals, screening, and air classification. The light material from the air classifier is principally aluminum.[2]

All three of the systems which recover copper from urban waste (Table 5–2) utilize the heavy-media technique to separate the copper-based metals.

In summary, the recovery of ferrous metals, aluminum, and copper-based metals from mixed urban wastes is technologically feasible. Mechanized systems to recover these metals and other resources from mixed urban wastes are being developed. Manual separation programs have been initiated in many cities, but only two are presently known to separate metals.

*The 1973 Thomas Register lists 14 manufacturers of magnetic separators.

Table 5-2. **Systems To Recover Metals and Other Resources from Mixed Urban Wastes**

Name	Recovered Metals	Other Recovered Products
1. St. Louis System	Ferrous metals	Fuel
2. CPU – 400	Ferrous metals Aluminum	Electricity
3. Chicago N.W. Incinerator	Ferrous metals	Steam
4. Black – Clawson	Ferrous metals	Pulp
5. U.S. B.M. (Raw Refuse System)	Ferrous metals Aluminum Copper-zinc	Paper Glass Plastics
7. National Center for Resource Recovery	Ferrous metals Aluminum Copper	Glass Fiber
8. Garrett Research and Development	Ferrous metals	Oil Char Glass
9. Monsanto Enviro-Chem System	Ferrous metals	Steam Char
10. Ecology, Inc.	Ferrous metals	Compost

Sources: References 1 and 2.

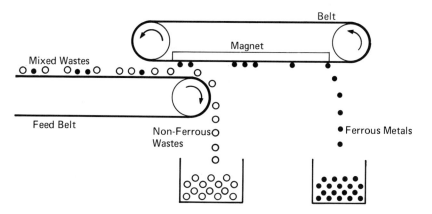

Figure 5-2. Principle of Magnetic Separation

CURRENT REFUSE PRACTICES
FOR SCRAP METAL

Metal scrap is generated at many points during the life cycle of a metal product. However, most metal scrap that is recycled into primary metal production is "new"–that is, recycled before being used by consumers–rather than consumer-discarded.

There are actually four broad categories of recoverable metal scrap:

1. *Home scrap or mill revert* is generated in primary metal production and is reincorporated by the producer directly in his production processes, without ever entering the scrap market.

2. *Industrial scrap or prompt scrap* results from the fabrication of primary metals into consumer-usable products, shapes, or forms; this is still a high quality metal, and can be recycled through conventional scrap channels back into primary metal production.

3. *Obsolete scrap* consists of large consumer or industrial products which can be readily separated; obsolete scrap may be from very high quality sources such as obsolete ships, rails, dismantled chemical plants, and shredded auto scrap. It may also contain impurities, such as "noncompatible" metals or alloys. Obsolete scrap usually requires significant handling and processing before it can be reused in primary metal production.

4. *Mixed waste scrap* is the metal contained in the mixed solid wastes discarded by residential, commercial, and industrial generators and collected by municipalities or private contractors. Very little of this metal is presently recovered for recycling, but, as will be seen later, the potential is significant. On the basis of 1972 data, we estimate that 70,000 tons of ferrous metals and 50,000 tons of aluminum (mostly cans collected at special collection centers) are recovered annually from urban refuse, and virtually no copper is presently thus recovered.

Figure 5–3 illustrates the overall flow of primary metals, metal products, and metal scrap through their life cycle. A large portion of the metals contained in mixed wastes are simply disposed of with no effort made at recovery. However, these discarded metals have become a valuable "ore" worthy of recovery instead of an economic liability.

IRON AND STEEL

Scrap is used extensively in the production of raw steel. Most of the scrap used, however, is home scrap, or mill revert, that is recycled routinely in the steel production process. For the past 20 years, about 50 percent of the total charge in raw steel production has typically been ferrous scrap (Figure 5–4); however, the proportion of "purchased" scrap–that is, scrap that is not reused in the home plant–consumed in raw steel production over this period has declined

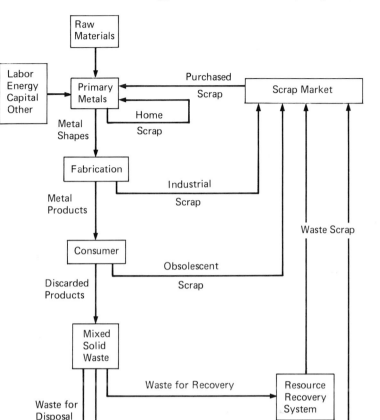

Figure 5-3. Flow of Primary Metals and Metal Scrap

from about 40 to 45 percent to about 35 percent of the total scrap component (see Figure 5–5). This has happened primarily because the Basic Oxygen Process (BOP) furnace has been replacing the open-hearth furnace; the BOP uses less scrap and therefore that generated in the plant is able to supply a higher percentage of the total scrap requirement. At the same time the installation of electric furnaces which use 100 percent scrap has not proceeded as rapidly as the phase-out of the open-hearth process. The availability of scrap in one locale, transportation, and economics of the steel industry are very complex; electric

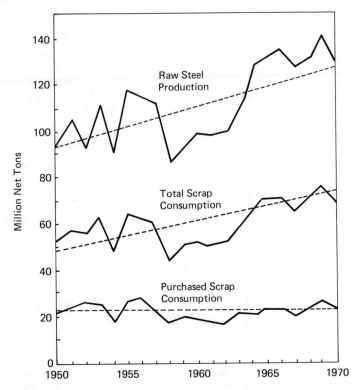

Figure 5-4. Raw Steel Production and Scrap Consumption,
1950-1970[3]

furnaces must compete with BOP and other types of furnaces. Nonetheless electric furnaces are being built as economics and scrap availability prove favorable.

The types of scrap used in iron and steelmaking vary considerably with the type of furnace used, operating practice, scrap quality and price, the iron or steel product, and past practice.[3] The proportions of scrap in the charge for the open hearth, basic oxygen, and electric furnace processes are, respectively, 40 to 45 percent, 30 percent, and 98 percent. These proportions have not changed significantly over the past 10 years.[4] The principal factors governing scrap usage are related to operating practices and the size, shape, bulk, density, and impurities present in the scrap.

Obsolete scrap occurs in many physical and chemical conditions and presents the greatest problems in scrap quality. Processing—shredding, separation, compaction—is required to obtain usable forms. Undesirable elements such as copper, lead, and tin are extremely difficult to remove and, if present, place a technical limitation on the amount of scrap usable in the furnace charge because

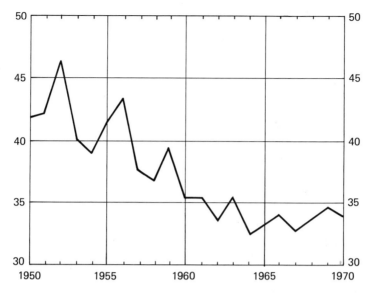

Figure 5-5. Purchased Scrap Percent of Total Scrap Consumption, 1950-1970[3]

they cause the finished product to be "off spec." However, this is more of a furnace charge limitation than a recycling limitation on the industry as a whole. Therefore this impure scrap should be distributed throughout the steel industry, and will thus constitute a sufficiently small proportion of each furnace charge. Thus, no insurmountable recycling limitation on the industry is presented.

1. *Blast furnace*: In typical blast furnace practice in the U.S.A. the scrap usage is about 5 percent of the pig iron production. Research in this area could probably result in larger scrap charges. In fact, National Steel has made tests that show about 50 pounds per ton of furnace charge could be steel cans (exclusive of "normal" scrap use).

2. *Open-Hearth (OH) steelmaking*: Open-hearth steelmaking in the U.S.A. currently accounts for about 35 percent of the total steel production. An intrinsic feature of the open-hearth furnace is its versatility in raw materials, permitting scrap usage in any amount from zero to nearly 100 percent; typically, it has been about 45 percent (but a large part of this is home scrap). However, the higher efficiency and production rate of the basic oxygen furnace (BOF) has caused a steady decline in open-hearth steelmaking which is expected to continue. For this reason, scrap recycling in the open-hearth furnace will decline in the future.

3. *Basic oxygen furnace (BOF) steelmaking*: BOF steelmaking in the U.S.A. currently accounts for about 50 percent of the total steel production. The BOF process is less capable of using scrap than open-hearth steelmaking and

is presently limited to scrap charges of about 30 percent. This is because in the BOF fuels external to the process are not used; the process heat is obtained by rapid, exothermic oxidation by oxygen-blowing of carbon, silicon, and manganese in the pig iron. The "heat balance" of the process is the major scrap limitation, since only the excess heat over that required to bring the steel to the tapping temperature can be used economically to melt the scrap. "Excess" scrap also tends to increase the charge-to-tap time and consequently slow the rate of production. Various schemes for preheating scrap or obtaining sources of heat have been and continue to be investigated in an effort to increase scrap use in the basic oxygen furnace. There is a genuine interest and effort by the steelmaking industry to increase BOF scrap charges, and prospects for doing so appear promising.

4. *Electric furnace steelmaking*: The electric furnace currently produces about 15 percent of the total U.S. steel production. This process uses an average of 98 percent scrap in the charge. Potential increases in productivity and reductions in the cost of electric furnace steel could result from continuing research efforts in continuous charging of prereduced iron ore, preheating of scrap, and higher power furnaces.[5] An increase in the production of electric-furnace steel would increase scrap usage by an equivalent amount.

5. *Q-BOP steelmaking*: 1973 marked the second year of commercialization of the bottom oxygen-blowing process (called Q-BOP by United States Steel Corporation) of steelmaking. Current existing and scheduled worldwide capacity is 17.3 million tons.[6] The potential of the process is still being debated in the industry, but it has been estimated that an explosive growth potential exists for a worldwide capacity of over 400 million tons of Q-BOP steel by 1980.[7] The process is an improvement over the BOF in raw materials versatility, and can accept maximum scrap charges in the range of 45 to 60 percent. Success of the Q-BOP process could thus increase scrap usage dramatically.

While the steelmaking industry is extremely complex and estimates of the potential for increasing scrap usage are difficult from a technological viewpoint, increasing scrap usage is entirely feasible. In addition, significant export of steel scrap adds to potential demand for scrap derived from urban waste.

ALUMINUM

Most "new scrap," generated in the production of primary aluminum or during the fabrication of aluminum products, is used by primary aluminum producers because of its availability and known and controlled compositions.* "Old

---

*Terminology in the aluminum industry is somewhat different from steel. *Run around* and *home scrap* are terms equivalent to each other, as are *new scrap* and *prompt scrap*, as well as *old scrap* and *obsolete scrap*.

scrap," derived from obsolete products, is rarely used by primary producers. (The exception to this rule is scrap aluminum cans which are reused in sheet aluminum.) The reuse of old scrap (other than cans) constitutes only about 4.5 percent of the aluminum industry's total production. The greater part of unrecovered aluminum scrap is "old scrap," most of which is found in urban wastes or special wastes. Old scrap is consumed primarily by the secondary aluminum smelters and small aluminum fabricators. The production of aluminum and reuse of scrap in the aluminum industry can be summarized as follows:[8]

1. *Primary producers*: These are companies which produce aluminum from alumina. Some primary producers are fully integrated, in that they own their own bauxite sources, alumina plants, and facilities for producing aluminum shapes from primary ingot. The industry's recently instituted and substantial drive to recycle aluminum cans—the single source of old scrap that is suitable for primary producers and unsuitable in secondary smelters—is a very promising development. About one-sixth of all aluminum cans are now being recycled by primary metals producers making sheet for aluminum cans.

2. *Nonintegrated fabricators*: These fabricators buy aluminum ingot, billet, and/or scrap, melt these source materials, and fabricate wrought products.

3. *Secondary smelters*: Secondary smelters purchase aluminum scrap and process it into secondary aluminum alloys (casting alloys, low-purity aluminum used in deoxidizing iron and steel, aluminum pig, and master alloys). These companies are the principal users of old aluminum scrap but are not its primary potential market. This is true because aluminum cans—by far the main component of such scrap—have a high magnesium alloy content that makes them difficult for secondary smelters to process.

Variations in alloy composition of aluminum scrap appears to be the only major technological problem in recycling aluminum scrap from urban wastes. However, Alcoa, Reynolds, and Kaiser are successfully recycling aluminum cans back into can stock and have the capability to increase their use of scrap derived from urban waste.

COPPER

The U.S. copper industry is composed of integrated primary producers (from ore to fabricated product), copper wire and brass fabrication, and the secondary copper industry. As shown in Table 5–3, recycled copper scrap constitutes about 45 percent of total U.S. copper consumption. Most of the copper and copper-base scrap not made into refined products is recycled by ingot makers (remelters), secondary smelters and refiners, brass mills, and foundries into useful products. Ingot makers use a wide variety of scrap to provide specification ingots to foundries. Secondary smelters use lower grade

Table 5-3. U.S. Copper Production and Scrap Recycling, 1969

Source	Domestic Copper Production (1,000 Tons)	Percent of Total Domestic Copper Produced
Copper ore	1,742.8	54.8
Recycled copper[a]		
Secondary copper	948.8	29.8
Scrap (refined)	491.0	15.4
Total produced	3,182.6	100.0

Source: *A Study to Identify Opportunities for Increased Solid Waste Utilization, vol. III, Copper.* Battelle Columbus Laboratories, June 1972.
[a]About 66 percent is old scrap, constituting about 30 percent of total production.

copper scrap and residues to produce blister copper (relatively pure copper) prior to electrolytic refining.

When copper scrap obtained from urban wastes becomes available, there appear to be no real technical problems in recycling it. The economics of recovery may govern the degree to which the copper and copper-base scrap is upgraded and thus determine the urban-waste copper market.

QUALITY OF SCRAP RECOVERED FROM URBAN WASTES

The most important factors governing the quality of ferrous scrap for recycling are: size, shape, bulk, density, and the impurities present. The major impurities in ferrous scrap (principally cans) are: (1) tin, (2) copper deposits on cans that have been incinerated, and (3) lead solder on can seams. All of these have an adverse impact on the finished steel or steel furnace refractories. Typically, ferrous scrap metal from urban wastes contains 88 to 98 percent iron.[9] All of the ferrous scrap produced (65 tons/month) by the Black-Clawson plant in Franklin, Ohio, is currently being used by the Armco Steel Corporation in an open-hearth furnace.[10] The scrap is 1.39 percent of the charge, and demonstrates the feasibility of using ferrous scrap from urban wastes in steelmaking. In addition, Granite City Steel (National Steel) is now testing ferrous metal scrap recovered from the St. Louis/Union Electric demonstration project.

Little nonferrous scrap is being produced from mixed urban wastes at present. However, can collection programs recover about 16 percent of aluminum beverage cans used, with the percentage continuing to rise.

ENERGY CONSERVATION POTENTIAL OF SCRAP METAL RECOVERY

Significantly less energy is required to produce metals from recycled materials than from virgin raw materials. Recyclable materials provide metal in a relatively pure form so that energy-consuming chemical reactions are not needed to extract the metal atoms from combinations with oxygen, their naturally occurring partner in ore.

The energy savings attributed to recycling must include the energy expended in collecting and preparing scrap for recovery as well as in the actual recycling process. In this chapter, the energy requirements for producing each of the three major metals from ores—considering the whole process, from the mine to finished metal—are computed and compared with the corresponding values for finished metals produced from scrap. Then an assessment is made of energy savings that could be realized with a comprehensive system of recycling metals in urban wastes.

STEEL MANUFACTURE—ORE VS. SCRAP

Steel From Ore

Steel is manufactured from iron ore, coal, limestone, and oxygen, with the predominant raw materials being iron ore and coal. Another major ingredient in steelmaking is scrap, some of which is shipped in from other locations, but most of which is home scrap—scrap generated on-site at the steel mill. A generalized materials flow diagram for a hypothetical basic oxygen-furnace steel-making operation is given in Figure 5–6, using only virgin ores and home scrap.

The energy for producing one ton of finished steel is also shown in Figure 5–6. These values include the energy for mining minerals, manufacturing oxygen and lime, transporting the materials, and manufacturing finished steel plate. These data show that most of the energy (93 percent) is expended in the steel manufacturing steps.

Table 5–4 compares energy values from three independent studies. These three studies are not directly comparable because of differing assumptions of transportation, efficiencies of electrical generation, scrap treatment methods, and so forth. However, remarkable agreement exists on the total energy requirement for steel manufacture. The range is from 48 million Btu/ton to 50.4 million Btu/ton, with the average being 49.0 million Btu/ton. We use this average as the estimate of the total energy required for steel produced from ore which includes internally generated scrap.

Steel from Scrap

As discussed previously, large quantities of steel scrap are used in the normal steelmaking processes. This scrap is used primarily in the open-hearth steel furnace and, to a lesser degree, in the BOP steel furnace. The blast furnace can also accommodate some scrap usage, but usually not more than 5 percent of pig iron production is scrap-derived. However, an alternative means of producing steel from scrap is widely used and increasingly preferred in the industry. This is charging scrap into an electric furnace designed specifically for melting scrap.

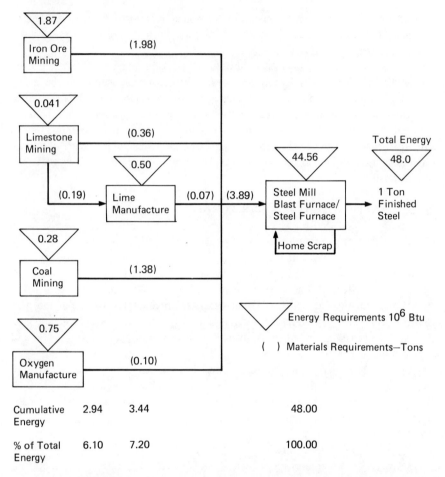

Figure 5-6. Materials and Energy Requirements To Produce One Ton of Steel

Locating electric furnaces near supplies of urban scrap is perhaps one of the most promising prospects for increased use of scrap.

It should be emphasized that in this discussion of the energy-saving potential of ferrous scrap, we do not include home scrap or mill revert, which is routinely recycled and re-recycled in the production of steel from ore. We are considering three basic sources of purchased scrap: industrial scrap from production of consumer products; obsolete, or source-separated scrap, such as junked auto bodies; and scrap from mixed urban refuse.

The energy required to obtain scrap varies somewhat with the source. However, the primary processing steps are usually shredding and transporting. For industrial scrap and obsolete scrap, these are basically the only steps required to prepare the steel for remelting.

Table 5-4. Energy Requirements for Finished Steel Manufacture (Million Btu/Ton Finished Steel)

Operation	MRI	Hannon	Bravard[a]
Mining, manufacturing, processing, and transporting raw materials	3.44	4.42	2.72
Manufacture of finished steel	44.56	46.00	45.78
Total	48.00	50.42	48.50
Average 49.0			

Sources: Midwest Research Institute, *Resource and Environmental Profile Analysis of Nine Beverage Container Alternatives* (Washington, D.C.: U.S. Environmental Protection Agency, Office of Solid Waste Management Programs, 1974); Bruce M. Hannon, "Bottles, Conservation, Energy," *Environment* 14 (No. 2, March 1972: 11–21); J.C. Bravard, H.B. Flora II, and Charles Portal, *Energy Expenditures Associated with the Production and Recycle of Metals,* ORNL-NSF-EP-24, 1972.

[a]Conversion factor of 1.516 tons of raw steel per ton finished steel, and 3,413 Btu per kwhr were used to convert this data to Btu.

Urban refuse must first be sorted to obtain salable fractions of material. This can be done by a variety of processes, but the output is generally a shredded product similar to shredded industrial scrap, although usually not as pure.

The energy requirements to obtain shredded scrap are summarized in Table 5–5. The values for scrap preparation vary considerably from 0.1 x 10^6 Btu/ton to 0.9 x 10^6 Btu/ton, with the exception of the Black-Clawson system (12.0 x 10^6 Btu), which is a wet pulping operation that rejects metals out of the pulper while defibering the organic materials. These values, although significantly large, are on the order of less than 2 percent of the energy to manufacture steel. For purposes of this study an average value for scrap preparation of 1.0 x 10^6 Btu/ton is used. This is close to the value for shredding and the magnetic

Table 5-5. Energy Requirements for Production of One Ton Shredded Steel Scrap

Source of Scrap	Energy (10^6 Btu/Ton)
Industrial or source-separated scrap shredding	0.3 to 0.6
Urban mixed waste	
Shredding and magnetic separation	0.9
Black-Clawson wet separation	12.0[a]
Bureau of Mines incinerator residue	0.1 to 0.3

Source: MRI, 1974.
[a]Excludes possible credits from energy recovery.

Table 5-6. Energy for Transportation of Steel Scrap

Mode	10^6 Btu/ 1,000 Ton-Miles		Average Ton-Miles/ Ton Scrap		10^6 Btu/ Ton Scrap
Rail	0.81	X	0.5 thou. ton-miles	=	0.40
Truck	2.5	X	0.025 thou. ton-miles	=	0.06
Total					0.46

Source: MRI, 1974.

separation process that will probably be the most common separation technique for steel in mixed waste.

The other energy-consuming step in providing scrap to a steel mill is transportation. Table 5–6 contains energy data for two modes of transportation. We have assumed that on the average, steel will travel 500 miles by rail and 25 miles by truck. The result is that approximately 0.46 x 10^6 Btu/ton is required to transport scrap. This figure combined with the 1.0 x 10^6 Btu for scrap processing gives us an estimated energy requirement of 1.5 x 10^6 Btu to prepare and transport scrap to a steel mill.

The next step is to determine the energy needed to melt steel scrap and form a finished ingot. Data were not available on the energy requirements of melting steel scrap in the open hearth or BOP steel furnace, so data for electric steel furnaces—which use close to 100 percent scrap—were taken as representative of scrap melting energy requirements for all types of furnaces.

Table 5–7 shows that 5.25 x 10^6 Btu are required to produce a steel ingot. Adding to this 1.5 x 10^6 Btu for scrap preparation and transportation results in a total energy requirement of 6.75 x 10^6 for one ton of steel produced from scrap. This is 14 percent of the 48 million Btu required to produce steel from ore.

ALUMINUM MANUFACTURE—ORE VS. SCRAP

Aluminum from Ore

Aluminum is produced from bauxite ores in two steps. First, the bauxite is refined by leaching with a caustic agent to produce a relatively high-purity aluminum oxide. The oxide is then processed in electrolytic cells

Table 5-7. Energy Requirements for Producing One Ton Steel Ingots by Electric Furnace Method

500 kwhr X 10,500 Btu/kwhr = 5.25 X 10^6 Btu

Source: MRI, 1974.

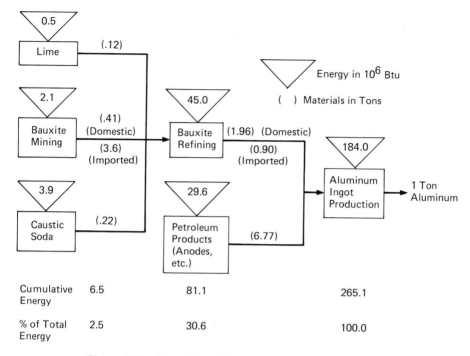

Figure 5-7. Materials and Energy Requirements To Produce One Ton of Aluminum

where a large quantity of electricity is used to separate the aluminum atom from its oxygen partners. The pure metal is then ready for processing and rolling.

Figure 5-7 is a material and energy-flow diagram for aluminum manufacture. As shown, there are three important materials required besides bauxite: lime, caustic soda, and petroleum pitch. The manufacture and delivery of these materials account for 13 percent of the total energy. However, the most important point of energy consumption is the electrolytic smelting which requires 184.0 million Btu/ton aluminum, or 69.4 percent of the system total.

Table 5-8 is a comparison of energy requirements from four independent sources. The respective totals vary from 222 million Btu/ton to 290 million Btu/ton, the latter being 31 percent higher than the former. Inconsistencies in sources of information, assumptions concerning the Btu value of electrical power, and scope of inclusion of secondary energy effects explain these variations. The Atkins data are lower than MRI and Hannon data. Atkins' data are derived from internal operating data of the industry; MRI and Hannon data come from published sources. The Bravard total is low because of the low value used for smelting. The average of all four has been selected the estimate nearest the true value of aluminum ingot requirements. This value is about 251 million Btu/ton.

Table 5-8.   Energy Requirements for Aluminum Manufacture (Million Btu/Ton Finished Aluminum)

Operation	MRI	Hannon[a]	Atkins[b]	Bravard[c]
Mining and transport of ore	2.1	5.7	3.8	9.45
Mining and manufacture of associated materials	34.0	—	30.8	11.9
Bauxite refining	45.0	284.6[c]	21.43	42.1
Aluminum manufacture	184.0	—	170.9	158.9
Total	265.1	290.3	226.9	222.4

Source: MRI, 1974; Hannon, 1972; Bravard, Flora, and Portal, 1972; and P.R. Atkins, *Aluminum—A Manufactured Resource,* (Aluminum Company of America, Undated report received by MRI in June 1973).

[a] Assuming 22.4 tons per million aluminum beer cans.

[b] Assuming 10,500 Btu/kwhr.

[c] Includes rolling and finishing.

Aluminum from Scrap

Aluminum scrap may be utilized in either of two distinct aluminum manufacturing segments. Clean industrial scrap (especially relatively pure aluminum) may be added to ore-derived aluminum at rolling mills with almost no preparation other than shredding. On the other hand, aluminum alloys or contaminated aluminum scrap is frequently sold to secondary smelters which produce aluminum products from nearly 100 percent scrap. Post-consumer or obsolete scrap has historically been sold principally to secondary smelters, but some recent changes have taken place. It has now become apparent that beverage cans and other post-consumer scrap will be used with ore-derived aluminum without serious degradation of product quality. These consumer products are suitable for "closed loop" recycling and are less satisfactory for secondary aluminum smelting.

Clean aluminum scrap is a valued commodity because of its ease in recycling and low energy requirement.

Data are not available on the energy required to melt aluminum scrap in a virgin ore plant, but numbers are available on energy requirements to melt batches of scrap. We have used these data to estimate the energy required to produce aluminum ingot from scrap.

Table 5-9 presents data from two sources on energy requirements in aluminum recycling. The average for the two values, 9.5×10^6 Btu/ton, is used to estimate energy conservation potential. This value is only 4 percent of 251×10^6 Btu, the value for producing aluminum from ore. Thus, a very impressive savings of energy could be realized in recycling aluminum, especially the type found in urban waste.

Table 5-9. Energy Requirements for Production of One Ton Aluminum Ingot from Scrap

Fuel Mix	Energy Conversion Values		MRI	Atkins
Distillate oil	5.7 gal. × 139,000 Btu/gal.	=	0.79×10^6 Btu	
Residual oil	5.3 gal. × 150,000 Btu/gal.	=	0.80×10^6 Btu	
Natural gas	4,651 cu ft × 1,030 Btu/cf	=	4.79×10^6 Btu	
Electricity[a]	360 kwhr × 10,500 Btu/kwhr	=	3.78×10^6 Btu	6.84×10^6
			$\overline{10.16 \times 10^6}$ Btu	100 kwhr × 10,500 Btu/kwhr = 1.05×10^6
Transportation			$\underline{1.0 \ \times 10^6}$ Btu	$\overline{7.89 \times 10^6 \text{ Btu}^b}$
			11.16×10^6 Btu	

Source: MRI, 1974; Atkins, 1973.
[a]Includes 250 kwhr for shredding.
[b]Includes transportation and shredding.

Copper from Ore

Copper is extracted from ores in which copper content ranges from 0.3 to 8 percent. In recent years reserves of high-percentage copper ores which can be economically mined in the U.S. have been depleted. Today U.S. copper ores average about 0.6 percent copper, occurring as copper sulfide.

Considerable processing of the ore is necessary to extract the low percentage of copper. After the ore has been mined (primarily by open-pit mining) it is crushed, ground, and subjected to flotation. The recovered copper concentrate is then smelted in a two-step process consisting of heating in a reverberatory furnace (that is, a furnace lined with heat resistant brick) followed by oxidation and removal of most of the impurities. The "blister copper" is then further refined in an electrolytic cell.

A summary of the energy requirements for the various steps in copper processing are found in Figure 5–8. These numbers correspond to a copper ore containing 0.65 percent copper. The most energy-consuming step is the mining and milling step which requires 58 percent of the total system energy. About one-half of this energy is expended in simple mechanical grinding of the ore. Because approximately 200 tons of ore must be ground for each ton of copper produced, a large energy expenditure is inevitable.

The Bravard reference is the only source of data used for energy in producing copper. The value of 71 million Btu/ton for each copper ingot is used as the working estimate of the true energy requirement in assessing energy conservation potential.

Copper from Scrap

As reserves of copper ores decline, the use of recycled copper as a primary source of the metal becomes increasingly important. As is the case in most metals industries, copper scrap is already an important commodity, but considerable potential exists for recovery of even more.

Table 5–10 shows the energy consumption necessary for 98 percent

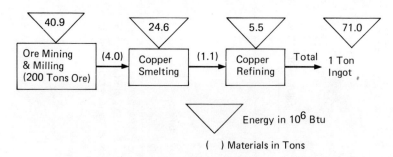

Figure 5–8. Materials and Energy Requirements To Produce One Ton of Copper. Source: Bravard.

Table 5-10. Energy Requirements for Production of One Ton Copper Ingot from Scrap

Energy Requirement	*98 Percent Pure*			*Energy Requirement—Impure Scrap*			
254 kwhr × 10,500 Btu/kwhr	=	2.67×10^6 Btu		600 kwhr × 10,500 Btu/kwhr	=	5.7×10^6 Btu	
Shredding and transportation	=	$1.0 \ \times 10^6$ Btu		Shredding and transportation	=	1.0×10^6 Btu	
Total		3.67×10^6 Btu				6.7×10^6 Btu	

Source: Bravard, Flora, and Portal, 1972.

pure and for impure copper. For pure copper, only remelting and electrofining are needed to produce copper ingot. In the case of impure copper, more fluxing and pretreatment is needed. Incremental supplies will mostly come from impure sources; thus we will assume that 6.7 x 10^6 Btu represents the best estimate of the true energy requirements for producing copper from scrap. This value is 9 percent of the value of 71 x 10^6 Btu/ton copper produced from ore.

Energy Conservation Potential

As can be seen from the previous discussion, considerable potential exists for conserving the nation's energy reserves by replacing ore-derived metal with scrap-derived metal. Table 5–11 summarizes the potential energy savings attributable to the three metals discussed in this report. The greatest percent of savings is for aluminum with 96 percent savings gained by replacing virgin-ore-derived aluminum with secondary aluminum. However, the savings of 91 percent and 87 percent for copper and steel, respectively, are also quite impressive.

In order to determine the feasible recovery of metals now occurring in urban waste, it is necessary to estimate the recovery potential of the three metals. In previous work[11] we have estimated that only that metal discarded in SMSA's (Standard Metropolitan Statistical Areas) will be discarded in sufficient quantity and concentrations to justify the installation of waste recovery processes. In addition, any mechanical or chemical recovery technique will not be 100 percent efficient. Therefore, a recovery efficiency factor must be applied.

Thus to determine the feasible recovery quantity, we apply two adjustments to total waste metal generated in urban waste: for population density and for mechanical efficiency. The data for MRI estimates of waste generation in 1975 are given in Table 5–12.

The potential recovery of metals may now be translated to an energy conservation potential. If the metals that can feasibly be recovered for recycling are actually recovered, and if directly substituted for virgin ores, then the potential energy savings is as follows: ferrous metals 291 x 10^{12} Btu; aluminum 105 x 10^{12} Btu; copper 6.8 x 10^{12} Btu. The total potential energy savings is 403.1 x 19^{12} Btu, based on 1975 estimates of recoverable waste metal generation (Table 5–13).

Table 5-11.   Energy Conservation Potential Resulting from Recycling

Metal	10^6 Btu/Ton from Ore	10^6 Btu/Ton from Scrap	Energy Savings Per Ton–10^6 Btu (Col. 1 – Col. 2)	Percent Savings
Steel	49.0	6.75	42.25	86
Aluminum	251.0	9.5	241.5	96
Copper	71.0	6.7	64.3	91

Source: MRI.

Table 5-12. Potentially Recoverable Metal in Urban Waste, 1975 (in Thousand Tons)

Metal	Total Generated	Percent in SMSA's	Available in SMSA's	Estimated Recovery Efficiency Percent	Potential Recovery
Steel	11,580	70.0	8,110	85	6,895
Aluminum	960	69.5	668	65	435
Copper	200	70.0	140	75	105
Total	12,740		8,918		7,435

Source: MRI, based on Franklin et al, 1974.

This potential savings is equivalent to 3.22 billion gallons annually of gasoline at 125,000 Btu/gallon. The energy conservation potential is, therefore, quite significant even after adjustments have been made for nonrecoverable quantities of metals in urban waste. The amount available in waste will rise annually as demand for the metals grows in response to the economic growth of the nation.

THE ECONOMICS OF METALS RECOVERY FROM URBAN WASTE

Municipalities are confronted with a bewildering array of potential solutions to their solid waste management problems. A methodical analysis of all feasible alternatives is needed to discover and implement the most cost-effective system. Such an economic determination, of course, involves increasingly complex questions of environmental quality and reserve conservation.

In general, there are three basic strategies that can be followed for municipal solid waste disposal:

1. Sanitary landfill, presently the lowest-cost, environmentally acceptable means of solid waste disposal in most areas.

Table 5-13. Potential Energy Conservation from Recycling Metals Recoverable from Urban Wastes

Metal	Potential Recovery from Urban Waste (1,000 Tons)	Energy Savings by Recycling (10^6 Btu/Ton)	Potential Energy Savings (10^{12} Btu)
Ferrous metal	6,895	42.25	291.3
Aluminum	435	241.5	105.0
Copper	105	64.3	6.8
Total	7,435		403.1×10^{12}

Source: MRI.

2. Incineration for disposal, usually employed only where suitable landfill sites are either unavailable or uneconomical.

3. Resource recovery, where wastes are processed for recovery as marketable commodities in some form.

Figure 5–9 is a highly simplified flow chart showing the movement of mixed municipal solid wastes, and depicting some of the major solid waste management alternatives available to municipalities.

Within each of the three broad waste management concepts, a wide range of possibilities exists. The sanitary landfill, for example, can be located at a close-in site, or can involve a remote location with a local transfer station. A number of small incinerators may be constructed, or a single large one may be strategically located. Should resource recovery be the waste management strategy adopted by a municipality, dozens of alternatives are presented,

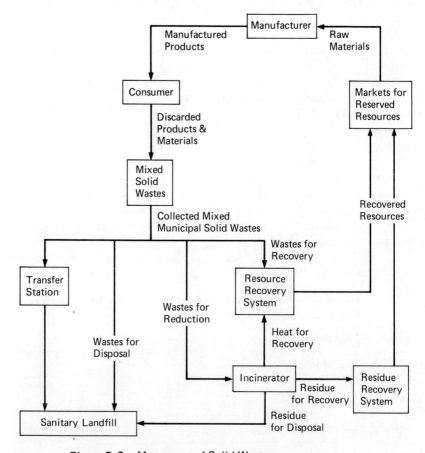

Figure 5-9. Movement of Solid Wastes

covering raw materials recovery, chemical and biological conversion processes, power generation, fuel preparation, and numerous others.

Table 5–14 summarizes the costs of disposing of mixed municipal wastes by incineration and by sanitary landfill, the conventional disposal methods. As shown in Table 5–13, net disposal costs may run from less than $2.50/ton in a large-scale, close-in sanitary landfill, to more than $10.00/ton in small municipal incinerators.

These mixed wastes contain substantial quantities of metals and other useful resources, with economic considerations determining the desirability of resource recovery. A thorough and objective analysis, weighing the cost of recovering these resources against the cost of disposing of them if they are not recovered, is essential before reaching a decision regarding the economic feasibility of resource recovery.

RECOVERY SYSTEMS COSTS

A number of mechanized resource recovery systems were discussed in an earlier section of this report. These systems can be grouped roughly into three categories:

1. *Comprehensive materials recovery* where the total mixed waste stream is processed for recovery of all usable materials—usually including ferrous metals, aluminum, copper (sometimes including zinc and other nonferrous metals), glass, and paper or fiber. This type of system is the ultimate in terms of materials recovery.

2. *Incidential metals recovery* where the primary objective of the resource recovery system is to produce substantial quantities of some marketable commodity, and, in the process, recover metals and other salable inorganic materials. Three examples of incidental metals recovery systems are included here: (a) *fuel recovery*, (b) *pyrolysis*, and (c) *composting* (see Appendix B).

3. *Incinerator residue recovery* where the noncombustible portion of

Table 5–14. Disposal Costs for Mixed Municipal Wastes Via Conventional Means

Plant Size (Tons/Day)	*Incineration ($/Ton)*	*Close-In Sanitary Landfill ($/Ton)*	*Remote Sanitary Landfill ($/Ton)*
250	10.37	2.81	6.52
500	8.98	2.69	6.22
1,000	7.68	2.57	5.94
2,000	6.65	2.45	5.67

Source: "Trend of Affairs," *Technology Review* 75 (May 1973:47).

the mixed waste stream is processed for metal and glass recovery following the incineration process, instead of being routed to a landfill for disposal.

In the detailed economic tables in Appendix B the quantities and values of the various recoverable resources and scrap recovery costs, and the overall system economics, are summarized. It should be emphasized that these economics are based on experimental recovery systems and do not reflect actual known operating results on commercial-sized plants. The costs and investment requirements are very likely to be understated relative to the current construction and operating cost trends.

Market values for the materials recovered from mixed municipal wastes may vary substantially from those quoted for specific grades in trade press publications such as *Iron Age*; this is largely because of the uncertainty regarding scrap quality and purity level of scrap derived from mixed waste.

SUMMARY OF RECOVERY ECONOMICS
FOR METALS IN URBAN WASTE

As was seen earlier, large quantities of recoverable metals are available in mixed municipal solid wastes, although most municipalities are presently more concerned with disposal rather than recovery. Economic considerations, however, are likely to change the situation, increasing the emphasis on resource recovery over the next decade. A number of different approaches can be taken to resource recovery, with systems available for raw materials recovery, chemical and biological conversion, power generation, fuel preparation, and other types of recovery. The economics of the different resource recovery systems vary widely, with metal recovery costs for a 1,000 ton/day plant estimated in Table 5–15.

The price commanded by scrap is dependent upon variable and sometimes volatile market demand.* The most sensitive economic parameter is the price of the commodity, and at this writing prices are rising rapidly. MRI estimates the market value for urban waste recovered primary metals at \$15 to \$30/ton for steel (\$10 to \$20/ton for steel from incinerator residues), \$200 to \$300/ton for aluminum, and \$400 to \$800/ton for copper. In addition, recovery credits can further reduce a municipality's net disposal costs. It should be noted here that these costs are subprocess recovery costs and generally assume that the metals are recovered in conjunction with other waste-processing/recovery operations for the organic fraction of mixed waste.

As the technology for metals recovery becomes available, municipalities should be able to provide a viable alternative to conventional disposal. The metals are the most valuable constituents of urban waste and will be sought by industry in the next decade.

---

*See, for example, Merilyn Wenenmeyer, "For Scrapmen, These are 'Tinsel Days'," *Fortune*, August 1974 (Vol. XC, No. 2), pp. 150 ff.

Table 5-15. Recovery Costs for a 1,000-Ton-Per-Day Plant[a]

| | Recovery Costs ($/Ton) | | |
System Type	Ferrous Metals	Aluminum	Copper
Comprehensive materials recovery	17.92	85.64	134.88
Fuel recovery	12.75	–	–
Pyrolysis	31.27	182.77	220.51
Incinerator residue recovery	9.41	51.69	82.50

[a]Development of the detailed economic data is in the Appendix.

POLICY CONSIDERATIONS OF METALS RECOVERY

At the federal level the Office of Solid Waste Management Programs of the Environmental Protection Agency has been the focal point for resource recovery, including metals recycling. In addition, the U.S. Bureau of Mines has explored the technology of metals recovery extensively. In the private sector the steel industry and aluminum industry have both explored, encouraged, and developed new techniques for recovery and recycling of metals from solid waste. Private sector companies have also developed most of the resource recovery technology with private funds and/or assistance from federal programs.

The Resource Recovery Act of 1970[12] and its predecessor the Solid Waste Disposal Act[13] were significant legislative steps in the stimulation of recycling of solid wastes. In recent years the principal thrust of the federal program has been: (a) demonstration of recovery technology; (b) technical assistance to governmental units; (c) policy background studies in solid waste, resource recovery and resource conservation; and (d) "source reduction" studies—options for selective reduction in the demand for materials and services (such as one-way beverage containers).

Government Policy Affecting Recycling

At present there are several significant and unresolved policy issues that bear directly on the recycling of metals and resource recovery in general. These fall into three separate categories.

1. Taxation policies of the federal tax codes provide depletion allowances, capital gains treatment, and foreign tax credits and other direct tax benefits to producers of virgin materials; similar benefits are not applicable to recycling activities. To an undetermined degree these tax policies reduce the relative virgin cost of materials, stimulate preferential consumption of virgin materials, and inhibit the growth of recycling operations.

The principal proposed act to provide similar benefits for recycled materials is the Griffith Bill[14] which is designed to amend the Internal Revenue

Code of 1954 to provide for "reasonable and necessary income tax incentives and to encourage the utilization of recycled solid waste materials and to offset existing income tax advantages which promote the depletion of virgin natural resources." The bill proposes a tax deduction of 15 percent for recycled copper and ferrous metal and 22 percent for aluminum.[15]

Recently, however, it has been reported that this approach may be dropped in favor of proposed reductions in depletion allowances for virgin natural resources. While the issue is fundamental to resource use questions, it is very complex and unlikely to be resolved for some time to come. Additionally, whether or not "reform" would lead to significant increases in the recovery of metals in mixed wastes is still undemonstrated.

2. Freight rate policies have been at issue for years. There is evidence that current rail freight rates for ferrous scrap are high relative to rates for competing materials. Certainly scrap dealers are directly affected, but again, the extent to which rate adjustment would stimulate recycling is problematical. This issue, too, is likely to remain for years.

3. Federal procurement policies have both a direct and indirect effect on the use of raw materials. Federal purchasing specifications are widely used in the purchase of goods and services by all levels of government and private sector organizations. There is now an effort by federal supply agencies, such as the General Services Administration, to develop guidelines for the inclusion of recycled materials to the extent practical in products purchased by the Federal government.

The Environmental Protection Agency (EPA) is also studying the possibility of instituting product design controls that would encourage resource conservation and reduce waste disposal and other environmental effects. However, this broad policy area is only beginning to be studied in detail.

Source reduction measures—that is, actions that would reduce consumption rather than increase recycling—are also gaining favor. Perhaps the most publicized source reduction focus has been on the beverage container. EPA has established that returnable containers have lower overall environmental effects than one-trip containers. Recently EPA has supported in principle the concept of a mandatory deposit on beverage containers proposed in the Hatfield Bill (S.2062), the effect of which could be to remove metal beverage container from the waste stream. Similar measures for automobiles, packaging, and rubber tires are under study. Since removal or reduction of the (virgin ore derived) metals in the waste stream would in itself have an energy- and materials-conservation effect, source reduction promises a conservation benefit similar to recycling of metals already in the waste stream.

Other Trends Affecting Recycling of Metals
Perhaps the most important developments of the last two years that appear to be paving the way to increased metals recycling are reflections of "free market forces." The increasing scarcity and rising costs of raw materials and

efforts to control the environmental effects of materials processing have led to more intense interest in recovery and recycling of metals, including those in mixed solid wastes. The economics of metals recovery from solid wastes will improve for several reasons: waste disposal costs are rising as more environmentally sound disposal practices come into use; land for disposal sites is rising in value and growing more scarce; and the value of recovered wastes is likely to rise rapidly in the future—especially the energy content of the organic or combustible fraction of mixed urban wastes. As technology for such energy recovery becomes economically feasible, metals recovery will follow as a processing/recovery subprocess.

The markets for the three metals in question are relatively open if the minimum specifications are met. Thus, the real policy considerations lie at the level of local jurisdictions:

- To provide the legal and jurisdictional encouragement for resource recovery.
- To provide the capital for construction of facilities to recover metals— directly, indirectly by grant from another agency, or investment by the private sector.
- To install the appropriate recovery technology.
- To establish marketing arrangements that guarantee outlets for recovered materials.

There is some activity on the part of the states to stimulate resource recovery from solid wastes. The State of Connecticut's Legislative Committee on the Environment recently (March 1973) approved a bill to establish a Resources Recovery Authority.[16] The bill provides the Authority with bonding and contracting powers to design, build, and operate a statewide solid waste system. The basic strategy will be to separate the combustibles from noncombustibles in the waste streams, with emphasis on recovering energy value of the combustibles, while marketing the noncombustibles such as ferrous metals and aluminum* In November 1972, the voters in New York State approved an environmental bond issue in which $175 million is allocated to finance solid waste recycling facilities.[17] Wisconsin and Hawaii[18] are also reported to be planning statewide solid waste recycling programs.

Some local governments have or are planning facilities to recover resources, including metals, from mixed urban solid wastes. Among these are Chicago, Illinois;[19] St. Louis, Missouri;[20] San Francisco, California;[21] Baltimore, Maryland;[22] San Diego County, California;[23] New Orleans, Louisiana;[24] Franklin, Ohio;[25] Lowell, Massachusetts;[26] Houston, Texas;[27] and others.

Thus the move toward implementation has begun. To the extent metals recovery can be stimulated, an energy-conserving recycling step will be accomplished as demonstrated in an earlier section—in most cases, a savings in energy of over 90 percent over the production of the virgin materials.

*For a discussion of energy recovery from organic wastes, see Alan Poole, "Potential Energy Recovery from Organic Wastes," a draft report to the EPP, July 1974.

The Quantity and Composition of Post-Consumer Solid Waste;* Estimates for 1971

Many of the issues relating to resource recovery and source reduction could be brought into much sharper focus with the use of detailed and consistent base-line data on waste quantities and compositions. Although there is no entirely satisfactory data base at present, Table 5A–1 contains EPA's most recent estimate of the total quantity and material composition of post-consumer solid waste. This table also provides a cross-classification of the waste stream by product category.

With the exception of the food, yard, and miscellaneous inorganic fractions, all the product and material figures are derived from analyses of aggregate U.S. industrial material production and product marketing data, together with estimates of average product lifetime and material recovery rates. These estimates have thus been developed entirely independently of refuse collection data and sample refuse composition measurements. The food, yard, and miscellaneous inorganics categories, on the other hand, are based on average proportions of these materials reported in published refuse collection studies.[28] The data thus represent an estimate of aggregate U.S. post-consumer waste generation, net of current material recovery.

The "as-generated" waste tonnages assume typical moisture content of the material prior to discard or collection. Thus, paper, textile, and wood materials have an "air-dry" moisture of approximately 7 to 15 percent; food and yard wastes contain 50 to 70 percent moisture; and all other materials are assumed to contain zero moisture. Because most published refuse composition studies reflect the moisture content of mixed wastes delivered to incinerator or landfill sites, the "as-disposed" tonnages have been adjusted to reflect moisture transfer en route to the disposal site. In making interpretations and comparisons,

*This Appendix was taken directly from: *Second Report to Congress, Resource Recovery and Source Reduction*, prepared by the U.S. Environmental Protection Agency, OSWMP, 1974, pp. 2–4.

Table 5A–1. Municipal Solid Waste Generation by Material and Source, 1971

Type of Material	Newspapers, Books, and Magazines	Containers, and Packaging	Major Household Appliances	Furniture and Furnishings	Clothing and Footwear	Food Products	Other	As Generated 10^6 Tons	As Generated Percent	As Disposed 10^6 Tons	As Disposed Percent
Paper	10.3	20.4	–	Trace	Trace	–	8.4	39.1	31.3	47.3	37.8
Glass	–	11.1	Trace	Trace	–	–	1.0	12.1	9.7	12.5	10.0
Metal:											
Ferrous	–	6.1	1.9	.1	Trace	–	3.8	11.9	9.5	12.6	10.1
Aluminum	–	Trace	.1	Trace	–	–	–	.8	.6	–	–
Other nonferrous	–	Trace	.1	.1	–	–	–	.4	.3	–	–
Plastic	Trace	2.5	.1	.1	.2	–	1.3	4.2	3.4	4.7	3.8
Rubber and leather	–	Trace	.1	Trace	.5	–	2.7	3.3	2.6	3.4	2.7
Textiles	Trace	Trace	–	.6	.5	–	.7	1.8	1.4	2.0	1.6
Wood	–	1.8	–	2.3	Trace	–	.5	4.6	3.7	4.6	3.7
Food	–	–	–	–	–	22.0	–	22.0	17.6	17.7	14.2
Subtotal	10.3	41.9	2.1	3.2	1.2	22.0	18.4	99.1	79.3	104.9	83.9
Yard waste								24.1	19.3	18.2	14.6
Miscellaneous inorganics								1.8	1.4	1.9	1.5
Total								125.0	100.0	125.0	100.0
Percent product source composition	8.2	33.5	1.7	2.6	1.0	17.6	14.7	–	79.3	–	83.9

Source: Environmental Protection Agency, Office of Solid Waste Management Programs.

the as-generated weight composition is thus more relevant from the standpoint of evaluating potential material recovery from solid waste, whereas the as-disposed weight composition should be more comparable to other published composition studies based on measured samples.

The data presented will differ from measured municipal refuse collection samples in a number of respects. For example, most sampling has typically excluded the so-called bulky refuse—major home appliances, furniture, and automobile tires—which, according to EPA estimates, accounts for about 7 million tons. In addition, the given estimates attempt to account for most but not all container and packaging waste, including a portion of that which originates at industrial plant sites and is often disposed of privately. Furthermore, virtually all composition studies have been highly localized, and most have not covered the complete spectrum of residential, commercial, institutional, and other post-consumer waste sources.

Table 5A–1 explicitly excludes sewage sludge, demolition, and contract-construction-type wastes, as well as obsolete automobiles. (Data on automobiles were presented earlier.)

The total waste generation estimate of 125 million tons per year (3.32 pounds per capita per day) for 1971 is significantly lower than the widely quoted 190 million tons per year (5.3 pounds per capita per day) result estimated from the *1968 National Survey of Community Solid Waste Practices.*[29] A portion of this difference exists because the *National Survey* results included some industrial demolition and construction wastes not included in the present estimates. An additional small part of the difference could probably also be accounted for by the fact that some net moisture is added to the solid waste stream, both in the household from kitchen activities and in the storage and collection system en route to the disposal site. Nevertheless, it appears that the *National Survey* tended to somewhat overestimate the national solid waste stream. In this regard it should be noted that the *National Survey* results were themselves principally based on collected tonnage estimates (as opposed to systematic measurements) prepared by the reporting local solid waste agencies. The present estimates for total waste are judged to be accurate to within 20 percent, given the waste categories covered.

The figures for product categories represent the first attempt to estimate physical weight quantities for the product sources of the solid waste stream. The first two categories (newspapers, books, and magazines, and containers and packaging) are judged to be accurate to within 10 percent. Other categories are judged to be accurate to within 25 percent.

MATERIAL COMPOSITION

Eighty percent of the waste stream is organic (including synthetics) and 20 percent inorganic (9.7 percent glass, 9.5 percent metals, and 1.4 percent miscellaneous inorganics). Of the materials recoverable as recyclable materials, only the paper, glass, and ferrous fractions each comprise more than 8 percent of the total waste stream. Other individual recyclable materials each comprise less than 3 to 4 percent of the total. Twenty to 25 percent of the total material weight is contributed by moisture originating principally in the food and yard waste fractions.

PRODUCT COMPOSITION

About 80 percent of solid waste (generation weight data) is derived from market product sources (as opposed to yard and garden-type wastes). Excluding food wastes, market product sources account for about 60 percent of the waste flow. It is this 75 to 80 million ton fraction at which product source reduction and material recycling programs are principally directed. If we define and measure the waste stream in terms of dry weight, the nonfood product sources account for 78 percent. Container and packaging materials currently contribute about one-third of total post-consumer waste, 42 percent of product waste, and 54 percent of nonfood product waste. The container and packaging fraction currently accounts for about 72 percent of the total mineral (combined glass and metals) fraction. In terms of individual materials, this source category contributes well over 90 percent of the glass, 75 percent of the aluminum, and at least 45 to 55 percent each of the ferrous metal, paper, and plastic fractions of the waste stream. Consumer durable goods, including household appliances, furniture, recreational equipment, and the like, account for about 10 to 12 percent of total wastes. Newspapers, books, and magazines account for about 8 percent.

Appendix B

Economics of Metals Recovery from Mixed Wastes

Recovery costs for the different materials have been allocated as fairly as possible among the recovered resources, considering both the quantity and value of the resources. Even so, any cost allocation is partially arbitrary and must be recognized as such. (The same as a petrochemicals plant producing a variety of products.) The problem is best illustrated by the mixed waste fuel recovery process (see Table 5B–4) where ferrous metals are removed magnetically from the solid waste stream, leaving everything else. The separation process in this case accomplishes two objectives—removing the noncombustible magnetic metals from the fuel resource, and separating the non-magnetic wastes from the marketable iron and steel scrap. Thus, one process—magnetic separation— produces two marketable commodities, and its costs must somehow be allocated between these two commodities. Only by making such an allocation can the economics of recovering a specific commodity be properly evaluated.

Substantial economies of scale are possible in resource recovery plants (just as in most other types of production plants) and the allocated recovery costs have been adjusted to reflect these economies at different scales of operation.

The economic feasibility of recovering a specific material from the mixed waste stream is artificial; the "profits" realized by recovering copper, for example, may well be far more than offset by the losses incurred as a result of recovering paper, glass, or ferrous metals at the same time. The total system economics must be considered when evaluating the relative merits of any recovery process.

The net gain (or loss) incurred as a result of resource recovery is found by taking the market value of the recovered resource, less its recovery cost at the prescribed scale of operation, times the quantity of the resource recovered. For example, in a comprehensive materials recovery plant operating at a scale of 1,000 tons/day, the net result for ferrous metal recovery would be

($12.00 – $17.92) x 21,152 = –($125,220)

while aluminum recovery under the same conditions is found to be

($162.50 – $85.64) x 2,184 = $167,862.

These net profits or loss figures do not consider the alternative cost of disposing of unrecovered metals.

The economics of each of the five major categories of resource recovery systems will be briefly discussed in the following sections.

1. MATERIALS RECOVERY

Comprehensive materials recovery from mixed urban wastes can be accomplished in a wet system such as the Black-Clawson/Fibreclaim unit, or by means of a dry separation process typified by the National Center for Resource Recovery system. Either way, provisions are made for the recovery of paper, glass, aluminum, and ferrous metals. Tables 5B–1, 5B–2, and 5B–3 summarize the pertinent economic characteristics of this type of recovery system.

Table 5B–1 shows the market value of each of the five recovered resources: ferrous metals, aluminum, copper, glass, and paper. The quantities recovered are based on an operating schedule of 312 days per year, with the 1,000 TPD plant processing 312,000 tons of mixed wastes annually.

Recovery costs for the various resources are summarized in Table 5B–2. Here, the cost of ferrous metal recovery is estimated at $17.92 per ton at the 1,000 TPD scale, while aluminum recovery costs are estimated at $85.64; copper (with zinc) at $134.88; glass at $17.30; and paper at $21.00. If it were possible to separate only the aluminum and copper at those costs, the project would be quite attractive. However, as shown in Table 5B–3, the profits allocated to these nonferrous metals are more than offset by the losses associated with ferrous metal, glass, and paper recovery. Comprehensive materials recovery cannot, by itself, be considered economically attractive (except in extremely large plants).

However, if a municipality's only alternative were incineration at a cost of $7.68 per ton (Table 5–6), the relative desirability of resource recovery changes substantially. Incineration of 312,000 tons per year of mixed wastes at $7.68 per ton would cost the municipality nearly $2.4 million annually, far more than the cost of recovering and marketing the potentially available resources in the solid waste stream. Consequently, as municipalities are confronted with these decisions in the future, resource recovery is likely to gain increased acceptance.

Table 5B-1. Quantity and Value of Recovered Resources from Comprehensive Materials Recovery Plant

Recovered Resource	Market Value As Recovered ($/Ton)	Quantity Recovered (Tons/Year)				
		250 TPD	500 TPD	1,000 TPD	2,000 TPD	4,000 TPD
Ferrous metals	12.00	5,288	10,576	21,152	42,304	84,608
Aluminum	162.50	546	1,092	2,184	4,368	8,736
Copper	200.00	312	624	1,248	2,496	4,992
Glass	10.00	4,992	9,984	19,968	39,936	79,872
Paper	15.00	3,120	6,240	12,480	24,960	49,920

Source: National Center for Resource Recovery, *Materials Recovery System*, 1972.

Table 5B-2. Scrap Recovery Costs from Comprehensive Materials Recovery Plant

Plant Size (Tons/Day)	Allocated Recovery Cost ($/Ton)					Average Recovery Cost for all Materials ($/Ton)
	Ferrous Metals	Aluminum	Copper	Glass	Paper	
250	26.42	126.25	198.85	25.51	30.96	34.69
500	21.76	103.98	163.77	21.01	25.50	28.57
1,000	17.92	85.64	134.88	17.30	21.00	23.53
2,000	14.76	70.53	111.09	14.25	17.30	19.38
4,000	12.16	58.09	91.49	11.74	14.24	15.96

Source: MRI estimates.

2. WASTE FUEL RECOVERY PROCESS.

The preparation of mixed waste for use as a fuel in an unconverted form offers an interesting possibility for the recovery of energy and ferrous metals. The model for this approach is the St. Louis/Union Electric process now in operation in St. Louis, where wastes are being utilized as supplemental fuel for an electric utility boiler furnace. This process uses the organic fraction of the waste after removal of the ferrous metals by magnetic separation. In addition, the other inorganics are partially removed by an air classifier unit.

The value of the fuel portion of the waste stream is estimated at $0.30 per million Btu or $2.90 per ton (see Table 5B–4). Ferrous metals are assumed to have a market value of $12.00 per ton, the same as in the previously-described comprehensive materials recovery system. The quantities of waste handled are approximately the same as in the previous system, except that a 300-day operating schedule is used here.*

Recovery costs for ferrous metals range from $19.36 per ton to $8.40 per ton at the 4,000 TPD level (corresponding roughly to the mixed wastes from a population of 1.5 to 2.0 million); fuel costs vary from $7.99 per ton down to $3.46 per ton over the same range (see Table 5B–5). Iron recovery costs, then, are somewhat higher than in the comprehensive materials recovery system, and the net results are somewhat less attractive (as shown in Table 5B–6). Still, costs are substantially less than for conventional incineration at the same operating levels, and the recovered resources from this system are perhaps more readily marketable than in the others.

*Operating schedules based on system developers' recommendations.

Table 5B-3. Economics of Comprehensive Materials Recovery from Mixed Municipal Wastes

Plant Size (Tons/Day)	Net Gain or Loss ($/Year)					
	Ferrous Metals	Aluminum	Copper	Glass	Paper	Total
250	(76,253)	19,793	359	(77,426)	(49,795)	(183,322)
500	(103,222)	63,904	22,608	(109,924)	(65,520)	(192,154)
1,000	(125,220)	167,862	81,270	(145,766)	(74,880)	(96,734)
2,000	(116,759)	401,725	221,919	(169,728)	(57,408)	279,749
4,000	(13,537)	912,126	541,682	(138,977)	37,939	1,339,233

Source: MRI.

Table 5B–4. Quantity and Value of Recovered Resources from Mixed Waste Fuel Recovery Process

Recovered Resource	Market Value As Recovered ($/Ton)	Quantity Recovered (Tons/Year)				
		250 TPD	500 TPD	1,000 TPD	2,000 TPD	4,000 TPD
Ferrous metals	12.00	5,100	10,200	20,400	40,800	81,600
Fuel	2.90	69,900	139,800	279,600	559,200	1,118,400

Source: Midwest Research Institute, *Resource Recovery—The State of Technology* (Report prepared for the Council on Environmental Quality, NTIS PB 214 149, February 1973).

Table 5B–5. Scrap Recovery Costs from Mixed Waste Fuel Recovery Process

Plant Size (Tons/Day)	Allocated Recovery Cost ($/Ton)		Average Recovery Cost for All Materials ($/Ton)
	Ferrous Metals	Fuel	
250	19.36	7.99	8.76
500	15.71	6.48	7.11
1,000	12.75	5.26	5.77
2,000	10.35	4.27	4.68
4,000	8.40	3.46	3.80

Source: MRI, based on cost data reported in *Resource Recovery,* 1973.

3. PYROLYSIS.

Several different pyrolysis processes are currently in various stages of development. Different products can be produced from the pyrolysis process, ranging from gases to synthetic fuel oils. The model used here is based on the Garrett system, generating an oil roughly equivalent to about two-thirds the Btu value of Number 6 fuel oil. Inorganics—metals and glass—are recovered in the preparation of mixed wastes for pyrolysis. The economics of this system are described in Tables 5B–7, 5B–8, and 5B–9.

The recovered resources (except for oil) are essentially the same as in any other mixed waste separation system employing magnetic and gravity separation. The oil yield from pyrolysis is reported to be approximately one barrel per ton of mixed waste input. A 1,000 TPD plant, then, would be expected to produce 300,000 bbls of oil annually, having a gross thermal content of 1.44×10^{12} Btu, at a value of $0.70/10^6$ Btu. Table 5B–7 summarizes the quantities and values of recovered resources.

As indicated in Table 5B–8, recovery costs for the various

Table 5B–6. Economics of Resource Recovery from Mixed Waste Fuel Recovery Process

Plant Size (Tons/Day)	Net Gain or Loss ($/Year)		
	Ferrous Metals	Fuel	Total
250	(37,536)	(355,791)	(393,327)
500	(37,842)	(500,484)	(537,966)
1,000	(15,300)	(659,856)	(675,156)
2,000	67,320	(766,104)	(698,784)
4,000	293,760	(626,304)	(332,544)

Source: MRI, based on cost data reported in *Resource Recovery,* 1973.

Table 5B-7. Quantity and Value of Recovered Resources from Pyrolysis System

Recovered Resource	Market Value As Recovered ($/Ton)	Quantity Recovered (Tons/Year)				
		250 TPD	500 TPD	1,000 TPD	2,000 TPD	4,000 TPD
Ferrous metals	12.00	5,100	10,200	20,400	40,800	91,600
Aluminum	162.50	188	375	750	1,500	3,000
Copper	200.00	113	225	450	900	1,800
Glass	10.00	4,200	8,400	16,800	33,600	67,200
Oil	21.33	11,813	23,625	47,250	94,500	189,000

Source: MRI, *Resource Recovery*, 1973.

Table 5B–8. Scrap Recovery Costs from Pyrolysis System

Plant Size (Tons/Day)	Allocated Recovery Cost ($/Ton)					Average Recovery Cost for All Materials ($/Ton)
	Ferrous Metals	Aluminum	Copper	Glass	Oil	
250	42.33	247.44	298.53	39.60	55.05	51.96
500	36.38	212.66	256.57	34.03	47.31	44.66
1,000	31.27	182.77	220.51	29.25	40.66	38.38
2,000	26.88	157.08	189.52	25.14	34.95	32.99
4,000	23.10	135.00	162.88	21.61	30.03	28.35

Source: MRI, based on cost data reported in *Resource Recovery*, 1973.

commodities are relatively high, averaging $38.38 per ton overall. As a result, this pyrolysis system would not pay its own way through the sale of recovered products (see Table 5B–9).

Even so, the pyrolysis process may offer an economical alternative to conventional incineration for disposal, since net costs (figured on the raw waste input) result in a substantially lower disposal cost than incineration at the same scale of operations. As an added benefit, the process yields a readily marketable fuel product, likely to increase in value over the next few years.

4. INCINERATOR RESIDUE RECOVERY.

The U.S. Bureau of Mines has done considerable work in developing a system to recover the noncombustible materials remaining in the residue following incineration of mixed wastes. The residue recovery plant is generally sized at from 20 to 25 percent of the input tonnage to a municipal incinerator. To achieve maximum economies of scale, it is desirable to utilize the residue from several incinerators, shipping them to a central residue recovery plant.

The quantities and values of recovered products are shown in Table 5B–10. Ferrous metals recovered from incinerator residues will have slightly lower market values because of lower quality than when recovered from a raw waste ($10.00 per ton instead of $12.00). Nonferrous metals and glass are valued the same as in the other recovery systems. Recoverable quantities of marketable ferrous metals are lower than is possible by preincineration recovery because of the loss of scale, slag and small nonrecoverable pieces that takes place during incineration.

Scrap recovery costs (Table 5B–11) are quite reasonable in comparison with alternative systems, ranging from $12.77 per ton down to $6.94 per ton for ferrous metals; $70.12 to $38.10 for aluminum; $111.92 to $60.81 for copper; and $12.25 to $6.65 for glass.

Table 5B-9. Economics of Resource Recovery by Pyrolysis of Mixed Municipal Wastes

Plant Size (Tons/Day)	Net Gain or (Loss) ($/Year)					
	Metals	Aluminum	Copper	Glass	Oil	Total
250	(154,683)	(15,969)	(11,134)	(124,320)	(398,334)	(704,440)
500	(248,676)	(18,810)	(12,728)	(201,852)	(613,778)	(1,095,844)
1,000	(393,108)	(15,203)	(9,230)	(323,400)	(913,343)	(1,654,284)
2,000	(607,104)	8,130	9,432	(508,704)	(1,287,090)	(2,385,336)
4,000	(1,016,760)	82,500	66,816	(780,192)	(1,644,300)	(3,291,936)

Source: MRI, based on cost data reported in *Resource Recovery*, 1973.

Table 5B–10. Quantity and Value of Recovered Resources from Incinerator Residue Plant

Recovered Resource	Market Value As Recovered ($/Ton)	Quantity Recovered (Tons/Year)				
		50 TPD	100 TPD	200 TPD	400 TPD	800 TPD
Ferrous metals	10.00	3,965	7,930	15,860	31,720	63,440
Aluminum	162.50	208	416	832	1,664	3,328
Copper	200.00	156	312	624	1,248	2,496
Glass	10.00	6,175	12,350	24,700	49,400	98,800

Source: R.M. Sullivan and M.H. Stanszyk, *Economics of Recycling Metals and Minerals from Urban Refuse*, Bureau of Mines Technical Progress Report, April 1971.

Table 5B–11.   Scrap Recovery Costs from Incinerator Residue Recovery Plant

Plant Size (Tons/Day)	Allocated Recovery Cost ($/Ton)				Average Recovery Cost for All Materials ($/Ton)
	Ferrous Metals	Aluminum	Copper	Glass	
50	12.77	70.12	111.92	12.25	15.07
100	10.96	60.21	96.09	10.52	12.94
200	9.41	51.69	82.50	9.03	11.10
400	8.08	44.38	70.83	7.75	9.53
800	6.94	38.10	60.81	6.65	8.18

Source: MRI, based on cost data reported in *Resource Recovery,* 1973.

As a result, the residue recovery system shows a favorable economic picture, as indicated in Table 5B–12, *providing* incineration is necessary anyway. With incineration the only practicable disposal technique available to a municipality for its solid wastes, the residue recovery system can substantially reduce the net costs of disposal. If low-cost sanitary landfill can be employed, the cost of incineration must be added to the cost of residue recovery for comparative purposes.

Table 5B–12.   Economics of Resource Recovery from Incinerator Residue

Plant Size (Tons/Day)	Net Gain or (Loss) ($/Year)				
	Ferrous Metals	Aluminum	Copper	Glass	Total
50	(10,983)	19,215	13,740	(13,894)	7,988
100	(7,613)	42,553	32,420	(6,422)	60,938
200	(9,357)	92,194	73,320	23,959	198,830
400	60,902	196,552	161,204	111,150	529,808
800	194,126	414,003	347,418	330,980	1,286,527

Source: MRI, based on cost data reported in *Resource Recovery,* 1973.

Notes to Chapter Five

1. National Center for Resource Recovery, *Materials Recovery System, Engineering Possibilities Study*, Washington, D.C., December 1972.
2. Midwest Research Institute, *Resource Recovery Processes for Mixed Municipal Solid Wastes, Catalogue of Processes*, Report prepared for Council on Environmental Quality, February 1973.
3. U.S. Environmental Protection Agency, *Marblehead Materials Operations, Marblehead, Massachusetts*, preliminary data, 18 June 1973.
4. *Ibid.*
5. *Ibid.*
6. American Metal Market Company, *Metal Statistics*, 1971.
7. *Ibid.*
8. Battelle Columbus Laboratories, *A Study to Identify Opportunities for Increased Solid Waste Utilization*, vol. II, Aluminum, June 1972.
9. D. Bendersky, S-Y Chiu, J. Hancock, and L. S. Shannon, *Quality of Products from Selected Resource Recovery Processes and Market Specifications*, Special Report, Midwest Research Institute, 28 February 1973.
10. *Ibid.*
11. William E. Franklin et al., *Baseline Forecasts of Resource Recovery, 1972 to 1990*, Final Report, Project No. 3736-D, Midwest Research Institute, May 1974.
12. *Resource Recovery Act of 1970*, Public Law 91-512, 26 October 1970.
13. *Solid Waste Disposal Act*, Public Law 89-272, 20 October, 1965.
14. H.R. 1508 93rd Congress, 1st Session, Introduced in the House of Representatives by Congresswoman Martha W. Griffiths, 8 January 1973.
15. *Ibid.*
16. *Connecticut Solid Waste Management News* 1 (8 April 1973).
17. *Solid Waste Report*, 13 November 1972.
18. *Solid Waste Report*, 5 February 1973.

19. Marshall Saloway, Chief Engineer, City of Chicago, personal communication, 27 April 1972.

20. F. E. Wisely et al., "Use of Refuse As Fuel in Existing Utility Boilers," *Proceedings* from National Incinerator Conference, June 4–7, 1972.

21. T. Meichtry, Solid Waste Transfer Systems, San Francisco, personal communication, 14 April 1972.

22. *Solid Waste Report,* 5 February 1973.

23. *Solid Waste Report,* 18 September 1972.

24. *Solid Waste Report,* 19 March 1973.

25. J. C. Dale, Director of Environmental Services, Aluminum Association, personal communication, May 1973.

26. *Solid Waste Report,* 18 September 1972.

27. Mr. Doepke, Browning-Ferris Industries, Kansas City, Missouri, personal communication, 18 May 1973.

28. Battelle Columbus Laboratories, *A Study,* vol. II.

29. Franklin et al., *Baseline Forecasts.*

Chapter Six

The Potential for Energy Recovery from Organic Wastes

Alan Poole

Every year the United States generates about 700 million dry tons of organic wastes. This represents over 10 quadrillion Btu of potential energy.

Until quite recently, however, energy recovery from this resource received only scant attention. But concern over resource limitations and pollution problems has altered the picture. Awareness of the environmental problems associated with conventional disposal systems for different kinds of organic solid waste has aroused interest in new alternatives. The energy crisis has focused this interest on alternative waste management systems which can recover energy from these wastes. At present—and for some years to come—a chief objective of waste recovery systems will be to reduce fossil fuel dependency.

There are several sources of wastes for energy production. The one receiving the most attention at present is mixed urban refuse, since high disposal or incineration costs make the alternative of resource recovery economically attractive in many cities. There is a general consensus in the private sector and at all levels of government that resource recovery from urban refuse and other post-consumer wastes will increase dramatically in the coming decade and

The Energy Policy Project of the Ford Foundation sponsored this study on the potential energy available from organic wastes as part of its two-year review of the full spectrum of energy issues.

The author would like to thank the entire staff of the EPP for their interest and cooperation, and in particular Dr. Robert Williams who initiated this study. Thanks are also due many individuals in the EPA, the U.S. Department of Agriculture, and National Science Foundation, private industry and various institutes, as well as to private citizens who freely gave their time, knowledge, and criticisms. Many are acknowledged by name in the text, but their contributions exceed the specific citations.

The views expressed in this report are the author's and do not necessarily reflect the views of the Energy Policy Project staff. Readers desiring to pursue further any points made in this study are invited to contact the author through the Institute for Public Policy Alternatives, State University of New York, Albany.

thereafter.[1,2,3] The wood and pulp industry, too, is already an important and growing energy source, providing about 540 trillion Btu each year.

On the other hand, relatively little serious attention has been given to resource recovery from the organic wastes generated in agriculture. Dry organic material in crop residues plus manure from feedlots amounts to about five times that found in all post-consumer wastes. Organic wastes from agriculture could eventually provide three or four times as much useful energy as urban refuse. The lack of interest in them so far is largely due to the fact that, with the exception of some feedlot manure wastes, there is no urgent disposal problem, and it is therefore not possible to credit a resource recovery system with alternative disposal costs.

This report will assess the conservation-production potential of energy recovery from the organic waste materials generated at present; it will also explore the possibilities of organic waste recovery in the future until 2000, in the framework of scenarios constructed by the Energy Policy Project in its final report.

In the case of mixed residential and commercial refuse, inorganic materials will be also considered, since projects designed to recover energy or materials from the organic fraction of urban refuse are nearly all designed also to recover separately the different classes of inorganic material commonly found in refuse (glass, ferrous metals, and aluminum). Integration of glass and metals recovery processes with organic materials and energy recovery processes makes each kind of recovery more economical. This is because many components (for example shredding and air classification) are common to all the recovered product streams.

A complete analysis requires the following as a minimum to design a feasible resource recovery system model and predict its probable output and impact: (a) estimates of significant or potentially significant materials flows; (b) estimates of the costs, materials balances, and economies of scale of resource recovery processes; and (c) estimates of the market value of the products and other benefits of resource recovery.

From the outset, there are limitations. Figures for solid wastes are still incomplete; few resource recovery processes have yet progressed beyond the demonstration plant phase. Thus, estimates of materials flows often must be tentative, and projected costs and benefits or resource recovery systems are subject to change. The estimates in this study, can, of course, be no more accurate than the studies on which they are based. All estimates, except for crop residues, are based on secondary sources rather than on raw data.

In spite of the dearth of firm data, cities and states throughout the country are formulating real orders for real resource recovery plants. It would appear appropriate to begin to assess the future potential of this recently recognized class of energy resources.

This report should be read as such a beginning, with the accent on exploring the potential for energy recovery in the context of contemporary or near-term technological capabilities.

Energy recovery systems from both urban refuse and agricultural waste are considered in some detail. Energy recovery from the organic wastes generated in forestry and forest industries, though potentially important, is reviewed only in brief.

The study is divided into four parts. In the first part, current estimates are made of the magnitude of different sources of organic waste in the United States. A large part of the total waste flow is related to the output of relatively few industrial sectors. For example, the output of the paper products and plastics industries is the major component of the organic fraction of urban refuse. On the basis of this observation, an attempt has also been made in this section to *begin* to project future waste generation by a method somewhat more valid than extrapolation of past trends. As a first approximation, future rates of organic waste generation are related to a *range* of outputs of specific industries. These ranges of industrial outputs are, in several cases, those used in the scenarios of the Energy Policy Project and are themselves not mere extrapolations of past trends.*

The second part will discuss the technical processes which will probably be part of future energy recovery systems. The main intent is to give readers who do not have much familiarity with resource recovery technology a brief overview of the status, problems, and characteristics of major processes which are now being actively developed and which are likely to be the basis of energy recovery in the foreseeable future. Readers interested in a more precise evaluation might refer to a study carried out by International Research and Technology, Inc., for the Environmental Protection Agency (EPA),[4] bearing in mind that it is now somewhat out of date.

*A note of explanation is needed on the three scenarios developed by the Energy Policy Project in its final report. "The scenarios are not offered as predictions," says the introductory chapter of *A Time to Choose.* "Instead, they are illustrative, to help test and compare the consequences of different policy choices." The scenarios are put to similar use in the present study: as tools for comparative examination of future energy-use possibilities.

The first of these scenarios is *Historical Growth*, which "assumes that energy use in the United States would continue to grow till the end of the century at about 3.4 percent annually, the average rate of the years from 1950 to 1970," with steadily rising demand and no deliberate conservation effort. Annual energy use would be about 187 quardrillion Btu by 2000. The second scenario, called *Technical Fix*, "reflects a conscious national effort to use energy more efficiently through engineering know-how" and assumes an energy growth rate of about 2 percent a year, with energy consumption reaching 124 quadrillion Btu annually by 2000.

The *Zero Energy Growth* Scenario assumes a concentrated energy conservation effort. It would not require any significant sacrifice of economic growth, but would emphasize better services rather than more goods. Energy use would continue to grow, but at a declining rate, until about 1990 when it would level off at about 100 quadrillion Btu.

In the third part, two examples of energy recovery systems are presented. Such systems have many possible variations and may be organized at a local, regional (intrastate), or state level. The examples presented here are intended to illustrate the sorts of impact and problems to be expected. One model is based on energy recovery from urban refuse and is basically a synopsis of the Connecticut Plan, which is now being carried out in that state. The second model investigates the possibility of energy recovery from agricultural wastes, particularly crop residues. This model is presented in considerable detail because of the enormous potential of agricultural wastes and the apparent lack of systematic studies. Agricultural wastes constitute by far the largest source of waste-derived energy. There is strong evidence that agricultural waste energy recovery is surprisingly close to economic viability. Clearly, research funding is now warranted.

In the fourth part, estimates will be made of the overall potential for energy recovery from organic wastes at present and in the year 2000, using data and conclusions from the first three parts. The impact of possible solid waste legislation on resource recovery will also be evaluated. An *upper* estimate of possible net energy supply (after conversion) from urban refuse, feedlot manure, and crop residues is 4 quadrillion Btu per year at present and perhaps 9–10 quadrillion Btu per year in the year 2000. It is possible that half this amount might actually be developed. Other savings from materials recovery and secondary effects, plus the total energy value of wastes used for fuel in the wood and paper industries, may approach 3 quadrillion Btu by the year 2000. By comparison, coal consumption in 1973 was 13.4 quadrillion Btu. Although by no means a giant energy source or universal panacea, organic wastes could provide energy on a scale and within a time that warrants more than the limited research and development effort currently being made.

MATERIALS FLOWS

The human ecosystem depends both directly and indirectly on the organic products of photosynthesis. "Direct dependence" refers to the biomass, i.e., organic materials, actually harvested by man—plants and livestock for food, wood for paper and other products, and plant fibers for other uses, such as textiles.

Eventually, all of this biomass is oxidized. The oxidation takes place, however, in many different forms and at different stages in the life cycle of any material. Distinctions between the waste stream and the product stream, and between wastes generated at various points in the cycle of harvest-processing-production-disposal of consumer goods are important to an understanding of waste energy potential.

Materials flow analysis offers a means of improving our understanding of these cycles in the human ecosystem. Although materials flow analysis (and energy flow analysis) has been a central theme of both classical ecology and chemical engineering for many years, the application of this methodology to the human economic ecosystem has been relatively recent. One of the first attempts was *Economics and the Environment; A Materials Balance Approach*, by Kneese, Ayres, and d'Arge (1970).* It was soon apparent that an accurate picture of the extraordinarily complex solid waste situation in this country would depend on a series of studies using the methodology of materials flow rather than on piecing together ad hoc local estimates and samples of industrial and urban refuse, as was done, for example, with the data from the *1968 National Survey of Community Solid Waste Practices*[5] to derive the commonly quoted figure of 190 million tons per annum of urban refuse.

Perhaps the first major study applying materials-flow analysis to solid waste was the report prepared by the International Research and Technology Corporation (IR&T) for the Environmental Protection Agency in 1972 entitled *Problems and Opportunities in Management of Combustible Solid Wastes*.[6] Although the report covers all sources of organic waste, its primary original contribution was a materials-flow analysis of the organic wastes generated in industry based on the 1967 *Census of Manufactures*. A more up-to-date study of the organic wastes generated by industry is currently being prepared for the EPA by the International Research and Technology Corporation (IR&T). It has been found that the quantities of organic waste generated by industry are smaller than previously assumed.

Recently the EPA has begun to revise its earlier estimates of household and commercial refuse generation on the basis of materials-flow analysis, and the result has been a substantially reduced estimate of quantities of refuse. The value of materials-flow type analysis can be illustrated here by the following example: Earlier studies estimated that paper constitutes 35 percent to 50 percent of urban solid waste, with total annual urban solid waste generation ranging from 145 to 190 million tons. The minimum amount of paper waste would, then, be in the range of 50 to 65 million tons. However, the actual total of annual production and imports of paper products—less recycled paper—was only 43 million tons in 1967 (see Figure 6–1), and a significant fraction of this never entered the waste stream. The materials-flow approach makes it clear that the earlier estimates, either for solid waste generation, or for the paper product composition of solid wastes, were too high—probably the former, since estimates for the proportional amount of paper have been generally regarded as the more reliable.

*See also F. A. Smith, "The Economics of Industrial Waste Production and Disposal," Doctoral dissertation, Northwestern University, 1968.

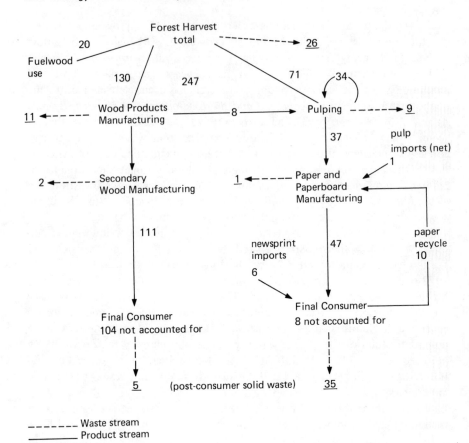

Figure 6-1. Forest Products Materials Flows, 1967 (in Million Dry Tons Organic Matter). Sources: General production and recycle data—*Statistical Abstract of the States*, 1972; Industrial processing wastes and fuel recovery in pulping—IR&T, 1972;[4] Post-consumer wastes—OSWMP, F.A. Smith,[98] 1974; F.L. Smith, 1974.[7]

Work on materials flows is far from complete. This section will attempt, however, to present highly aggregated materials flows for two of the three most important product streams: forest products and plastics (see detailed discussion of Figure 6–1 below).

Information from present-day materials flows permits the development of fairly useful projections of future "waste streams" from future product stream projections of the industries concerned. The product stream projections used here are the individual industry projections for the year 2000 in the Zero Energy Growth and Historical Growth scenarios developed in the Energy Policy Project's final report, *A Time to Choose.*

Forest Products

The following discussion of Figure 6–1–the first of six materials-flow diagrams–may further clarify this approach. Figure 6–1 shows a total forest harvest of 247 million dry tons (mdt) of organic matter. Of this total, 26 mdt become process waste in the initial logging process; 20 mdt are sold as fuelwood; the rest (201 mdt) forms the product stream. The larger part of this product stream (130 mdt) is used to make lumber for wood products. In this process, 11 mdt enter the process waste stream, while 8 mdt more are recycled at this point into pulping operations; and 111 go to secondary wood manufacturing–that is, to making furniture, frame structures and so forth. In this process, 2 mdt become waste, and the aggregate of useful products that then goes out to consumers is equivalent to about 109 mdt. In the post-consumer stage of the cycle, finally, 5 mdt go to the incinerator or city dump as solid waste and 104 mdt–in this case a huge proportion of the total–are designated "not accounted for."

The remaining 71 mdt in the product stream from the forest harvest are used for paper manufacture, beginning with pulping operations (along with 8 mdt recycled from primary wood manufacture). The pulping processes are fueled with 34 mdt waste wood (illustrated by a circular arrow), another example of process waste recycling. Process wastes entering the waste stream from pulping operations amount to 9 mdt. Paper and cardboard products are made from the 37 mdt pulp output (to which is added 1 mdt from net pulp imports). Recycled paper adds an additional 10 mdt and a total of 53 mdt–47 mdt of domestically manufactured paper plus 6 mdt of imported newsprint–go to the consumer; 35 mdt go to the waste heap, and 8 mdt are called "not accounted for."

The term "not accounted for" as used in these materials-flow diagrams simply designates a disparity between consumption of products and final output of waste in a given year, and covers a multitude of situations. In the case of wood products, where 104 mdt are so labelled, one factor is simply that durable goods, such as furniture do not become "waste" as fast as new goods are produced. A growing population with more homes to furnish accounts for some of this; much wood waste, too, is undoubtedly burned for fuel and nevers gets to any central dump where it can be counted. What is *measured* as waste today, then, is only a small fraction of what actually enters the waste stream. Moreover, many wooden homes and furnishing, barring accidental fires or freak accidents, have indefinite lifespans, considered in the time frame of recent human history.

In the case of paper, on the other hand, the figure for post-consumer wastes is over four times that not accounted for. The great bulk of paper, of course, is not durable at all and—like newspapers, periodicals, stationery—has a short life cycle. Some factors explaining the 8 mdt not accounted for are permanent storage of books and documents (libraries, archives) and irretrievable dissipation of such products as cigarette paper.

These observations help demonstrate that the use of not accounted for is simply a convenience and in no way implies that a mass of material comparable to initial harvest or production in a given year *should* be accounted for in waste output.

Ongoing work at EPA[7] and elsewhere is refining the methodology of analysis of this discrepancy between input to and output from the consumer, which is the most problematic part of materials-flow analysis applied to urban solid waste.

Generally speaking, post-consumer waste includes most of the components of "urban refuse," but the terms are not synonymous. Household and commercial-institutional wastes, demolition, sewage, and automobile wastes are included in post-consumer waste; construction wastes are also frequently so labelled, but this seems illogical to the author. "Commercial-institutional" wastes generally include, for example, used crates and other packaging from industrial plants, since these cannot strictly be considered as "processing wastes." Household and commercial-institutional wastes are by far the major components of post-consumer wastes, as can be seen in Appendix A. The final consumer input includes much long-lived construction (particularly in the wood products stream) which may be in industrial plants. Since we have not included demolition wastes, there may be somewhat of an underestimate of post-consumer solid waste in the wood products stream. However, as shown in Appendix A, demolition wastes are not large.

The flow chart in Figure 6–2 is in accord with both the Historical Growth and Zero Energy Growth scenarios of the Energy Policy Project's final report, *A Time to Choose*. Important assumptions are that:

1. Wood products consumption will increase at the same rate as during the 1950–1970 period.

2. Fuelwood consumption will increase at the same rate as wood products.

3. Consumption of paper products will be 170 million tons per annum.

4. The proportion of supply from imports will remain constant while 25 percent of the paper consumed (29 percent of the paper produced) will be recycled, compared to 19 percent in 1970.

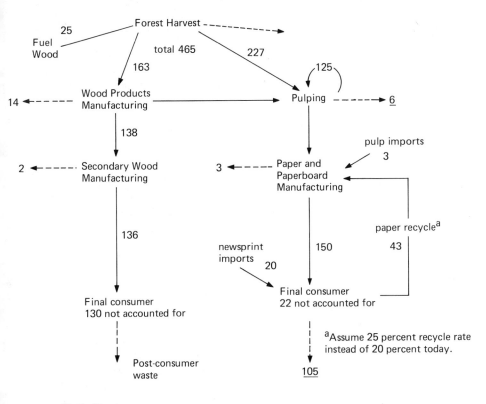

25
Fuel
Wood

Forest Harvest

total 465

227

163

125

Wood Products
Manufacturing

Pulping

6

14

138

pulp imports

3

2

Secondary Wood
Manufacturing

3

Paper and
Paperboard
Manufacturing

paper recycle[a]

136

newsprint
imports
20

150

43

Final consumer
130 not accounted for

Final consumer
22 not accounted for

[a]Assume 25 percent recycle rate
instead of 20 percent today.

Post-consumer
waste

105

— — — — — — Waste Stream
——————— Product Stream

Note: Figures underlined indicate organic matter entering
the waste stream.

Figure 6-2. Forest Products Materials Flow, 2000: Historical
Growth and Zero Energy Growth Scenarios (in Millions of Tons
Dry Organic Matter).

5. Fossil fuel conservation measures as discussed in *Potential Fuel
Effectiveness in Industry*,* are generally adopted in the pulping industry.

Assumption 3, the most critical, is based directly on the scenarios in
A Time to Choose.

Assumption 5, although the author's own, reflects a trend in the
pulping industry. The ThermoElectron study demonstrated that a net savings of

*By Gyftopoulos, Lazarides and Widmer, Ballinger Publishing Co., Cambridge,
Mass., 1974.

about 1100 kwh per ton of paper could be expected with current technology. Instead of requiring about 500 kwh of electricity per ton of paper produced, the industry could export 585 kwh/ton. In addition, use of purchased fossil fuels drops from 19.5 to 11.7 million Btu/ton of paper produced, so that total fuel savings (including fuel for utilities) could be about 18.7 million Btu/ton of paper produced. Use of on-site wood wastes and spent pulp liquor increases from 14.5 million Btu to 18.0 million Btu per ton of paper produced.

It may be possible to sbustitute wood product wastes even further for purchased fuels if off-site wastes are available.

This raises the possibility of using forest debris from logging as fuel for nearby pulping plants. This possibility has generally been ignored,[8] but rising fossil fuel costs and the recently demonstrated feasibility of expanded use of forest debris now make its consideration worthwhile. Moreover, the development of silvicultural (forest cultivation) techniques such as "windrowing" of debris to reduce the danger of intense forest fires[9,10*] suggests further that collection of forest debris for fuel in forest associated industries deserves more attention.

Plastics

A materials-flow chart for plastics in 1970 is shown in Figure 6–3. Growth rate in the consumption of plastic in the Historical Growth scenario is shown in Figure 6–4, section (a). Although lower than in the past, it is close enough so that we may adopt the same relative proportion of plastic in the waste stream for 2000 as for the present time (see the discussion of time lags above). In the Zero Energy Growth Scenario (Figure 6–4, Section (b)), however, growth in the use of new plastic products would be appreciably slower. Therefore, the *proportion* (though not the absolute quantity) of plastic entering the waste stream increases slightly, even after allowing for a 50 percent increase in the average use time (currently about seven or eight years). Virtually no post-consumer waste plastic is recycled at present, and unless there are major economic or technical breakthroughs, the probability of significant recycling in the future is small.

Agricultural Products

To do justice to the size and complexity of agricultural materials flows would require a major study, particularly if a serious attempt were made to measure the nutritional balances of domestic animals. Such a flow chart would be valuable for its inbuilt checks on consistency. Here, however, a simpler

---

*This report USDA Study notes that forest fires in logged areas are seven times as intense as in unlogged areas, with increased environmental harm both to the forest and the atmosphere. This increase in intensity is a direct result of the presence of large quantities of logging debris on the ground.

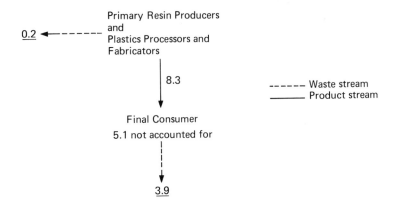

Note: Figures underlined indicate organic matter entering
the waste stream.

Figure 6-3. Plastics Materials Flow, 1970 (in Millions of Tons Dry
Organic Matter). Sources: Data for processing wastes—Marynowski,
1972; Data for consumption—Glausz et al., 1973; Data for post-
consumer wastes—F.A. Smith, 1974.[98]

hierarchy diagram (Figure 6–5) showing calculated waste outputs, with
agricultural output unquantified, will suffice.

A notable point that emerges from this hierarchy diagram and the
accompanying figures is the small amount (6 million tons) of dry solid waste
from food processing, particularly since 5.5 million tons of this are bagasse from
the processing of sugar cane.* (A significant but unknown fraction of this
bagasse is now used as fuel.) Food processing generates large quantities of
byproducts, but these cannot be considered wastes since they are almost all used
in other parts of the agricultural sector (generally as feed). The quantities of
food processing wastes are likely to decline in the future rather than increase
since the application of water pollution restrictions has encouraged the
development of technologies that retain a larger percentage of the raw food
material in the product or byproduct stream.[11]

The figure for sewage solids is for sludge after treatment, and is the
figure generally used. (A more accurate reckoning would be possible if the
amount of *organic matter* in raw sewage were measured instead, since raw
sewage could quite conceivably be integrated into energy recovery systems now
being developed.[12,13] It is likely that the figure would then be about 50 percent
higher.)

No diagram for the year 2000 has been constructed since there are

---

*It should be noted that except for bagasse, this refers to net waste *after*
resource recovery of byproduct materials.

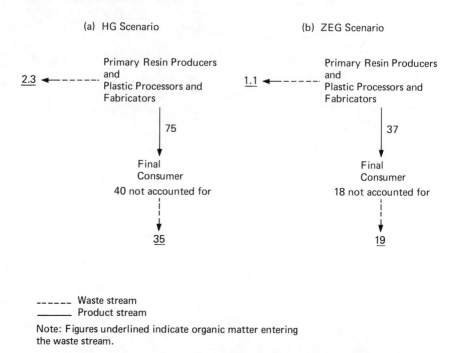

(a) HG Scenario　　　　　　　　　　　　　(b) ZEG Scenario

2.3 ◄─────　Primary Resin Producers and Plastic Processors and Fabricators　　　　1.1 ◄─────　Primary Resin Producers and Plastic Processors and Fabricators

75　　　　　　　　　　　　　　　　37

Final Consumer　　　　　　　　　　　Final Consumer

40 not accounted for　　　　　　　　18 not accounted for

35　　　　　　　　　　　　　　　　19

- - - - - Waste stream
───── Product stream

Note: Figures underlined indicate organic matter entering the waste stream.

Figure 6–4.　Plastics Materials Flows, 2000 (in Million Dry Tons Organic Matter). Source: Calculations are based upon projections for consumption in 2000 from EPP's final report *A Time to Choose*, scenarios.

no satisfactory projections for agricultural production. This is largely because of uncertainties about the future extent of export expansion,[14] domestic demand for meat—particularly beef—and use of feedlots vs. range and pasture by the animal production sector. These unpredictable elements result in a tremendous range of realistic projections, particularly of food and feed crops. (A simple and highly speculative projection of crop residues and feedlot wastes for 2000 is made in the concluding chapter.) Two points are clear, however: provided that the fertility of the land is not impaired, the surplus productive potential of American agriculture is vast if there is a strong and consistent policy of development,[15] and exports of American food products will remain substantial. The United States will almost undoubtedly remain the world's dominant exporter of agricultural commodities.

Gross Energy in Currently Generated Waste

A more complete evaluation of the available energy content in wastes will be made, based on energy recovery processes and systems data in the

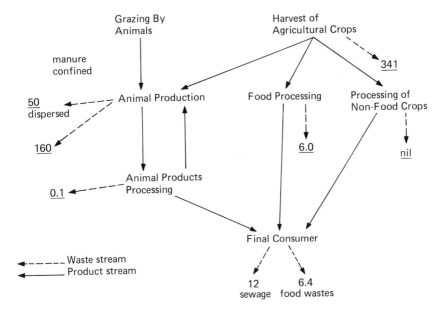

Figure 6-5. Hierarchy Diagram of Waste Generation from the Agricultural Product Stream, 1973 (in Million Dry Tons Organic Matter). Sources: Bases for waste outputs from field residues and animal manure (two largest sources)—Appendix A; Data for plant product processing, animal product processing, sewage wastes— International Research & Technology (IRT) Corporation study; Data for food in post-consumer solid waste—F.A. Smith, 1974[98] (figure for food could be in error by up to 25 percent).

final section of this report. However, the general magnitude of energy in currently generated wastes may be usefully indicated here.

Figure 6–6 shows major waste flows (in tons of dry organic matter) with the net total dry organic wastes produced each year at about 700 million tons (see Appendix A for details). At 16 million Btu per ton of dry organic matter, the gross energy in wastes is 11.2 quadrillion Btu. This is by no means a trivial resource, particularly since it is almost all renewable.

The gross energy in urban solid refuse is a fraction of this amount. The EPA currently estimates it to be 1.1 quadrillion Btu (based upon 125 million tons of waste at 4,500 Btu per pound in 1971).[16] An alternative estimate, based on the energy content of the components of urban refuse (66 million tons dry organic matter, 3 million tons rubber, 4.2 million tons plastic) is 1.3 quadrillion Btu gross energy, or 5,200 Btu per pound.

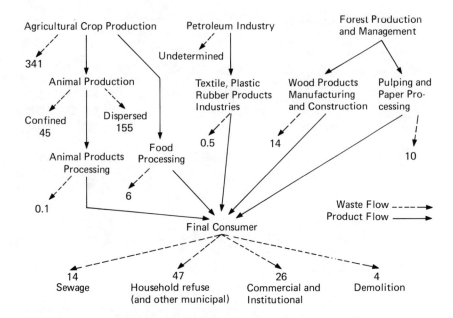

Agricultural Crop Production   Petroleum Industry

Forest Production
and Management

341

Undetermined

Animal Production

Textile, Plastic
Rubber Products
Industries

Wood Products
Manufacturing
and Construction

Pulping and
Paper Pro-
cessing

Confined
45

Dispersed
155

0.5   14

Animal Products
Processing

Food
Processing

10

6

0.1

Waste Flow ----→
Product Flow ——→

Final Consumer

14
Sewage

47
Household refuse
(and other municipal)

26
Commercial and
Institutional

4
Demolition

Notes: 1. Detailed product and byproduct flows between processing sectors not shown.
2. Product flow quantities are unknown in some cases; hence, no quantification is given here. Product flows are simply indicated with solid lines.

Figure 6–6. Major Processing and Post-Consumer Organic Waste Sources and Related Product Flows, ca. 1970 (in Million Dry Tons Organic Matter)

RESOURCE RECOVERY PROCESS CONCEPTS APPLICABLE TO ORGANIC AND MIXED ORGANIC AND INORGANIC WASTES

Organic wastes can theoretically yield a range of products, including: (a) fuel or thermal energy; (b) feed or food energy or protein; (c) soil conditioners and fertilizer nutrients; and (d) industrial raw materials.

A large number of process concepts have been developed or are being developed to recover one or more of these products.[17,18] Attention here will be directed to those processes which yield fuel energy or can be integrated with fuel-yielding processes.

Any review of process concepts for resource recovery is limited at this time by frequent gaps and conflicts in the available data for costs and operational parameters. In particular: (a) reported costs for any given concept may vary; (b) sound figures for net energy conversion efficiency appear to be lacking (the EPA is preparing to analyze systematically the net conversion efficiency of each concept that it is funding); (c) data on scale-cost relationships are limited and uncertain; (d) data are inadequate to compare different process "packages" that are being developed (for example, the Garrett oil pyrolysis demonstration plant consists of a materials separation process yielding metal, glass, and residue as well as the actual pyrolysis process which yields oil, char, and low Btu gas); (e) difficulties in costing the products are great.

These difficulties are perhaps inevitable. With a few exceptions (such as a few isolated ferrous metal and paper recycling operations, composting and spreading manure on land), development of resource recovery from urban refuse at the pilot plant scale commenced only after 1970.[19, 20]

With these provisos, discussion will begin with a brief description of some of the most advanced of the major processes currently under development. These processes are becoming well known, and more detailed and encyclopedic presentations are readily available elsewhere;[21,22] consequently, the status of each concept—and the major attendant problems—will be described simply and briefly.

Materials Separation Processes

Most recent research and development on resource recovery from solid wastes has dealt with urban refuse. Refuse is, along with most other post-consumer wastes, a mixture of different classes of materials. Estimates of the composition of urban refuse are shown in Tables A6–7 and A6–8 in Appendix A. In order to recycle any particular refuse material, it is necessary to separate it from the general mixture; furthermore, most of the energy recovery processes using urban refuse require that the organic matter be separated from the bulk of the inorganic matter and be shredded or milled.

Since these last two operations are common both to many energy recovery processes and to processes designed to recover recyclable materials, there are cost advantages in integrating certain materials separation processes and energy recovery concepts. Major energy recovery concepts that currently have "front-end" materials separation—that is, separation before fuel recovery—and that also prepare the combustible material are: (a) CPU–400; (b) supplementary solid fuel; (c) Garret oil pyrolysis; (d) methane fermentation. These are discussed in detail below.

Two types of front-end materials separation processes are under development at present: "dry separation" and "wet separation." The major distinction is that the separation of the light organic fraction from the heavier inorganic fractions is achieved using air processes in dry separation, while in the wet separation water is first added to make a slurry.

Many dry separation processes are under development in con-junction with the energy recovery concepts listed above. In addition, the Bureau of Mines has developed a complete materials recovery pilot plant at College Park, Maryland, which is based on dry separation of the organic and inorganic fractions and subsequent materials recovery.[23] Specialized techniques for use with either wet or dry processes in the further segregation of inorganic fractions (ferrous metals, aluminum, and glass in particular) have also been developed elsewhere. An example is the Glass Container Manufacturer's Institute process for recovering aluminum and glass.

A simplified block diagram for a dry materials separation process yielding solid combustible fuel, ferrous metals, glass, aluminum, and residue is shown in Figure 6–7. Typical separation efficiencies are shown in Table 6–1.

Wet materials separation has been mainly developed in the Black-Clawson demonstration plant in Franklin, Ohio. The principal objective in this EPA project is recovery of paper in the form of long-fibered pulp. The refuse is first shredded and slurried with water.

As shown in the flow chart of Figure 6–8, unpulpable materials such as large inorganic objects and other unsatisfactory materials for paper fiber recovery (small bits of aluminum, plastic, and glass and short-fibered or nonfibrous organics) are progressively removed from the stream. Substantial amounts of organic material are left for energy recovery after separation of the recoverable paper fiber. The wet separation process can be modified to provide combustible fuel for boilers with or without paper fiber recovery. The conversion efficiency is somewhat less than in dry separation because the product of the wet separation process must be dried for use in most boilers. This process, unfortunately, presents a marketing problem because the paper pulp it yields does not match any current general grade specifications. Another

Table 6-1.   Typical Separation Efficiencies of Component Sub-processes of Dry Materials Separation (From Wise, 1974)[13]

	Percent of Component Reporting with Fraction					
	Magnetic Separation		Screening		Air Classification	
	Magnetic Fraction	Non-magnetic Fraction	Oversize Fraction	Fines Fraction	Heavy Fraction	Light Fraction
Paper	Trace	100	100	Trace	5	95
Yard waste	Trace	100	100	Trace	23	77
Food waste	Trace	100	100	Trace	50	50
Wood, plastic, rags, rubber	Trace	100	100	Trace	50	50
Glass	Trace	100	25	75	85	15
Ash, rock, dirt	Trace	100	50	50	85	15
Ferrous	85	15	100	Trace	96	4
Aluminum	15	85	100	Trace	94	6
Other nonferrous	15	85	100	Trace	94	6

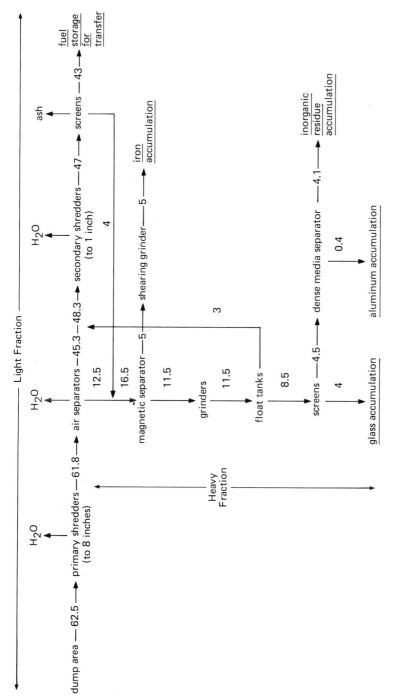

Figure 6-7. Flowchart for a 1,000-Ton/Day Dry Materials Separation Process[a] (in tons per hour)

[a]From General Electric, Connecticut, 1973.[19]

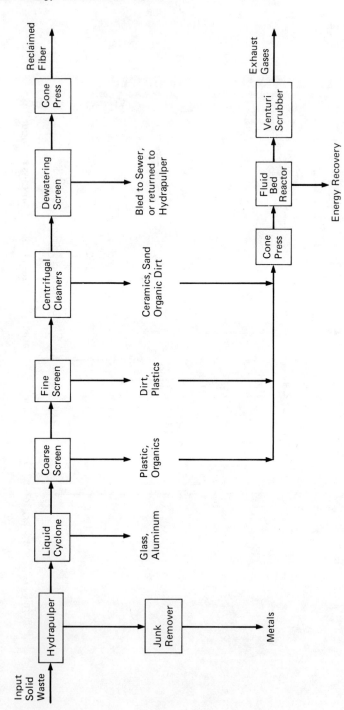

Figure 6-8. Flow Diagram for a Wet Materials Separation Process[a]

[a]From IR&T, 1972.

difficulty is that since the wastes are slurried *before* separation of the pulpable fraction, the amount of soluble and settleable contaminants added to the suspending water is very large. The water is too contaminated to release into sewers, nor can it be recycled in the process without some form of treatment. In an alternative process for paper fiber recovery (the Trezek process), wet separation comes after initial shredding and air-classification with the consequence that contamination of the suspension water is much lower. The pulp produced is also of better quality (C. G. Golueke, personal communication*).

Though there is controversy on this point, such low-technological *approaches* to fiber-recovery as hand-picking from a dry material separation stream (8 to 10 percent recovery) or separate collection of newsprint seem to be increasingly popular.[24,25]

Energy Recovery Processes

The following energy recovery concepts will be reviewed: (a) combustion of organic wastes as solid fuel for steam-electric generators; (b) electricity generation from combustion gases; (c) supplementary solid fuel for utility and industrial boilers; (d) pyrolysis; (e) producing steam for space heating and cooling; and (f) anaerobic methane fermentation.

Despite the widespread publicity it has received, the deoxygenation process has not developed substantially since it was last reviewed.[26] The author has not studied the most recent work on the biological conversion of cellulose-rich materials to ethanol, but results up to 1973 have not been particularly encouraging (K. Selby, personal communication*). These two concepts will therefore not be reviewed.

Combustion of Organic Wastes as Solid Fuel
for Steam-Electric Generators

Use of organic waste material as the sole or primary energy source for steam-electric generation is an established technology. Many plants in the wood and paper industries generate substantial amounts of electricity and industrial steam on site from waste materials. Central power plants also use wastes; for example, a plant in Portland, Oregon, uses wood wastes, and plants in Milan, Paris, and various sites in Germany use urban refuse.

In the wood and paper industries, the use of wood-related wastes in total energy systems yielding electricity and industrial steam is very promising. A report to the Energy Policy Project[20] shows that 75 percent of the energy requirements in papermaking could be supplied by process wastes as opposed to the present 37 percent. Most virgin paper is produced in integrated pulp and paper mills. The production of paper from pulp in 1967 (as shown in Figure 6-1) was 37 million tons. Energy from wastes amounts to 0.5 quadrillion Btu. In 2000, virgin paper production may be as high as 107 million tons (see Figure 6-2) with wastes providing 2 quadrillion Btu of fuel energy annually.

*Names and addresses of these and other correspondents are listed on p. 308, following the chapter notes.

Outside of total energy systems such as these, however, steam-electric generation from organic wastes is rather less promising. Such steam-electric plants will generally have to be smaller than their fossil fuel counterparts because of smaller quantities of available fuel, and unit costs tend to be substantially higher. For urban refuse, incineration combined with steam-electric generation was found to have the highest total operating cost and net disposal cost of any resource recovery process. It also appears that the efficiency of electricity generation from organic wastes alone is lower than that from fossil fuels. The efficiency of thermal generating plants is a function of steam pressure and thus ultimately of temperature. The larger particle size of most organic wastes and the impurities in urban waste keep the temperatures at which boilers can be operated lower than those for fossil-fueled plants.

Although the smaller plants used are also less efficient, if they are fueled 50 percent or more by waste and the rest by coal or oil, they should achieve somewhat higher efficiencies than plants fired by wastes alone. Either partially or totally waste-fueled plants could be ideal if integrated into district heating and cooling schemes which could utilize the waste heat, from a small plant much more easily than from large plants. Such a system has been developed in Nottingham, England, and is part of the MIUS (Modular Integrated Utility System) developed by United Aircraft for the U.S. Department of Housing and Urban Development.

Electricity Generation from
Combustion Gases

An alternative concept for generating electricity from organic wastes is the CPU-400 being developed by the Combustion Power Corporation in Menlo Park, California, with a grant from the EPA. After the organic material is separated from the refuse, it is combusted in a fluidized bed reactor. The hot gases from the reactor are cleaned and then used to drive a gas turbine. According to the IR&T study,[27] this process promises to be less expensive than steam-electric generation. However, there have been serious difficulties with submicron particles in the combustion gases which plate the turbine blades and can cause failure of the turbine after only five hours of operation (S. Levy, personal communication). Present technology appears unable to reduce the quantity of these submicron particles in the combustion gases to the very low levels required for turbine functioning. Excessive heat loss and loss of medium from the fluidized bed are other major difficulties (C. G. Golueke, personal communication). Unless substantial improvements can be made, this process does not seem technically feasible for urban refuse. If, however, condensation of an aluminum oxide aerosol in the gases is responsible for the turbine failure—as has been suggested—this process might yet be applied successfully to organic wastes that are not mixed with metallic aluminum. If this proves to be the case, the concept would be quite promising. An attractive possibility is the development of plants, using the still hot exhaust gas from the turbine to generate steam to drive a steam turbine. Combined cycle plants have a higher efficiency than single cycle plants, and a number are currently under construction using natural gas as a fuel.

Supplementary Solid Fuel for Utility and Industrial boilers

In this concept, organic waste material is used as a supplement to fossil fuels in fossil-fuel-fired boilers. This concept is now being developed for shredded organic wastes separated from urban refuse, as previously seen in Figure 6–7. The shredded waste is fired together with the fossil fuel in the boiler. Several advantages of this concept are:

1. Many existing boilers with ash handling capabilities can use the fuel once it is suitably prepared. In this way the high cost of building steam-electric power plants for use with organic wastes alone is avoided.

2. Since large fossil fuel plants are considerably more efficient than waste-fueled plants (33 percent conversion efficiency compared to 20 percent),[28] and this efficiency appears to be unimpaired by adding organic materials from mixed urban wastes,[29] it follows that organic waste material can be put to more efficient use as a fossil fuel supplement than as a primary fuel.

3. Implementation can be rapid.

A demonstration plant in St. Louis funded by EPA has shown the feasibility of this concept for coalburning boilers.[21] The most difficult problem at present is emission of atmospheric pollutants. Recent tests were inconclusive, but indicated particulate emissions levels above those for boilers fired entirely with coal. Particulate emissions, however, do not pose an insoluble problem. Emissions are, in any case, far lower than when the organic material alone is incinerated. Earlier difficulties with high ash content and wear of the boiler feed lines have been reduced by the development of a more complete front end materials-separation process. But the St. Louis plant is still characterized by the use of refuse-derived fuel which has a relatively high ash content. If a still more complete materials-separation system is used, particularly with screening of the light fraction of refuse after air classification, as seen later in Figure 6–7, the ash content will be further reduced. This should lower particulate emissions.

Although experience gained so far has been exclusively with coal-fired boilers,* it is anticipated that shredded organic waste can also be used as a supplement in oil- and gas-fired boilers with ash-handling facilities. A demonstration plant to test this is currently being planted by the EPA.

As shown in Table 6–2, energy recovery from this system is relatively high, while costs appear to be relatively low. The study for the solid

---

*It is reported that some major utility boiler manufacturers are now routinely installing facilities for firing refuse-derived solid fuel as optional equipment in new fossil-fuel boilers for electricity generators.

Table 6-2.   Costs, Products, and Net Energy Conversion Efficiency of Concepts for Processing Urban Refuse

	Capital Cost ($ per Ton per Day Capacity)	Recovered Products	Net Conversion Efficiency (in Percents)
Supplementary solid fuel			
a. With dry materials[a] separation	(13,500)[b] 6300–14,000[d]	Fe, solid fuel	70
b. With wet materials[a]	14,500[b]	Fe, solid fuel	65
Garrett oil pyrolysis[a]	16,730[e]	oil, char, low btu gas, Fe	37
Tovax gas pyrolysis	11,000[g]	low Btu gas Fe	65
Monsanto gas-steam pyrolysis	–	steam, Fe	46
Union Carbide gas pyrolysis	–	low btu gas	63
Tovax-steam (four units-330 each)	$(17 \times 10^5$–17,000^5[g]	steam, Fe	55
Incineration with steam generation	17,480[e]	steam	57
Anaerobic methane[a] fermentation	7,500[f]	high Btu gas, Fe	42

[a]Cost and efficiency of process effected by materials separation step which yield a glass and aluminum stream which may be recovered as well.

[b]GE-Connecticut, 1973;[19] the costing given in this study generally represent the upper end of the range of costs (S. Natof, personal communication).

[d]Range of bids for Bridgeport, Connecticut, supplementary solid fuel plant, (F.M. Smith, personal communication—mid-1974 dollars.

[e]Dataquest, Inc., *Energy Recovery from Wastes*, 1974—early 1974 dollars.

[f]Ghosh and Klass,[42] 1974, Ghosh (personal communication). All cost data for this process based on a detailed engineering evaluation of a plant for Indianapolis, Indiana, in 1972 dollars.

[g]S. Natof (person communication) in mid-1974 dollars for 1,000-ton-per-day plant with adequate redundancy (four 330-ton-per-day units).

waste plan for Connecticut[30] and a recent EPA study[31] consider this concept to be capable of the most rapid implementation. The latter study projects an energy recovery capacity of 85 trillion Btu per year from a total 36,290 tons of dry solid waste a day by 1980. Of this capacity, 28,400 tons will be used as fossil-fuel supplement. Both estimates are considered conservative, since they include only those communities which have *already* taken definite steps toward implementation of an energy recovery system. But since interest is growing and plants ordered in 1978 could be on line by 1980, actual implementation could well be substantially greater. On the other hand, growth could be limited by institutional and marketing difficulties. Investor-owned utilities, for example, have been reluctant to commit themselves to using refuse-derived solid fuels.

The same EPA report studied the areas where energy recovery

systems based on the fossil fuel supplement concept could be feasible by 1980. The criteria were:

    1. A Standard Metropolitan Statistical Area (SMSA) with a population of at least 100,000 (although some smaller communities have, in fact, already begun to implement this concept).

    2. High alternative disposal costs. Areas with abundant available landfill capacity such as Los Angeles and San Francisco were therefore not included.

    3. Generally higher alternative fuel costs.

    4. A coal-burning electric utility boiler in the SMSA. (Extension of the concept to include ash-handling oil-burning electric utility boilers and large industrial boilers with ash-handling facilities is nevertheless likely.)

    Communities satisfying these criteria had a total population of 72 million in 1970 and are anticipated to have a total population of 78 million in 1980 (Series E projections of the Bureau of Census). Their waste generation rate in 1980 is anticipated to be 170,000 tons per day or 62 million tons per year with recoverable energy totalling 558 trillion Btu.

Pyrolysis

    Pyrolysis is the thermal decomposition of organic substances in an oxygen-deficient atmosphere. Combustible gases (primarily CO, H_2, and CH_4), char, and pyrolytic acid tars are produced in varying proportions, depending on conditions inside the reactor. Different variations of the concept are under development, though no full-scale commercial systems are operational yet.

    The four most advanced processes are designed for energy recovery from urban refuse. They are: (a) the oil pyrolysis process developed by Garrett Research and Development Corporation with some EPA support; (b) the gas pyrolysis process developed by Union Carbide Corporation; (c) the gas pyrolysis process developed by Monsanto Enviro-Chem Systems with EPA support; and (d) the gas pyrolysis process developed by the Carborundum Company.

    The Garrett pyrolysis process involves front-end separation of the organic and inorganic fractions, after which the organic material is finely milled. The material is then decomposed at $1000°F$ in an atmosphere from which all oxygen is excluded. Low-Btu gas and considerable quantities of char and acid tars are produced. The product of the pyrolytic acid tars which condense is called "oil," but is not chemically related to petroleum oil. If the temperature of the reactor is increased, the process will yield medium-Btu gas, though the developers favor oil.

    There are at least two major difficulties with this process. First, it has proven to be technically difficult to mill the organic waste material to the required fineness at reasonable cost. Second, the "oil" is very viscous. It must be heated to approximately $160°F$ in order to flow and is corrosive at that temperature. It therefore requires special storage and feed facilities. Feedlines used for pyrolytic oil must be purged with residual oil before shutting down. The end product of the Garrett process is therefore not as attractive as it might appear to be at first sight.

The Monsanto gas pyrolysis process was originally designed to achieve maximum volume reduction of urban refuse as an alternative to incineration. It can be modified to produce either steam or low-Btu gas. The process differs from the Garrett process in two important ways. First, the reaction is carried out at a higher temperature (approximately 1400°F) and yields gas and small quantities of char mixed with inorganic solids. Second, although shredding is required, the process does not require materials separation before pyrolysis. Of course, it could be designed with front-end materials separation and recovery of different inorganic fractions if desired. In the plant being built for Baltimore with EPA support, a materials separation step (recovery of ferrous materials) occurs *after* pyrolysis rather than before. The development of back-end materials separation plants in this country has been pioneered by the Bureau of Mines[32] for use with municipal incinerators, and a 250 ton/day back-end materials separation plant is being constructed in Lowell, Massachusetts, with EPA support. This technology could be applied to processes such as the Monsanto gas pyrolysis.*

The Union Carbide process resembles the Monsanto system in that a low-Btu gas is produced and no front-end materials separation is required. Back-end separation, however, is not possible here because of the high temperature of the partial oxidation reaction.** Because pure oxygen is used at this stage, temperatures are in the range from 2600° to 3000°F. Metals alloy at these temperatures and thus cannot be separated.

The use of oxygen instead of air results in a gas product undiluted with nitrogen and therefore having a somewhat higher energy value (300 Btu/standard cubic foot instead of 150 Btu/scf). This gas may be transported somewhat further if necessary (one or two miles is considered economical). Although this process has been quite favorably accepted,[33] the requirement for an on-site oxygen facility adds complication. One feature of the Union Carbide process which is extremely attractive is that preliminary shredding or treatment of the input material is optional.

The Torax system developed by Carborundum resembles the Union Carbide process in many ways. The pyrolysis unit is vertical and feedstock enters at the top. Preliminary shredding and feed preparation are optional. The

---

*The relative merits of front-end versus back-end materials separation processes have not yet been determined. Back-end systems appear to be somewhat cheaper to operate (since smaller quantities of material are handled), but also suffer from a lower product value. There appears to be more general and varied interest in front-end processes at present.

**Air or oxygen are used only in one stage of the pyrolysis process in order that combustion of some of the input material will produce higher temperatures for the true pyrolysis reaction which later occurs in an oxygen-deficient atmosphere.

temperature of reaction is slightly lower—approximately 2300°F. A major difference, however, is that the Torax system does not use pure oxygen. The output gas is therefore diluted with inert nitrogen and has an energy value of only about 170 Btu/scf, but the complication of an on-site oxygen plant is avoided.

A different application of pyrolysis is also being developed by Carborundum and is another example of how different processes and concepts may be integrated into new subsystems. In this instance, the pyrolysis plant is used both to produce low-Btu gas and to prepare high quality, refuse-derived solid fuel. The rationale for this is as follows: the residence time of fuel in the combustion chamber of a modern coal-fired boiler is approximately 6 to 9 seconds. Only small particles of fuel can be completely oxidized in such a short time. If, using normal materials-separation processes, an attempt is made to maximize the amount of organic material recovered as fuel, a significant fraction of the fuel may end up completely or partially unburnt in the ash pond. Much of this wasted fuel is from the heavier organic fractions, which will typically be found in the heavy fraction after air classification (see Table 6–1 and Figure 6–7). It is possible to pyrolyze this heavy fraction after removing whatever inorganic materials can be removed economically. The pyrolysis process itself can be adjusted to yield varying quantities of gas, carbonaceous particulates, (or char) or tars. Carborundum, for example, estimates that its process can be adjusted to yield 50 percent carbonaceous particulates or tars. These may be added to the processed light fraction from the air classification step (Figure 6–7). Waste heat and gas from the pyrolysis unit are used to dry the material. The resulting refuse-derived solid fuel has a higher energy content per unit weight and volume, and it can be stored indefinitely. Oxidation of the fuel in the combustion chamber is far more complete. It is estimated that 70 percent net of the higher heating value of refuse can be applied as boiler heat using this technology (S. Natof, personal communication).

Other concepts are possible and may prove to be more economical. Some pyrolysis units are being designed, for example, to produce steam as a final product. The point here is the potential versatility of pyrolysis development. Problems, of course, remain—some of which were detailed above.

One more frequently mentioned difficulty merits attention here. This is the apparent need for the very close proximity of the pyrolysis plant to the consumer. Figures of one-half mile to two miles are considered maximal. This may pose a considerable constraint on the marketing of the gas, placing limitations on the number of consumers—a situation to be avoided if possible. The author has not had an opportunity to investigate this limitation adequately, and it is not immediately obvious why it should be economic to pipe natural gas at 1,000 Btu/scf for 2,000 miles, while it is uneconomic to pipe gas at one-third to one-sixth of this energy density more than 2 miles. Many technical factors are involved, but at least one nontechnical factor seems important. Present refuse-derived fuel contracts do not exceed 10 years. Industry decision-makers have concluded that these pipelines must be depreciated within that period. Natural gas pipelines are depreciated over a longer time span. The extent of the impact of this policy—and its rationale—warrant study.

Producing Steam for Space Heating and Cooling

Using refuse in water-wall incinerators to produce steam for district heating and cooling and industrial manufacturing is technically the best developed method for recovering the energy value in solid waste. Marketing the steam may be difficult, however, because it is not storable and can only be transported over short distances.

This form of energy recovery has not been strongly encouraged in this country because of the anticipated difficulties with marketing. However, the apparent success of the Nashville (Tennessee) Thermal Transfer Corporation (which provides district heating and cooling) may change this assessment. The plant is to be operational in the very near future. District heating and cooling fueled entirely by refuse (except during emergencies) will be provided by steam and chilled water and will result in very substantial savings to customers. At the same time, revenues from these sales will pay for *all* capital and operating costs (including distribution costs) and the city will be able to dump its waste at the plant at no charge (or a very small charge). The city must, however, dispose of the relatively small quantities of ash from the incinerator.

No other energy recovery process being considered at this time for urban refuse is claimed by its sponsors to cover all costs at today's product prices. The experience in Nashville will therefore be watched very closely by other municipalities. One drawback for other cities may be high land costs in areas where such plants must be situated, in order to have the required access to high density markets. Unique circumstances in Nashville permitted plant siting on relatively inexpensive ground.

It would appear that the decisive factor in the apparent success of the Nashville scheme was the integration of district heating and cooling. The chilled water for cooling can be sold competitively at a much higher price per million Btu than steam for heating, with a relatively smaller increase in costs. Production of chilled water also insures use of the plant over the year and therefore increases the load factor.

Anaerobic Methane Fermentation

In contrast to the other energy recovery technologies discussed here, the anaerobic methane fermentation is a biological process. As such it has a number of characteristics that distinguish it from all the other energy recovery technologies discussed above.

1. There is no necessity for a combustion process to produce the energy product (methane).

2. The conversion takes place in an aqueous environment. There is therefore no penalty associated with the use of wet organic materials unless they are in dilute suspension (less than 5 percent suspended solids).

3. There is a greater sensitivity to rather small changes in the composition (reflected in greater variations in the yield and rate of reaction) of the input material. Plastics are not digestible, and the digestion of wood is very much slower, for example, than that of manure, paper, or leafy plant matter. Certain organic compounds and inorganic ions are also toxic to the micro-organisms in relatively small quantities.[34]

4. The retention time in the reactor is very much longer, being measured in days rather than in minutes or seconds. The reactor (digester) must therefore be very much larger to process a given amount of material. This consideration, at least, partly offsets the advantages gained in simplicity of reactor construction resulting from (1) above.

5. A significant amount of organic residuum remains at the end of the process. This is considered by many to be one of the primary handicaps facing this process. At least in some cases, however, the possibility of using the residuum as fertilizer or animal feed may make it valuable enough to compensate for the additional cost of handling it. This aspect will be discussed at some length later in the report.

Although methane fermentation has been a basic primary sewage treatment process in many parts of the world throughout this century, its serious development for energy production in this country was largely neglected until recently.* This research and development work has just entered the pilot plant stage, but it is being done in many places.**

There is now no consensus on optimal digester design or growth conditions for the micro-organisms; but despite the complexities, there has been enormous progress in recent years.

Development efforts have been most successful in increasing the loading rate of digesters (pounds of feedstock introduced into the digester per cubic foot of digester volume) and in decreasing the capital costs per unit volume of digester capacity. Both of these developments will result in lower

---

*I refer here to what may be termed "second-generation" methane digestion. Earlier simpler digesters have been used for producing methane in rural areas for many years.

**Among the most prominent are: The University of Illinois;[35] University of California;[36,37] University of Pennsylvania;[38] United Aircraft, Inc;[39,40] Institute of Gas Technology;[41,42] and Dynatech Corporation.[43] Much of this recent work is summarized in the proceedings of the *Bioconversion Energy Research Conference.*[44] Most work is being done with urban refuse and animal manure. Independent private investigators such as L. John Fry[45] and Biogas of Colorado, Inc. (located in Denver) also appear to be making serious contributions.

energy conversion costs, and judging from data used later in this report (without considering the removal of the residuum), anaerobic methane fermentation appears to be one of the cheapest available processes for converting organic material to usable fuel. Evidence also suggests that beyond a certain rather modest scale, the digestion process is rather insensitive to scale.[46,47] Most energy recovery processes appear to require rather large-scale plants (generally well above 500 tons/day) before the scale cost curve begins to flatten out.

Later in this report, a model of an energy recovery system will be presented which is based on different agricultural wastes and uses anaerobic methane fermentation as a conversion process. A major disadvantage of the process as defined in the model is the relatively low net energy conversion efficiency* (Table 6–2). No adequately documented process models available to the author exceed 42 percent efficiency when account was taken of heating and power requirements. Gross energy conversion efficiency (1), using materials high in cellulose, did not much exceed 50 percent with these systems. However, the theoretical gross conversion efficiency* is approximately 80 percent. Developments in technique show promise of considerably increasing the efficiency of the digestion. One possibility is two-phase digestion which has been shown to increase the yield (and hence efficiency of conversion) by 40 percent for some materials.[48,49] Another is to decrease process losses for heating by using solar heating instead of gas. Finally, the systems which have been available for analysis by the author are not those with the highest net conversion efficiencies. This is in part because these systems have used urban refuse as a feedstock, which does not appear to be an optimal substrate for the fermentation point. This will be discussed in more detail later.

Although admirably suited for the conversion of such materials as animal manure or crop residues,* there is some question as to whether the process will be sufficiently reliable when it uses heterogeneous urban refuse. In particular, the rising proportion and importance of plastics (see Figures 6–3 and 6–4) should be considered. A pilot plant will be begun later this year by the National Science Foundation to test the concept as applied to urban refuse. If this plant demonstrates strong advantages, it may be worthwhile to think seriously about planning the contents and limiting the introduction of certain materials into "standard urban refuse." Some such thought is probably warranted in any case due to the increase in such hazardous materials as radiological wastes from hospitals and laboratories. The unlimited heterogeneity of contemporary urban refuse causes many engineering and perhaps safety problems for other types of resource recovery processes as well (S. Natof, personal communication).

A very different concept based on anaerobic methane fermentation

*Bio-Gas of Colorado, Inc., is building a plant for Montfort of Colorado's Gilcrest feedlot in Greeley, Colorado, which has 100,000 head of beef cattle. This is the largest feedlot in the country, according to the *High Country News* of May 10, 1974.

has been under development since 1972 by the Department of Water and Power and the Department of Public Works of the City of Los Angeles. In this concept, methane is recovered from wells under covered landfills.[50,51] Methane gas is generated during the course of the anaerobic fermentation, which occurs spontaneously in all sanitary landfills.

The gas may either be used directly for electricity generation or be cleaned for distribution together with natural gas. The first approach is currently being tested in a four-month demonstration project, and the second on a semi-commercial basis under a development contract with NRG Technology, Inc., of Newport Beach, California.

The major engineering problem in this concept is the design of a system of wells in the landfill area that will yield a reliable continuous supply of gas of acceptable quality over a 10- to 15-year period. Work to date has resulted in wells yielding a stable output of gas at approximately 525 Btu per scf. Whether output can be reliably maintained over a 10- to 15-year period will be difficult to predict until experience indicates the yield of gas from a landfill of a given size and type. It is estimated at present[52] that one ton of household refuse in the landfill will produce 17,000 scf of gas at 525 Btu per scf. It is also estimated that the half-life of gas production is approximately 50 years. One landfill being investigated at present contains 6 million tons of material (as disposed) and is expected to yield 600 million scf of medium Btu gas per year over a 10- to 15-year period. However, until there is extended experience, such estimates will remain tentative.

Long-term uncertainty about yields should not deter initial development of methane recovery from the larger landfills, however, if current development efforts meet with success (defined as reliable gas production over a one- to three-year period). The low cost of the gas produced is an immediate benefit. It is estimated that a methane recovery system yielding 1 billion scf per year of unprocessed gas at 500 Btu per scf would involve an initial total investment of $300,000. with 11 percent interest and a 10-year amortization, annual capital costs are only 12.6¢ per million Btu. Other operating costs in the landfill methane recovery system are low and should add less than 2¢ per million Btu.

Assuming that the unprocessed gas can be sold at 40¢ per million Btu* (well-head price), the entire investment could be returned in about two years. It is likely that as the concept develops and reliability is established (probably at little extra cost), a higher well-head price can be charged.

This concept promises to be one of the most successful energy recovery processes. Most urban communities cannot continue to use landfills, and must seek energy recovery technologies that substantially reduce the volume of refuse; but application of this concept should allow communities such as Los

---

*This was the average regulated well-head price for natural gas in early 1974.

Angeles (that will, in any case, continue through the foreseeable future to use landfill) to carry out related energy recovery programs.

It is also possible that substantial quantities of gas can be recovered in the coming years from old landfills throughout the country, though to what extent this will be possible is still difficult to estimate. Implementation could be very rapid.

Evaluation of Processes

A definitive evaluation would still, of course, be premature. Cost estimates vary substantially and efficiency data are still uncertain. Any scale-cost estimates for particular processes can only be approximate. The author has been able to assemble only limited cost data, shown in Table 6–2. The large range seen in the table in bids for a single supplementary solid fuel plant emphasizes the difficulties in comparing different concepts. The quality of these data should improve substantially in the next few months as more projects get underway.

Another complication is the variation in prices for the products of the different processes. The price per million Btu is not the same for steam, pyrolytic oil, supplementary solid fuel, and low-Btu gas. Furthermore, some processes as costed yield iron, paper, and a stream potentially yielding aluminum and glass, while others (notably high-temperature incineration and the Union Carbide pyrolysis), as costed at present, do not. The prices of the products have also changed dramatically in recent months.

It is not the purpose of this study to analyze and recommend a particular process for, say, urban refuse, but to discuss more broadly the feasibility and potential of energy recovery from organic wastes. Hence discussion will be brief. Several points however, have emerged.

First, with existing technology, front-end materials separation substantially reduces the net efficiency of the energy-conversion processes.* This is in part due to the energy consumption of the separation process, but it is largely a result of inefficiencies in the separation of organics from inorganics with present technologies (Table 6–1). The overall effect is clearly illustrated for different preparation concepts for supplementary solid fuel. The earliest concept, with ferrous recovery only, seemed to be highly efficient. However, large quantities of inorganics were left in the solid fuel; these proved to cause many problems in the operation of the boilers. Furthermore, the high efficiency may have been apparent rather than actual, since a significant fraction of the low quality refuse-derived fuel was not in fact burned during its residence in the boilers. Adding a materials-separation step that removed most of the inorganics—in addition to iron—considerably enhanced the value of the solid fuel product, but resulted in substantial penalties in both cost and net energy-conversion efficiency. Obviously, improvement in the efficiency of removal of

---

*We ignore here the compensating energy-conservation value of the recovered inorganic materials. This will vary according to the composition of the refuse.

organic matter from inorganic matter could affect the relative overall efficiencies and, therefore, the net operating costs of different processes.

Second, there appears to be little basis for choice between the supplementary solid fuel concept and the various gas pyrolysis technologies in terms of capital cost, operating cost, and efficiency. It is estimated that at present, most 1,000-ton-per-day processing plants have a total capital cost of about $12,000 for each ton per day capacity, and operating and maintenance costs of about $4.20 to 6.10 per ton (excluding capital charges). Materials handling modifications to the boilers will require an additional $1.6 million to $3 million capital costs for the fossil-fuel preparation plant, while pyrolysis plants will require pipeline installations (S. Natof, personal communication).

Total net processing costs will be sensitive to interest rates, payments in lieu of taxation, and the value of the products. The major economic variable is the value of the fuel, which is likely to be very site-specific. Other factors, such as interest rates and average scrap prices, are likely to vary less than energy prices. The impact of changing energy prices can be great. With certain assumptions* the total net processing cost for either pyrolysis or supplementary solid fuel systems might vary from about $3.00 per ton, if energy is sold at $1.20 per million Btu to about $9.00 per ton if the energy is sold at $0.60 per million Btu. Utilities throughout the country are paying widely different prices for fuel, often in excess of $1.20 per million Btu.

The economics of these two major concepts for energy recovery will be largely dependent on specific marketing situations. At present it seems that energy in the form of refuse-derived fuel is being sold at the bottom of this range with accompanying higher net operating costs. This is apparently due in part to institutional resistance, which decrees that this low-sulfur fuel be sold at bargain prices. Institutional resistance may decline, however, as the technology matures, and as the reliability of refuse-derived fuel supply (in many ways more important than price to large consumers) is demonstrated. Given the possibility of greater public involvement in electric utilities in the future, there may be less resistance from some utilities to innovations that seem to be in the public interest.

Third, where suitable markets exist, production of steam and cooling water from refuse-fired boilers appears to be very economical. Although such markets may be limited, a thorough evaluation is needed of the potential and trade-offs in district heating and cooling with solid waste-derived energy and heat recovery from power plants (particularly smaller plants).

Fourth, methane fermentation appears promising as a low-cost

---

*Assumptions: 1. Processing plant investment cost at $12,000 per day capacity. Interest, depreciation, payment in lieu of taxes, and insurance at 18 percent of investment per year. Operating and maintenance costs at $6.10 per ton. 2. Transport costs at $1.00 per ton. 3. Boiler modifications, investment cost of $2,400,000. Capital charges as above at 18 percent of investment. Operating and maintenance costs at 4 percent of investment. 4. Ferrous scrap recovery, 8.5 percent ferrous content in waste with scrap value of $35 per ton before shipment. 5. Plant operation 300 days per year.

energy-recovery technology, producing a fuel that is more marketable than either supplementary solid fuel or pyrolytic gases and oils. Its efficiency, however, according to most reports, is rather low at present. Later in the report a model energy recovery system for agricultural wastes based on methane fermentation will be discussed in some detail.

Fifth, processes which use waste as the sole or major fuel for electricity generation have many advantages over supplementary fuel processes from a marketing and institutional point of view, if technical problems and high costs can be overcome. There is a limited market for supplementary solid fuel and pyrolytic products. Potential large consumers of these fuels are often reluctant to commit themselves, less out of technological considerations than out of fear that they may become locked into a public waste management system. They are wary that they will lose the flexibility to change to other kinds of fuel systems which might prove more economical or attractive in the future. Plants that consume fuels from wastes might become indispensable links in the waste disposal system.

For example, a utility that plans to rely on nuclear power for base-load generation in the 1990s will not be enthusiastic about contracting for supplementary solid fuel, use of which implies a long-term commitment to fossil-fuel fired plants with ash-handling capabilities for base load electricity generation. If a utility attempted to close down a fossil-fuel plant which was an essential part of the local waste management system there could be a substantial conflict between the city's interest in disposing of its waste and the power plant's interest in shifting to a different system.

An important consideration throughout this discussion is the relationship between scale and cost. Although absolute costs cannot yet be assigned, there is some consensus on relative scale cost relationships of plants. At present, there appear to be sharply increasing unit capital and operating costs at a scale below 750-1,000 tons per day capacity[53] for pyrolysis, supplementary solid fuel, and incineration with energy recovery. Of the small-scale energy-recovery processes, anaerobic fermentation to produce methane seems to be the least expensive; and, if not associated with materials separation from urban refuse, it is the least sensitive to economies of scale. If tied with materials separation from urban refuse, then there may be a substantial advantage in larger plants.

RESOURCE RECOVERY SYSTEMS CONCEPTS

As noted earlier, resource recovery must be integrated into whole systems rather than operated as isolated processes. Resource recovery systems include the following operations: (a) transport of wastes to the recovery systems; (b) one or more resource recovery processes; and (c) product distribution.

The nature of resource recovery systems and the extent of their development will be largely dependent on: the minimum "wasteshed" area necessary to provide the smallest economically feasible processing plant; whether the waste resources are concentrated or diffuse; institutional constraints; the type of waste; and the relative cost of waste management without resource recovery processing.

For any particular source of organic wastes to become available as a practical resource, it is necessary that a resource recovery system be developed which can function within the constraints set by the particular waste source. In this section we will consider simple models of resource recovery systems based on three organic waste sources: urban refuse, animal manure, and agricultural crop residues.

Urban Refuse

Development of resource recovery processes and their integration into systems has been particularly rapid for urban refuse. The impetus for this development has arisen from increasing disposal costs in many parts of the country (caused in part by increased environmental awareness) and the growing value of the recoverable products.

Urban refuse has traditionally been disposed of by incineration and dumping. Increasingly strict air pollution emissions standards have escalated incineration costs per ton of refuse to the point where they equal or exceed the costs of most resource recovery processes—even before credit is taken for sale of recovered products.[54]

Concern over water pollution and disease vectors has fostered a preference for sanitary landfill over the traditional dump, but land scarcity is becoming a critical problem. Whereas the dump was simply the cheapest and most convenient land available, the site selected for sanitary landfill must satisfy certain geologic, hydrologic, and engineering requirements. Suitable land may be neither cheap nor readily available.[55] Land acquisition problems are particularly acute in the more heavily populated parts of the country. The Department of Environmental Protection of the State of Connecticut found that the average life expectancy of landfills was only 5.4 years in 1973. The options are increasingly remote sites, giving rise to jurisdictional problems and increasing costs, installation of high-cost incinerators, or volume reduction by resource recovery. The need for volume reduction of refuse to avoid the high net costs of incineration has thus been a primary motive for the interest of communities in the relatively novel technologies associated with resource recovery. Both energy and materials recovery processes will probably spread quite rapidly in the coming years. As noted earlier, communities with a total projected population of 78 million are potential candidates by 1980 for implementation of one process (solid fuel supplementation for coal-fired electric utility boilers).

In recognition of this potentially rapid growth, communities and states have begun to plan resource recovery systems. An example of such a system is the solid waste management plan for Connecticut.[56] This plan includes a model, the "baseline system design," for Connecticut to follow in building new facilities and phasing out old ones. Though this model will certainly be modified with time, it provides a starting point for a more precise discussion of resource recovery systems based on urban refuse.

Before discussing the model, it should be noted that the proposed plan for solid waste management has been approved by the state legislature, and a Resource Recovery Authority to organize and finance actual construction and operation has been established. Bids for a supplementary solid fuel plant in the Bridgeport SMSA have been taken, and a contractor is being named. It is anticipated that this plant will be on line in mid-1976, thereby keeping to the schedule outlined in the plan. Implementation depends on the voluntary participation of local communities both large and small, but so far no community reluctance or noncooperation has been apparent. It is, in fact, possible that orderly development cannot proceed fast enough to satisfy these communities.

In the study made for this plan, three major technical conclusions were reached:

1. Sufficient technical processes exist now (or will soon exist) to allow disposition of Connecticut's solid waste on a statewide basis.

2. Conversion of the combustible segment of the state's waste into a supplementary solid fuel for use by electric utility companies is the best short-term concept.

3. Oil or gas pyrolysis is the best long-term approach.

The first conclusion is prerequisite to initiating any statewide resource recovery program at all. The next two conclusions are the basis for the proposed schedule of resource recovery plants, shown in Table 6–3.

Table 6-3. Schedule of Resource Recovery Plants

Location	Earliest Date on Line	Type of Plant	1985 Tonnage (Tons/Day)
Greater Bridgeport	Mid-1976	Dry fuel	1,814
New Haven area	1977	Gas pyrolysis	1,694
Hartford area	1978	Oil pyrolysis	2,185
New Britain	Mid-1979 to 1980	Dry fuel or gas pyrolysis	1,915
Southwestern	1980	Gas pyrolysis or dry fuel	1,821
Montville	1981	Pyrolysis	1,325
Waterbury	1981	Pyrolysis	1,621
Valley	1982	Dry fuel or pyrolysis	785
Danbury	1983	Pyrolysis	953
East Windsor	1984	Pyrolysis	1,806

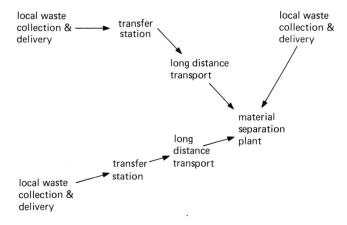

Figure 6-9. The Wasteshed

  The major innovation resulting from the study and incorporated in the model is the wasteshed concept in which waste from a number of towns is collected, deposited at transfer stations and taken by longer distance transport to resource recovery plants. The concept is illustrated in Figures 6–9 and 6–10. This wasteshed concept allows smaller communities together to use current resource recovery technology that would otherwise be uneconomical. Transport costs average $2.15 (in 1973 dollars) per ton in the model, including the cost of hauling refuse from the transfer station to the plant, hauling residue from the plant to the disposal site, and hauling fuel to market. Despite its simplicity, this concept has not yet been applied to organic waste management in this country. All current estimates of "available" waste are limited to SMSA's of over 100,000; should the wasteshed concept prove successful, much larger quantities would be available for energy recovery.

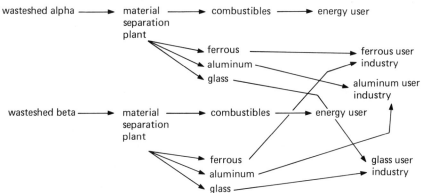

Figure 6-10. A Wasteshed System

The Connecticut plan anticipates that by 1985 the system will be processing 84 percent of the state's waste, from 133 of the 169 towns. The remaining 36 towns are lightly populated and are scheduled to join the system during the period from 1985 to 1993 using existing resource recovery plants. Thus, by 1993 the entire state should be participating.

A further development of the waste shed concept is the wasteshed—material shed—energyshed concept illustrated in Figure 6—11. The basis for this concept is that the cost of a plant for further separating and recovering the different materials in the inorganic fraction of the refuse is very sensitive to scale, while transporting these materials is relatively inexpensive. After separating the heavy inorganics from the organic combustible material, it is cheaper, presumably, to ship all of the inorganic material to a central inorganic materials-separation and recovery plant.

A remarkable result of the model is that the cumulative capital requirements for the resource recovery system are in fact less than the cumulative capital requirements of the conventional waste disposal facilities that were planned prior to the development of the statewide plan. (This point is highlighted in Figures 6—12 and 6—13.)

The estimated cost per ton of refuse as calculated in the study, including revenue credits and payment in lieu of taxes, is $14.47 per ton. Recent price changes for the products of the resource recovery process (including energy price changes since mid-1973) will decrease the net total cost. It is interesting to note that total net cost of a system based entirely on supplementary solid fuel, as costed in the study, would be $8.30 per ton. On this ground alone one may query the priminence given in the Connecticut plan to pyrolysis.* The response offered is that coal-fired stations will be phased out for base-load electricity generation as nuclear power is developed. Gas- and oil-fired plants will be used for peak demand periods, and a storable, transportable fuel is required for flexible marketing.

At present, however, it is not at all certain that coal-fired stations will be phased out for base-load generation. It is likely that the supplementary solid fuel concept can be applied to ash-handling oil-fired boilers as well. Pyrolysis gas is less storable than solid waste, and the difficulties of handling pyrolytic oil reduce its flexibility as a fuel source.

Finally, developments in processing refuse-derived solid fuel have resulted in a cleaner fuel with a lower moisture content and a higher energy density per unit (volume or weight) improving its storability, transportability, and general handling characteristics. These advantages of solid fuel ought to be considered in the development of a large-scale integrated resource recovery plan.

---

*It should be noted that costs quoted here may well be too high and the spread between supplementary solid fuel and gas pryolysis too large, according to a study by S. Natof (personal communication). However, since we are contesting the internal logic of the plan, we felt it appropriate to employ the figures used in it.

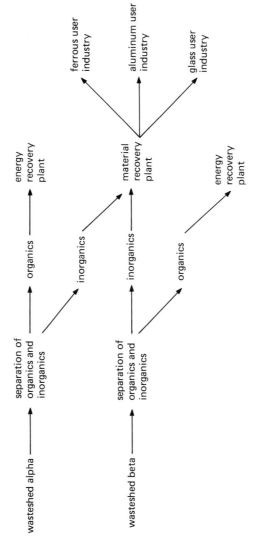

Figure 6–11. A Wasteshed–Material Shed–Energy Shed System

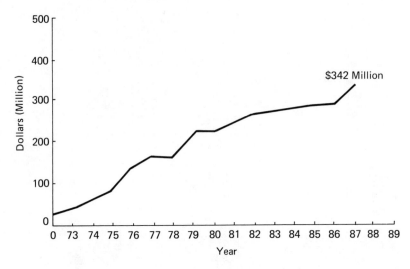

Figure 6-12. Cumulative Capital Requirements for Conventional Solid Waste Management System in Connecticut to 1987[a]

[a]From: *Summary—A Proposed Plan of Solid Waste Management for Connecticut*, General Electric Company; and the Department of Environmental Protection, State of Connecticut.

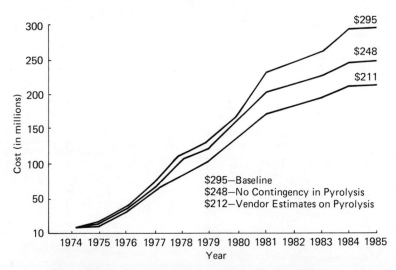

Figure 6-13. Estimates of Cumulative Capital Cost Requirements for Connecticut Resource Recovery System to 1985[a] (In Millions of Dollars, 1973)

[a]From: *Summary—A Proposed Plan of Solid Waste Management For Connecticut*, General Electric Company; and the Department of Environmental Protection, State of Connecticut.

Crop Residues

As shown earlier, crop residues represent the single largest potential source of organic waste material. This potential resource has a number of characteristics that distinguish it from urban refuse, and thus a system designed to exploit it will differ substantially from systems designed for resource recovery from urban refuse.

Crop residues are relatively diffuse, and from our point of view, relatively homogeneous compared to urban refuse. They are not a waste problem, except when they are present in large quantities or when they harbor crop pathogens—and even then the problem is marginal—so there can be little credit for removing them from the fields. This last characteristic is in strong contrast to urban refuse, the removal of which can earn the resource recovery system a very substantial credit. It may indeed be argued that if there is permanent removal of the organic matter in these residues, the fertility of the soil will gradually be reduced. However, many farmers here and abroad have burned and still do burn large amounts of residues, such as wheat straw, in their fields.

These features indicate that a resource recovery system should: (a) be able to market the products at a profit without any credit for removal of the waste; (b) include a materials collection subsystem that is not expensive; (c) use resource recovery processes without high costs per unit output on a relatively small scale; (d) return inorganic matter to the areas from which crop residues were taken in order that the fertility of soils not be endangered; and (e) induce farmers to make their crop residues available for processing.

Materials separation, an expensive step preceding most energy recovery processes using urban refuse, is not necessary. Still, these are rigorous conditions. Any resource recovery system capable of satisfying them would be technically and economically close to successful development as a system for bioconversion of solar energy on a large scale in many parts of the world. Thus the ultimate significance of a successful resource recovery system for crop residues could be enormous.

Is such a resource recovery system feasible? In seeking to answer this question, a baseline model system will be proposed and discussed. The model is intended as a preliminary quantification of a concept which has been discussed but apparently not yet costed.[57, 58] It is intended simply as a scenario and has not been optimized. In fact, it is likely that the baseline model is too conservative (that is, estimated costs are high).

The primary energy recovery process in this model will be anaerobic methane fermentation, for these reasons: (a) it allows organic matter to be recycled to the soil (assuming that this is necessary); (b) it appears to be the energy recovery process which is least cost sensitive to scale and is relatively inexpensive (particularly if the energy conversion step alone is considered); and (c) it yields a relatively valuable product which is easily marketable.

For the purpose of discussion, the model is set in a major

agricultural region of the country, represented by the Federal Power Commission Regions numbers 4, 5, and 6 (see Figure 6–14). It will assume as a simplification that corn stover (mature cured stalks of corn from which the ears have been removed) is the only field crop residue collected.

The system may be briefly described as follows. Corn stover is collected from the fields by the farmer with a conventional silage chopper. The chopped material is then taken by wagon to a convenient transfer point (assumed to be two miles from the field) and left. The material is purchased and carried by truck to be unloaded and stored at the energy recovery plant. A secondary shredder further reduces the size of the chopped bits of organic material. After some storage and slurrying with water, the material is introduced into the methane digester. After a detention time of 10 days the digested sludge residuum is removed and dewatered to a 60 percent moisture content. A small portion of this residuum is fed to ruminants (and possibly nonruminants) under feedlot conditions. The residuum has substantial value as a feed. In return for a high protein feed at no cost, the feedlot provides animal manure at no cost, which is digested in either the same or a separate digester as the corn stover. The digested sludge residuum which is not fed to animals is made available to farmers in the area for fertilizer, at a price which offsets hauling and spreading costs. Application of the fertilizer would be carried out by a private specialist contractor.

A detailed flow diagram showing inputs and outputs and the costs and credits of each step is shown in Figure 6–15. The cost and energy assumptions upon which this flow chart is based are systematically laid out in Appendix B which should be studied by the reader who is entertaining technical questions. Examination of this flow chart will, however, raise a number of important questions which will be discussed briefly here.

Prominent among these questions are: first, what is the basis for assuming that methane can be sold at the indicated price in the future? Second, what is the basis for the scales of organic matter inputs indicated? Third, what basis is there for assuming the indicated feed value? Fourth, how can it cost so little to use digested sludge residuum as fertilizer? Fifth, what is the basis for the cost and efficiency parameters used for the important digestion step?

The energy and economic costs of residue collection are obviously also of great importance, and have been detailed in Appendix B.

The Price of Methane

In assessing any concept's potential, a realistic value must be assigned to its products. Little thought appears to have been given to this point in most published studies on methane fermentation. In the recent Bioconversion Energy Research Conference,[59] a value of $0.75 per million Btu was used for methane, for example, apparently without any analysis.

In an effort to arrive at a meaningful value for methane in a state

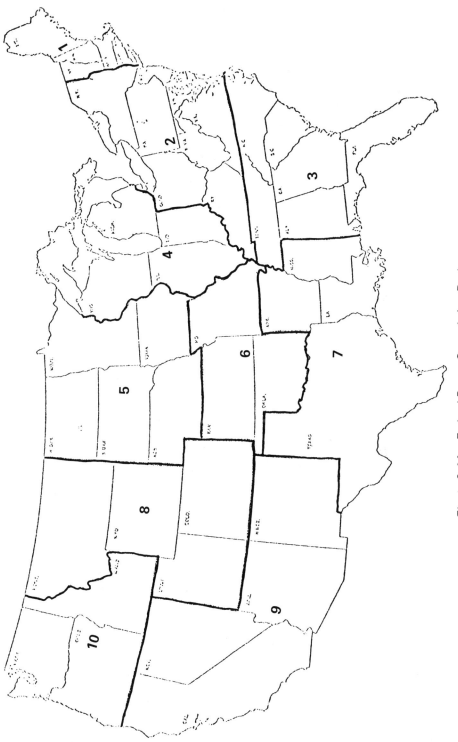

Figure 6–14. Federal Power Commission Regions

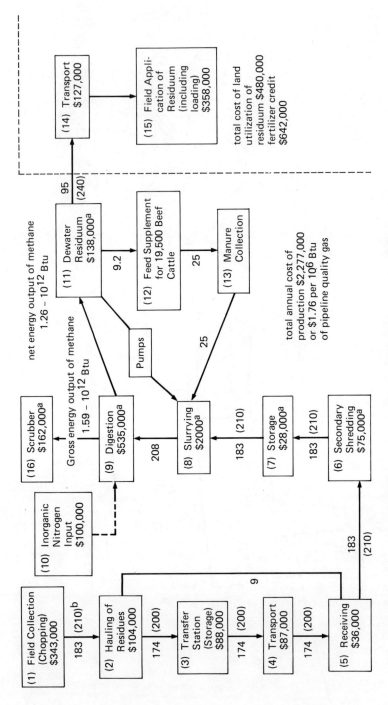

Figure 6-15. Flow Diagram of Baseline Model of a 570-Ton-Per-Day System

^{a}Cost does not include labor.
$^b\frac{183}{(210)}$ Dry organic matter moved from one step to next annually
in thousands of tons, number in parenthesis is wet weight.

Notes:
1. Net annual energy output of methane equals gross annual energy
output less the following annual energy inputs =

$200\text{-}10^9$ Btu (Digestion)
$\ 80\text{-}10^9$ Btu (Scrubbing)
$\ \ 3\text{-}10^9$ Btu (Dewatering)

Other energy inputs are given in Appendix B and are included in
costs.
2. operation
   annual cost
   of operation
3. The fertilizer credit for steps 13 and 14 is only for the value of
nutrients in the residuum which have been added to the crop residues
after their collection. The value of all the nutrients in the residuum is
very much higher. The reason for using the lower valve is discussed in
the text. The credit for fertilizer is ignored when calculating the cost
of gas production.
4. Additional Annual Expenses include:
   a. Labor for Steps 6, 7, 8, 9, 10, 15 as follows:

   2 men shredding @ $11,000/year = $22,000
   1 man continuous digester monitoring @ $5/hr = $44,000
   1 man continuous dewatering @ $5/hr = $44,000
   1 technician @ $13,000/year = $13,000
   1 supervisor @ $17,000/year = $17,000

                        Total: $140,000.

   b. Secretarial expenses $30,000. Technical expenses $10,000.
   c. Local taxes 2 percent and insurance 1 percent of fixed invest-
      ment.
   d. Pumps and piping $60,000 @ 15 percent = $9,000. Office—
      $100,000 @ 15 percent = $15,000.
   e. Maintenance at 2 percent of installed investment = $130,000.

Figure 6-15. [Notes & Explanations]

closely resembling contemporary natural gas—at the time when this model is
assumed to be implemented on a wide scale (1990–2000)—two approaches have
been used. First, the price index forecasts (adjusted to constant dollars) of the
National Gas Survey of the Federal Power Commission[60] for prices to industrial
consumers in 1990 have been used and applied to FPC Regions 4, 5, and 6
(Figure 6–14). Firm industrial prices in 1970 in Chicago, Minneapolis and St.
Louis[61] were taken as the basis for the price index forecasts. On this basis, prices
to industrial consumers in Chicago, Minneapolis, and St. Louis are anticipated to
be $1.56, $1.76, and $1.22 per million Btu respectively (constant dollars) in
1990.

The second approach is to consider the possible ceiling imposed by coal gasification technology. In a Resources for the Future, Inc., report to the Energy Policy Project,[62] it is estimated that synthetic natural gas (SNG) from Eastern bituminous coal will cost $2.05 to $2.15 per million Btu (early 1974 dollars) if the new processes develop as planned and coal is available at 40¢ to 60¢ per million Btu. Estimates of the cost of coal (in regions 4, 5, and 6 of Figure 6–14) for utilities indicate a cost of coal in the range from 50¢ to 70¢ (constant dollars) per million Btu (baseline Foster Associates, 1974; projection Federal Power Commission, 1973) by 1990; hence SNG costs are likely to be in the upper part of the range indicated. Western coal may produce SNG at a cost of $1.60 to $1.70 per 10^6 Btu, but additional gas transmission costs of 25¢ to 30¢ per million Btu would be required to supply the area in question.[37] There are also severe limitations imposed by water shortages on the potential size of an SNG industry based on Western Coal. Shipment of coal would increase the cost by between 35¢ and 50¢ per million Btu of gas produced. The SNG costs quoted here are somewhat higher than those normally used, since we have used estimates based on a 12 percent discount rate, as recommended for analysis purposes in the Resources for the Future study, rather than lower utility rates. This discount rate more closely resembles that used in industry in general and in the primary energy industry in particular. The costing in the model also assumes a 12 percent discount rate.

One may note also that there has been a succession of escalations of coal gasification estimates, and many sources doubt that present cost estimates are realistic.[63] Coal gasification to SNG standards presents formidable technological problems.

Although there is some uncertainty regarding reserves and the effects of federal pricing policy, there can be little doubt that the relatively limited quantities of domestic natural gas will continue to increase in cost. Contracts are presently being signed for liquified natural gas at $1.50 per million Btu. The going rate for unregulated intrastate gas in Louisiana and Texas is now $1.20 to $1.40 per million Btu for large utility and industrial users (according to *The Wall Street Journal*, May 8, 1974, p. 8, and *The New York Times*, September 28, 1974, p. 39). It is only a matter of time until alternative sources of gas become competitive. That time may come sooner than the above price projection discussion indicates, even if Arctic gas and oil are widely exploited. There are, however, severe environmental problems associated with offshore drilling in the Arctic[64] which may limit exploitation of the large oil and gas fields located there. As shown above, competition with coal gasification appears to be entirely feasible at this time on economic grounds alone.

Scale of Organic Matter Inputs
Because cost and energy input estimates are available for plants with a 550 to 600 ton (volatile solids a day) capacity, a plant of this size has been assumed in the model. In any case, there are indications that the cost of

digestion and dewatering is, unlike that associated with most energy recovery processes, fairly insensitive to scale.

It is, however, unlikely that 550-600 tons per day of crop residue organic matter (the rate of input used in the model) is the optimal scale. Development of plants of 150 tons per day or less might be preferable, if possible (though marketing problems might be more difficult). Within a radius of about four miles, it is possible for farmers to deliver the waste directly to the plant from the fields, thereby eliminating the rather expensive first transfer step. Given the relatively low net efficiency of the model at present, even slight reductions in the cost of the input material can result in substantial savings in the cost of the output gas.

Other advantages of smaller plants would be the lower cost of hauling sludge residuum to the fields and the smaller numbers of farmers involved in plant operation. Plants could perhaps take the form of gas co-ops. Administrative and technical costs and talent could be shared throughout a network of such plants in an agricultural region.

The relative scale of manure and crop residue inputs has also been chosen rather arbitrarily and is illustrative of possibilities; the system has not been optimized. The manure has been added as a cheap source of nitrogen and phosphate.

Crop residues by themselves contain inadequate nitrogen and phosphate for maximum rates of fermentation. For example, the optimum carbon to nitrogen ratio for fermentation is approximately 30:1, while the ratio of carbon to nitrogen in corn stover is approximately 50:1. While fermentation will proceed without supplemental nitrogen, the rate will be slower. It is possible that under certain conditions it would be cheaper not to add nitrogen and to accept slower fermentation rates; however, since the model assumes high fermentation rates, it also assumes, by necessity, the use of supplemental nitrogen. This nitrogen may come from either of two sources—inorganic nitrogen fertilizers or sources of organic nitrogen with a carbon-to-nitrogen ratio smaller than 30:1 (virtually all animal excreta fall in this category).

The cost of inorganic nitrogen is high. Using the model with a supplement of inorganic nitrogen, as a basis for calculation, the cost of gas would be $2.03 per million Btu.* This does not include phosphate inputs which would also be considerable.

On the other hand, adding manure is potentially a cheap way to acquire the required carbon to nitrogen ratio. If all the nutrients required in the model were supplied from cattle manure added to the crop residues (at no net cost), the cost of the gas in the model would be only $1.62 per million Btu.**

---

*Nitrogen inputs costed as in Appendix B, Item 10, including storage costs. Scrubber, dewatering, and digester costs in baseline model reduced to 88 percent due to elimination of manure inputs. Gas production reduced to 88 percent due to elimination of manure inputs.

**Digester, scruber and dewatering costs assumed to increase by 15 percent due to increased input of manure. Gas output increased 15 percent.

This large decrease is in part due to the increased gas production, resulting from the huge inputs of manure.* There is, however, a problem inherent in this requirement. To supply a plant of this size, about 56,000 tons (dry matter) would be required each year. This would require about 43,000 head of cattle in an area of 237 square miles, the area covered in the model. There are relatively few areas in the United States with this concentration of livestock.

For this reason, we have chosen to use both inorganic and organic supplemental nutrient sources in our model. The relative proportion of crop residue and manure inputs was set rather arbitrarily to reflect the national proportion of crop residues to feedlot manure (about 7.5:1). Since the higher the proportion of manure inputs the lower the unit gas production costs (using the assumptions in the model), it is likely that in the real world plants will start up in the vicinity of large feedlots, as in the midwest, and use manure inputs, largely or entirely.

As systems are optimized and experienced gained, and if local natural gas prices are favorable, increasing energy recovery from crop residues may be expected.

It must be assumed that any widespread system of this kind will require supplemental inorganic nitrogen and perhaps phosphate inputs. As the work of Pfeffer and Liebman[65] shows, this is technically feasible—indeed one set of experiments on which this model's digestion parameters are based used inorganic supplements for virtually all the nutrients. The cost disadvantages involved in using inorganic supplements have been noted; however, these may not be as severe as assumed, if it is possible to capture some of the value of the nutrients in the residuum. The value of the fertilizer credit will be discussed in detail later on. Here we may simply note that the residuum which is returned to the fields has a total nutrient content valued at *$1,690,000*. Of this, nutrients worth *$642,000* are returned which were not in the original crop residues and represent a net input. Transport and field application cost less than $500,000.

Feed Value

The model assumes high concentrations of cattle near the plant, providing a cheap source of nitrogen and phosphate. The digester may in turn prove to be a cheap source of cattle feed supplement, as assumed in the model

---

*To illustrate, let us consider the hypothetical case of a digester containing crop residues. The ratio of carbon to nitrogen is 50:1, so if there are 100 tons of carbon, there are 2 tons of nitrogen. This ratio must be reduced to 30:1. If we add 1.3 tons of inorganic nitrogen (in a form such as ammonia, which contains no carbon) we will have 100 tons of carbon and 3.3 tons of nitrogen, achieving the stipulated 30:1 ratio.

If we rely on cattle manure instead (which has a carbon to nitrogen ratio of about 15:1) to lower the ratio, we will be adding 2.7 tons of nitrogen and 40 tons of carbon. If we added only 1.3 tons of nitrogen, as in the case of ammonia, we would at the same time have added 19 tons of carbon, so that the carbon-to-nitrogen ratio would still be too high – about 36:1. Thus, more nitrogen must be added when manure is the nutrient source.

(Step 12). Although this concept is still unproven and its incorporation is not critical to the successful operation of intermediate and larger scale plants, it is included in order to suggest one way the system can function to recover resources other than energy from agricultural wastes. Moreover, the feed value component might indeed be critical to the development of small-scale plants.[66]

Hamilton Standard, working with the U.S. Department of Agriculture, has begun research on use of residuum from the anaerobic digestion of feedlot beef cattle manure as a high protein feed. This residuum has twice the crude protein content and three and a half times the amino acid content of manure. Preliminary nutritional experiments using the residuum as a protein supplement in chick diets indicate that when present at 7 to 14 percent of the dry weight of the diet, it may substitute for traditional protein supplements such as soybean.

The concept of using manure from animals as a feed supplement is not new and has been successfully applied for a number of years. Anthony,[67] for example, developed "wastelage," in which hay and manure are ensiled for a short time before feeding cattle. This material can at least partially replace feedgrain and traditional high protein supplements and has a crude protein level of 14 percent. Anthony has found this ensiled mixture to be superior to manure alone.

The concept can also be applied to animals other than ruminants. In fact, rations composed or 40 percent *steer manure* (from animals on high-concentration diets) have been fed to *laying hens* with no apparent differences in egg production compared with layers fed conventional diets.[68]

The residuum from digestion of manure of cattle fed high concentrate diets appears to be nutritionally superior to both manure and wastelage.

A major difficulty in the past with manure feed concepts, and a predictable one in the development of feeding residuum from the anaerobic digestion of manure, is the health problem. It is not yet known whether any of these products are safe for consumption by animals or that meat and byproducts from animals consuming these products are safe for human consumption. In the case of farm wastes, drug and pesticide residues and pathogenic organisms must all be shown to be absent before the material can be used as a feed, according to Food and Drug Administration regulations. Such proof does not yet exist. There is still some doubt regarding viruses, which are difficult to measure. Drugs and pesticides are in many cases degraded, though specific tests must be made in each case.

While this difficulty may inhibit the development of digester residuum from manure as feed, there is little reason it should limit the use of digester residuum from crop residues as feed any further than the associated feedgrains and foodgrains are limited in use.

The feed value of residuum from crop residues is estimated to be about the same, on a dry-weight basis, as that of alfalfa. Assuming that the crude protein content of corn stover is 6.4 percent, the crude protein level of the residuum should be approximately 12 to 13 percent. Comparison of the proximate composition corn stover with manure of cattle on a high concentrate diet shows that, with the exception of crude protein concentration, the two materials are similar. Digestion of the manure yields a residuum with the composition shown in Table 6–4.

The value of the digested residuum from crop residues may be estimated to be about $25 per ton dry matter in 1971 prices[69] (assuming that its value would resemble that of wastelage). The value of the residuum from digestion of cattle manure is estimated to be approximately $40 dry ton in 1971 prices and $44 in 1973 prices.[70] It is probable that the value of the digested residuum from crop residues with nitrogen added during fermentation would approximate that from manure. The addition of inorganic nitrogen to the fermentation would result in higher crude protein (and true protein) levels in the residuum, since the nitrogen is incorporated in the cell material. The value of the residuum is basically dependent on its protein and amino acid content, rather than on the digestible energy content, which is, in any case, mediocre.

Land Utilization of Digested Sludge Residuum

Disposal of digested sludge residuum is generally regarded as a key problem in the overall economics of the methane fermentation, and is at present regarded as an expensive process. A study by Dynatech Corporation for the National Science Foundation,[71] for example, attaches a penalty of $30 per ton of residuum (dry solids) from digested urban refuse. This penalty may be realistic for residuum from digested urban refuse, though this is debatable. It is almost certainly unrealistic when applied to digested agricultural residues; our model assumes no penalty cost for disposal. A detailed justification of this cost assessment will be made in this section, since assumptions regarding the net cost

Table 6–4. Proximate Analysis of Corn Stover, Manure from Beef Cattle Fed High Concentrate Diets, and Residuum from the Anaerobic Digestion of Such Manure

	Corn Stover	Manure Waste[a]	Residuum Product
Crude protein (%)	6.4	12.9	25.2
Fat (%)	33.1	1.0	1.3
Fiber (%)	34.2	33.1	22.8
NFE (%)	51.0	47.8	40.4
Ash (%)	6.8	5.2	10.3

[a]EPA figures (Denit, 1973)[17] for crude protein even in biodegraded manure of cattle fed concentrates are substantially higher. The ash content is also higher.

of residuum disposal can be critical to the overall economics of the system. It may be noted in advance that the firms involved in the construction of the Greeley, Colorado, plant anticipate a net credit for residuum disposal.

As discussed above, digested residuum can be used as a feed. The model assumes that the energy recovery plant is associated with one or more feedlots. In such cases, the feed portion of the residue can be disposed of at no cost to the plant, with net savings (after handling costs) for the feedlot.

However, only a portion (8 percent) of the digested residuum has been used as feed in the model, as discussed earlier. The cost of removing the remaining 92 percent will be decisive.

In the model, residual sludge is used as organic fertilizer, so discussion of the costs of removal will center on the economics of using sludge as a fertilizer-mulch.* This option is possible because methane fermentation conserves essentially all of the nutrients in the input.

Given, first, that farmers will accept the residuum, costs of loading, hauling, and spreading it, using techniques for handling animal manure would probably be lower for large installations than has been assumed. Certainly capital costs per ton of manure spread per day drop sharply as the scale increases beyond that normally encountered on farms. This is illustrated in Figure 6–16. A key example is a beef feedlot in Texas with 80,000 head.[72] A private contractor hauls and spreads the biodegraded manure from the feedlot onto surrounding farms at a rate of five tons per acre or more at a cost of $1.10 per ton plus 5¢ per ton-mile. Farmers apparently pay the contractor, but receive a subsidy of 50¢ per ton from the feedlot. It is interesting to note that the farmers using this manure report higher average silage yeilds (up to 27 tons/acre from 20 tons), though the earlier husbandry practice was not specified.

The figures in this example have been used as the basis for the costing in this model. Given approximately 240,000 tons per annum of wet residuum (95,000 tons dry organic matter) and an average haul of 8.0 miles, the total annual cost of hauling and spreading the manure is $389,000. If we assume a 25 percent inflation rate since early 1973 in these costs, total costs are $486,000.

Against this cost may be weighed the benefits of the residuum to the soil. The quantity of plant nutrients in the residuum is substantial. In order to be

---

*It is ecologically sound in that it recycles the nutrients and organic matter required for soil fertility; purely disposal-oriented technologies are at present expensive and have no potential for resource recovery credits; other use-oriented concepts are hardly beyond the pilot plant stage and would be difficult to quantify.[73] However, Pfeffer,[74] in a personal communication to the author, has suggested that the residuum be used as fuel. This is possible because the characteristics of the residuum allow it to dewater to a moisture content of 60 percent without further drying. The alternative of fuel use should be carefully considered and may be particularly applicable if the methane fermentation is applied to urban refuse, since toxic materials from refuse (or sewage) *may* limit use as an organic fertilizer.

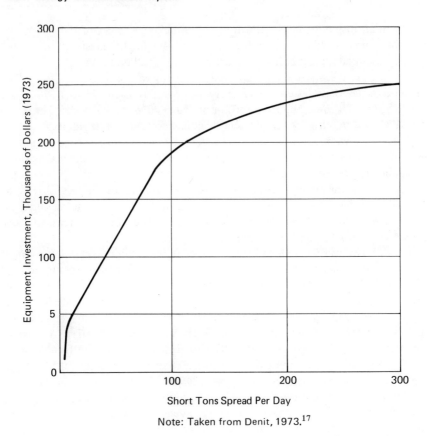

Short Tons Spread Per Day

Note: Taken from Denit, 1973.[17]

Figure 6-16.   Land Utilization Investment Cost-Solid Manure

as strict as possible, however, it was assumed that only those nutrients in the residuum which were *not* present in the crop residues would be used to calculate the fertilizer value of the residuum. Hence, only the value of net inputs of fertilizer nutrients to farms participating in the resource recovery system would be calculated. In the model, therefore, only the nutrients recovered from the feedlots and from the ammonia input to the digester (step 10 in Figure 6-15), are calculated. Quantities of nutrients per head are from Table 1 in Denit[75], and assume fresh manure. The total per annum is:

	from feedlot	from ammonia input to digester	total
nitrogen	935 tons	550 tons	1,485
phosphorus	240 tons	—	240
potassium	650 tons	—	650

Calculating the value of these nutrients is complicated by the fact that authorities differ in their estimates of the effective fertilizer equivalent, pound for pound, of nutrients in such related materials as manure or sewage sludge. One estimate[76] for animal manure is as follows:

Animal manure	*equivalent to*	*inorganic fertilizer*
1 lb nitrogen		0.5 lb nitrogen
1 lb phosphorous		0.67 lb phosphorus
1 lb potassium		0.75 lb potassium

Evidence is accumulating, however, that this conventional assessment (which has strongly influenced decisions on whether to use organic fertilizers) is inaccurate, particularly as regards the nitrogen equivalence. Several points should be made to substantiate such an assertion. First, as noted in the same publication,[77] organic nitrogen is released gradually into the nitrate form for plant uptake. Only half the nitrogen is released in the year of application, half of the remainder in the subsequent year and so forth.[78] Thus, though only 50 percent is recovered by the crop in the first year, most of the remainder is eventually released and will add to subsequent fertility if applications are continued. It is widely known that farms that begin using animal manure experience an initial drop in yields, but yields steadily increase thereafter when applications of manure are kept at the same level over a period of years.

A second point is that soil does not actually recover 100 percent of nitrogen in inorganic fertilizer, and therefore studies assuming that no leaching or runoff of inorganic nitrogen takes place are significantly misleading. Apparently about 33 percent of the applied inorganic nitrogen is lost in leaching and runoff[79] at present rates of fertilizer application. In fact, runoff of nitrogen (as well as phosphorus and potassium) from manure fertilized fields had been shown to be four to eight times *less* than from fields treated with inorganics.[80] It is likely that there is similarly less leaching. Furthermore, these results are for manure rather than anaerobic sludge. Anaerobic sludge (from anaerobically digested cattle manure) appears to reduce runoff losses of all nutrients essentially to zero (even on an 11 percent slope) and substantially enhance nutrient recovery by plants.[81] Clearly, anaerobic sludge could well prove superior to both manure and inorganic fertilizer.

Another often neglected factor, but one of critical importance, is the effect of organic fertilizers on the crude protein content of the harvested crop. It has been noted that as yields of important American crops have increased, the crude protein content has declined.[82] The crude protein content of corn appears to have dropped approximately 50 percent in 45 years. Evidence from practice in Iowa[83] suggests that organic fertilizers work to reverse this trend.

In the Iowa case, a farmer applying 15 tons of manure (assumed to contain about 240 pounds of nitrogen) per acre achieved an *average* yield of 145 bushels per acre at 12.3 percent crude protein in 1972. The county average was 112 bushels per acre at 5 to 8 percent crude protein with applications of 110 pounds of nitrogen. Taking account of the crude protein level (assuming 7 percent to be average for the county), the nitrogen effectiveness per pound of nitrogen applied appears to be slightly higher with organic fertilizer. This is particularly remarkable when it is noted that the application rate of nitrogen in the manure was more than twice as high as that of the inorganic fertilizer; application rates of inorganic fertilizers at that level—that is, 200 pounds or more per acre—dramatically reduce the effectiveness of the nitrogen on a pound-for-pound basis.[84]

The greater nitrogen effectiveness of organic fertilizers seems to be further corroborated in a study by Tietjen and Hart.[85] Their research was carried out on compost from municipal refuse. Since this compost has a very low fertilizer value (in terms of nitrogen, phosphorus, and potassium), almost all the fertilizer application was in an inorganic form. The experiment was carried out over a nine-year period. A three-year rotation of potatoes-rye-oats was used. Compost was applied at a rate of 44.5 tons per acre at the beginning of the first three-year rotation and at 40 tons per acre at the beginning of the second and third rotations. Supplemental chemical fertilizers were used, and a control with an equivalent total amount of inorganic fertilizer was established. Average total yields with ripe compost were 11.1 percent higher. Interestingly, they also noted increased nutrient content in each of the harvested crops; however, precise quantification is not possible since the wording in the paper is rather ambiguous:

> Potatoes grown on composted plots averaged 6 percent more nitrogen, phosphorus, and potassium per pound of crop harvested than did those grown on uncomposted but equivalently fertilized plots. Compost-grown rye averaged a 4 percent higher nutrient content, and compost-grown oats averaged a 9 percent higher nutrient content. These increases are considered significant in the nutrient content of the harvested crops . . . .

It must be emphasized, however, that this compost has qualities very different from those of either manure or anaerobic residuum; most notably, this fertilizer was a mixture of low nutrient organic matter and inorganic fertilizer nutrients. What does emerge clearly is that a fertilizer that contains organic matter seems to have definite benefits, both for crop yield and crop quality. Little useful experimental work has been done on this subject, but the implications are critical and warrant high priority attention in light of the worldwide shortage of fertilizer foreseen for the coming decade. Extrapolations of the Iowa data (above) suggest that organic fertilization of the land growing the 158 million tons of corn produced in the United States in 1973 could (assuming no increase in yield) increase annual crude protein production by 7,900,000 tons; and if we assume a similar increase in yield (29 percent), crude protein production would increase by 10 million tons. These are tremendous figures, equal to an amount of protein equivalent to 40 percent and 50 percent, respectively, of the 1973 soybean crop, which covered 56.4 million acres (corn covered 61.8 million acres).

This point will not be pursued further here since the basic data are incomplete. This brief review does, however, suggest the magnitude of the phenomenon and indicate that addition of inorganic nitrogen to anaerobic methane digesters before field application should be seriously considered since it is unlikely that recycled nitrogen in manure and sewage would be adequate (see Table 6–5).

Finally, it has been noted[86] that in spite of the high levels of inorganic nitrogen application in the Corn Belt, soil nitrogen and organic material are declining at 0.5 percent a year (see Table 6–6). If this continues, the land will lose its fertility. The consequences would be of global significance, given the importance of this area in world trade of agricultural commodities.

A similar decline in fertility has been noted in England.[87] It appears that increasing inorganic nitrogen applications will not reverse this trend.[88] On the other hand, the level of soil nitrogen (and soil organic matter) increases when organic fertilizers are applied.[89] Though this effect is not shown in tables on the equivalance of organic to inorganic nitrogen in this study, it is nevertheless of crucial importance for national agricultural policy.

Given these doubts about the validity of the conventionally accepted nutrient equivalents in organic and inorganic form, an upward revision seems to be warranted. A rather conservative estimate, in light of the previous discussion,

Table 6–5. Total Nitrogen, Phosphorous, and Potassium in Major Waste Sources in the USA, ca. 1970

Source	N	Percent	P	Percent	K	Percent
Confined animals	2.4	(23)	0.5	(21)	1.2	(18)
Dispersed animals	3.7	(35)	1.0	(42)	2.4	(35)
Residues (major crops only)	2.8	(27)	0.3	(13)	2.9	(43)
Sewage solids	1.6	(15)	0.6	(25)	0.3	(4)
	10.5	100	2.4	101	6.8	100

Source: Unpublished calculations by the author, available on request.

Note: By comparison, agricultural consumption of these fertilizer nutrients in 1973 was: nitrogen 8,300,000 tons; phosphorus, 2,100,000 tons; potassium, 3,700,000 tons. Obviously most of the nutrients from dispersed animals and crop residues are already recycled in agriculture, as are an undetermined fraction of nutrients from confined animals. Thus, only a relatively small part of the total nutrients (perhaps 30 to 35 percent) may be considered wasted at present. This is nevertheless a substantial quantity.

Table 6-6.   Nitrogen Balance Sheet—Illinois: Corn/Soybean Acreage (16.7 Million Acres), 1969

Nitrogen Entering Soil *(Million Pounds of N)*		*Nitrogen Leaving Soil* *(Million Pounds of N)*	
Fertilizer[a]:	1,058	Corn Crop[c]:	855
N Fixation[b]:	424	Soybean Crop[d]:	707
		Denitrications[e]:	157
		Leaching[f]:	336
Total	1,482	Total	2,055

Deficit: 573 million lbs. N
     or 34 lbs./acre,
     or 0.57 percent of Soil N (6,000 lbs./acre)

Source: Commoner, 1972.[79]

[a]Computed as 90 percent of total fertilizer N used in Illinois (1,175 million pounds N).
[b]Computed as 60 percent of N in soybean crop.
[c]Computed from 0.9 lb. N/bu. of corn and total crop of 950 million bu.
[d]Computed from 3.2 lb. N/bu. of soybeans and total crop of 221 million bu.
[e]Estimated as 15 percent of applied fertilizer N.
[f]Estimated from nitrate carried by Sangamon River, and fertilizer N applied to the relevant watershed, as 32 percent of applied fertilizer N.

is the set of equivalents developed for sewage sludge residuum in England,[90] although this residuum has important differences from crop residue digested residuum.

organic material *(sewage sludge)*	*equivalent to*	*inorganic fertilizer*
1 lb nitrogen		0.85 lb nitrogen
1 lb phosphorus		0.7 lb phosphorus
1 lb potassium*		0.75 lb potassium

In the model, the fertilizer equivalent of the *incremental* nitrogen, phosphorus, and potassium returned to the soil in the residuum is therefore:

nitrogen   . . . . 1,260 tons
phosphorus . . . . 170 tons
potassium . . . . 470 tons

At current prices per ton of nutrients—$350 for nitrogen.** $789 for phosphorus, and $166 for potassium [see Table 6–7]—the value of the incremental fertilizer equivalent (we emphasize again that the gross 1,830 tons

*Relative potassium availability was not discussed in the report cited.
**Weighted average cost of nitrogen from major sources in Table 6-7.

Table 6-7. Prices of Plant Nutrients in USA, 1974

Fertilizer	Cost of Fertilizer as Sold per Ton April 15, 1974	Cost of Relevant Nutrient Element (N, P, or K) per Ton	Index of Cost (Cost as of 4/5 1973 at 100)
A. *Farmgate Prices*			
Nitrogen fertilizers			
Anhydrous ammonia (82% N)	$183	$ 223	208
Ammonia nitrate (33.5% N)	$139	$ 415	194
Urea (45–46% N)	$180	$ 400	199
Nitrogen solution (30% N)	$111	$ 370	190
Phosphatic fertilizers			
Superphosphate (20% P_2O_5; 8% P)	$ 91	$1,143	170
Superphosphate (46% P_2O_5; 19% P)	$150	$ 789	171
Potassium fertilizer			
Potash (60% K_2O; 49% K)	$ 81	$ 166	132
B. *Bulk prices*			

Large lots of ammonia are currently selling for $110–130 f.o.b. New York.
This is $134–159 per ton of nitrogen.

Source: *April Price Report*, Crop Reporting Service, Statistical Reporting Service, US Department of Agriculture.

of nitrogen, 165 tons of phosphorus, and 1,650 tons of potassium from the digested crop residues is *not* included, despite its nutrient worth of more than $1,045,000 to the recipient farmers) is $642,000. This substantially exceeds the cost of hauling and spreading the residuum throughout the wasteshed area.

The high inorganic fertilizer costs cited above are likely to remain high for three reasons: first, it is anticipated that worldwide demand for fertilizer will press hard against supply (with the possible exception of potassium sources) certainly into the 1980s, and with the spread of new farming techniques in the poor countries to cope with rapidly increasing demand for food, probably beyond.[91,92] Second, the cost of nitrogen fertilizer is very strongly dependent on the cost of hydrogen.* The cheapest source of hydrogen in this country is

---

*It has been estimated that 96 percent of the cost of bulk ammonia is accounted for by the cost of the natural gas. Contracts for gas made in the mid sixties when the last capacity was installed were 25¢ per million Btu; any new capacity must buy gas at more than $1.30 per million Btu intrastate (new regulated gas is probably unavailable). See the article by D.R. Safrany, "Nitrogen Fixation-Thermodynamics and Economics Rule Ways of Making Nitrogen from Compounds," *Scientific American*, 231:4, p. 64, October 1974. We could, of course, build all our new capacity in the Middle East at a lower economic cost, but one may doubt whether the implications of such a strategy would be politically acceptable to the vast majority of Americans. Neither the United States nor the world can afford to let our food production be dependent on the vagaries of Middle Eastern politics. If we opt for our traditional independence in food production we must accept higher nitrogen costs.

natural gas, and (as noted earlier) the price of natural gas, particularly *new* gas, is anticipated to increase steadily. Although coal will undoubtedly be cheaper than natural gas, the technology for using it as a hydrogen source is considerably more expensive and energy-intensive.[93] Third, agricultural scientists are beginning to support the use of less volatile nitrogen fertilizers and time-release fertilizers to increase efficiency.[94] Such fertilizers appear to be more expensive than, say, simple anhydrous ammonia. One might note in conclusion that fertilization via digester residuum would be consistent with this trend in agronomic thinking.

We have sought to argue in this section that the residuum from anaerobic methane digesters using crop residues and/or manure has a fertilizer value to farmers that is higher than normally assumed. We have noted in the course of this discussion a number of important advantages that the residuum may have over inorganic fertilizers, though evidence is incomplete. It is conceivable that the best way to apply inorganic fertilizer is to add it routinely to methane digesters, convert it to organic form and spread it in the residuum. Such a policy deserves serious study since it may combine the potentially enormous nitrogen-fixing capacity of our chemical industry,* with the possible agronomic advantages of organic fertilizers. While such developments are possible and should be pointed out, it must be emphasized that the intention in this section has *not* been to deny the usefulness of inorganic fertilizers but simply to revise upward the presumed value of the residuum from anaerobic methane digesters and suggest its great potential to agriculture in the future.

Digester Conversion Efficiency and Cost

Two very important parameters defining system costs are the capital cost per unit volume of digester capacity and the energetic efficiency of converting organic matter to methane. The values used in this model for both parameters are based on the published work of Pfeffer and Liebman[95] funded by the National Science Foundation. This work was chosen as a data base because the microbiological input is reliable, the yield results *at the loading rate used* were corroborated for an agricultural residue (cattle manure) by work at Hamilton Standard, and costings were available in a form that made it possible to use them in the model. Much more favorable costings, based on the work of Ghosh and Klass,[96] were not used because they were not available in a form that could be used in the model.

Without detracting from the value of Pfeffer and Liebman's work, it

---

*An objection often cited about the use of inorganic fertilizer is the energy intensiveness of fertilizer production. Given the fundamental importance of food, U.S. energy use in fertilizer production is relatively small—less than 1 percent of total energy use. In fact, it can be argued that with a system of energy recovery from crop residues, it is often the case that synthetic nitrogen fixation is a "breeder" reaction. That is, the energy required to produce synthetically one ton of nitrogen in fertilizer form is less than the energy recovered from gas produced by fermenting the *increment* of crop residues resulting from the fertilizer application; and meanwhile food is also produced.

is important to realize that, at least in the case of agricultural residues, it is likely to yield cost estimates that are too high. We may illustrate this point by referring to the digester which Biogas of Colorado, Inc., is about to build for the Montfort feedlot in Greeley, Colorado. This plant is to yield approximately 2.2 x 10^9 scf of methane net per annum (approximately 70 percent more gas than the plant in the model) and will be financed entirely from the private sector.

Although it was not possible to obtain hard data from the contractor for detailed analysis in this report, several points emerged from conversations. First, capital cost per unit volume of digester capacity may be lower than assumed in Pfeffer and Liebman's work. The Biogas of Colorado, Inc., plant claims to be much cheaper than other designs on a unit-volume basis, though it is not possible here to give an accurate figure since a breakdown of costs was not available. It is claimed that reductions in costs are in part a result of using cheaper construction materials (but again details were unavailable for proprietary reasons). Interestingly enough, these costs include installation of solar heating units. Similarly low costs per unit volume of digester capacity are implicit in Ghosh and Klass's work (see Table 6–2), but any cost breakdown or details were also unavailable for proprietary reasons.

The second important parameter is the yield of gas from a given input of substrate. Based on pilot plant experience, yields of 4 to 5 scf methane per pound of volatile solids (dry organic matter) can be anticipated. This is substantially higher than the methane yield of 3.3 scf per pound volatile solids assumed in the model. Even higher yields have been recorded for crop residues.[97,98,99] It is possible that agricultural residues are a superior substrate for fermentation compared to the organic fraction of urban waste, which was the substrate studied by Pfeffer.

The Biogas of Colorado plant uses solar energy for maintaining the digester at 95°F. This is a natural application of solar heating because of the characteristics of the digester: it works at relatively low temperatures, has considerable thermal inertia, and can be designed to achieve low rates of heat loss. An advantage of using solar heating is that gas is not used to heat the digester, as assumed in the model. The final net yield of high value gas is therefore increased still further relative to the model.

Increasing the efficiency of conversion to methane has as an important result a decrease in the absolute raw material cost per million Btu of gas. For example, the cost in the model of crop residues which are introduced into the digester (after collection, transport, storage, and shredding, etc.) is about $4.10 per ton or $0.26 per million Btu. At a net conversion efficiency, as assumed in the model, of 37 percent, the raw material cost per million Btu of gas is 70¢. At a net conversion efficiency of 55 to 60 percent, (representative of the Colorado plant) the raw material cost per million Btu of gas (net output) is only about 45¢. All this suggests that it is possible to produce more methane per unit input at about the same cost. This is apparently achieved by allowing lower loading rates (and longer detention times at lower temperatures) and compensating for this by designing digesters with lower capital costs per unit volume of capacity.

It is interesting to speculate on the effect of substituting into the model the values based on the Biogas of Colorado plant for those based on Pfeffer and Liebman. Referring back to Figure 6–15 and the accompanying notes, we will assume that the costs of steps 1 through 7 and 12 through 15 remain constant, that the cost of 16 varies linearly with the gas output, and that, for the costs of 8, 9, and 11 and the output of 9, the costs and output values of the Biogas model are substituted. These are derived as follows:

One pound of dry organic matter yields 4.5 scf of methane. Assuming that 95 percent of the 208.000 tons of dry matter is dry organic matter, we have an input of 197,000 tons of dry organic matter and an output of 1.8×10^9 scf of methane or 1.8×10^{12} Btu per year. Assuming solar heating, energy requirements for digestion become insignificant. The scrubber is 94 percent efficient, so net methane production is about 1.7×10^9 scf.

The Biogas of Colorado plant capital cost is $4 million (early 1974 dollars). Given the greater designed output of the Colorado plant (2.2×10^9 scf per year), we may assume a plant of the same size in the model without being excessively optimistic. Assuming discounting and depreciation at 16 percent, the annual cost of steps 8, 9, and 11 is $640,000.

Annual scrubber costs increase from $162,000 with 1.34×10^9 scf gas entering the scrubber to $217,000 with 1.8×10^9 scf of gas entering the scrubber. Of the additional annual expenses in the notes to Figure 6–15, maintenance, taxes, and insurance decrease by $2,000. Labor costs are also apparently lower in the Colorado plant, but will not be changed in the model.

Total annual costs* are now $2,235,000.00 with an output of 1.7×10^{12} Btu or at a price of $1.31 per million Btu. *This is competitive with current intrastate natural gas prices.*

Finally, it is possible that a net profit may be earned on the sale of residuum. Biogas of Colorado expects that income from residuum sales for fertilizers will exceed hauling and spreading costs. It is possible therefore that the plant in the model here can capture a part for the fertilizer credit in the residuum. This might in turn permit greater use of inorganic nitrogen inputs to the digester without increasing gas production costs as derived in this chapter.

Conclusion

A baseline model system for the production of methane from crop residues and animal manure at a cost of $1.76 per million Btu has been described above (and in Appendix B). It should be emphasized again that there are many variables that could change the cost of gas; for example, the costs of gas production could well

---

*A word on our use of the word "costs" in this model. Costs here includes a 12 percent discount rate (constant dollars) on capital invested, hence our assumption that the gas can be sold at a price equal to costs.

be lower (as noted above) than the estimate in the model. In that case, immediate development of this energy resource would become feasible in many parts of the country. Given the simpler technology involved, lead times for development and construction should be shorter than for coal–Synthetic Natural Gas plants now being planned. Materials and technical bottlenecks should also be less of a problem. Finally, while it is not suggested that this system could supply more than a fraction of natural gas demand, it is certainly worthwhile to note that production of, say, 1 trillion cubic feet of methane (essentially the same as natural gas or SNG) from this system should involve substantially less social dislocation and environmental degradation than coal-SNG plants. Additional farm income, tax revenues and employment would follow, too, in many rural areas now suffering depopulation.

It is interesting to explore how this system could someday supply an amount of energy (in the form of methane) greater than that in the fossil fuels used to operate farm equipment and produce farm chemicals. This analogy may help to put our energy-intensive agriculture into perspective, especially when we consider transporting it to underdeveloped countries. Pimentel et al.[100] found that one Btu of fossil fuel input yielded 2.86 Btu of food energy in corn. Assuming—as we have in the model—that the residue coefficient of corn is 0.85 (see Table 6A–4 of Appendix A), 2.86 Btu of energy as food in corn will yield about 2.4 Btu of energy in residues. Conversion at a net 37 percent efficiency yields 0.89 Btu of fossil-fuel equivalent. If we accept the residue coefficient (1.2) from a study by Stanford Research Institute study (discussed below), 2.84 Btu of corn yield 3.4 Btu of energy in residues or 1.25 Btu of methane. At the conversion efficiency claimed in the Colorado plant the net yields of methane would be 1.35 Btu (.85 residue coefficient) and 1.95 Btu (1.2 residue coefficient) per Btu of fossil-fuel input required to grow the corn. It is fair to say, therefore, that with an energy recovery system, the agricultural sector could easily be a net exporter of fossil-fuel equivalent (i.e., methane). *There need be no energy subsidy for modern agriculture.* While this conclusion in itself need not be of great importance to the United States in the near future, the potential of scaled-down versions of this system in rural areas of the underdeveloped countries could be very great. Plants such as this may be the basic energy source for the decentralized power needed to irrigate millions of acres in the next few years.*

One final thought. It has been observed that when pulverized coal is added to organic matter it can be fermented to yield methane.[101] It has even been suggested that addition of coal may enhance the fermentation, although the author has seen no evidence. It is intriguing to speculate whether it might be

---

*The fuller significance of this finding is discussed in a forthcoming EPP book, *Energy and Agriculture In the Third World,* by Arjun Makhijani with the Collaboration of Alan Poole. In terms of fossil fuels American agriculture is energy-intensive. However, in broader energy terms, the author believes much traditional peasant agriculture is more energy-intensive.

possible to substitute the methane fermentation, or biogasification, of coal for at least some conventional coal gasification. One possible advantage of biogasification as opposed to conventional gasification of coal is the potential for water conservation, a major advantage in the West. Biogasification of coal might require less than one-third of the quantity of water required for conventional coal gasification. In fact, if the residuum were applied to the soil, there would be virtually no water loss. However, the residue from the digestion of a coal-agricultural waste mix might not be suitable for soil application.

It is difficult to make a reasonable estimate of the current potential of the system. If it is assumed that all crop residues which are present in a density of two tons per acre or more are available as in the model (see Appendix A, Table A6–5), approximately 160 million tons of dry organic matter are available. Another 44 million tons are available in feedlots (see Appendix A, Table A6–6). A total of 200 million tons of dry organic matter may therefore be considered available with present agricultural systems. The gross energy available is therefore approximately 3.2 quadrillion Btu. At 37 percent efficiency, it is possible to produce 1.2 quadrillion Btu of methane in the baseline model. If, however, the higher net efficiency claimed by the Biogas of Colorado plant is assumed (55 to 60 percent), about 1.8 quadrillion Btu of methane could be produced.

Even if we discount the possibility of using crop residues at lower densities, this figure could still be an underestimate. The great bulk of residue available at an average density of two tons per acre or more consists of corn (see Appendix A, Table A6–4 and A6–5). The quantity of corn and other residues has been derived from data on harvests by using "residue coefficients," largely based on estimates by various crop experts in the U.S. Department of Agriculture. It must be emphasized that *these are estimates*, and, in the case of corn at least, there is some doubt about the accuracy of the coefficients. A higher coefficient (1.2) was obviously used (though not specified) in the calculations in the Stanford Research Institute's study for the National Science Foundation.[102] If we use the SRI coefficient of 1.2 (instead of 0.85), we find an additional 60 million tons of corn residues. On this basis a total of up to 2.4 quadrillion Btu (instead of 1.8) of methane might be produced—an increase of over 30 percent. This discrepancy highlights the need for a study of crop residue quantities based on a real field survey.

Secondary energy savings could also be substantial, though impossible to quantify at present. For example, if it is true that sustained application of organic fertilizer nutrients enhances the yield and protein content of corn (as discussed earlier in this study), assuming the original source of all the nitrogen to be synthetic ammonia added as a supplement in digesters, then the net secondary energy saving would be approximately 0.2 quadrillion Btu. The saving is calculated on the assumption that less soybeans would be required than at present to make up for protein deficiencies in corn.

Other secondary savings would result from recycling organic fertilizer nutrients which are now wasted and perhaps from possible feed value of the residuum. In the latter case, grain which is replaced does not have to be planted, cultivated, fertilized, harvested, dried, and transported to feedlots.

All these calculations must be speculative, but it is possible that secondary energy savings taken together might amount to 0.4 to 0.5 quadrillion Btu.

NET ENERGY AVAILABLE
FROM ORGANIC WASTES

The gross energy available in wastes generated today was summarized earlier in this report. Present development and the projected use of waste-derived fuels (according to EPA) were summarized in the section on "supplementary solid fuel for utility and industrial boilers." This will probably be the most rapidly implemented of the processes discussed here. As also shown in the introductory discussion to the urban refuse resource recovery model, many factors contribute to decisions to recover resources from urban refuse. The rate of development, however, will surely be sensitive to energy and materials price trends. It seems certain that energy and materials prices will increase rather than decrease up to the year 2000; this would encourage recovery of these materials from refuse.

On the other hand, it is becoming clear that *source reduction*, either alone or combined with resource recovery, is in many ways preferable to *resource recovery* alone as an optimal strategy for inorganic materials in urban refuse. The situation is much less clear for paper and plastic. Source reduction means, simply, generating less solid waste; for example, use of returnable bottles is a source reduction strategy, as opposed to the comparable materials recovery approach—recycling glass from one-way bottles. The growing popularity of source reduction could, of course, lessen the extent of resource recovery.

A recent EPA study comparing a materials recovery (recycling) scenario with a partial source-reduction scenario (all beverages marketed in returnable bottles) illustrates the point very well.[103] Assuming "maximum possible" materials recovery in 1972, 172 trillion Btu of energy would have been saved. Much more energy—244 trillion Btu—would have been saved if beverages had been marketed in glass bottles, refilled an average of 10 times. However, since substantial amounts of glass, aluminum, and steel have been removed from the waste stream (assuming that steel and aluminum beverage cans cannot be used because they cannot be refilled) 6.2 million tons of material that would have been recovered in the recycling scenario are not availabe for recovery in this partial source-reduction scenario; hence, energy savings from recycling would be reduced by 73 trillion Btu to 98 trillion Btu. A combined returnable beverage bottle and materials-recovery scenario would therefore save 244 + 98 = 342 trillion Btu in 1972, compared to only 172 trillion Btu in the materials-recovery-only scenario. Similar reasoning could be applied to other waste sources, particularly aluminum foil which should be reused at home as it still is in Europe to a large extent. (It is possible that sufficient reduction of aluminum and glass in the waste stream would make the recovery of the remainder uneconomic. Ferrous recovery probably is sufficiently inexpensive to remain viable, even under a maximum possible resource reduction strategy.) An all returnable bottle strategy plus ferrous-material recovery (no aluminum or glass recovery) would involve a total net energy savings of 244 + 65 - 309 trillion Btu in 1972.

It is possible that legislation enforcing certain kinds of source reduction will be considered by the end of the decade. Two major programs are being actively studied at present—marketing of all beverages in returnable glass bottles and almost complete recycling of newspaper. Stuart Natof (personal communication) has studied the impact these two programs combined would have on the viability of resource recovery plants. His unpublished preliminary calculations, shown in Table 6–8, indicate that from the point of view of composition of the refuse it is unlikely that energy, glass, or ferrous recovery would be rendered uneconomic. The gross throughput of the plant could decrease (about 13 percent in the calculations shown) but this should not have much effect on unit costs, particularly of larger plants. Thus, anticipated legislative action on source reduction should not reduce the rate of development of resource recovery.

Table 6–8. Impact of Returnable Bottle and Newspaper Recycling Legislation on Mean Solid Waste Composition

	Current Composition Percent and Pounds/100 Pounds	Change Multiplier	Composition Pounds	Composition Percent
Steel	6.7	0.8	5.36	6.13
Aluminum	0.5	0.5	0.25	0.29
Glass	10.0	0.8	8.0	9.15
Combustibles (not including news-papers)	70.0	1.0	70.0	80.08
Newspaper	10.0	0.1	1.0	1.14
Other inorganic	2.8	1.0	2.8	3.2
Total	100%, 100 lbs	–	87.4 lbs	100.0%

Note: This multiplier estimates the impact of legislation on the absolute amount of each waste material generated. For example, out of 100 pounds of typical refuse today, 6.7 pounds are steel. Legislation would reduce steel to 80 percent of this amount (hence the multiplier is 0.8). Adding the impact on different materials of the different change multipliers, we find that where 100 pounds of refuse were generated only 87.4 pounds are now generated. Thus, after legislation, even though steel in refuse has declined by 20 percent, the relative fraction of steel in refuse has only declined from 6.7 percent to 6.1 percent.

Energy recovery from organic wastes in the year 2000 will be estimated here only for agricultural wastes and urban refuse—the two types of waste for which model systems have been discussed here. Projected energy recovery of approximately 1.8 quadrillion Btu from forest industry-related wastes is not included.

The available energy in organic wastes at present and in the future is a function of the gross energy in wastes, the efficiency of collection of waste material, and the efficiency of processing waste material into a form suitable for consumption. A simplified projection of gross energy in agricultural and urban organic wastes is given in Table 6–9. Collection efficiency projections are more difficult and are subject to wide ranges of error. For urban refuse, a commonly used criterion is that only refuse in Standard Statistical Metropolitan Statistical Areas is available for collection. It is estimated that 75 percent of the waste stream in urban refuse is collectable according to this criterion[104] when account is taken of the higher rate of per-capita waste generation in urban areas (3.6 pounds per day per capita compared to a national average of 3.3 pounds per day per capita). This collection efficiency will therefore be used in the projections for the year 2000, although there has been a tendency for areas outside of SMSA's to be included in resource recovery plans, as exemplified by the Connecticut plan.

A collection efficiency of 75 percent represents a realistic, conservative, upper limit based on present technology and to a certain extent on present commodity prices. Whether actual collection efficiency will be less, equal to, or above this level, and at what rate it will increase, are more dependent on public

Table 6-9. Gross Energy and Collectable Energy of Organic Wastes, 1972-73 and 2000

	1972/73 Gross Energy[a] (Quadrillion Btu)	2000 Gross Energy (Quadrillion Btu)	1972/73 Collectable Energy (Quadrillion Btu)	2000 Collectable Energy (Quadrillion Btu)
Crop residues	5.4	10.5–12.3[b]	n/a	n/a
Feedlot manure	0.7	2.0	n/a	n/a
Organic matter in urban refuse	1.3	3.0–3.4[d]	1.0[c]	2.3–2.6[d]

[a]Energy content of dry organic matter assumed to be 16 million Btu/ton and of plastics 32 million Btu/ton.
[b]Range dependent on 2.5–3.1 percent growth rate in residues.
[c]Assumes all organic wastes in SMSA's are collectable for energy recovery, either with supplementary solid fuel, steam generation, or methane from landfill concepts.
[d]Higher estimate assumes Historical Growth Scenario, lower estimate assumes Zero Energy Growth Scenario.

policy than technology. For example, energy and materials recovery plants serving all of Connecticut's SMSA's are scheduled to be on line by 1985, using now-available technology.

It is far more difficult to establish a reasonable estimate of the collection efficiency for agricultural wastes. In the resource recovery model discussed earlier for animal manure and crop residues, it is assumed that once the system is in operation, manure will be collected from a large percentage of the feedlots in the area, while crop residues at a density of two tons per acre or more would be economically collected. Several factors, however, complicate our projections. If, for example, crop-harvesting procedures were modified to include simultaneous collection of residues (a characteristic of traditional harvesting technologies), crop residues at a density of less than two tons per acre might be collected. Furthermore, residues such as straw in wheat fields lie mainly in windrows and are easier to collected than stover, which is chopped (as assumed in the model). Here again residues at a density of less than two tons per acre might be collected.

It is rather difficult to project the growth of feedlots relative to increases in animal production. Conventional projections of one class of feedlots (beef) show an increase from 14 million head in 1973 to 37 million head in 1980. High feedgrain prices might, however, arrest the growth not only of beef feedlots, but of other classes of feedlots as well. Speculations on the availability of wastes from different classes and sizes of feedlots are also unsatisfactory. Thus, projections of collection efficiency of feedlot animal wastes and crop residues would be highly arbitrary. For this reason, gross quantities of agricultural wastes in 2000 are roughly estimated in Table 6–9.

The calculation of gross quantities of organic agricultural wastes for Table 6–9 is based only on feedlot waste estimates and crop residues. Dispersed animal wastes are ignored. It is assumed that manure from animals in confined conditions will increase by 4 percent per annum, on the basis of an assumed 3 percent annual increase in meat consumption to 1985 (projected by Martin)[105] and the trend in animal husbandry in the recent past toward confining livestock. A range of growth rates in crop residues is indicated, based as a first approximation on extrapolations to 2000 of certain major crop projections to 1985.[106] The range is 2.5 percent to 3.1 percent per annum.

The calculation of the gross energy in organic wastes in urban refuse in 2000 for Table 6–9 is based on the paper and plastic materials flows in Figures 6–2 and 6–4 and assumes a conservative 0.5 percent annual increase in energy from other sources combined (rubber, leather, wood, garbage, yard waste).

Processing efficiency will vary according to the process. Three factors must be considered. If the processing involves urban refuse and front-end materials separation is necessary, there is, with present technology, a loss of combustible material from the energy recovery stream. This loss is estimated to be overall (including energy expenditure during the materials separation step) about 25 percent.[107] Second, if the process involves conversion to another form of fuel (such as pyrolysis or methane fermentation), the efficiency of the energy conversion step must be accounted for. Third, heat loss due to the moisture content of material must be considered. Table 6–2 summarizes these data.

For simplicity in calculating potential net energy output, it is assumed that all energy recovery from urban refuse will be with the solid fuel supplementation concept, while all energy recovery from agricultural wastes will use the methane fermentation concept. Presently achieved processing efficiencies are assumed. Calculations assume the collection efficiencies in Table 6–9 where applicable. The results, for 1972-73 and 2000, are shown in Table 6-10.

It is evident that a concerted policy of energy recovery from organic waste materials could make a significant contribution to domestic energy supply in the later part of this century. It is reasonable to expect that 5 quadrillion Btu of energy, the equivalent of 200 million tons of coal annually, could be provided directly by the organic waste sources listed in Table 6–10.

However, as shown repeatedly in this report, it is an interesting feature of energy recovery systems that the actual production of energy constitutes only a part of their impact on the energy economy. Energy recovery from urban refuse permits large-scale materials recovery which would otherwise be uneconomic; in this area, we may conserve up to 1 quadrillion Btu annually. Energy recovery from agricultural wastes may, as in the model, reduce demand for fertilizer and supply a significant animal feed input. These secondary savings may amount to a significant fraction of the primary net output.

In spite of a very modest research and development effort relative to other energy sources, progress in commercializing the relevant technologies has been very rapid, due to their simplicity and short lead times. We must not, however, restrict ourselves to technologies. Development of suitable systems, such as those described, deserves much more attention than it has received.

Table 6-10. Net Energy Potentially Recoverable from Urban Refuse, Crop Residues, and Feedlot Manure, 1972–73 and 2000

	Net Efficiency of Energy Conversion Process	*Conversion Product*	*Net Energy 1972/73 (Quadrillion Btu)*	*Net Energy 2000 (Quadrillion Btu)*
Crop residues	37%–55%[a]	High Btu gas	2.0–3.0	3.9–6.8[b]
Feedlot manure	37%–55%[a]	High Btu gas	0.3–0.4	0.7–1.1[b]
Urban refuse	70%	Coal or oil supplement	0.7	1.6–1.8

[a]Efficiency range discussed in model in text.

[b]Based on gross energy in Table 6–9 and range of efficiency indicated.

Many institutional factors require study and perhaps modification. Resource recovery technologies may influence packaging (for example, materials high in chlorine may be limited) and the handling of refuse in homes and institutions. The trade-offs must be carefully assessed.

Energy recovery from organic wastes is essentially a way of using solar energy. Most waste, of course, is a renewable energy source, and waste-derived fuels can substitute in part for fossil fuels as these become scarcer and more expensive. Recovery appears to be economical, and—unlike most forms of energy—it actually reduces pollution problems instead of compounding them. These are some of the present advantages of energy recovery from organic wastes.

In the future, the nature of the benefit may change, waste could become a major source of a specific carbon-based fuel instead of the range of refuse derived fuels now being developed on an ad hoc basis. As fossil fuels decline, such newer sources as solar, geothermal, wind, and nuclear power may begin to take their place. These provide heat and electricity, but do not provide storable fuels. There are some specific uses for particular fuels—such as propelling the internal combustion engine automobile—for which other energy sources are not readily adaptable. Hydrogen, which is often called the fuel of the future, is so far much more expensive and harder to handle than any contemplated waste-derived fuel analyzed in this study.

In the years ahead, not only may organic wastes be used for their fuel content, but crops may actually be grown specifically as a source for carbon-based fuel. The same technology that processes organic wastes may be a part of a "solar farm" system which uses photosynthesis to convert solar energy to carbon-based fuel. This form of solar energy fixation might prove to be relatively simple, inexpensive, and nonpolluting.

The ideas outlined here could eventually be an indispensible component of the future energy economy.

We have in waste-derived energy a potential "oil well that will never run dry." If this report has contributed to understanding and interest in this area, its purpose has been fulfilled.

Appendix A

Current Generation of Organic Waste in the United States

The amount of organic waste currently generated in the United States each year is estimated to be approximately 690 million tons (dry matter). Included in this estimate are organic wastes from the sources listed in Table 6A–1. The annual quantity of organic waste from each source is also given in this table. With the exception of crop residues and food processing wastes, these represent *net* wastes after current resource recovery. The food processing wastes include a large proportion of bagasse from sugar cane, much of which is currently used

Table 6A–1. Current Generation of Organic Waste in the United States as Estimated in This Report

Source	Dry Weight (10^6 Tons)	Base Year
Residues from production of agricultural crops	341	1973, (1967)
Manure and bedding from animal production		
−Confined animals	45	1973
−Dispersed animals	155	1971
Animal products processing	0.1	1967
Food processing	6.0	1973, (1967)
Processing of nonfood crops	nil	1967
Textile, plastic, and rubber products industries	0.5	1967
Residues from managed forests	26	1967
Pulp mills	8.9	1967
Saw mills	11.2	1967
Pulp and paper processing	1.3	1967
Secondary wood manufacturing	2.0	1967
Sewage solids	14	1973
Residential & municipal solid refuse	43–50 (47)	1971
Commercial & institutional solid refuse	26.4	1970
Construction	1.3	1967
Demolition	4	1967
Total	689.7	

(though how much is used is unknown). Some crop residues are also used as feed and bedding; however, in this case the data represent only a rough estimate, and it is not certain to what extent current use (also unknown) would interfere with resource recovery.

This estimate of total organic wastes is intermediate to those of Anderson[108] for the Bureau of Mines, and of the International Research and Technology Corporation[109] for the Environmental Protection Agency. Anderson's estimate of total organic wastes generated in 1971 was 880 million tons (dry matter), while IR&T's estimate from a combination of data for 1967 and 1970 was 571 million tons (dry matter). A breakdown by source is given for the Anderson and IR&T estimates in Tables 6A-2 and 6A-3, respectively. Generally speaking, Anderson's estimates of organic matter from urban refuse, industrial waste, and miscellaneous sources appear to be high, while IR&T's estimate of agricultural crop waste appears to be low, and its estimate of household and municipal organic waste appears to be high, as will be shown in the rest of the Appendix.

A discussion of the derivation of the major waste estimates follows:

DERIVATION OF SOURCE ESTIMATES—
PRODUCTION OF AGRICULTURAL CROPS

The wastes from this source are composed of field residues of harvested crops. The general method for estimating the quantity of field residues for a particular crop is first to define the portion of the crop plant which is to be considered field residue and, second, to calculate from physiological and anatomical data a residue coefficient which relates the dry matter content of the residue to the weight of the harvested crop (at the moisture content used in agricultural

Table 6A-2.   Estimates of Organic Wastes Generated in the USA in 1971 and 1980 (Millions of Tons of Dry Organic Matter)

Source	1971	1980
Animal manure	200	266
Urban refuse	129	222
Logging and wood manufacturing residues	55	59
Agricultural crops and food processing waste	390	390
Industrial wastes	44	50
Municipal sewage solids	12	14
Miscellaneous organic wastes[a]	50	60
Total	880	1061

Source: Anderson, 1972.

[a]Includes, among other things, organic wastes from federal installations, antibiotic fermentation residues, wastes and carcasses from dogs, cats, horses, and marine animals.

Table 6A-3. Estimate of Total Organic Wastes Generated in the USA—International Research and Technology Corporation (Millions of Tons of Dry Organic Matter)

Source	Amount	Base Year
Agricultural crop residues	166	1967
Animal manure	207	1967
Forest logging residues	26	1967
Household and municipal refuse	84	1970
Commercial and institutional refuse	30	1970
Wood processing industries	27	1967
Sewage sludge	13	1970
Industrial plant trash	12	1967
Demolition	4	1967
Construction	1	1967
Food processing and other manufacturing	1	1967
Total	571	

Source: IR&T, 1972.

statistics). No single coefficient, of course, will always be valid for a particular crop, due to the varying effects of crop variety, growth conditions, and harvested yield. (For example, the residue coefficient of cotton *increases* with increasing lint and seed yield, hence, the higher the yield the greater the *proportion* of residues). This method does, however, permit the use of the vast compendium of conventional agricultural statistics.

The most complete source of residue coefficients is in the report by the International Research and Technology Corporation.[110] However, the residue coefficients (called waste coefficients in the report) which are given appear to be excessively conservative. Consequently, a reevaluation of the residue coefficients of major agricultural crops was carried out with the Assistance of Dr. Robert Yeck of the Agricultural Research Service of the U.S. Department of Agriculture. The corrected residue coefficients are given in Table 6A-4. The coefficients used in the IR&T report are also given for comparison. It should be emphasized here that the corrected residue coefficients are based on estimated moisture content in most cases and generally use conservative base data.

When deriving the residue coefficients of any crop, only above-ground portions of the crop plant which are not harvested are defined as residue. The roots, which comprise anywhere between 20 percent to 50 percent (more in the case of tuber and root crops) of the biomass of a mature plant, are ignored. Decay of the root material of harvested crops is considered to be the most significant source of soil humus, even when above ground crop residues are left in the field as a mulch. This point may have considerable importance when discussing the availability of crop residues, since it is often assumed that the

Table 6A–4.   Residue Coefficients for Major Crops

Crop	Corrected Residue Coefficient[c] (Pound Dry Residue/ Pound Harvested Crop)	IR&T Residue[d] Coefficient
Soybean	0.85[a]	0.55
Corn	0.85	0.55
Cotton[b]	3.00	1.20
Wheat	1.50	0.47
Barley	1.25	0.82
Rice	0.85	0.38
Rye	1.70	1.20
Oats	1.50	0.95
Grain sorghum	0.85	0.50
Sugar beet	0.17	0.07
Sugar cane	0.20 bagasse 0.03 field residue	0.13

Note: Residue coefficients were determined by individual crop experts and forwarded by Dr. Robert Yeck of the Agricultural Research Service. IR&T estimates included for comparison.

[a]The residue coefficient for soybean is very dependent on the condition of the crop at the time of harvest. This figure assumes that all the leaves have fallen and are unavailable. Coefficients three times as high have been recorded.

[b]Both lint and seed are included in the harvested crop.

[c]A moisture content of 15 percent is assumed for grains and beans at the time of harvest.

[d]To the knowledge of the author, who spoke with the president of IR&T, the coefficients developed there were intended to derive gross above-ground residues from harvested crop data. The reason for the discrepancy, therefore, remains obscure.

removal of these residues results in the removal of all humus-forming organic matter from the land.

The residue coefficients for the major crops in Table 6A–4 have been used to estimate the quantities of residues generated by these crops in 1973. These estimates and related data are given in Table 6A–5. The total figure is, therefore, probably rather conservative, since minor crops and horticultural wastes are not included.

ANIMAL PRODUCTION

Wastes from this source have been divided at the outset into two categories: those produced by animals in confined conditions and those produced by dispersed animals. The distinction between the two categories, however, is inexact, since there are intermediate production systems also, particularly in the dairy and swine industries.

Data for wastes from confined animals have been assembled from a detailed U.S. Environmental Protection Agency study on feedlots.[111] Feedlots have been divided into 18 subcategories in the EPA study, defined by the type of animal and the production system. Our figures for confined wastes do not

Table 6A–5. Total Residues Generated by Major Agricultural Crops in the USA in 1973

Crop	*Harvested[a] Product (10⁶ Tons)*	*Residue[b] Generated (10⁶ Tons Dry Matter)*	*Average Density of Dry Residues (Tons/Acre)*
Soybean	47.0	39.9	0.71
Corn	158.0	134.3	2.17
Wheat	51.3	77.0	1.43
Barley	10.2	12.7	1.21
Rye	0.7	1.3	1.21
Oats	10.6	15.9	1.13
Grain sorghum	26.2	22.3	1.40
Sugar beet	24.5	4.2	3.41
Sugar cane[d]	27.5	0.8	1.10
Cotton[c]	8.5	25.4	2.12
		333.9	1.45

[a]Crop production data for 1973 from the Statistical Reporting Service, U.S. Department of Agriculture.

[b]Calculated from crop production data using the corrected residue coefficient in Table 6A–4.

[c]Harvested product for cotton includes lint and seed.

[d]Does not include bagasse, which is considered a food-processing waste.

include all the wastes of all these subcategories, either because they were considered numerically insignificant or because a part of the wastes produced were, in fact, dispersed. To determine this latter case, the criterion used as in the EPA study was whether a pasture lot could absorb the wastes without deterioration of the pasture. These subcategories are in fact partial confinement systems, and a rough estimate based on data in the EPA study was made of the confinement time averaged through the year and used to help determine the average daily rate of manure generation given in the table.

Table 6A–6 lists the categories of confined animal waste, together with related data. The figures used in the EPA report for dry organic matter of manure waste per animal per day often differ quite substantially from figures found elsewhere in the literature. However, since feedlot conditions are special, the EPA figures have been used whenever they are available. Wastes produced by dispersed animals are estimated to be approximately 155 million tons dry weight. Total manure generated by animals in Table 6A–6 was subtracted from the generally accepted total figure of 200 million tons.

FOOD PROCESSING

The estimate of wastes generated annually by food-processing industries is taken directly from the IR&T study, with the exception of sugar cane bagasse which amounts to 5.5 million tons. Although bagasse is normally counted together

Table 6A–6. Dry Organic Waste Generated by Major Farm Animals Under Confined Conditions

Animal	EPA[b] Feedlot Category	Number of Animals (000)	Manure[a] Dry Organic Solids (Pound/ Day/Head)	Total (000 Tons)
Beef cattle[c]	I	13,400	5.8	14,070
Beef cattle[c]	II	600	5.8	770
Dairy cows	III	6,800	7.8	9,660
Dairy cows	IV	1,815	15.3	5,060
Dairy cows	V	2,920	6.4	3,390
Swine	VI	15,400	0.4	1,120
Swine	VII	9,200	0.4	680
Swine[d]	VIII	37,000	0.23	1,550
Broilers	IX	468,000	0.022	1,880
Layers	X, XI	478,000	0.049	4,300
Sheep	XII, XIII	2,270	2.0	830
Lambs	XII, XIII	1,940	1.2	420
Turkeys	XIV	19,700	0.18	650
Total				44,380

Source: Denit, 1973.

[a] Accounts for differences in housing, bedding, age of manure, and confinement time.

[b] See Denit, 1973.

[c] Assumes fresh manure.

[d] This category is marginal—in some cases animals will be in feedlot conditions, while in others they will not.

with crop residues, it was felt to be more logical to count is as a food-processing waste since it is the residue left after sugar extraction. Considerable quantities of bagasse are already used as fuel in sugar mills, and it is not clear what fraction of the 5.5 million tons can be considered as waste today.

The remainder of the food-processing industry generates only relatively small amounts of waste, though it is possible that the IR&T estimate of 0.5 million tons may be somewhat low. There is a trend toward lower food-processing wastes per unit input.[112]

OTHER PRE-FINAL USER WASTE SOURCES

Estimates for these sources have all been taken directly from the IR&T study. That study's treatment of the forest products, textile, rubber, plastics, and various food-processing industries is systematic and well documented.

Table 6A-7. Material Flow Estimates of Residential and Commerical Solid Waste Generation, by Kind of Material, 1971

Kinds of Materials	"As-Generated"[a] Basis		"As Disposed"[b] Basis	
	10^6 Tons	Percent	10^6 Tons	Percent
Paper	39.1	31.3	47.3	37.8
Glass	12.1	9.7	12.5	10.0
Metals	11.9	9.5	12.6	10.1
Ferrous	10.6	8.5		
Aluminum	0.8	0.6		
Other nonferrous	0.4	0.3		
Plastics	4.2	3.4	4.7	3.8
Rubber & leather	3.3	2.6	3.4	2.7
Textiles	1.8	1.4	2.0	1.6
Wood	4.6	3.7	4.6	3.7
Nonfood product totals	77.1	61.7	87.2	69.7
Food wastes	22.0	17.6	17.7	14.2
Product totals including food	99.1	79.3	104.9	83.9
Yard wastes	24.1	19.3	18.2	14.6
Miscellaneous organics	1.8	1.4	1.9	1.5
Total waste	125.0	100.0	125.0	100.0
Percent product source composition		79.3		83.9

Source: F.A. Smith & F.L. Smith RRD/OSWMP/U.S. EPA, September, 1973.
[a]"As-Generated" = weight at time of disposal, including moisture.
[b]"As-Disposed" = weight after redistribution of moisture content in disposal receptacle.

URBAN REFUSE—RESIDENTIAL AND MUNICIPAL; COMMERCIAL AND INSTITUTIONAL

The estimate of dry organic wastes generated from this source is based on a recent study in the Office of Solid Waste Management Programs (OSWMP) in the U.S. Environmental Protection Agency.[113] Recent materials flow studies indicate that the estimates based on the *1968 National Survey of Community Solid Waste Practices*[114] are too high, including the updated analysis based on the complete 1968 survey data made by Paul Britton which were in turn used in the IR&T study for residential organic wastes. On this same basis, the IR&T study estimates of commercial waste also appear to be high.

The results of the OSWMP study are reproduced in Tables 6A–7 and 6A–8 for their interest. Table 6A–7 summarizes data for the commercial and

Table 6A-8. Material Flow Estimates of Residential Solid Waste Generation, by Waste Material Category, 1971

Waste Material Categories	Oven-Dry Weight Basis 10^6 Tons	As-Generated Weight Basis 10^6 Tons	As-Disposed Weight Basis 10^6 Tons
Nonbulky product waste:			
Paper	21.6	23.2	28.8
Glass	10.8	10.8	11.1
Metals	7.1	7.1	7.5
Plastics	3.2	3.3	3.7
Rubber & leather	1.0	1.0	1.1
Textiles	0.9	1.0	1.2
Wood	0.5	0.6	0.6
Subtotal: Nonfood	45.1	47.0	54.0
Food waste	5.3	17.8	15.0
Subtotal: nonbulky product waste	50.4	64.8	69.0
Yard waste	9.0	18.1	13.9
Misc. inorganics	1.0	1.0	1.0
Total: Nonbulky material	60.4	83.9	83.9
Add: Bulky wastes	6.4	6.4	6.4
Total residential	66.8	90.3	90.3

Source: F.A. Smith & F.L. Smith, Resource Recovery Division, Offices of Solid Waste Management Programs, U.S. EPA, February, 1974.

residential sectors together, while Table 6A–8 is for the residential sector only. From Table 6A–8 it is estimated that 40.6 million tons (oven-dry weight) of organic wastes are generated annually from the residential sector, and 26.4 million tons from the commercial and institutional sector (which includes industrial plant trash).

A source not studied in the OSWMP study is "other municipal," comprising street and alley cleanings, tree and landscaping, park and beach, and catch-basin solids. These were estimated to be from 6 to 22 million tons in the 1968 National Survey. Dry organic wastes may amount to from 2 to 10 million tons.

SEWAGE SOLIDS

Most estimates related to this source are for sewage sludge, which is estimated to be about 12 million tons dry weight (see Table 6A–2, for example). Sewage sludge, however, is the residue which is left in sewage treatment plants after biological treatment. If sewage solids before treatment are estimated, the figure would be 19 to 21 million tons dry weight, assuming a daily rate of 0.5 to 0.6

pounds per person, and dry organic matter is approximately 70 percent of this or 14 million tons.[115]

DEMOLITION AND CONSTRUCTION

Estimates of organic wastes from these sources are taken directly from the IR&T study. However, there is very great uncertainty about the estimate for demolition wastes (K. Shuster, personal communication).

Appendix B

Notes for Model System for Energy Recovery from Agricultural Residues

1. FIELD COLLECTION

Assumptions
65 horsepower tractor
corn chopper operating at two acres per hour
moisture content of stover is 15 percent
2 tons of dry organic matter of stover per acre

Economic Costs
$3.75/acre
  (a) $1.50 for tractor includes gas, oil, housing, taxes, insurance, depreciation (assuming 700 to 800 hours annual use)
  (b) $1.00 for labor
  (c) $1.25 for chopper (high rate of depreciation to account for less use than tractor)

At two tons of residue per acre, the cost is $1.88 per ton of dry organic matter. Assuming 16 million Btu per ton of dry organic matter, the cost per million Btu is 11.75¢. This may be compared with the cheapest coal produced in America (Western strip-mined coal), which costs 19.3¢ (1972 dollars) per million Btu; and the geographically more comparable Eastern strip-mined coal which has a cost of 25.3 per million Btu.[116]

The farmer can be a very cost-effective "miner."

Costs of field collection per ton of product will vary with the "density" of residues in the field, since up to a point the cost of chopping is constant per acre regardless of the density of residues. Since average corn yields are anticipated to be approximately 120 bushels per acre in 1985, an average density of 2.85 tons dry organic matter of stover may be anticipated. The cost per ton would therefore be $1.31 and per million Btu, 8¢.

In general, one may say that the economics of field collection of residues will improve as crop yields improve, although the effect of dwarf varieties must be quantified. (One may note in passing here that wheat in this country, despite many years of breeding for short stems, has one of the highest residue coefficients of any crop. In light of this, it is difficult to see how the residue coefficient for corn, already surprisingly low, could be substantially reduced.) This is in contrast to all fossil fuels, for which extraction will tend to become increasingly expensive.

Modification of harvesting procedures might further reduce costs. However, this model has been designed to fit current farm practice.

Energy Inputs
Assuming the tractor is gasoline-powered, 1.2 gallons of gasoline are required per acre. At 125,000 Btu per gallon, this is 150,000 Btu per acre or 75,000 Btu per ton dry organic matter, or 0.45 percent of the gross energy of the material harvested. (The data base for these economic and energy inputs was provided by Dr. Ralph Patterson of the Extension Service, United States Department of Agriculture.)

2. HAULING OF RESIDUES

Assumptions
65 horsepower tractor
two two-ton wagon loads per trip at 15 mph and stops
moisture content of stover is 15 percent
stover hauled two miles and dumped, empty trip back

Economic Costs
$1.15 per acre
   (a) $0.50 for tractor as in (1)
   (b) $0.25 for labor
   (c) $0.25 for wagons, equipment, and delays
   (d) 15 percent of total above to account for moisture
One may note that a two-mile haul may be more than necessary.

Energy Inputs
Assuming the tractor is gasoline-powered, 0.11 gallon of gasoline is required to haul one ton of dry organic matter off the field and two miles. This is 13,000 Btu per ton or 0.08 percent of the energy value of the material Data base provided by Dr. Patterson as in (1).

3. TRANSFER STATION

Assumptions
All fields more than 2.5 miles from the plant deliver residues to a transfer station, which is simply a convenient point for the farmer to pile the material to be kept under canvas, much as a haystack. Loading for transport will occur later. The costs here are assumed to include stacking and loading costs and land costs for an aggregate of 50 acres of storage area.

Economic Costs
$0.57 per ton dry organic matter
  (a) four men @ $11,000 per year each
  (b) four four-cubic yard front end loaders @ $40,000 each.[117]
      Interest and amortization at 20 percent annually. (Discount rate @ 12 percent, depreciation @ 8 percent
  (c) land cost for 60 acres @ $1,000 per acre, interest at 12 percent annually (includes simple land preparation)
  (d) fuel and materials @ $5,000 per year

Energy Inputs
Undetermined but small

4. TRANSPORT

Assumptions and Economic Costs
$0.50 per ton dry organic matter
Cost of delivery is dependent on the distance that material must be transported; this in turn is dependent on the area of the wasteshed.

A 500-ton per day plant requires 182,500 tons dry matter per year. At a yield of two tons per acre, 91,000 acres are required, or 142 square miles. Assuming that 60 percent of land in area surrounding the plant is in harvested cropland providing the system with residue, the wasteshed area is 237 square miles. (By way of comparison, approximately 57 percent of the area of Iowa was harvested cropland in 1969.)

Assuming the wasteshed is circular with the plant at the center, the radius of the wasteshed from the plant is 8.7 miles. Assuming waste is available more or less evenly over the area, the average distance of transfer stations from the plant is 5.8 miles. Farmers have already hauled wastes to transfer stations with the exception of those within 2.5 miles, who deliver directly to the plant. Road patterns add 20 percent to distance. The average distance will therefore remain 6.0 miles. At 7¢ per ton-mile the transport cost is 42¢ per ton average. Allowing for 15 percent moisture, the cost is 50¢ per ton of dry matter.

Energy Inputs

Hirst[118] estimated 2,800 Btu per ton-mile for intercity freight transport by truck. Allowing for country roads, etc., 3,500 Btu per ton-mile is reasonable. With an average trip of six miles, 1,000 Btu per ton-mile is added for return trips, bringing the total to 27,000 Btu per ton. Fifteen percent must be added to account for moisture, bringing the total to 31,000 Btu per ton of dry organic matter. This is 0.2 percent of the energy value of the material.

There can be no question that the energy inputs for field collection and transport of residues to the plan are trivial and do not represent an obstacle, contrary to conventional wisdom on this subject.

5. RECEIVING

Assumptions and Economic Costs
$0.18 per ton dry matter

Costs of labor, weighing station for trucks, and front-end loader are included

(a) two men @ $11,000 per year each
(b) one four-cubic-yard front-end loader at $40,000[119], with interest and amortization at 20 percent annually. Discount rate 12 percent, 8 percent depreciation.
(c) one truck weighing station @ $32,000,[120] discounting and depreciating at 20 percent annually.

Energy Inputs
Undetermined but very small.

6. SECONDARY SHREDDING

Assumptions

Secondary shredding, as the term is used in solid waste handling, involves further shredding material which has undergone primary shredding to approximately six-inch length strips. The material is now shredded to one-half inch to one-inch long bits. The operation is assumed necessary in this model, but there are two reasons why it may not in fact be necessary. First, material is already shredded during harvest, although the author has not yet determined the size of the shredded bits. Secondly, there is disagreement regarding the size of particle which should be introduced into the digester. Pfeffer[121] found no difference in digestion of particle size between one and two inches and the small fibers from a hydropulper. Gosh and Klass[122] however, have found a dramatic difference in gas yields from refuse shredded or milled to different sizes with finely milled material yielding far more methane than coarser material, as shown

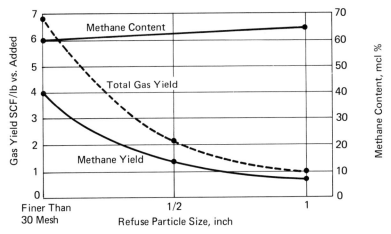

Notes:
1. Digester deed contained 80 percent refuse and 20 percent sludge solids on a dry basis.
2. All runs were conducted at 35°C., a detention time of about 12 days, and a loading of about 0.11 pounds of volatile solids per cubic foot per day.

Figure 6B-1. Effect of Particle Size on Mesophilic Digestion of Refuse-Sludge Mixture[a]

[a]From Ghosh and Klass, 1974

in Figure 6B-1. Finally, Boshoff[123] found one-half-inch particles to be optimal, though it is uncertain over what range of particle sizes he experimented. Differences of this magnitude between established workers in the field highlight the difficulties involved in trying to optimize the methane fermentation at present. Our understanding is simply deficient.

Economic Costs
[19¢ per ton dry organic matter]
Two 50-ton-per-hour shredders @ $80,000 per unit and installation estimated at 50 percent of purchase price,[124] discounting at 12 percent and depreciating at 6 percent. Annual cost at $43,000, not including labor. Electricity costs @ 2¢/Kwh are $32,000 annually.

Energy Inputs
A 50-ton-per-hour plant has 600 horsepower. Ten hours of operation are required per day, or 6,000 horsepower-hours (15.3 million Btu). Assuming electricity is generated on-site, with unscrubbed gas with an overall efficiency of 25 percent, a daily input of 61 million Btu is required. Or 120,000 Btu per ton

of dry organic matter. This is 0.75 percent of the gross energy in the material. It might be cheaper to buy electricity, and in the model this has been done. Annual requirements are 1,600,000 Kwh.

7. STORAGE

Assumptions and Economic Costs

Milled material is stored in a 600-ton capacity silo at a total cost of $189,000[125] with discount rate at 12 percent, depreciation at 3 percent.

8. SLURRYING

Mixing tank and slurry pump at $17,500.[126]

9. DIGESTION

Assumptions

Capital cost of digester is $3,570,000, discounting at 12 percent and depreciating at 3 percent. The capital cost of digester and energy inputs given in Figure 6–15 are taken from the report by Pfeffer and Liebman to the National Science Foundation.[127] These figures are based on computer simulations based on present digester design and experimental data for digestion parameters. The digestion parameters used in this study are:

temperature: 60°C
detention time: 8 days
feed concentration: 10 percent
volatile solids concentration: 90 percent

The loading rate used in this study (0.75 lbs/cu. ft./day volatile solids per day) is relatively conservative compared to some of the loading rates used in Pfeffer's work, and the results are corroborated by work at the Hamilton Standard Division of United Aircraft Laboratories.[128]

The digester costed by Pfeffer and Liebman handles 1,000 tons of dry solids per day, while that costed here handles approximately 630 tons per day, assuming 10 percent outage (the capital cost of the digesters includes reserve quoted above capacity equal to 10 percent of total capacity).

Wise, Sadek, and Kispert[129] indicates that unit capital cost variation should not be significant in this range. Labor and operating costs for digestion have been accounted under a separate heading in the notes to Figure 6–15.

10 INORGANIC NITROGEN INPUT

Economic Assumptions

(1) 550 tons of nitrogen for $82,000. Bulk price for large lots of ammonia is $110 to $130 (f.o.b. N.Y.) or $135 to $160 per ton of nitrogen (see Table 6–7 in text). It is assumed that plants could qualify for such prices.

(2) $120,000 capital cost for storage, assuming approximately 300 tons of storage capacity (see item 7 in this Appendix).

11. DEWATER RESIDUUM

Capital cost $865,000, discounting at 12 percent and depreciating at 4 percent. Dewatering costs are similarly based on the work of Pfeffer and Liebman.[24] Labor, energy, and maintenance costs have been accounted for in the notes to Figure 6–15. Personal communications with Dr. Pfeffer as well as Dr. S. Ghosh indicate that a dry matter content of 40 percent should be expected after dewatering, rather than the 25 percent figure quoted in the reference above.

12. FEED SUPPLEMENT FOR 19,500 BEEF CATTLE

Discussed in main text; no net costs accounted to system.

13. MANURE COLLECTION

The possible value of the residuum as a feed supplement for beef cattle and nonruminants was discussed in the main text, as was the basis for the relative magnitudes of crop residues, feed supplement, and cattle manure in the model. The quantity of residuum used per head is 2.6 pounds per day.[130]

Given the relatively high value of the material as feed (which is given free of charge), it is assumed that the small cost of handling it is borne entirely by the feedlot, as is delivery of the manure to the slurry tank.

14. TRANSPORT OF RESIDUUM

The cost of transporting residuum to the fields was discussed in the main text. On the basis of (4) in this appendix, the energy inputs would be on the order of 30,000 Btu per ton of wet residuum, assuming that the average trip is seven miles.

15. FIELD APPLICATION OF RESIDUUM

The economics of this were discussed in the main text. Energy inputs are, according to Pimentel et al.[131] 1.1 gallon per ton or 133,000 Btu per ton.

16. SCRUBBER

Installed cost $1,015,000, discounted at 12 percent and depreciated at 4 percent. The only gas that will be scrubbed is the gas to be marketed. Unscrubbed gas will be used for all plant operations. Costs for a scrubbing unit of almost exactly the same size are given by Wise, Sadek, and Kisper.[132] The unit used, however, is not the same and has a thermal efficiency of 94 percent. Costings for such a unit were obtained from the EPA for smaller plants and closely resembled those of comparably sized MEA plants. Research is currently underway to develop CO_2 scrubbers that are more suited for small scale applications such as this plant. It is anticipated that scrubbers will be cheaper than estimated here (Ghosh, personal communication; Pfeffer, personal communication).

Energy Accounting
All significant energy inputs have been quantified in this model. However, only those for secondary shredding, digestion, dewatering, and scrubbing have been used to determine the net efficiency and net output. This is partly because the other energy costs have been included in the available economic cost figures. To have included them in determining net output would therefore involve double counting. There impact on net energy conversion efficiency is quite small.

PERSONAL COMMUNICATIONS

Sambhunath Ghosh, Institute of Gas Technology, Chicago, Illinois 60616
Clarence Golueke, Sanitary Engineering Research Laboratory, University of California, Berkeley, Calif. 94700
Steven Levy, Office of Solid Waste Management Programs, U.S. Environmental Protection Agency, Washington, D.C. 20460
Stuart Natof, Carborundum Co., Inc., Hagerstown, Maryland 21740
John Pfeffer, Department of Civil Engineering, University of Illinois, Urbana, Illinois 61801
Keith Selby, Rank-Hovis, Ltd., London, England
Kenneth Shuster, Office of Solid Waste Management Programs, U.S. Environmental Protection Agency, Washington, D.C. 20460
Frank A. Smith, Office of Solid Waste Management Programs, U.S. Environmental Protection Agency, Washington, D.C. 20460

Notes to Chapter Six

Notes to Chapter Six

1. "Converting the Garbage into Energy," *Business Week* (30 March 1974: 42-43).
2. National Academy of Sciences, *Composition of Cereal Grains and Forages*, NAS Publication 585, 1958.
3. Office of Air and Water Programs, *Processes, Procedures, and Methods to Control Pollution Resulting from Silvivultural Activities*, Report No. EPA 430/9-73-010, U.S. Environmental Protection Agency, Washington, D.C., 1973.
4. International Research and Technology Corporation (IR&T), *Problems and Opportunities in Management of Combustible Solid Wastes*, Report prepared for the Environmental Protection Agency, 1972.
5. D. J. Muhich, A. J. Klee, and P. W. Britton, "Preliminary Data Analysis: 1968 National Survey of Community Solid Waste Practices," Public Health Service Publication No. 1867 (Washington, D.C.: U.S. Government Printing Office, 1968).
6. IR&T, *Problems and Opportunities.*
7. Fred L. Smith, Unpublished draft of a report, Resource Recovery Division, Office of Solid Waste Management Programs, U.S. Environmental Protection Agency, Washington, D.C., 1974.
8. L. L. Anderson, "Energy Potential from Organic Wastes: A Review of the Quantities and Sources," Bureau of Mines Information Circular, 8549, 1972.
9. Ann O'Laughlin, *Organic Gardening and Farming* (November 1973: 37-40).
10. U.S. Department of Agriculture, *Wastes in Relation to Agriculture and Forestry*, Miscellaneous Publication 1065, 1968.
11. S. R. Hoover, "Prevention of Food Processing Wastes," *Science* 183 (824-828).

12. S. Ghosh, J. R. Conrad, and D. L. Klass, "Anaerobic Acidogenesis of Sewage Sludge," *Journal of Water Pollution Control* 46 (1974).

13. D. L. Wise, S. E. Sadek, and R. G. Kispert, *Fuel Gas Production from Solid Waste*, Semi-Annual Progress Report from Dynatech R/D Company to the National Science Foundation, Report No. NSF/RANN/SE/C-827/PR/73/4, 1974.

14. L. R. Martin, "Agriculture as a Growth Sector—1985 and Beyond," Unpublished report to the Energy Policy Project, 1974.

15. *Ibid.*

16. R. A. Lowe, *Energy Conservation Through Improved Solid Waste Management* (Washington, D.C.: Office of Solid Waste Management Programs, U.S. Environmental Protection Agency, 1974).

17. J. D. Denit, *Development Document for Proposed Effluent Limitations Guidelines and New Source Performance for the Feedlots Point Source Category* (Washington, D.C.: Effluent Guildelines Division, Office of Air and Water Programs, U.S. Environmental Protection Agency, EPA 440/5-73/004, 1973.

18. IR&T, *Problems and Opportunities.*

19. General Electric—Connecticut, *A Proposed Plan of Solid Waste Management for Connecticut: Summary*, G. E. Corporate Research and Development, State of Connecticut, Department of Environmental Protection, 1973.

20. C. B. Kenahan et al., "Bureau of Mines Research Program on Recycling and Disposal of Mineral-, Metal-, and Energy-Based Wastes," Bureau of Mines Information Circular 8595, 1973.

21. Denit, *Development Document.*

22. IR&T, *Problems and Opportunities.*

23. Kenahan et al., "Bureau of Mines Research Programs."

24. S. Lingle, "Paper Recycling Through Source Separation," Article available at Resource Recovery Division, Office of Waste Management Programs, U.S. Environmental Protection Agency, Washington, D.C., 1974.

25. G. E. Smith, "Economics of Water Collection and Recycling," Working paper 6, Autonomous Housing Study, Department of Architecture, University of Cambridge, England, 1973.

26. A. L. Hammond et al., *Energy and the Future* (Washington, D.C.: American Association for the Advancement of Science, 1973).

27. IR&T, *Problems and Opportunities.*

28. *Ibid.*

29. R. A. Lowe, *Energy Recovery from Waste*, U.S. Environmental Protection Agency Report No. SW 36d, 1973.

30. G. E.—Connecticut, *A Proposed Plan.*

31. Lowe, *Energy Conservation.*

32. Kenahan et al., "Bureau of Mines Research Program."

33. R. O. Ramseier, "How to Melt the Arctic and Warm the World," *Environment* 16 (4:7-14).

34. J. T. Pfeffer, *Reclamation of Energy from Organic Waste,* EPA 670/2-74-016, National Environmental Research Center, Office of Research and Development, U.S. Environmental Protection Agency, Cincinnati, 1974.

35. J. T. Pfeffer and J. C. Liebman, *Biological Conversion of Organic Refuse to Methane,* Semi-Annual Progress Report to National Science Foundation, No. NSF/RANN/SE/GI-39191/PR/73/4, Washington, D.C., 1973.

36. C. G. Golueke, P. H. McGauhey, and S. A. Klein, "Comprehensive Studies of Solid Waste Management," 3rd Annual Report, SERL Report No. 70-2, Sanitary Engineering Research Laboratory, University of California, Berkeley, 1970.

37. S. A. Klein and C. G. Golveke, "Comprehensive Studies of Solid Waste Management," Final Report, SERL Report No. 72-3, Sanitary Engineering Research Laboratory, University of California, Berkeley, 1972.

38. M. Altmann, *Technology for the Conversion of Solar Energy to Fuel Gas,* Report No. NSF/RANN/SE/GI 34991/PR/73/2, submitted to the National Science Foundation, Rann Program, Washington, D.C., 1973.

39. *Ibid.*

40. U.S. Department of Agriculture (USDA)–Hamilton Standard (a division of United Aircraft, Inc.), *Proposal for Thermophilic Fermentation of Feedlot Wastes–Pilot Project Evaluation,* 1974.

41. Ghosh, Conrad, and Klass, "Anaerobic Acidogenesis."

42. S. Ghosh and D. L. Klass, "Conversion of Urban Refuse to Substitute Natural Gas by the Biogas™ Process" (Paper presented at the Fourth Mineral Waste Utilization Symposium, Chicago, 1974). Ghosh and Klass are at the Institute of Gas Technology, 3424 South State Street, ITT Center, Chicago 60616.

43. Wise, Sadek, and Kispert, *Fuel Gas Production.*

44. F. A. DiGiano, A. R. Hoffman, and W. L. Short (eds.), *Proceedings–Bioconversion Energy Research Conference,* sponsored by the National Science Foundation under Grant No. GI 39215, June 25 and 26, 1973.

45. L. J. Fry and R. Merrill, *Methane Digesters for Fuel Gas and Fertilizer,* Newsletter No. 3 (Santa Barbara, California: New Alchemy Institute, 15 West Anapamu, 1973).

46. Ghosh and Klass, "Conversion of Urban Refuse."

47. Office of Air and Water Programs, *Processes, Procedures and Methods to Control Pollution.*

48. Ghosh, Conrad, and Klass, "Anaerobic Acidogenesis."

49. Altmann, *Technology.*

50. J. E. Bigger, "Methane Recovery Demonstration Project January to May 1974," Department of Water and Power, City of Los Angeles, 1974.

51. R. E. Schwegler, "Energy Recovery at the Landfill" (Paper presented at

the 11th Annual Seminar and Equipment Show of the Governmental Refuse Collection and Disposal Association, November 7-9, 1973. R. E. Schwegler is Section Engineer, County Sanitation District of Los Angeles County.

52. Bigger, "Methane Recovery."
53. G. E.–Connecticut, *A Proposed Plan.*
54. *Ibid.*
55. Council of State Governments, *Our Effluent Society–The States and Solid Waste Management*, Lexington, Kentucky, 1974.
56. G. E.–Connecticut, *A Proposed Plan.*
57. D. J. Dugas, *Fuel From Organic Matter* and *Fuel from Organic Matter: Possibilities for the State of California,* The Rand Paper Series No. P-5100 and P-5107, Rand Corporation, Santa Monica, California, 1973.
58. R. Yeck, "Agricultural Biomass Byproducts and Their Effects on the Environment" (Paper presented at the International Biomass Energy Conference, Winnepeg, Canada, May 15, 1973).
59. DiGiano, Hoffman, and Short, *Proceedings.*
60. Federal Power Commission, "Natural Gas Demand Forecasts," National Gas Survey, FPC Report of Distribution Advisory Task Force Feneral Draft, April 1973.
61. Foster Associates, Inc. *Energy Prices: 1960-1973*, Research Study for the Energy Policy Project (Cambridge, Mass.: Ballinger, 1974).
62. N. Searl, "Economics of the Production of High-Btu Gas from Coal," Appendix in "Resources for the Future," *Supply Reports*, 1974.
63. *Ibid.*
64. Ramseier, "How to Melt the Artic."
65. Pfeffer and Liebman, *Biological Conversion.*
66. C. Tietjen and S. A. Hart, "Compost for Agricultural Land," in *Proceedings for the American Society of Civil Engineers–Journal of the Sanitary Engineering Division* 95 (SA 2, April 1969: 269-287).
67. W. B. Anthony, "Cattle Manure as Feed for Cattle," in *Livestock Waste Management and Pollution Abatement* St. Joseph, Mich,: American Society of Agricultural Engineers,1971).
68. J. C. Taylor, "Regulatory Aspects of Recycled Livestock and Poultry Wastes," in *Livestock Waste Management and Pollution Abatement* (St. Joseph, Mich,: American Society of Agricultural Engineers, 1971).
69. W. H. M. Morris, "Economics of Waste Disposal from Confined Livestock," in *Livestock Waste Management and Pollution Abatement* (St. Joseph, Mich.: American Society of Agricultural Engineers, 1971).
70. USDA–Hamilton Standard, *Proposal.*
71. Wise, Sadek, and Kispert, *Fuel Gas Production.*
72. Denit, *Development Document.*
73. *Ibid.*
74. Pfeffer, *Reclamation of Energy.*
75. Denit, *Development Document.*

76. *Ibid.*
77. *Ibid.*
78. *Ibid.*
79. B. Commoner, *A Study of Certain Ecological, Public Health and Economic Consequences of the Use of Inorganic Nitrogenous Fertilizers,* First year progress report to the office of Interdisciplinary Research, National Science Foundation, submitted by the Center for the Biology of Natural Systems, Washington University, St. Louis, Missouri, May 5. 1972.
80. R. R. Hensler et al., "Effect of Manure Handling Systems on Plant Nutrient Cycling," in *Livestock Waste Management and Pollution Abatement* (St. Joseph, Mich.: American Society of Agricultural Engineers, 1971).
81. *Ibid.*
82. M. J. Perelman, "Farming with Petroleum," *Environment* 14 ((8:8-13).
83. National Center for Resource Recovery, Inc. "Resource Recovery: A Status Report," *NCRR Bulletin* 4 (1:2-10).
84. Commoner, *A Study.*
85. Tietjen and Hart, "Compost for Agricultural Land."
86. Commoner, *A Study.*
87. Ministry of Agriculture Fisheries and Food, *Modern Farming and the Soils* (London: H. M. Stationary Office, 1970).
88. Commoner, *A Study.*
89. Tietjen and Hart, "Compost for Agricultural Land."
90. Water Pollution Research Laboratory, "Agricultural Use of Sewage Sludge," Notes on Water Pollution, No. 57, June 1972. (Available from the Director, Water Pollution Research Laboratory, Elder Way, Stevenage, Herts., England.)
91. Economic Research Service, *United States and World Fertilizer Outlook: 1974 and 1980* (Washington, D.C.: U.S. Department of Agriculture, February 22, 1974).
92. Martin, "Agriculture as a Growth Sector."
93. Economic Research Service, *United States.*
94. *Ibid.*
95. Pfeffer and Liebman, *Biological Conversion.*
96. Ghosh and Klass, "Conversion of Urban Refuse."
97. W. H. Boshoff, "Methane Gas Production by Batch and Continuous Fermentation Methods," *Tropical Science* 5 (1963: 155).
98. F. A. Smith, "The Quantity and Composition of Community Solid Waste," Unpublished report, Office of Solid Waste Management Programs, U.S. Environmental Protection Agency, Washington, D.C., 1974.
99. G. E. Smith, "Economics of Water Collection."
100. Pimentel, "Food Production."
101. G. E. Johnson, "Production of Methane by Bacterial Action on a Mixture of Coal and Sewage Solids," U.S. Patent 3,640,864.
102. Stanford Research Institute, "Effective Utilization of Solar Energy to

Produce Clean Fuel," Report submitted to the National Science Foundation, Report No. NSF/RANN/SE/GI 38723/FR/2, 1974.
103. Lowe, *Energy Conservation.*
104. *Ibid.*
105. Martin, "Agriculture as a Growth Sector."
106. *Ibid.*
107. G. E.–Connecticut, *A Proposed Plan.*
108. Anderson, "Energy Potential."
109. IR&T, *Problems and Opportunities.*
110. *Ibid.*
111. Denit, *Development Document.*
112. Hoover, "Prevention of Food Processing Wastes."
113. Smith, "The Quantity and Composition of Community Solid Waste."
114. Muhich, Klee, and Britton, *Preliminary Data Analysis.*
115. D. P. Chynoweth and R. A. Mah, "Volatile Acid Formation in Sludge Digestion," *Anaerobic Biological Treatment Processes,* Advances Chemistry Series, No. 105. (Washington, D.C.: American Chemical Society, n.d.).
116. Searl, "Economics of the Production of High-Btu Gas."
117. Wise, Sadek, and Kispert, *Fuel Gas Production.*
118. E. Hirst, "Transportation Energy Use and Conservation Potential," *Bulletin of the Atomic Scientists* 29 (9:36-42).
119. Wise, Sadek, and Kispert, *Fuel Gas Production.*
120. *Ibid.*
121. DiGiano, Hoffman, and Short, *Proceedings.*
122. Ghosh and Klass, "Conversion of Urban Refuse."
123. Boshoff, "Methane Gas Production."
124. Wise, Sadek, and Kispert, *Fuel Gas Production.*
125. *Ibid.*
126. USDA, *Wastes.*
127. Pfeffer and Liebman, *Biological Conversion*, p. 31.
128. USDA–Hamilton Standard, *Proposal.*
129. Wise, Sadek, and Kispert, *Fuel Gas Production.*
130. USDA–Hamilton Standard, *Proposal.*
131. Pimental et al., "Food Production."
132. Wise, Sedak, and Kispert, *Fuel and Gas Production.*

NOTE: The personal communications cited were from the following: Sambhunath Ghosh, Institute of Gas Technology, Chicago, Illinois; Clarence Golueke, Sanitary Engineering Research Laboratory, University of California, Berkley; Steven Levy, Kenneth Shuster, and Frank A. Smith, Office of Solid Waste Management Programs, EPA; Stuart Natof, Carborundum Co. Inc., Hagerstown, Md.; John Pfeffer, Department of Civil Engineering, University of Illinois, Urbana, and Keith Selby, Rank-Hovis Ltd., London.

Chapter Seven

Energy Needs for Pollution Control

John Davidson, Marc Ross, David
Chynoweth, Ann Crampton Michaels,
David Dunnette, Carl Griffis, J. Andrew
Stirling, and Don Wang*
University of Michigan

Environmentalists—long proponents of energy conservation—sometimes now appear to be on the other side of the fence. They seem to be caught in a bind, for pollution control technology often involves an increased use of energy— especially when control equipment is added on to an existing process.

Take the automobile as an example. Cars with pollution control devices often suffer reduced gasoline mileage, and the end result is a need for *more* fuel. Thus, any effort to determine future energy needs must include a close inspection of the demand for energy presented by environmental quality goals.

This chapter—a summary of a University of Michigan study—focuses on the specific issue of what impact pollution controls will have on energy consumption. It is primarily concerned with the energy penalties and gains associated with controlling important conventional types of pollution. It excludes pollution from nuclear power plants and does not deal with delays or dislocations in energy supply which may be caused by controls.

While only conventional kinds of pollution are discussed here, it is important to note that our natural environment is also degraded in many other ways, through inappropriate use of land and other resources and through daily assaults on the senses of sight and hearing. At risk are the esthetic pleasure of "unspoiled" land and our opportunity to be alone in the wilderness; the ability of species other than man to keep a secure niche; and the opportunities, health and safety of future generations. Unrestrained, man now has the power to cause catastrophic destruction in all these areas.

In 1970, the total wastes put into the air in the U.S. equaled 0.8 pounds of material per person per day.[1] In a number of areas in the country these pollutants regularly reach levels injurious to human health and life.

*The authors wish to thank Jonathan Buckley and Dale Briggs for their helpful suggestions in the course of this study

309

The principal pollutants entering the air include sulfur oxides, particles, nitrogen oxides, hydrocarbons, carbon monoxide, and lead. The first three are largely associated with fixed sources such as industry. The latter pollutants are directly connected with motor vehicles. Table 7–1 shows the Nationwide Atmospheric Emmissions for 1970 by source.

The situation with water pollution is equally serious. More than one pound of waste per person enters U.S. waters every day.[2] Much of this wastewater from "point" sources is subject to inadequate treatment. "Nonpoint" sources—runoff from agricultural, construction, and mining activities—have been even less carefully controlled.

Urban solid wastes, along with air and water pollutants, add to the noxious burden in our environment. These solid wastes today average about 8 pounds per person-day, of which 3.4 pounds is personal garbage.[3,4] And the control of agricultural solid wastes is becoming a more serious environmental problem with the rapid increase in numbers of confined animals (as in feedlots).

While many efforts to regulate and control waste disposal were made prior to the mid 1960s by both the states and the federal government, more recent efforts are having major impact. The principal new regulations are: The Air Quality Act of 1967 and Clean Air Act Amendments of 1970, the Water Quality Improvement Act of 1970 and 1972 Amendments to the Federal Water Pollution Control Act, and the standards established by states and by the U.S. Environmental Protection Agency (EPA) under these acts.

This study has been divided into five major areas: (a) air pollution standards and transportation; (b) fixed-source air pollution control; (c) waste heat management for power plants; (d) control of industrial wastewater; (e) management of agricultural and municipal wastes.

Special emphasis has been given to the two air pollution areas which present the most serious energy difficulties: transportation and fixed-source air pollution.

In the study, we define "energy penalty" as the *full* energy consumption associated with the activity to which the control technology is attached *less* the full energy consumption of the activity as carried on without the control. Energy quantities are expressed in fuel value terms—thermal Btu. A British thermal unit (Btu) is the energy required to raise one pound of water one degree Fahrenheit. "Thermal" Btu represent the total heat energy required—it takes roughly three units of thermal energy to produce one unit of electrical energy. (The 1973 Per Capita U.S. Energy Consumption was about 360 million Btu.)

Full energy includes, in addition to direct energy consumption, all energy associated with material flows and capital construction. This is important since it removes much uncertainty associated with indirect implications of new processes. These indirect energy uses are calculated using an energy input-output model developed by Herendeen.[5] (See Appendix A for discussion of input-

Table 7-1. Nationwide Atmospheric Emissions, 1970 (10^6 Tons/Yr)

Source	CO Tons	CO Percent	Particulates Tons	Particulates Percent	SO_X Tons	SO_X Percent	HC Tons	HC Percent	NO_X Tons	NO_X Percent	Total Emissions Tons
Transportation	111	74.6	.8	3.1	1.0	2.9	19.5	55.9	11.7	51.3	144.0
Fuel combustion in stationary sources*	.8	.5	6.7	25.6	26.4	77.5	.6	1.7	10.0	43.9	44.5
Industrial processes	11.4	7.7	13.3	50.1	6.4	18.7	5.5	15.8	.2	.9	36.8
Solid waste disposal	7.2	4.9	1.4	5.3	.1	.3	2.0	5.7	.4	1.7	11.1
Miscellaneous	18.3	12.3	4.0	15.9	.2	.6	7.3	20.9	.5	2.2	30.3
Total	148.7		26.2		34.1		34.9		22.8		267
(1968 data)											
*Breakdown into											
Utilities				63		69				40	
Industrial				30		21				51	
Residential-commercial				7		10				9	
Total				100		100				100	

Source: *Compilation of Air Pollutant Emission Factors (2nd ed.)*, U.S. Environmental Protection Agency, April 1973.

output analysis.) This analysis is an economic tool which permit summation of all energy inputs from supplier, to supplier's supplier, and so on. It yields an average energy per dollar of cost of product.

The calculation of the amount of energy used by a specific pollution control technology has been made in two stages: first, particular examples of the technology are carefully examined and an energy penalty is deduced. Next, this result is combined with estimated levels of activity in the U.S. where this technology is used. These two steps give us a projection of a national energy penalty.

AIR POLLUTION STANDARDS
AND TRANSPORTATION

Controversy concerning the energy impact of "moving-source" emission standards has centered on the automobile. Standards for automobiles and other "Light-Duty Vehicles" are more stringent than for large trucks and other "Heavy-Duty Vehicles." Initial emissions standards for aircraft first went into effect in early 1974, and emissions standards for motorcycles are still being formulated.

Federal automotive exhaust emissions standards now set limits on the amounts of pollutants per mile that can be released into the air. These standards have evolved over the years as new data have become available. The most recent change occurred when Congress passed the Energy Supply and Environmental Act of 1974. In effect, it relaxed standards for the 1976 and 1977 model automobiles.

When federal exhaust emissions controls were first required in 1968, the degree of impairment in fuel economy to be expected was uncertain. Credible estimates comparing the fuel economy of the 1973 models to that of the precontrol vehicles (pre-1968) showed decreases in fuel efficiency ranging from as low as 7 percent to high as 20 percent. But, in the past year, the uncertainty has been substantially reduced. There is now little disagreement on the overall effect, though there is still disagreement on the size of the effect for small cars, with some indication that the penalty for them is negligible. (Figure 7–1).

Austin and Hellman,[6] using EPA data, found an average fuel economy loss of 10.1 percent for 1973 automobiles. This number was obtained by first comparing the fuel economy of pre-1968 and 1973 vehicles of comparable weight, and then averaging these numbers according to recent sales figures. Ford Motor Company, in a similar study, has indicated an average penalty of 13.6 percent over their model line.[7]

These two studies are by far the most complete and statistically significant. Averaging the findings of these two reports probably gives the best estimate of the penalty: a 12 percent overall sales-weighted decrease in fuel economy due to emission controls for 1973 model cars.

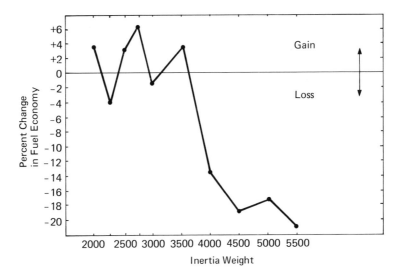

Figure 7-1. Percent Change in Fuel Economy Between Uncontrolled and '74 Models vs. Inertia Weight. Source: DeKany and Austin, "Automobile Emissions and Energy Consumption," 1974.

While the loss in fuel economy for 1974 model automobiles remained similar to 1973, the outlook for 1975 models is brighter. The use of "catalytic converters" on the 1975 models to reduce emissions permits engines to be "retuned" to more efficient operating conditions. EPA has reported an improvement of from 7 to 8 percent over 1973-74 models.[8,9] And a more recent EPA report suggests a potential improvement of approximately 10 percent.[10] Using the more conservative figure, this means that pollution controls for 1975 automobiles should have about a 5 percent fuel economy penalty over pre-control models.

Possible fuel economy penalties resulting from what are now the 1977 and 1978 model year emissions standards are not well established.[12,13,14,15] The stringent 1978 nitrogen oxide standard of 0.4 grams/mile may again be delayed since the EPA has suggested that the 2.0 grams/mile standard be maintained until the 1982 models.[16]

Much of the decrease in fuel economy often attributed to emission controls, actually has been due to increases in the weight of vehicles. Energy consumption, for the most part, is directly proportional to vehicle weight. Neglect of this factor has resulted in much confusion. Energy consumption (Btu per mile) versus vehicle weight is shown in Figure 7-2.

Implementation of safety standards and alterations in design have been the primary reasons for the increases in vehicle weight. General Motors has listed the factors which resulted in a 502 pound increase for its fullsize V-8

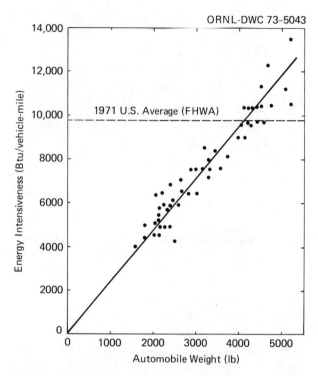

Figure 7-2. Automobile Fuel Consumption As a Function of Vehicle Weight for 1971 and 1972 Model Cars. Source: Hirst, 1973.

Chevrolet four-door automobile between 1968 and 1973.[17] Ford Motor Company has reported about a 9 percent decrease in fuel economy between 1967 and 1973 models due to increases in vehicle weight and displacement.[18]

When the effects of weight increases, emissions controls and the greater use of energy-consuming accessories are combined, the total decrease in fuel economy can be as high as 20 to 30 percent. The gasoline shortage led consumers to shift their purchasing habits from full-sized automobiles to smaller vehicles (Figure 7-3).

Engineering improvements, weight reductions, and the use of alternative engines (such as the light-weight diesel and certain stratified charge engines) would permit substantial improvements in fuel economy and regulated exhaust emissions.[19,20] Figure 7-4 compares fuel economy versus vehicle weight for conventional and diesel-powered vehicles. Unfortunately, the diesel vehicles used to generate the dashed curved had low power-to-weight ratios and thus overstate the expected improvement in fuel economy. On a comparable performance basis, the diesel would have a 20 to 30 percent greater fuel economy.[21] The introduction of an alternative engine would require long lead

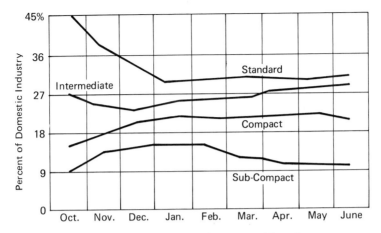

1974 Models: Sample Sizes; Subcompact-Vega; Compact-
Nova; Intermediate-Chevelle; Standard-Chevrolet.

Figure 7-3. Car Sales and Sizes (Percent of Domestic Industry).
Source: Agis Salpukas, "What the Energy Crisis Taught Auto
Makers," *New York Times*, July 21, 1974.

times for mass production. Commitments would be needed now for a phase-in
beginning in the late 1970s or early 1980s.[22] These alternative engines have
potential (but unquantified) problems with presently unregulated pollutants.

Federal exhaust emission regulations were set for new heavy-duty
diesel engines beginning in 1973. Available data indicates these standards will be
met without penalties in fuel economy.[23] The penalty for meeting federal
emissions standards for new heavy-duty gasoline engines is less certain. Available
data suggest a penalty of about 5 percent.[24]

Recently established aircraft emissions control standards will
become effective in several stages between 1974 and 1981. These standards set
emissions limits for hydrocarbons, carbon monoxide, oxides of nitrogen, smoke,
and fuel-venting emissions. The EPA has indicated that standards promulgated
for piston-type aircraft are expected to save fuel, while no penalty is expected
for aircraft using turbines.[25,26]

To estimate the 1985 national energy penalty for transportation,
several assumptions must be made:

1. All light-duty vehicles suffer a 5 percent decrease in fuel economy
due to emissions controls. (The use of 1974 and earlier vehicles should be
negligible by 1985. It is assumed that design improvements, weight changes,
and/or delay of 1978 emissions standards will keep the average fuel penalty at
projected 1975 levels.)

2. Heavy-duty gasoline vehicles suffer a 5 percent decrease in fuel
economy due to emissions controls.

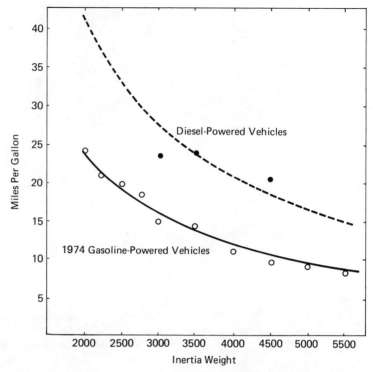

Figure 7–4. Fuel Economy vs. Vehicle Weight for Conventional and Diesel-Powered Vehicles. Source: DeKany and Austin, "Automotive Emissions and Energy Consumption," 1974.

3. Without emissions controls, the percentages of total U.S. energy consumed by light-duty vehicles and heavy-duty vehicles would remain at 1970 levels: 14.4 percent and 4.4 percent, respectively.[27]

4. An additional 0.07 million Btu are required for each dollar invested in pollution controls.[28] Twelve million controlled vehicles are sold per year; pollution controls add $200 to the purchase cost.

5. No additional penalties are incurred.

Using these assumptions, a penalty amounting to 1.1 percent of total 1985 energy consumption is found for the transportation sector. Table 7–2 lists the separate contributions.

FIXED SOURCE AIR POLLUTION CONTROL

On April 30, 1971, the U.S. Environmental Protection Agency established national ambient air quality standards and a schedule for their application. The

Table 7-2. National Energy Penalty Associated with Moving Source Air Pollution Control

	Percent of Total National Energy
Fuel penalty—light-duty vehicles	0.72
Fuel penalty—heavy-duty gasoline vehicles	0.22
Fuel penalty—heavy-duty diesel vehicles	0.0
Fuel penalty—aircraft	0.0
Energy required to manufacture emissions control systems	0.14
Total	1.1

EPA required each state to submit an implementation plan which can require emission controls stricter than federal standards. In addition, the EPA established regulations for new stationary sources with an energy input greater than 250 million Btu per hour.* The sulfur standards could be met using coal with at most 0.75 percent S by weight or oil with at most 0.6 percent S. For fuels with higher sulfur content, stack gas controls would be required.

The principal pollutants from fixed source combustion processes are sulfur oxides, nitrogen oxides, and particles. Particles are the main pollutant in the noncombustion processes with the greatest emissions in the iron and steel, cement and asphalt industries.[29] Technology for control of particles is in wide use and the energy penalties are small.**

Particles from fossil-fuel plants can be controlled in most cases by using wet scrubbers, often in combination with sulfur removal equipment or electrostatic precipitators. Electrostatic precipitators are effective in removing particles from the burning of coal. Their effectiveness is impaired with use of low sulfur coal, although it appears this problem will be solved. There are several effective means of particle control in noncombustion processes: cyclones, wet collectors, baghouses and electrostatic precipitators.

The electrostatic precipitator energy penalty (thermal) has been given as 0.1 percent of the power plant consumption.[31] The energy involved in capital, i.e., in construction materials and equipment, was calculated using input-output analysis. We adopt the figure, for the Standard Industrial Classification "New Construction, Public Utilities" of 0.076 million Btu (MBtu)

*Equivalent to about 75 megawatts of electrical power or the burning of 10 tons per hour.
**Technologies for control of small particles less than about two microns in diameter are of limited effectiveness. These particles appear to be inordinately important when health effects are considered.[30] Standards leading to the control of small particles are expected to be forthcoming, but there is inadequate information available to estimate what the energy penalty would be for these controls.

per dollar of 1963 construction costs.[32] This value corrected for inflation to 1972 is 0.041 MBtu/$. Using a capital cost of $6 per kilowatt of electrical capacity and a 15-year life for the equipment, this results in an energy penalty associated with this capital of 0.02 percent of plant power. Thus the total energy penalty for particle removal at a power plant is 0.12 percent.

The technologies for controlling nitrogen oxides (NO_x) are uncertain. Research is taking place on combustion modification, reducing excess air supply, catalytic decomposition of nitrogen oxides in the flue gas, and removing (NO_x) from the flue gas. Combustion modification is most advanced. It eliminates high local temperatures which can fix atmospheric nitrogen. Present tangentially fired boilers can meet the present NO_x standard and even operate well with a stricter standard.[33] However, a study made for the EPA concluded that combustion modification techniques are satisfactory in oil- and gas-fired plants, but flue gas treatment methods are needed for coal since it contains nitrogen compounds.[34] It is not clear that standards will require flue gas treatment. We conclude that although units may be derated in controlling NO_x, there would be no significant direct energy penalty. Control equipment capital and capital costs (and shortages) associated with energy needs caused by derating also appear negligible.

The most difficult problem is that of sulfur dioxide emissions. Presently, the use of natural low sulfur fuels is perhaps the best way to protect air quality, but this is not sufficient since these fuels are in short supply. The greater number of electrical power plants and the continued dependence on high sulfur coal and oil therefore demand that adequate sulfur removal technology be developed. Its application will involve considerable effort in the 1970s.

The most advanced technologies for sulfur removal are: add-on devices that remove pollutants from the stack gas, desulfurized oil, and low sulfur synthetic fuel made from coal. It may also prove feasible to remove sulfur (and ash) in the combustion process using fluidized-bed boilers.*

We first consider add-on devices. It is not certain which scrubbing systems will be widely used in the late 1970s and early 1980s. At present, lime and limestone scrubbers have involved the greatest effort, and several large devices have operating experience. Our energy penalty estimates based on these will be indicative of scrubber operations even if other types are adopted.[35]

There are two classes of sulfur dioxide scrubbers: regenerative and throwaway. The regenerative process uses a chemical substance to react with the sulfur dioxide typically forming a compound that can then be separated into the original compound plus a feed stream for a sulfur or a sulfuric acid plant. A throwaway process like lime or limestone, involves only the first step; the disadvantage is a serious waste disposal problem.[36]

---

*In a fluidized-bed boiler, the air required for combustion is blown up through a thick layer, or bed of granular particles. When limestone particles are added sulfur dioxide emissions are reduced.

The energy penalty can be expressed as a fraction of the plant energy, which is equally well thought of in the case of a power plant as a fraction of fuel input or of electrical output. Direct energy requirements are for pumps and fans and for reheat of stack gases. About 40 to 60 percent of the energy penalty is in reheat, necessary to give the flue gas enough buoyancy to rise after it leaves the stack. The indirect (construction) energy is found to be negligible.

Four large power plants with scrubbers were investigated, and we found penalties in the range of 5 to 10 percent (Table 7–3). We project a 7 percent average energy penalty. This compares closely with a recent estimate of 4 to 7 percent.[37] As shown in the table, the energy required for capital construction is small. If there would be a regenerative step, it would add to the energy penalty. We found it of interest that the reversible thermodynamic (i.e., absolute minimum) energy penalty for separation of SO_2 from the stack gases is about 0.2 percent.

A typical eastern coal containing 3.5 percent sulfur and 10 percent ash requires a scrubber that removes 80 percent of sulfur oxides and 99 percent of particulates to meet new plant emission standards. The problem with demonstration scrubbers has not been in meeting such emissions standards, but in reliability.[38] A study by Battelle suggests that several types, including

Table 7–3. Penalties Associated with Limestone Scrubbing Devices

	Scrubber 1[a]	Will County[b]	Detroit Edison[c]	Widows Creek[d]
Power plant capacity	800	177	172	500
°F gas reheat (ΔT)	75°	72°	125°	e
Type reheat	steam	steam	oil	steam
Capital cost ($/kW)	55	96	46	60
Percent SO_2 control		83		
Percent particle control		98		
Percent reheat energy	3.9	2.5	5.4	3.2
Percent equipment energy[f]	4.7	4.0	4.1	1.7
Percent energy in capital construction	0.3	0.5	0.2	0.3
Percent total fuel energy for pollution control	8.9	7.0	9.7	5.2

[a]Proprietary information.

[b]*Will County Unit 1 Limestone Wet Scrubber*, D.C. Gifford, presented at ASME Air Pollution Control Division National Symposium, April 24–25, 1973.

[c]Personal communication with John Cross and Richard Austin, Detroit Edison Company, Detroit, Michigan, May 1973.

[d]Personal communication between A.V. Slack, Chief Chemical Engineer, Tennessee Valley Authority, and Eric Hirst, Oak Ridge National Laboratory.

[e]Gas reheated to 175°.

[f]Equipment includes pumps, fans, limestone mills, and waste disposal.

lime-limestone, could establish reliability by 1976–77.[39] One type which has created enthusiasm is a double alkali scrubber developed by General Motors for a process steam facility at Parma, Ohio. The EPA has determined various types of sulfur scrubbing technology to be sufficiently adequate for utilities to place orders.[40,41]

Orders by power companies for scrubbers have been relatively low.[42] The high cost of scrubbers, up to about 10 percent of new plant cost, uncertain scrubber technology, and the uncertainty of the fuel and regulatory situation, all contribute to the utilities' resistance.

We next turn to oil desulfurization. Some crude oil is available with 0.1 percent S by weight. However, most oil has 1 percent to over 3 percent. The strictest local regulations require burning 0.2 percent S oil, while in many areas use of 1 percent S oil is permitted. Desulfurization of oil is a well-established process for removing sulfur to levels below 0.5 percent S by weight.

Most process schemes for desulfurization of hydrocarbon liquids are basically the same, although their commercial trade names vary. A typical process involves the following steps: the liquid feed combines with a hydrogen-rich gas stream, passes through a heat exchanger and furnace, and then enters a catalytic reactor. In the reactor some of the sulfur in the feed combines with hydrogen to form hydrogen sulfide (H_2S) in the presence of the catalyst. The reactor effluent exchanges heat with the incoming feed, is cooled, and then passes to a separator where the dissolved H_2S is removed.

To evaluate adequately the overall thermal efficiency of oil desulfurization processes, a single case was selected from the literature.[43] This was necessary because many of the available processes did not give sufficient published data to make a complete evaluation. The processing scheme was chosen because fairly complete data were available concerning inputs, outputs, and fuel requirements. Complete processing of the H_2S is included so that sulfur from the oil leaves the process in a very pure, elemental form.

The refinery is intended to be completely self-sufficient, supplying all of its required energy from the naptha which is separated out of the crude feed by distillation. It is somewhat unusual in that whole crude, rather than reduced crude or residuum, is principally used to make fuel oil. In most refineries, a wide spectrum of products is made from whole crude.

We found that this processing scheme will have the following overall thermal efficiencies:

1. The efficiency is 94.4 percent when processing 100,000 barrels per stream day (BPSD) of light Arabian crude oil containing about 1.7 wt percent sulfur to make about 72,800 BSPD of fuel oil containing about 0.5 wt percent sulfur and 22,000 BPSD of naphtha containing about 0.04 wt percent sulfur. At the same time approximately 170 long tons per day of essentially pure sulfur will be produced.

2. If the process is modified to produce fuel oil containing 0.3 wt percent sulfur, the overall thermal efficiency drops to about 94.1 percent.

3. If the plant were used to process 100,000 BPSD of heavy Arabian crude oil with 3.05 wt percent sulfur, the overall thermal efficiency would be about 92.1 percent and 77,100 BPSD of 0.5 wt percent sulfur fuel oil would be produced along with 16,400 BPSD of 0.03 wt percent sulfur naphtha. Three-hundred sixty-eight long tons per day of pure sulfur would also be produced.

To isolate the energy costs associated with desulfurization, the overall thermal efficiency of a process to produce fuel oil and naphtha from a relatively sulfur-free crude oil feed was evaluated. The case studied was the processing of 100,000 BPSD of Brega crude oil from Libya containing 0.17 wt percent sulfur to produce 30,500 BPSD of naphtha containing 0.02 wt percent sulfur.[44] The sulfur content of the feed is so low that no desulfurization is required. The overall thermal efficiency of this process was found to be 97.9 percent. Thus, the energy penalty associated with fuel oil desulfurization is roughly from 3.5 to 5.8 percent, depending upon the type of feed and extent of desulfurization.

In all cases, the heating value of the sulfur was credited to the process, but it made a difference of only a few tenths of a percent in the overall thermal efficiency. When compared with calculations made using available data on other desulfurization processes,[45] the above efficiencies were consistent. The above calculated efficiencies are slightly lower than other calculated efficiencies which do not include the energy consumption necessary to convert gaseous H_2S into elemental sulfur.

The energy involved in capital construction can be estimated from a study of a 40,000 BPSD facility for desulfurization of 4 percent S Kuwait residuum to produce 0.5 percent S fuel oil.[46] When the construction cost is combined with the energy-per-dollar coefficient discussed in the previous section, and a plant life of 15 years is assumed, one finds a construction energy penalty of 0.15 percent of the energy of the fuel processed. This is negligible compared to the processing losses, which we take to be 5 percent.

For the longer term, synthetic fuels made from coal offer a more basic approach to pollution control by allowing pollutant removal prior to combustion. Since refined coal and low-Btu gasification are not likely to have a substantial impact by 1985, we do not consider them in our national penalty.

To make a national energy penalty estimate for 1985, several assumptions must be made:

1. The total energy required to produce electricity is 30 percent of the national energy total of 115 QBtu (quadrillion Btu—10^{15} Btu).

2. Of this electrical energy, 42 percent is obtain from coal and 17 percent is obtained from oil, as in 1972.

3. Of the coal used in power plants, the ratio of low sulfur coal to coal used in plants equipped with scrubbers is 1:1. Of the oil used, the ratio of low sulfur oil to desulfurized oil is 1:1. No synthetic fuels are considered.

4. The ratio of industrial consumption of coal and oil to electrical industry consumption in 1972 will be maintained. Industrial coal consumption is primarily low sulfur coal. Of the industrial oil used, the ratio of low sulfur oil to desulfurized oil is 1:1.

5. One-half of the low sulfur coal production is Western coal subject to a transportation energy penalty.

Sulfur dioxide and particle control penalties are included, while nitrogen oxide control penalties were found to be negligible, as explained earlier.

In this scenario for 1985 the projected scrubbers would be on generators with capacity of roughly 150,000 Megawatts (electric), the projected rate of oil desulfuration for utilities and industry would be roughly 4 million barrels per day, and the low sulfur Western coal shipped would be roughly 400 million tons per year. The process penalties for various control methods have been calculated above and are reviewed here briefly: the sulfur dioxide scrubbers are taken to require 7 percent of the power plant's energy. Oil desulfuration is assumed to require 5 percent of the fuel energy. Transport of Western coal implies a penalty of 3.4 percent of the fuel value.* Particle pollution is assumed to come primarily from coal combustion and from noncombustion industrial use. These control energy penalties are 0.12 percent of fuel value and 0.008 percent of national energy use, respectively. (For a discussion of the energy penalty for noncombustion industrial sources see Appendix B.)

Table 7–4 lists the resulting national energy penalties. If one attempts to break down the penalty into that due to sulfur standards and that due to particle standards, one finds that it's almost all associated with control of sulfur oxides; only about a 0.03 percent penalty is associated with particle control.

The 1 percent national energy penalty for fixed source air pollution is seen to be small when compared with the investment in new technologies and supplies necessary for pollution control. The issues, therefore, are the rate of development of certain new technologies and the capital cost of new facilities,

---

*Although substantial reserves of low sulfur oil and natural gas exist and there are substantial reserves of low sulfur coal in the East, 90 percent (by weight) of the easily recoverable strippable reserves of low sulfur coal in the U.S. are in the Rocky Mountain-Northern Great Plains area. (On a Btu basis the percentage is lower.) Substantial growth in coal production from this area is likely to occur in response to sulfur emissions standards, and we associate an energy penalty with its transportation. Since 65 percent of all strippable reserves are in the West, it is not clear how much of this production will be in response to pollution controls alone. We arbitrarily assign an energy penalty associated with 1,000 miles extra transportation for low sulfur coal shipped from the Western mining states. At 20 million Btu/ton heat of combustion for the coal and 680 Btu/ton-mile for rail haulage, we find an energy penalty of 3.4 percent of the fuel energy.

Table 7-4. National Energy Penalty Associated with Fixed Source Air Pollution Control

	Percent Total National Energy
Electrical generation	
Scrubbers for high S coal	.44
Low sulfur coal	.11
Oil desulfurization	.13
Subtotal	.68
Industrial	
Low sulfur coal	.12
Oil desulfurization	.23
Subtotal	.35
Total	1.0

and not the relatively small amount of energy which is actually diverted for pollution control.

MANAGEMENT OF WASTE HEAT AT POWER PLANTS

The Environmental Protection Agency has proposed guidelines to limit thermal pollution from steam electric power plants (Table 7–5).

Cooling of power plants is accomplished either by once-through circulation of water from lakes and rivers or by recirculated water from a cooling tower or pond. The use of cooling towers or ponds as required by the federal guidelines, leads to a fuel penalty. This penalty results from the following factors:[47,48]

• Additional fuel required to operate the closed cycle cooling system (e.g., about 1 percent).
• Additional fuel required per kilowatt hour of electricity because of higher steam condenser temperatures (e.g., about 2 percent).

The EPA has examined this problem carefully. The total penalty for an individual plant depends on many factors, such as the cooling system used to meet the standards, turbine and condenser design parameters, and climatic conditions. Nevertheless, an average penalty for an *individual plant* required by the guidelines to install cooling towers or ponds is about 3 percent (confirmed by both our own calculations and by reference[47]). The energy required to build the systems is negligible in comparison.

Table 7-5.   Draft Summary of Proposed Effluent Guidelines for Thermal Discharge: EPA Recommendation

Category (Type of Unit)	1977	1978	1979	1980	1983	New Sources
I. Large baseload[a]						
A. Existing units larger than 500 mw	–	ND	–	–	–	ND
B. Existing units 300–500 mw	–	–	ND	–	–	ND
C. Existing units smaller than 300 mw	–	–	–	ND	ND	ND
D. All units on line after July 1977	ND	–	–	–	–	ND
II. Small baseload[b]	NL	–	–	–	ND	ND
III. Cyclic[c]	NL	–	–	–	ND	ND
IV. Peaking[d]	NL	–	–	–	ND	ND
V. Exceptions[e]						

Source: *Economic Analysis of Proposed Effluent Guidelines [for] Steam Electric Plants*, U.S. Environmental Protection Agency, EPA–230/1–73–006, September 1973.

Note: ND = No discharge of heat except that blowdown may be discharged from cold side (e.g., closed cycle cooling system); NL = No technology-based limit (e.g., no restrictions on type of cooling system).

[a]The term large baseload unit will include all units with average boiler capacity factor (essentially the fraction of time the unit is in use) greater than .60 that won't retire before July 1983, all nuclear units, and all units, for which construction begins after October 1973.

[b]The term small baseload unit shall mean a unit which is a part with a rated capacity of less than 25 megawatts or part of a system of less than 150 megawatts.

[c]Units with capacity factors between .2 and .6 that won't retire before July 1983.

[d]Units with capacity factors less than .2.

[e]Exemptions are mentioned in the text.

The fuel penalty before exemptions* would be approximately 0.8 QBtu by 1983; the comparable figure after exemptions is 0.17 QBtu.[49] Assuming that this penalty increases by 15 percent between 1983 and 1985 (the date for our evaluation) leads to a national energy penalty of about 0.2 percent.

CONTROL OF INDUSTRIAL WASTEWATER

The effluent of manufacturing establishments (i.e., not including electrical utilities) is approximately 15 trillion gallons per year, about three times as great as that of the nation's sewered population. Approximately 90 percent of industrial water withdrawals is used for condensing and cooling, and 2 percent provides boiler feed so that 8 percent is process water used in direct contact with raw and finished materials.[50] The latter is our principal concern in this section.

*Section 316(a) of the Federal Water Pollution Control Act of 1972 specifies that whenever the owner or operator of any source subject to the *thermal discharge* guidelines can demonstrate that the effluent limitation proposed for the control of the thermal discharge for that source is more stringent than necessary to assure the protection of the environment, the EPA may impose an *alternative effluent limitation for thermal discharge*.

The National Water Pollution Control program—the federal government's effort to deal with this problem—has two phases. In the first, or 1977 phase, standards comparable to "secondary" treatment of municipal sewage will apply. The second phase covers 1981–1983, with the goal of "zero discharge" into bodies of water by 1985. To cope with the complexity of industrial wastewater treatment, we calculated the energy use associated with end-of-the-line treatment per dollar of operating costs. This characteristic is fairly independent of level and type of pollutants and treatment. The result is 0.2 million Btu per dollar (1968) of operating costs. (See Appendix C for a discussion of this calculation.)

The Council on Environmental Quality projects that 12 billion dollars (1972) will be spent to build end-of-the-line treatment facilities in the decade ending in 1981 with 2 billion dollars of associated annual operating costs.[51] An extension of this development to 1985 implies annual operating costs for all industrial wastewater treatment of $3.2 billion. This would imply energy consumption of 0.55 QBtu or 0.5 percent of the total U.S. energy consumption expected by the mid-eighties.

In phase two, we believe that in-plant (i.e., process) change will be adopted in most cases. The energy impact of in-plant changes over U.S. industry is impossible to predict. But process change to reduce effluent flows often tends to coincide with efforts to reduce energy consumption.* Therefore, it would be incorrect to predict that there must be an increase in energy consumption as U.S. industry moves from phase one to phase two. We are unable to make a quantitative estimate.

AGRICULTURAL AND MUNICIPAL WASTES

The water pollution potential of confined animal wastes, agricultural field practices, and pollution due to sewage presents serious problems to the environment. They are being regulated in a variety of ways and will be subject in the future to increasingly strict standards. Domestic and industrial solid wastes and some agricultural wastes, especially confined animal wastes, and the products of sewage treatment of municipal wastewater present a solid waste disposal problem. Disposal in landfill involves an energy penalty. Incineration, anaerobic digestion, and/or pyrolysis of agricultural and municipal wastes can result in a net energy gain.

---

*For example, the present practices of the paper industry require the withdrawal of 200 tons of water for every ton of paper produced. Most of this water must subsequently be removed from the paper so large quantities of energy are consumed during a drying process. One engineering firm has developed a process which permits the use of higher pulp contents in paper formation. This device can reduce water demand for this production phase by as much as 75 percent, providing savings in electrical and heating energy of up to 50 percent.

Table 7-6. National Energy Penalty and Potential Energy Recovery Associated with Control of Agricultural and Municipal Wastes (1985)

	Total National Energy Impact (Recovery (+) Penalty (-))	
	Units of 10^{14} Btu/Yr	Percent
Agricultural wastes		
Anaerobic digestion of 50 percent of confined animal manure	3.4	+0.3
Municipal wastewater		
Sewage treatment	−7.2	−0.6
Anaerobic digestion of sewage	0.8	+0.1
Municipal solid wastes		
Fossil fuel supplement (1/2)	7.3	+0.6
Pyrolysis or anaerobic digestion (1/2)	3.3	+0.3
Net energy gain	7.7	0.7

If the Council on Environmental Quality's capital investment projection of $48 billion for sewage treatment between 1971 and 1981 is extended to 1985, a total use of energy for sewage treatment equals 0.6 QBtu per year. (See Appendix D for a discussion of this calculation). A survey of current practices showed that more than half of the total is indirect energy—energy involved in the construction of the treatment facilities. This indirect energy does not play the major role in any of the other categories considered in this chapter.

The transportation and handling energy associated with suitable landfill disposal of solid wastes (garbage and confined animal manure) is unimportant on the national scale.*

However, organic wastes are an energy resource. We assume that one half of confined animal wastes, all municipal solid wastes and sludge from sewage treatment can be converted into convenient energy forms. Three processes are considered: (a) fossil fuel supplement in power plants;[52] (b) pyrolysis, or breakdown of complex organic molecules into simple fuels;[53] and (c) anaerobic digestion to produce methane.[54] A reasonable mix of these processes implies a 1.3 percent contribution to national energy needs. (See Appendix E.) Agricultural crop wastes could also be utilized in this way, but such a development would not be a waste disposal measure. Table 7-6 shows the

---

*The total animal waste subject to the problems associated with large quantities of highly concentrated waste material was estimated. Assuming an average haul distance of two miles, we obtained a national energy use per year for this operation of about 0.002 QBtu. This is only about 0.003 percent of current national energy consumption. Similarly, the energy presently required to dispose of residential and commercial solid waste was estimated and found to be only about 0.03 percent of total national energy use.

national energy penalty and potential energy recovery of agriculture and municipal wastes to result in a net energy gain of 0.7 percent.

SUMMARY

In each pollution control category we have projected a national energy penalty for 1985. These are summarized in Table 7–7. The national energy penalty is 2 percent of total energy use, or 2.3 QBtu.

These sample national energy penalties can be compared with studies by Hirst,[55] the National Petroleum Council (NPC),[56] and the EPA.[57] Our sample automotive penalty based on new information for 1975 models is intrinsically lower than that of others. Two other studies embody weight reductions substantially reducing the penalty that they project. Our fixed source air pollution penalty depends on the assumed availability of natural low sulfur fuels. We found that stack gas scrubbers are more energy-intensive than did Hirst, and Gakner and Jimeson.[58] Our closed cooling system penalty is somewhat smaller than that of others. Our industrial wastewater control penalty is smaller than NPC's and, by implication, smaller than any projection based on the Edison Electric Institute Study.[59] It seems that a significant part of normal industrial operations were attributed to control of waste in their survey. Our sewage estimate is somewhat below Hirst's (the latter is based on extension of secondary treatment to the entire population). the NPC's large sewage and fresh water energy value probably involves a very broad definition of provision and disposal of water.

Our sample gain (negative penalty) for organic solid wastes is somewhat larger than Hirst's since it involves a somewhat more ambitious scheme of waste conversion. Either one of these schemes would require considerable investment. For example, up to $10 billion is indicated as the capital cost of anaerobic digestion facilities.

Based on these sample national energy penalties, we conclude that the overall energy penalty associated with pollution control is small. The 2 percent penalty is less than half the typical increase of U.S. consumption in *a single year*.

Not only is the overall penalty small but so are individual penalties with respect to each process, with only the 5 percent automotive penalty and the 7 percent SO_2 scrubber penalties being especially large. The penalties are small considering growth is use of energy in every area. They are especially small compared to energy consumption reductions which could be made with readily available technologies for more efficient energy utilization, without substantial alteration in products or service, in every area. However, it should be noted that in several areas the pollution control technologies are not fully developed. The difficulty of implementation of these control technologies is not reflected in the energy penalties. Cost, technological reliability, and timing, not energy, are the important factors that bear on the implementation of pollution control.

Table 7-7. Sample National Energy Penalties Associated with Pollution Control, 1985

	Principal Assumptions	*Typical Energy Penalty in the Controlled Activity Evaluation in This Report*	*National Energy Penalty as a Percent of Total Energy Use*
Air pollution standards and transportation	Autos of 1975 type compared to pre-1968, and same weight as at present. Auto consumption is at 14% of the national total. Other transport with 5% or zero penalty.	5% of auto fuel	1.1%
Fixed source air pollution controls	Present ratios for use of coal and oil, scrubbers in half of coal fired power plants, low S coal otherwise. Desulfurized oil in half of oil use.	5–7% of fuel in the particular plants 3–4% for transport of western coal	1.0%
Waste heat management for steam electric power plants	New plants, adopt wet closed cycle cooling instead of once through cooling where available.	$\leqslant$ 3% of fuel in the particular plants	0.2%
Industrial waste water controls	Meet phase one type standards with $3.2 billion annual operating cost. The energy penalty is associated with this cost compared with 115×10^{15} Btu total.	$\dfrac{0.2 \text{ million Btu}}{\$ \text{ Operating Cost}}$	0.5%
Sewage treatment	Meet standards with $48 billion per decade capital investment rate. Energy penalty is relative to 115×10^{15} Btu total.	0.7×10^{15} Btu (thermal)	0.6%
Conversion or disposal of solid wastes	All "available" organic wastes i.e., all garbage sewage, sludge, and 50% of confined animal wastes, are converted to fuel or used as fossil-fuel supplement in power plants. Percentage is calculated for a 1985 projection relative to 115×10^{15} Btu total.	Production of 1.5×10^{15} Btu	–1.3%
Net penalty			2.1%

Appendix A

Input-Output Analysis

The inclusion of indirect energy requirements associated with material flows and capital construction is an important aspect of this study. These indirect energy uses are included by means of input-output (I/O) analysis, and, in particular, by means of a study provided to us in advance of publication by Herendeen.[60] The I/O analysis is an economic tool which in this case enables summation of energy inputs all the way from supplier, to supplier's supplier, and so on. The energy given by the analysis does not include energy used by employees or to support the employees outside of work. We assume that this energy would be consumed regardless of the nature of their employment (see below for a further remark). The basic ideas of I/O analysis are contained in the writings of Leontieff.[61]

There are limitations as to the accuracy of the I/O approach. Considerable averaging over activities exists. To choose a particularly bad case, it provides an energy content per dollar of average product of the "organic and inorganic chemicals" industry rather than energy content for particular products. While the cases important to this study suggest that this averaging process does not cause serious error, the summation of energy inputs accomplished by the analysis is based on a fixed national economic structure (that of 1963). Thus we do *not* evaluate changes in the rest of the economy due to adoption of a control technology. Another difficulty arises when an activity involves suppliers whose role in the economy is, at the time of interest, very different from that of 1963. We are not aware in this study of having made any gross misuse of the analysis in either of these categories.

Appendix B

Energy Requirements for Noncombustion Industrial Air Pollution Control

Although great emphasis has been placed on sulfur oxide and particulate emissions control from power plants, industrial emissions also are a significant fraction of total nationwide emissions. Noncombustion industrial emissions accounted for 36.8 percent weight fraction of total emissions in 1970, with particle emissions in this category reaching 50.1 percent of total particle emissions (Table 7–1). We find the energy penalty is small for noncombustion industrial air pollution, so therefore we will not make a very detailed analysis. Since the largest class of noncombustion industrial air pollution is particles and particle control is the most urgent problem, the energy penalty for particle collection alone will be calculated.

There are several types of control equipment used for particle control: cyclones, wet collectors, baghouses, and electrostatic precipitators. Cyclones are simple in construction, can handle high dust loading, and can operate under varying temperatures. However, they are inefficient for small particle sizes. Wet collectors are advantageous in simultaneous gas and particle control. However, the particles cleaned from the gas stream are transferred to the water, creating a water pollution problem. Electrostatic precipitators are sensitive to varying flow rates and dust loadings and are unable to collect some particles that have inappropriate electrical properties. Baghouses are efficient collectors, but high temperature and chemicals are hazards to bag life. For a few types of processes there are, indeed, no convenient adequate means of particle control: glass-making furnaces and coke ovens, among others.

The average "gas exit loadings" for iron and steel, cement and asphalt batching are 7 to 30, 5 to 20, and 24 to 82 gr/scf, respectively, where gr/scf is grains per standard cubic foot.[62] A grain is about 1.4×10^{-4} pound or the weight of 0.065 gram. The gas exit loading is the weight of particles per volume of air. These three industries contributed over 40 percent of total industrial particle air pollution in 1968. Taking an average gas exit loading and

331

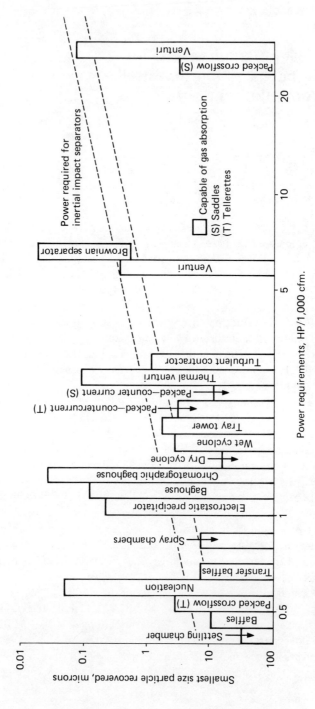

Figure 7B-1. Technologies for Particle Removal, Particle Size, and Power Requirements. Source: Teller, 1972, p. 93.

using the amount of industrial particles emitted in one year, an average flow rate can be calculated. Teller has tabulated horsepower requirements for various pollution control devices per unit flow rate as shown in Figure 7B–1. Precipitators, baghouses, and cyclones require between 1 and 2 horsepower per 1,000 cubic feet per minute (cfm). For this rough calculation, a horsepower requirement of 1.3 hp/1,000 cfm will be used. Taking a gas exit loading of 5 grains/scf and a 1970 emissions total of 13.3 x 10^6 tons of particles (corresponding to 7.2 x 10^7 standard cubic feet/min). the yearly demand for electricity is about 15 x 10^8 kilowatt hours (thermal).

At an average capital cost of $2.14 per cfm capacity[63] national investment of $150 million is projected. Assuming 15-year equipment life and the appropriate input-output energy coefficient, we obtain an energy penalty of .41 x 10^{12} Btu per year associated with capital cost. Capital and operating penalties sum to 5.7 x 10^{12} Btu per year. Using a national energy consumption of 67 x 10^{15} Btu in 1970, noncombustion industrial air pollution would require 0.008 percent of the national energy consumption.

Appendix C

Energy and Industrial Wastewater Treatment

The variety and complexity of inorganic and organic components of industrial effluents presents a serious wastewater treatment control problem. As a result of this variety of industrial effluent streams, generalizations can easily be misleading.

TERMINOLOGY

It remains useful to adopt the terminology of sewage treatment to discuss the varied problems of industrial wastewater treatment. Industrial waste measurement and the treatment processes—primary, secondary, and tertiary (see Table 7C-1)—have been borrowed from municipal sewage treatment practices, and thus have focused on the removal of organics and suspended solids. Although organic waste loads represent only part of the industrial waste control picture, they cause a substantial portion of our water pollution problem. In fact, 93.4 percent of the Biological Oxygen Demand (BOD) 89 percent of the Chemical Oxygen Demand (COD), and 85 percent of suspended solids in U.S. waste waters from point sources are contributed directly by production processes.[64] (See Table 7C-1 for terminology.)

There is a considerable range of wastewater treatment technology that is already in commercial use or will be ready in the near future. Processes comparable to biological treatment processes for secondary treatment of organic wastes have been successfully borrowed from domestic sewage treatment. Such processes as activated sludge, anaerobic or aerobic lagoons, and trickling filters are capital intensive generally requiring large initial capital outlay but relatively small annual operating costs.[65]

Lagooning, either anaerobic or aerobic, aerated or natural, is a reliable, natural, and effective waste treatment process. However, its implementation and effectiveness are declining as wasteloads are increasing and the amount of available land is decreasing.[66]

Table 7C-1.   Some Wastewater Control Terminology

Water Quality Parameters

Parameter	Defined Chemically	Defined Conceptually
Biological oxygen demand (BOD)	Amount of oxygen (mg/liter) utilized in microbial mediated oxidation of organic matter in specified amount of time (usually 5 days, sometimes denoted BOD_5)	A measure of the oxygen demand in microbial degradation of organic matter. Represents that fraction of organic matter capable of being oxidized by dissolved oxygen in water
Chemical oxygen demand (COD)	Amount of oxygen (mg/liter) consumed in chemical oxidation of organic (or inorganic) matter in water	A measure of the oxidizability of substances in water. Most of the substances oxidized are organic

Levels of Treatment

	Pollutant Removal	General Method
Primary	Removes 30 to 60% of oxygen demanding wastes, mainly particles	Mechanical screening
Secondary	Removes 85–90% BOD, or down to a level of 25–50 parts per million by weight, and suspended solids	Physical and biological treatment; see text
Improved secondary	Removes 90–95% BOD and suspended solids and 80–90% of phosphates	Addition of chemicals
Tertiary	Removes 95–99% BOD, suspended solids and certain dissolved inorganics	See text

Other Terms

Nonpoint sources	Sources of wastewater not discharged through a pipe, especially agricultural, mining and construction runoff.	
Zero discharge	No discharge of effluent to surface bodies of water, e.g., heavily concentrated effluent is pumped into a deep well or it is incinerated and residue is disposed of as solid waste.	

Trickling filter systems are applicable to large volumes of organic wastes.

Activated sludge treatment is also a useful system for large plants. BOD levels of 30 parts per million or better can be consistently realized. This system must support a very complex organism population of bacteria, protozoans, metazoans, and fungi which requires a definite temperature range and nutrient balance for growth and metabolism of the organic waste stream. This delicate system cannot withstand shock loads of organic and toxic wastes as well as a system of lagooning or trickling filtration. The required aeration pumps cause the energy requirements for activated sludge treatment to be proportionately higher than for other biological treatment processes.

The most prevalent tertiary treatment methods are ion exchange, activated-carbon absorption, and incineration. All of these processes involve complex chemical reactions and thus require constant supervision and highly skilled operation. In some instances, these processes can replace secondary biological treatment but have yet to receive wide acceptance. Nemerow summarizes the origin, character, and most prevalent waste treatments for food and drug, paper and allied products, and chemical and allied products effluent streams.[67]

OVERVIEW OF ENERGY ASSOCIATED
WITH END-OF-THE-LINE TREATMENT

Whereas industrial plant type, wastewater flows, pollutant mix, and treatment approach vary extraordinarily intra- as well as inter-industry, the energy expended per dollar of operating cost appears to be relatively constant for secondary treatment:[68]

> Few measures of pollution control activity serve as well as the continuing annual expenditures for the operation of pollution control equipment and programs. This expenditure translates into cost factors the investment made for capital equipment and provides a year to year basis for gauging the extent of pollution control activity.

For our purpose, "annual operating costs" consist of the sum of salaries and wages, electricity, chemical, fuel, other supplies, maintenance, and miscellaneous items required to operate a plant for a given year.

We have thus incorporated calculated energy costs into a number to represent the energy required per dollar of annual operating cost for end-of-the-line treatment. It appears that a well-managed facility expends on both direct and indirect energy approximatly 25 cents out of every dollar (1968) of operating and maintenance cost. The actual energy to cost ratio is 0.2 million-Btu (the equivalent of one and a half gallons of gasoline) consumed per dollar of operation and maintenance costs. Only some industries manage to spend a substantially larger fraction of each dollar on energy. These are usually industries where intense energy use and low labor use is obvious, such as primary metals, or some industries whose product is fuel-based, such as asphalt. This figure appears to be a reasonable *upper limit* for energy expenditure necessary to comply with the anticipated 1977 industrial effluent guidelines. Some facilities will buy such a large amount of energy with each operating dollar, many will buy less, and very few if any will buy more.

To give further understanding of the 0.2 million Btu-per-dollar figure, the national average energy use for all activities was 0.072 million Btu per dollar of Gross National Product (GNP) in 1968. Our calculation yields a result twice as large as that obtained from the 1963 input-output data, which gives a ratio of 0.10 million Btu per dollar (adjusted to 1968) for the industrial classification "Water and Sanitary Services."[69]

Wastewater treatment in industry, therefore, is energy-intensive.

We now discuss how the energy-to-cost ratio was obtained in several different cases.

MUNICIPAL ACTIVATED SLUDGE TREATMENT

The energy we consider is energy in the fuels originally consumed. Electricity figures both for purchased and in-plant generation have been converted from kilowatt hours electrical to thermal Btu by applying an efficiency factor of 0.30. The conversion factor is thus 0.0114 million Btu per kwh. In instances where the number of kilowatt hours used had to be determined from cost figures, the price of electricity was taken from the Federal Power Commission's *Typical Electric Bills*[70] or from direct information. To determine the energy value of chemicals used in the activated sludge process, we referred to Herendeen's input-output analysis.[71] Lime accounts for about two-thirds of the necessary chemicals. According to Herendeen, the total energy value for this category is 0.20 million Btu per 1963 dollar. Updated to 1968, this figure becomes 0.17, which we use to convert chemical costs to Btu. Any fuels such as gas for sludge disposal or process steam for space heating and prevention of pipe freezing are included when such information is available.

Finally, we attempt to account for the energy value of capital in the waste treatment facility, such as materials, construction, and equipment. Capital costs used are installed costs assumed to be equipment cost plus 30 percent and are depreciated over 15 years. For capital, we chose the classification "New Construction of Public Utilities" with a 1963 energy per dollar output value of 0.076 million Btu. In our calculation, this figure appears as 0.058 for 1968, having accounted for inflation of construction costs.

According to data compiled and analyzed by Michel[72] on the operation of a 1-million-gallon-per-day standard activated sludge treatment process for a municipal plant, electricity represents 22 percent and chemicals (not including chlorine) account for 2.9 percent of annual operating costs. (Full costs were not quoted.) After converting to a Btu value using the processes explained above, we calculated an energy value of (0.14 million Btu + fuel) per 1968 dollar operating cost (see Table 7C–2). The results for sewage plants up to 10 times larger and 10 times smaller (the 1 million gallon per day) flow are not substantially different.

In one comparison, we examined an activated sludge process treating

Table 7C-2. Total Energy Use Associated with Wastewater Treatment per Dollar of Annual Operating Costs (Million Btu per 1968 Dollar)

	Activated Sludge with Sludge Treatment			
	Sewage[a] (1 mgd)[e]	Mixed Municipal-Paper[b] (4 mgd)	Paper Industry Average[c]	Projection for Reverse Osmosis[d]
Electricity	0.128	0.098	0.09	0.12
Fuel	–	0.043		
Chemicals and nutrients	0.005	0.028		
Capital	0.024	0.024		
Total	.14 + fuel	.19		

[a]From Robert Michel, "Costs and Manpower in Municipal Wastewater Treatment Plant Operation and Maintenance 1964–1968," *Journal of the Water Pollution Control Federation* (November 1970; update 1972).

[b]From U.S. Environmental Protection Agency, Program Number 12070 GND, *Projected Wastewater Treatment Cost in the Organic Chemical Industry*, Datagraphics, Inc., Pittsburgh, Pennsylvania, July 1971 (update of an original study by Cyrus M. Rice and Company).

[c]From Testimony from Peter E. Wrist, American Paper Institute, Hearings before the Committee on Public Works, House of Representatives, Ninety-second Congress, First Session on H.R. 11896; H.R. 11895 to Amend the Federal Water Pollution Control Act, December 7, 8, 9, and 10, 1971.

[d]From Office of Research and Monitoring, U.S. Environmental Protection Agency, Project No. 12040EEL, *Reverse Osmosis Concentration of Dilute Pulp and Paper Effluents* (February 1972).

[e]mgd = million gallons per day.

municipal and paper mill wastes.[73] In summarizing the data for this facility, Robinson and Coughlin note that overall operation costs increase between 50 and 60 percent when plant capacity is doubled. Cost parameters analyzed by the Environmental Protection Agency indicate that economies of scale result in a declining number of manhours expended per unit load with increased plant size, but costs per unit of material and energy also decline. Accounting for the electricity, fuel, chemicals, and nutrients, and estimating the capital energy for this 4-million-gallon-per-day combined treatment plant, we calculate total energy use to be 0.19 million Btu per dollar of operating costs (see Table 7C–2).

As the required level of effluent treatment becomes more stringent and treatment costs escalate, municipalities charge proportionately higher rates for treatment of industrial wastewater. Accordingly, high waste-producing industries are forced to treat their own effluent. Wasteload estimates based on the "average quantity of pollutant per product unit" reveal that three Standard Industrial Classifications (SIC)—Chemicals and Allied Products; Paper and Allied

Products; and Kindred Food Products—generate 90 percent of the BOD in industrial waste water.[74] These are three of the six standard classifications which accounted for 66 percent of 1968 industrial energy consumption.[75] We have thus chosen to focus on the water pollution control effects of these three water and energy-intensive industries. In the following two subsections, we will develop the energy-to-cost ratio for activated sludge treatment of wastewaters of the organic chemicals and paper products industries.

ORGANIC CHEMICALS AND THE 1977 STANDARDS

The principal contaminants in the organic chemicals industry's wastewater are BOD, COD, oil, suspended solids, acids, heavy metals, and residue organic byproducts.[76] Since the production of organic chemicals results in so many types of effluent, wastewater treatments employed cover the range of known practical technology.

A 1972 study of wastewater treatment by the organic chemicals industry considers pretreatment by a primary treatment process, secondary treatment by an activated sludge process and final clarification for average BOD_5 removal of 84 percent. Capital costs were found to be a scattered logarithmic function of the wastewater volume, averaging $1.0 million per plant. Operating costs of the larger treatment palnts were roughly one-sixth of the capital costs—an average of $0.19 million per plant.[77]

More explicit capital and operating cost figures for a large wastewater treatment facility at a chemical plant complex enabled a calculation of the thermal energy required per dollar operating costs for the treatment facility. The major portion of energy use was for secondary treatment by activated sludge. We obtained a 0.20 MBtu per 1968 dollar operating costs excluding energy associated with capital,[78] independently confirming the energy-to-cost ratio discussed above.* This plant is reasonably close to meeting the presumed 1977 standards.

End-of-the-line wastewater treatment implies added energy consumption. It also adds to costs. The ratio total energy use per dollar of total cost, associated with a production facility or an industry, need not increase with increased treatment.

---

*We note that the total energy use per dollar of product of the organic and inorganic chemicals industry is 0.32 million Btu (1963).[79] (This high value is presumably associated in part with use of fuel as feed stock for the making of organic chemicals.) What this means is that added dollars spent for wastewater treatment in the chemical industry will tend to *lower* the energy-to-cost ratio characteristic of the chemical industry, since the treatment facilities alone have a lower energy-to-cost ratio.

PAPER AND ALLIED PRODUCTS AND
1977 STANDARDS

Experience to date shows that the average annual operating costs for wastewater treatment in the paper and allied products industry are one-sixth the capital investment in treatment facilities.[80] The total industry installed capacity was approximately 170,000 tons of product per day. Estimated operating costs for wastewater treatment in 1970 were $210 million per year, an average of $3.50 to $4.00 per ton of product. The average capital cost of wastewater treatment, based on a weighted average of the available data, was $5,000 to $7,000 per ton of daily capacity. Thus the total capital cost for the industry to meet 1977 standards is estimated to be in the range of $0.85 to $1.20 billion.

Peter Wrist, representing the American Paper Institute, testified at House hearings in 1971 that the power consumption of a typical secondary treatment facility was 0.8–1.2 kilowatt hours per 1,000 gallons of water treated.[81] At an industrywide average of 28,000 gallons per ton of product, power consumption was close to 30 kilowatt hours per ton of product or 0.09 million Btu per dollar of operating costs. (See Table 7C–2 for comparison of electricity categories.)

As in the case of the chemical industry, we can ask the hypothetical question: would adding end-of-the-line wastewater treatment facilities to an otherwise unchanged paper industry increase or decrease the total energy-to-cost ratio of that industry? The ratio of total energy use-to-operation and maintenance costs for treatment is 0.2 million Btu/$. Total treatment costs include capital, so the ratio of total energy to total costs for treatment is lower, and by coincidence is about the same (0.12 million Btu/$) as the total energy use per dollar average product of the paper industry.[82]

We conclude first that investment in wastewater control at the secondary treatment level will not alter the ratio of energy use-to-cost characteristic of the paper industry.

It has been estimated that the paper and allied products industry will spend $627 million for installed primary and secondary treatment for the period 1972–1975.[83] We estimate that this implies $105 million added, annual operating costs and therefore, on the basis of 0.2 million Btu per dollar of operating costs, 2×10^{13} Btu energy consumption per year. This represents 0.02 percent of total projected national energy use for the late seventies or about 1 percent added energy use by the paper industry.[84] So we conclude that feasibility and cost of, not energy for, wastewater treatment are the problems facing the paper industry.

Appendix D

Energy Associated with Treatment of Municipal Wastes

The energy demand associated with wastewater treatment has been divided into the following components: (a) electricity; (b) fuel, including gasoline, oil, and natural gas; (c) chemicals, and (d) capitalization energy.

ELECTRICAL ENERGY

Electrical energy is used at many points in wastewater treatment plants. Influent pumping and air diffusion account for 75 percent of the electrical energy use in a 10 mgd (million gallons per day) activated sludge plant.

To obtain the total electrical energy required by wastewater treatment plants, plots were first made of electrical energy requirements by type of plant and flow rate. The type of plants treated in this way were activated sludge, high-rate trickling filter, standard-rate trickling filter, conventional primary extended aeration, and waste stabilization. These types of plants serve approximately 86 percent of the sewered population.

An example of the plots used is given in Figure 7D–1 showing electrical energy requirements versus flow rate for three sets of data. The three curves of Figure 7D–1 are based on the data of (a) Michael and Johnson,[85] * (b) Smith,[86] and (c) a survey of 80 wastewater treatment plants conducted by one of the authors (D.D.). Where data are unavailable, the curves were extrapolated. A total flow rate for treatment plants was then calculated, based upon the 1968 National Inventory and an average per-capita flow rate of 100 gallons/day.[87, 88] The electrical energy required for all plants for each type were

*The FWPCA study evaluated electricity expenditure in terms of January 1968 dollar cost. For the present work, this was converted to kwh/yr by use of electricity cost data from the *Edison Electric Institute Statistical Yearbook* indicating the average cost of electricity for public authorities in 1968 to be 1.2¢/kwh. Since electricity costs vary depending upon quantity used/month, the actual costs used to calculate energy requirements were based on a range of 1.8-1.0¢/kwh and a curve relating cost to quantity used.

343

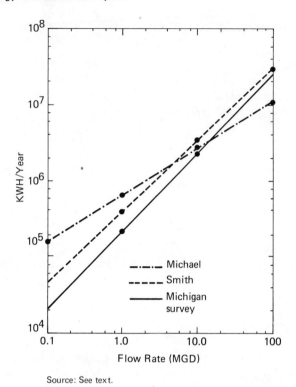

Source: See text.

Figure 7D-1. Electrical Energy Requirements for Municipal Treatment of Wastewater—Activated Sludge

then added together. Only the Michael and Johnson data were available for extended aeration and waste stabilization so that only a single value is given for this method of treatment. High rate and standard rate trickling filter plants were combined and treated as a single category under trickling filters. The results of the calculation procedure are summarized in Table 7D–1. The average of these for 1971 corrected for growth in sewered population from 1968 to 1971 is taken to be 53×10^{12} Btu.

Advanced processes of treatment (often referred to as tertiary) have been used at some plants to further purify the effluent. The advanced process train used depends upon the needs and requirements of those using the effluent water. Two sample tertiary treatment processes were considered here. The electrical power requirements for those systems average 4.2 million kwh/yr for 10 mgd beyond that required for secondary treatment. This compares to 0.85 million kwh/yr for a 10 mgd primary, 1.75 for a high rate trickling filter plant, and 3.26 million kwh/yr for a 10 mgd activated sludge plant. Removal of phosphorous and dissolved organics would require additional electrical energy. Total added energy requirements for tertiary treatment of nitrogen, phospho-

Table 7D-1. Estimated Electrical Energy Required for Municipal Wastewater Treatment by Type of Plant in U.S.[a]

Type of Plant	Electrical Energy Expended (Billions of kwh)		
	Michel and Johnson	Smith	Michigan
Primary	0.63	0.46	0.49
Trickling filter	1.06	1.55	1.08
Activated sludge	1.34	2.06	1.68
Waste stabilization	0.16	0.16	0.16
Extended aeration	0.33	0.33	0.33
Totals	3.52	4.56	3.74
Assuming 30% generation and transmission efficiency	11.7	15.2	12.47
Btu equivalent (trillions)	39.9	51.9	42.6

Sources: References in addition to this study include numbers 85, 86, and 88.
[a]Based Upon flow by plant type as given in the 1968 Inventory of Municipal Wastewater Facilities.

rous, and organics would be 120 to 270 percent of that required for standard secondary treatment, depending upon the type of secondary treatment employed.

CHEMICALS

The data of Michael and Johnson[89] was used to examine the relationship between dollar chemical cost versus plant flow from 0.1 to 100 mgd. Extrapolations were made for high flow rates when no data were available. Since chemical costs differ considerably from one type and capacity of plant to another, as does electricity, an estimate by summation of all costs determined from the aforementioned curves was made using data on the type and size of wastewater treatment plants.[90] The estimated annual chemical costs for the entire U.S. is given by treatment type for 1968 in Table 7D–2. In order to obtain an estimate of the primary energy represented by this cost of chemicals, the energy input-output study of R. Herendeen was used.[91] The energy coefficients listed for three different classifications of chemicals are:

Lime	0.20×10^6 Btu/$
Industrial chemicals	0.32×10^6 Btu/$
Agricultural chemicals	0.20×10^6 Btu/$

The average taken was 0.24 million Btu/$ for 1963. Corrected to 1968 dollars, this is 0.21 MBtu/$ and the approximate energy represented by the chemicals used in all U.S. wastewater treatment plants in 1968 is 6.1×10^{12} Btu.

Table 7D–2. Dollar Cost of Chemicals (1968 Dollars) for Wastewater Treatment Plant Operation in U.S. in 1968

Type of Treatment	*Chemical Cost ($ Millions)*
Primary	4.8
Extended aeration	1.4
High-rate trickling filter	5.9
Standard-rate trickling filter	2.8
Activated sludge	8.5
Waste stabilization	5.9
Totals	29.3
Btu equivalent (see text)	6.1×10^{12}

Source: Michel and Johnson.

Table 7D–3. Fuels, Natural Gas, Gasolines, and Oil in Wastewater Treatment per Year

		Activated Sludge	*Trickling Filter*	*Primary*
Natural gas	No. of plants surveyed	12	12	8
Michigan survey (1973)	Average design flow (mgd)	13.1	2.3	2.2
	Million scf gas used/mgd treated	1.38	.93	.58
	Billion Btu of gas/mgd treated	1.38	.93	.58
Gasoline and oil Michigan survey (1973)	No. of plants surveyed	15	20	14
	Gasoline and oil used thousands gals/mgd treated	2.04	.79	1.22
	Billion Btu of gasoline & oil/mgd treated	0.276	0.107	0.163
Wastewater flow in U.S. in 1968 (reference 90)	Population served (millions)	41	29	36
	Percent of total sewered population	31.6	22.7	28.3
	gpd/capita	123	89	122
	Estimated total bdg flow	5.04	2.58	4.39
Fuels required for wastewater treatment in U.S.	Btu equivalents in trillions/yr	8.4	2.7	3.3

Tertiary treatment requires the use of additional quantities of chemicals, particularly lime and carbon and ion exchange resins (polymers). The best data available is for the 7.5 mgd Lake Tahoe Plant[92] in which $319 worth of chemicals was used per day for the system which included nitrogen, phosphorous, and organics removal. An approximate energy equivalent, obtained using the input-output coefficients, is 3.2 billion Btu/yr per mgd/day. This would be 0.65 trillion Btu/yr for each 1 percent of the total U.S. sewered population on the Lake Tahoe-type tertiary system.

FUEL

Data used to calculate fuel (including gasoline, natural gas, and oil) was obtained by surveying (in 1973) 80 wastewater treatment plants in Michigan. It indicates approximately how much is used in U.S. wastewater treatment plants.

An average scf (standard cubic feet) value for natural gas used per million gallons treated was calculated and is given in Table 7D–3. Total gasoline and oil estimates were obtained in the same manner using Michigan Survey data as shown in this table. The number of plant surveys for this application were somewhat different than those for natural gas, but the average flow/plant was approximately the same. The total energy associated with gas, gasoline, and oil used was then approximated by multiplying the energy used per year per mgd flow by the U.S. total estimated flow for each type of treatment as given in Table 7D–3. The energy consumption associated with use of gas, gasoline, and oil in the three major types of treatment in the U.S. based on 1968 population data is found to be 14×10^{12} Btu/yr. The results for growth of sewered population to 1971 is 16×10^{12} Btu.

CAPITALIZATION

The energy associated with construction expenditures has been caculated from capital cost data from the 1973 annual Environmental Quality Council Report.[93] The new capital cost in 1971, taken to be 3.9 billion dollars (1972$) were converted to approximate Btu equivalents by use of the input-output data with "New Construction, Public Utilities" as the standard industrial classification. The total primary energy equivalent for this classification is given as 0.0755 million Btu/1963$. Corrected to 1972, this becomes 0.040 MBtu/$. The results are shown in Table 7D–4.

TOTAL ENERGY

Total energy requirements for municipal wastewater treatment found above are summarized in Table 7D–4 for 1971. In addition, an independent value is given for operation and maintenance calculated from overall expenditures[94] of 1.4

Table 7D-4. Use of Energy for Municipal Wastewater Treatment in the U.S. (Trillions of Btu)

	1971	*1981*
Operations[a]		
Electricity	53	
Chemical (1968)	6	
Fuel	16	
Total	75	
Operations and maintenance (based on expenditures)	125	260
Capitalization	160	290
Total	285	550

[a]From Tables 7D-1, 7D-2, and 7D-3 updated to 1971 and 1981 as discussed in text.

billion dollars (1972) and input-output data[95] using the classification, "Water and Sanitary Services" with an associated energy equivalent at 0.117 million Btu/1963\$, corrected to 0.089 MBtu/1972\$. A difficulty is that this energy coefficient in the input analysis is for water supply as well as treatment. The effect of this is uncertain. The energy for sewage treatment calculated on the basis of three individual components is seen in Table 7D-4 to be 75, while that calculated on the input-output basis is 125 trillion Btu. This is a very satisfactory agreement since the first figure is small on two counts: (a) some of the data are for 1968 rather than 1971 and do not cover the entire inventory of sewage facilities, and (b) some indirect energy such as for maintenance is not counted.

On the basis of these two counts, we estimate roughly that total 1971 energy use, for operations and maintenance, based on extending the partial vertical analysis, would be about 100 trillion Btu agreeing within 20 percent with the input-output analysis value.

Table 7D-4 also lists the energy required for U.S. Municipal Wastewater treatment for 1981. This was obtained by using the estimated 1981 expenditures[96] and the input-output data. Assuming that the rate of growth in total energy use for sewage treatment from 1971 to 1981 continues at the same rate to 1985, an estimate of 720 trillion Btu/year is obtained for Municipal Wastewater Treatment in 1985.

Appendix E

Energy-Conserving Waste Management Alternatives

In this Appendix we consider three of the most promising techniques for conversion of organic wastes into convenient forms of energy: combustion of solid waste as a fossil fuel supplement, pyrolysis to produce fuel, and anaerobic digestion to produce methane and a fertilizer-soil stabilizer. We determine the net useful energy that can be thus obtained from available municipal solids, animal wastes, and sewage sludge.

COMBUSTION OF SOLID WASTES AS A FOSSIL FUEL SUPPLEMENT

The concept of waste heat recovery from refuse is not new. Refuse can be burned to produce steam or to generate electricity. An especially efficient application involves using refuse as a supplement to coal in power generation.

In utilizing refuse in utility boilers the proportion of refuse to coal is relatively small so as to reduce the possibility of adverse effects on the combustion and power generation phases and on emissions. The availability of a refuse source close to power plants is an added advantage. Since equipment for processing, handling, and transporting refuse is available today, this waste heat recovery process could be implemented economically and quickly with little additional developmental effort.

Under a grant from the Bureau of Solid Waste Management this idea has been studied in St. Louis, Missouri. A 1970[97] report confirmed that the original premises of the study were basically valid. The plant is currently handling 300 tons per day of refuse on a 90 percent coal and 10 percent refuse heat basis. Prior to introduction into the boiler, refuse is shredded and magnetic materials are removed. The shredded refuse is then fed pneumatically to the boiler. Typical heat values for refuse range from 4,500 to 5,500 Btu/lb.[98] Some energy may be wasted in heating noncombustibles, so these figures may be high.

The quantity of collected domestic and commercial solid wastes was taken to be 3.4 pounds per day per capita. The total population served by refuse collection was estimated by using the total estimated sewered population in 1973 based upon EPA projections. The sewered population used was 160 million for 1973. Based upon a heat value of 4,500 Btu/lb, the available energy from all residential and commercial refuse is 0.90 x 10^{15} Btu, which is 1.2 percent of the 1973 consumption of energy of 76 x 10^{15} Btu.

PYROLYSIS

Pyrolysis is a destructive distillation process in which organic materials are heated in the absence of oxygen to temperatures ranging from 1000 to 1800°F to break down complex organic molecules. The temperature and pressure determine to a great extent the nature of the resulting products: char, oil, and combustible gases. The process is compatible with recovery of metals and glass when such processes become economically feasible. When used with domestic refuse, pyrolysis involves several steps: (a) shredding, (b) drying, (3) air classification for removal of combustibles, (d) secondary shredding, (e) pyrolysis, (f) collection of pyrolysis products, and (g) recovery of metal and glass. Most of these steps could be eliminated for animal wastes. An EPA pilot plant study in San Diego, California, indicates that 1.1 barrels of oil with two-thirds the heating value of standard heating oil can be obtained from one ton of refuse. Combustible gases and char may also be produced which can serve as process fuels. Using these values, the energy available from pyrolysis of residential and commercial solid wastes is 2,240 Btu/lb. For an estimated 1973 collection population of 160 million with 3.4 pounds solid waste per capita the total energy is 4.4 x 10^{14} Btu for 1973. This is equivalent to 0.6 percent of the 1973 energy consumption.

The energy involved in capital construction can be estimated from a 1973 study of a large (1,000 ton/day) plant which found that the capital cost would be $12,200 per ton/day capacity.[99] Using the energy per construction-dollar coefficient of Appendix D and a 15-year life for the facility, the energy in capital construction is found to be 0.1 x 10^{14} Btu per year for the nation. This somewhat underestimates capital costs that would have to be undertaken if pyrolysis of garbage were to become pervasive in the U.S. during the next decade. However, the construction energy is relatively small.

Pyrolysis of animal wastes has not been extensively developed. No energy benefit occurs if the manure has to be dewatered directly.[100] However, it has been estimated that a ton of dry manure (15 percent water) yields 0.41 tons of oil at 12,000 Btu/lb and 0.15 tons of char at 9,000 Btu/lb, a net fuel equivalent of 6,300 Btu/lb, plus gas which can be used to maintain the process.[101] It seems likely that the actual process would involve energy losses which would substantially reduce this energy equivalent. We are unable to evaluate pyrolysis of animal wastes quantitatively because of lack of information.

ANAEROBIC DIGESTION OF ORGANIC WASTES

The anaerobic digestion process for treatment of organic wastes is given special attention in this study for the following reasons: (a) it can effect a 50 to 80 percent reduction in the organic matter of most wastes; (b) the process yields methane as a product; and (c) the liquid-solid component of the digested waste has a high fertilizer value.

Historically, the use of this process for treatment of organic wastes and generation of fuel dates back to World War II when the Germans used the process during the fuel shortages. Since the war several developing countries, including India, Taiwan, and China, have developed digesters based on the German prototypes, and such digesters are currently in wide use on farms. In the United States fuel shortages have not been a problem until recently, but anaerobic digesters have nonetheless been widely used for treatment of municipal sewage sludges.

Basically, the anaerobic digestion process involves addition of organic sludges (4 to 15 percent total solids) to a closed vessel where it is mixed and maintained at 95°F. At regular intervals (2 to 5 per day) raw sludge is added and digested sludge removed at a hydraulic retention time of 20 to 30 days. The digested sludge contains 3 to 5 percent solids and is usually dewatered by centrifugation or vacuum filtration prior to land disposal. The gaseous product is typically 70 percent methane and 30 percent carbon dioxide, with trace amounts of hydrogen sulfide and hydrogen. Prior to use, the gas is usually purified to increase the methane concentration and to decrease the corrosive properties due to hydrogen sulfide.

In this study, energy budgets have been estimated for the methanogenic fermentation of animal wastes, urban refuse, and domestic sewage sludge based on estimates of production of these wastes in a concentrated form in the United States in 1973. Table 7E—1 presents the quantities of available wastes the gross energy yields estimated for the anaerobic digestion of these wastes, and the number of anaerobic digesters required for this treatment process.[102-111] These calculations are based on an average digester with the following dimensions: diameter—60 ft., height—25 ft., volume—70,650 cubic feet. The operational parameters are as follows: hydraulic retention time—25 days, temperature 98°F, continuous mixing, and volatile solids loadings of 0.25, 0.24 and 0.12 pounds of solid per cubic feet of fluid per day for animal wastes, urban refuse, and domestic sewage sludge, respectively.

The energy requirements for the anaerobic digestion process were estimated for the above "average digester" for ambient temperatures of 38°F and 70°F. These data presented in Table 7E—2 are based on energy requirements of heat loss by conduction, heating and maintaining the sludge at 98°F, continuous mixing, and pumping the sludge at the influent, effluent, and through the heat exchanger. It was concluded that the energy costs of purifying the digester gas are insignificant. A final average energy requirement per digester, 4.7×10^9

Table 7E-1.   Estimates of Annual Potential Energy Yields from Methanogenic Digestion of Organic Wastes (1973)

	Confined Animal Wastes	Urban[a] Refuse	Sewage[a] Sludge
Total dry solids/year (pounds)	0.81×10^{11}	1.58×10^{11}	0.125×10^{11}
Annual production volatile solids (pounds)	0.65×10^{11}	1.09×10^{11}	0.094×10^{11}
Percent volatile solids destruction	70	80	70
Gas production (ft^3/lb vs. des.)	12	11	16
Total gas yield (cu. ft.)	5.4×10^{11}	9.59×10^{11}	1.05×10^{11}
Percent methane	60	50	70
Total methane (cu. ft.)	3.3×10^{11}	4.80×10^{11}	0.737×10^{11}
Gross energy production Btu	3.18×10^{14}	4.62×10^{14}	0.710×10^{14}
Number of "average" digesters required	10,000	17,600	3,030

Source: Based on references 102 through 111.
[a]Based on 1973 Sewered Population 160,000,000. For urban refuse the population is that which is sewered.

Btu/day, calculated by averaging the energy requirements at the two temperatures, is used in all subsequent calculations involving the energy costs of anaerobic digestion. This is 15 to 20 percent of the gross energy credit for methane production. The net energy equivalent of methane produced is 2,850 Btu/lb of animal manure with 15 percent moisture and 1,800 Btu/lb of municipal solid with 25 percent moisture.

Two other adjustments can be made to the energy balance associated with anaerobic digestion of organic wastes: the debit for capital construction and a credit for fertilizer production from animal wastes. We can consider a $0.59 million capital cost for a 90,000 cubic ft. digester with peripheral facilities.[112] Another cost analysis for an urban waste digester finds a capital cost including receiving, shredding, metals separation digester, storage, sludge dewatering and gas purification of $15,300 per ton per day capacity at a large plant.[113] These correspond to 0.46 and 0.25 million dollars per average digester, respectively. Assuming the energy per construction dollar coefficient of Appendix D and a 15-year life for the facility, these two cost estimates correspond to an energy debit of 1.1×10^9 and 0.67×10^9 Btu per average digester, respectively. We take an average of 0.9×10^9 Btu per average digester or 2.8×10^{13} Btu to process the nation's 1973 wastes as listed in Table 7E-1.

The use of the sludge which results from anaerobic digestion of

Table 7E-2. Energy Requirements of the Anaerobic Digestion Process For "Average Digester"[a]

	Millions of Btu Per Day at Ambient Temperatures of 38° and 70°F	
	38°F	*70°F*
Heat loss by conduction	7.3	3.9
Sludge heating	6.9	3.7
Pumping sludge (influent, effluent, heat exchanger)	0.43	.38
Mixing	1.7	1.7
Total/day	16.3	9.7
Total/year	5,900	3,500
Average total/year		4,700

[a]Based on R. Smith, "Electrical Power Consumption for Municipal Wastewater Treatment," EPA, Cincinnati, Ohio, 1972; and Metcalf and Eddy, Inc., *Wastewater Engineering, Collection, Treatment, Disposal* (McGraw Hill, 1972) pp. 313–316.

animal wastes as a fertilizer implies an energy credit. We calculate this credit on the basis of the nitrogen content of the product. An average nitrogen content of cattle manure is 3.5 percent N by weight in dry manure.[114] The energy needed to dewater the digested sludge is about 0.6 kwh/lb of N content in a large plant.[115] The energy required to produce the inorganic fertilizer which is being replaced is about 30,000 Btu/lb of N.[116] Assuming that no fixed nitrogen is lost in the process of digestion and dewatering, there is a net credit of about 1,000 Btu/lb of dry manure.

Table 7E–3 presents an estimate of the annual energy budget for the

Table 7E-3. Energy Balance for the Methanogenic Fermentation of Organic Wastes, 1973 Levels

	(Trillions of Btu)			
	Animal Wastes[a]	*Urban Refuse*	*Sewage Sludge*	*Total*
Gross energy credit for methane	318	462	71	851
Operation energy debit	47	83	14	143
Net energy at digester	271	380	57	708
Percent of energy credit for operation	15	18	20	
Capitalization energy debit	10	18	3	31
Nitrogen fertilizer energy credit	80	–	–	80
Overall energy credit	340	360	54	760

[a]Total of confined animal wastes.

Table 7E-4. Energy from Three Categories of Available Organic Waste Using Various Different Techniques, 1973 (Units of 10^{14} Btu/Yr)

	Fossil Fuel Supplement	*Pyrolysis*	*Anaerobic Digestion with Methane Recovery*
Municipal solid waste[a]	9.0	4.4	3.8
Total confined animal waste			2.7
Sewage sludge			0.6

[a]The numbers for municipal solids are, in each case, for the total collected municipal solids.

methanogenic treatment of organic wastes. The total energy of the methane product of this treatment process is 851 trillion Btu. Subtracting the energy requirement of this treatment process, 143 trillion Btu, the energy in capital construction, 31 Btu, and adding the fertilizer energy credit of 80 trillion Btu, yields a net energy credit of about 760 trillion Btu or approximately 1.0 percent of national energy requirements in 1973.

The three energy conserving waste management alternatives are reviewed in Table 7E-4.

In order to estimate the potential energy recovery for 1985 shown in Table 7-6 of the main text, several assumptions had to be made. For municipal solid wastes, we assumed a 4 percent general growth and 100 percent availability of collected municipal solids, one-half for use in fossil-fuel supplement processes, and one-half for pyrolysis or anaerobic digestion processes. For agricultural waste we assumed that confined animal wastes will grow 2 percent annually, and one-half of these will be disposed of through pyrolysis or anaerobic digestion processes, the other half being disposed as landfill (energy associated with the latter item is negligible compared with the total). We assumed that all sewage sludge is available as an energy source, but this item is small. The total energy consumption for 1985 is taken at the nominal value of 115×10^{15} Btu/yr.[117]

Notes to Chapter Seven

1. U.S. Environmental Protection Agency, *Compilation of Air Pollution Emission Factors* (2nd ed.) Washington, D.C., April 1973.

2. U.S. Environmental Protection Agency, *Economics of Clean Water*, vol. 1, 1972.

3. U. S. Department of Health, Education and Welfare, "Preliminary Data Analysis, 1968 National Survey of Community Solid Waste Practices," Cincinnati, 1968.

4. National sampling of urban solid waste management practices and State of Michigan sampling of sewage treatment practices, conducted by David Dunnette for this study, 1973.

5. R. A. Herendeen, *An Energy Input-Output Matrix for the U.S. (1963)— User's Guide*, Center for Advanced Computation, University of Illinois, Urbana, March 1973.

6. Thomas Austin and Karl Hellman, "Passenger Car Fuel Economy — Trends and Influencing Factors," Society of Automotive Engineers Paper 730790, September 1973.

7. Clayton LaPointe, "Factors Affecting Vehicle Fuel Economy," Society of Automotive Engineers Paper 730791, September 1973.

8. Reports from automobile manufacturers vary widely but do not appear to be inconsistent with this figure. Industry estimates generally range from "no significant change" to "13 percent improvement." See notes 12 through 15.

9. U.S. Environmental Protection Agency, *Environmental News*, Washington, D.C., January 1974.

10. John P. DeKany and Thomas C. Austin, "Automobile Emissions and Energy Consumption," U.S. Environmental Protection Agency, Office of Air and Water Programs, May 1974.

11. U.S. Environmental Protection Agency, *Environmental News*.

12. Chrysler Corporation, "Report to the Environmental Protection Agency on Progress and Status of Light Duty Motor Vehicle Emission Systems for 1975–1976 Models," November 1973.

13. General Motors Corporation, "General Motors Advanced Emission Control System Development Progress" (Report submitted to Environmental Protection Agency, 19 November 1973.)

14. Ford Motor Company, "1975–77 Emission Control Program Status Report" (Submitted to the Environmental Protection Agency, 26 November 1973).

15. American Motors Corporation, "American Motors Efforts to Meet Light Duty Vehicle Emission Standards for 1975, 76, 77 Model Years" (Report submitted to the Environmental Protection Agency, 12 November 1973).

16. U.S. Environmental Protection Agency, *Environmental News*.

17. E. Starkman, "Statement on Conservation and Efficient Use of Energy, General Motors Corporation" (Submitted to the House Select Committee on Small Business, 10 July 1973).

18. LaPoint, "Factors Affecting Vehicle Fuel Economy."

19. DeKany and Austin, "Automobile Emissions and Energy Consumption."

20. Donald A. Hurter, *A Study of Technological Improvements in Automobile Fuel Consumption*. Preliminary evlauation prepared by Arthur D. Little, Inc., for the U.S. Environmental Protection Agency, October 1973.

21. DeKany and Austin, "Automobile Emissions and Energy Consumption."

22. International Research and Technology Corporation, *Economic Impact of Mass Production of Alternative Low Emissions Automotive Power Systems* (Amended report prepared for Department of Transportation, DOT-OS-20003, March 1973).

23. "Progress and Problems Concerning Standards and Approval of 1975 Heavy-Duty Engines and Vehicles," State of California, Air Resources Board, 19 September 1973.

24. George Hanley, General Motors Corporation, telephone conversation, 13 March 1974.

25. Robert W. Fri, "Control of Air Pollution from Aircraft and Aircraft Engines – Emission Standards and Test Procedures for Aircraft," *Federal Register*, 38 (136, pt. II, 17 July 1973).

26. Robert W. Fri, "Ground Operation of Aircraft to Control Emissions– Advanced Notice of Proposed Rule Making," *Federal Register*, 37 (239, pt. III, 12 December 1972).

27. Office of Systems Analysis and Information, Department of Transportation, *Summary of National Transportation Statistics*, November 1972.

28. This figure is an updating for inflation and energy use increase of a coefficient describing energy use per dollar of product cost from reference 5.

29. Aaron Teller, "Air Pollution Control," *Chemical Engineering Deskbook Issue* (9 May 1972).

30. J. F. Finklea, *A Conceptual Basis for Establishing Standards*, in *Proceedings of the Conference on Health Effects of Air Pollutants*, Report to the Committee on Public Works of the U.S. Senate, November 1973;

and D. P. Rall, *A Review of the Health Effects of Sulfur Oxides* (Report prepared by the National Institute of Environmental Health Sciences, submitted to the Office of Management and Budget, October 1973).

31. S. Oglesby and G. B. Nichols, *A Manual of Electrostatic Precipitator Technology, Part II Application Areas*, Southern Research Institute, August 1970.

32. Herendeen, *An Energy Input-Output Matrix.*

33. Gerald Hollinden, Power Research Staff, Tennessee Valley Authority, personal communication, August 1973; and C. E. Blakeslee and H. E. Burbach, "Controlling NO_x Emissions from Steam Generators" (Paper presented at the 65th Annual Meeting of the Air Pollution Control Association, June 1972).

34. Alexander Gakner and Robert Jimeson, "Environmental and Economic Cost Considerations in Electric Power Supply" (Paper presented at American Institute of Chemical Engineers National Meeting, New Orleans, March 1973).

35. Fluidized bed boilers to remove sulfur and ash in the combustion process have been under study by Pope, Evans and Robbins, Inc., and at Argonne National Laboratory.

36. Sulfur Oxide Control Technology Assessment Panel, *A Projected Utilization of Stack Gas Cleaning Systems by Steam-Electric Plants*, November 1972 (Reprinted by the Committee on Interior and Insular Affairs, U.S. Senate No. 93-12, p. I, June 1973).

37. U.S. Environmental Protection Agency, "National Public Hearings on Power Plant Compliance with Sulfur Oxide Air Pollution Regulations," January 1974.

38. National Electric Reliability Council, "Assessment of the State-of-Technology of Air Pollution Control Equipment and of Clean Air Regulations on the Adequacy of Electric Power Supply of North American Bulk Power Systems," October 1972; W. H. Downey, Commonwealth Edison Co., private communication, August 1973; and C. P. Quigley, Boston Edison Co., private communication, February 1974.

39. Battell Columbus Laboratories, *State of the Art Report on Status of Development of Process for Abatement of SO_2 Emissions by Stack Gas Treatment* (Report to American Electric Power Service Corporation, 1973).

40. U.S. Environmental Protection Agency, "National Public Hearings."

41. F. Princiotta, Environmental Protection Agency, personal communications, 1973.

42. U.S. Environmental Protection Agency, "National Public Hearings."

43. "Desulfurization Strategy Options Including Fossill Fuel Supply Alternatives for the Electric Power Industry," (Report prepared by Chemical Systems, Inc., 1971).

44. *Ibid.*

45. *Hydrocarbon Processing, 51* (9: September 1972, 111-222).

46. Stanford Research Institute, "Control of Sulfur Dioxide Emissions," April 1973.
47. U.S. Environmental Protection Agency, "Economic Analysis of Proposed Effluent Guidelines (for) Steam Electric Powerplants," EPA-230/1-73-006, September 1973.
48. U.S. Environmental Protection Agency, "Development Document for Proposed Effluent Limitations Guidelines and New Source Performance Standards for the Steam Electric Power Generating," EPA 440/1-73/029, March 1974.
49. *Ibid.*
50. U.S. Enviromental Protection Agency, *Economics of Clean Water*, vol. 1.
51. U.S. Council on Environmental Quality, *Environmental Quality* (1973).
52. Harner and Shifren, Inc., "Study of Refuse as Supplementary Fuel for Power Plants," St. Louis, Missouri, 1970; International Research and Technology Corporation, *Problems and Opportunities in Management of Combustible Solid Waste*, 1972.
53. H. Shultz, "Resource Recovery from Municipal Solid Waste," in *Proceedings Bioconversion Energy Research Conference*, University of Massachusetts, Amherst, 1973.
54. S. A. Hart, "Digestion of Livestock Manures," *Journal of Water Pollution Control Federation* 44 (1, 1972); S. A. Klein, "Anaerobic Digestion of Solid Wastes," *Compost Digest* 12 (6–11, 1971); John Pfeffer, University of Illinois, personal communication, July 1973; D. P. Chynoweth, "Volatile Acids Production in the Sludge Methane Fermentation," Doctoral dissertation, University of North Carolina, 1969; P. L. McCarty, "Anaerobic Waste Treatment Fundamentals," *Public Works* 95 (107-112, 123-126) and 96 (91-94, 95-99), 1964; L. C. Gramms, L. B. Polkowski, and S. A. Witzel, "Anaerobic Digestion of Farm Animal Wastes (Dairy, Bull, Swine, and Poultry)," *Trans. American Soc. Agri. Eng.* 14 (7, 1971); W. B. Coe and M. Turk, "Processing Animal Waste by Anaerobic Fermentation" (Paper presented at the Annual Meeting of the American Society for Microbiology, Miami Beach, Florida, 1973); D. L. Wise, S. E. Sadek, and R. G. Kispert, *Fuel Gas Production from Solid Waste*, Semi-Annual Progress Report, NSF Contract C-827, Dynatech R/D Company, Cambridge, Massachusetts.
55. E. Hirst, "Energy Implications of Several Environmental Quality Strategies," Oak Ridge National Laboratory, March 1973.
56. National Petroleum Council, *U.S. Energy Outlook* (December 1972: 52–55).
57. T. W. Bendixen and G. L. Huffman, "Impact of Environmental Control Technologies on the Energy Crisis," EPA, Cincinnati, Ohio, January 1974.
58. Gakner and Jimeson, "Environmental and Economic Costs Considerations."
59. Edison Electric Institute, "Power Needs for Pollution Control," *Electrical World* (April 1973).

60. Herendeen, *An Energy Input-Output Matrix.*

61. W. W. Leontieff, *Input-Output Economics* (Osford, 1966) and "Environmental Repercussions and Economic Structure: An Input-Output Approach," *Review of Economics and Statistics* 52 (1970: 262).

62. Teller, "Air Pollution Control."

63. J. E. Mutchler, G. D. Clayton Association, private communication, August 1973.

64. U.S. Environmental Protection Agency, *Economics of Clean Water*, vol. I.

65. George A. Sawyer, "New Trends in Wastewater Treatment and Recycle," *Chemical Engineering* 79 (29 July 1972).

66. Nelson I. Nemerow, *Liquid Waste of Industry—Theories, Practices and Treatment* (Reading, Mass.: Addison-Wesley, 1971).

67. *Ibid.*

68. U.S. Environmental Protection Agency, *Economics of Clean Water*, vol. 111.

69. Herendeen, *An Energy Input-Output Matrix.*

70. U.S. Federal Power Commission, *Typical Electric Bills,* December 1971.

71. Herendeen, *An Energy Input-Output Matrix.*

72. Robert Michel, "Costs and Manpower in Municipal Wastewater Treatment Plant Operation and Maintenance 1964—1968," *Journal of the Water Pollution Control Federation* (November 1970, update 1972).

73. Peter C. Robinson and Francis A. Coughlin, "Municipal Industrial Waste Treatment Costs," *TAPPI* 54 (1971: 2005—2010).

74. U.S. Environmental Protection Agency, *Economics of Clean Water*, vol. I.

75. Office of Science and Technology, Executive Office of the President, *Patterns of Energy Consumption in the United States,* Stanford Research Institute, 1972.

76. U.S. Environmental Protection Agency, *Projected Wastewater Treatment Cost in the Organic Chemical Industry, Datagraphics, Inc.* (Pittsburgh, Pa.: Program Number 12070 GND, July 1971 update of an original study by Cyrus M. Rice and Company).

77. *Ibid.*

78. S. Douglas Hall, Supervisor of Wastewater Treatment, Dow Chemical Company, Inc., personal conversations, Midland, Michigan.

79. Herendeen, *An Energy Input-Output Matrix.*

80. Testimony from Peter E. Wrist, American Paper Institute, Hearings before the Committee on Public Works, House of Representatives, Ninety-second Congress First Session on H.R. 11896; H.R. 11895 to Amend the Federal Water Pollution Control Act, December 7, 8, 9, and 10, 1971.

81. *Ibid.*

82. Herendeen, *An Energy Input-Output Matrix.*

83. Testimony from Peter E. Wrist.

84. Office of Science and Technology, *Patterns of Energy Consumption.*

85. R. L. Michel and W. J. Johnson, "Cost and Manpower Hours for Operation and Maintenance of Municipal Wastewater Treatment Plants: 1957–1970," Unpublished report supplied to authors by R.

C. Michel, Division of State and Local Water Programs, U.S. Environmental Protection Agency, 1970.

86. R. Smith, "Electrical Power Consumption for Municipal Wastewater Treatment," Environmental Protection Agency Advanced Waste Treatment Research Laboratory, Cincinnati, Ohio, 1972.

87. R. C. Loehr, "Variation of Wastewater Parameters Public Works" (May 1968), p. 81.

88. B. L. Goodman, *Design Handbook of Wastewater Systems: Domestic, Industrial, Commercial,* Smith and Loveless Division, Ecodyne Corporation, Lenexa, Kansas.

89. Michel and Johnson, "Cost and Manpower Hours."

90. K. H. Jenkins, "Statistical Summary of 1968 Inventory of Municipal Waste Facilities in the U.S.," Federal Water Quality Administration, U.S. Department of the Interior, 1970.

91. Herendeen, *An Energy Input-Output Matrix.*

92. D. R. Evans and J. C. Wilson, "Capitol and Operating Costs AWT," *Journal of Water Pollution Control Federation* 44 (1, 1972).

93. Council on Environmental Quality, *Fourth Annual Report,* 1973.

94. *Ibid.*

95. Herendeen, *An Energy Input-Output Matrix.*

96. Council on Environmental Quality, *Report.*

97. Harner and Shifren, "Study of Refuse as Supplementary Fuel."

98. IR&T, *Problems and Opportunities.*

99. Shulz, "Resource Recovery from Municipal Solid Waste."

100. Midwest Research Institute, "The Disposal of Cattle Feedlot Wastes by Pyrolysis," EPA Project 13040-EGH, 1971.

101. IR&T, *Problems and Opportunities.*

102. USDA, "Cattle on Feed, January 1, 1973," Washington, D.C., 1972.

103. USDA, *Statistical Yearbook 1972,* Washington, D.C., 1972.

104. E. Paul Taiganides and R. L. Stroshine, "Impact of Animal Production and Processing on the Total Environment," in *Livestock Waste Management and Pollution Abatement* (St. Joseph, Mich.: American Society of Agricultural Engineers, 1971), pp. 95–96.

105. E. Paul Taiganides, personal communication, July 1973.

106. Hart, "Digestion of Livestock Manures."

107. Klein, "Anaerobic Digestion of Solid Wastes."

108. John Pfeffer, University of Illinois, personal communication, July 1973.

109. Chynoweth, "Volatile Acids Production."

110. McCarty, "Anaerobic Waste Treatment Fundamentals."

111. Grams, Polkowski, and Witzel, "Anaerobic Digestion of Farm Animal Wastes."

112. Coe and Turk, "Processing Animal Waste by Anaerobic Fermentation."

113. Wise, Sadek, and Kispert, *Fuel Gas Production.*

114. J. R. Miner (ed.), *Farm Animal Waste Management,* North Central Regional Publication 206, Agriculture and Home Economics Experiment Station, Iowa State University, May 1971.

115. R. Smith, "Electrical Power Consumption for Municipal Wastewater Treatment," U.S. Environmental Protection Agency Advanced Waste Treatment Research Laboratory, Cincinnati, Ohio, 1972.
116. Harner and Shifren, "Study of Refuse as a Supplementary Fuel."
117. Energy Policy Project, *Exploring Energy Choices,* March 1974.

Bibliography

Altman, M. *Technology for the Conversion of Solar Energy to Fuel Gas.* Report submitted by the University of Pennsylvania to the National Science Foundation, Rann Program, Washington, D.C. Report No. NSF/RANN/SE/GI 34991/PR/73/2, 1973.

American Metal Market Company. *Metal Statistics.* 1971.

American Motors Corporation. "American Motors Efforts to Meet Light Duty Vehicle Emission Standards for 1975, 76, 77 Model Years." Report submitted to the U.S. Environmental Protection Agency, 12 November 1973.

American Transit Association. *1971 Transit Operating Report, Revenues, Expenses, Operating Statistics.* Pts. II and IV, 1971.

Anderson, L. L. "Energy Potential from Organic Wastes: A Review of the Quantities and Sources," Bureau of Mines Information Circular 8549, 1972.

"Annual Energy Requirements of Electric Household Appliances." New York: Electric Energy Association, 1971.

Anthony, W. B. "Cattle Manure as Feed for Cattle," In *Livestock Waste Management and Pollution Abatement.* St. Joseph, Michigan: American Society of Agricultural Engineers, 1971.

Atkins, P. R. *Aluminum—A Manufactured Resource.* Undated report from the Aluminum Company of America, June 1973.

Austin, Thomas, and Hellman, Karl. "Passenger Car Fuel Economy—Trends and Influencing Factors." Society of Automotive Engineers Paper 730790, September 1973.

Automobile Manufacturers Association, Inc. *1971 Automobile Facts and Figures,* 1971.

Barton, Russell. "Energy Requirements for Urban Vehicles," Report written as senior independent work, Princeton University.

Battelle Columbus Laboratories. *A Study to Indentify Opportunities for Increased Solid Waste Utilization.* Vol. II, *Aluminum,* and III, *Copper.* June 1972.

363

Battelle Columbus Laboratories. *State of the Art Report on Status of Development of Process for Abatement of SO₂ Emissions by Stack Treatment Report.* Report to the American Electric Power Service Corporation, 1973.

Bendersky, D., Chiu, S-Y, Hancock, J., and Shannon, L. S. *Quality of Products from Selected Resource Recovery Processes and Market Specifications.* Special Report, Midwest Research Institute, 28 February 1973.

Bendixen, T. W. , and Huffman, G. L. "Impact of Environmental Control Technologies on the Energy Crisis," Environmental Protection Agency, Cincinnati, Ohio, January 1974.

Bigger, J. E. "Methane Recovery Demonstration Project January to May, 1974." Los Angeles, California: Department of Water and Power, City of Los Angeles, 1974.

Blakeslee, C. E. and Burbach, H. E. "Controlling NOₓ Emissions from Steam Generators." Paper presented at the 65th Annual Meeting of the Air Pollution Control Association, June 1972.

Boshoff, W. H. "Methane Gas Production by Batch and Continuous Fermentation Methods," *Tropical Science,* 5 (1963): 155.

Boshoff, W. H. "Reaction Velocity Constants for Batch Methane Fermentation on Farms." *Journal of Agricultural Science* (1967).

Bravard, J. C., Flora, H. B. II, and Portal, Charles. *Energy Expenditures Association with the Production and Recycle of Metals.* ORNL-NSF-EP-24, 1972.

Buchanan, Lewis. "An Overview of the Motorcycle and Bicycle Problems." (Paper presented at the Cycle Safety Conference, Lansing, Michigan, January 1973).

Bullard, Clark, and Herendeen, Robert. *Energy Use in the Commercial and Industrial Sectors of the U.S. Economy, 1963.* (CAC Document No. 105.) Urbana: Center for Advanced Computation, University of Illinois.

Census Tracts, Trenton, N.J. SMSA. Bureau of the Census, U.S. Department of Commerce, Final Report PHC (1)-217.

Chrysler Corporation. "Report to the Environmental Protection Agency on Progress and Status of Light Duty Motor Vehicle Emission Systems for 1975–1976 Models," November 1973.

Chynoweth, D. P., and Mah, R. A. "Volatile Acid Formation in Sludge Digestion." *Anaerobic Biological Treatment Processes Advances in Chemistry Series, No. 105.* Washington, D.C.: American Chemical Society, n.d.

Chynoweth, D. P. "Volatile Acids Production in the Sludge Methane Fermentation." Doctoral dissertation, University of North Carolina, 1969.

Cochran, C. N. "Aluminum—Villain or Hero in Energy Crisis?" Pennsylvania: Alcoa Research Laboratories, 1973.

Coe, W. B. and Turk, M. "Processing Animal Waste by Anaerobic Fermentation." Paper presented at the Annual Meeting of the American Society for Microbiology, Miami Beach, Florida, 1973.

Commoner, B. *A Study of Certain Ecological, Public Health and Economic Consequences of the Use of Inorganic Nitrogenous Fertilizers.* 1st year progress report to Office of Interdisciplinary Research, National Science Foundation, submitted by the Center for the Biology of Natural Systems, Washington University, St. Louis, 5 May 1972, under NSF grant number GI-29920 X, 1972.

"Comparative Costs to Consumers of Convenience Foods and Home-Prepared Foods," Marketing Research Report No. 609. Marketing Economics Division, U.S. Department of Agriculture, June 1963.

"Converting Garbage into Energy," *Business Week,* 30 March 1973: 42–43.

Council of State Governments. *Our Effluent Society–The States and Solid Waste Management,* Lexington, Kentucky, 1974.

Council on Environmental Qualtiy. *Fourth Annual Report,* 1973.

Denit, J. D. *Development Document for Proposed Effluent Limitations Guidelines and New Source Performance for the Feedlots Point Source Category.* Effluent Guidelines Division, Office of Air and Water Programs, U.S. Environmental Protection Agency–EPA 440/1-73/004, 1973.

"Desulfurization Strategy Options Including Fossill Fuel Supply Alternatives for the Electric Power Industry." Report prepared by Chemical Systems, Inc., 1971.

DiGiano, F. A., Hoffman, A. R., and Short, W. L. (eds.) *Proceedings–Bioconversion Energy Research Conference,* 25 & 26 June 1973. Sponsored by the National Science Foundation under grant No. GI 39215, 1973.

Drake, William et al. "Ann Arbor Dial-A-Ride Pilot Project, Final Report." April 1973.

Dugas, D. J. *Fuel from Organic Matter* and *Fuel from Organic Matter: Possibilities for the State of California.* The Rand Paper Series No. P-5100, P-5107. Santa Monica, California: The Rand Corporation, 1973.

Economic Research Service. *United States and World Fertilizer Outlook: 1974 and 1980.* Washington, D.C.: U.S. Department of Agriculture, 22 February 1974.

Elmberg, Curt M. "The Gothenburg Traffic Restraint Scheme." Paper presented at the International Conference on Transportation Research, Bruges, Belgium, June 1973.

Energy Policy Project. *Exploring Energy Choices,* March 1974.

Edison Electric Institute. "Power Needs for Pollution Control." *Electrical World* (April 1973).

Evans, D. R. and Wilson, J. C. "Capitol and Operating Costs AWT." *Journal of Water Pollution Control Federation* 44 (1, 1972).

Federal Power Commission. *Natural Gas Demands Forecasts.* National Gas Survey, Federal Power Commission Report of Distribution Advisory Task Force General Draft, April 1973.

Fels, Margaret Fulton. "Comparative Energy Costs of Urban Transportation Systems." Transportation Program Report #74-TR-2, Princeton University, 1974.

Finklea, J. F. "A Conceptual Basis for Establishing Standards." In *Proceedings of the Conference on Health Effects of Air Pollutants.* Report to the Committee on Public Works of the U.S. Senate, 19 November 1973.

Folk, Hugh, and Hannon, Bruce. *An Energy, Pollution and Employment Policy Model.* CAC Document No. 68. Urbana: Center for Advanced Computation, University of Illinois.

Ford Motor Company. "1975–77 Emission Control Program Status Report," Report submitted to the Environmental Protection Agency, 26 November, 1973.

Foster Associates, Inc. *Energy Prices: 1960-1973.* Research study for the EPP. Cambridge Massachusetts: Ballinger Publishing Co., 1974.

Franklin, William E. *Baseline Forecasts of Resource Recovery, 1972 to 1990.* Final Report, Project No. 3736-D, Midwest Research Institute, May 1974.

Fri, Robert W. "Control of Air Pollution from Aircraft and Aircraft Engines— Emission Standards and Test Procedures for Aircraft." *Federal Register* 38 (136, Pt. II, 17 July 1973).

Fry, L. J., and Merrill, R. *Methane Digesters for Fuel Gas and Fertilizer.* Santa Barbara, California: New Alchemy Institute, 15 W. Anapamu, 1973.

Gakner, Alexander, and Jimeson, Robert. "Environmental and Economic Cost Considerations in Electric Power Supply." Paper presented at American Institute of Chemical Engineers National Meeting, New Orleans, March 1973.

General Electric–Connecticut. *A Proposed Plan of Solid Waste Management for Connecticut: Summary.* General Electric Company–Corporate Research and Development State of Connecticut–Department of Environmental Protection, 1973.

General Motors Corporation. "General Motors Advanced Emission Control System Development Progress." Report submitted to Environmental Protection Agency, 19 November 1973.

Ghosh, S., Conrad, J. R., and Klass, D. L. "Anaerobic Acidogenesis of Sewage Sludge," *Journal of Water Pollution Control* 46 (1974).

Ghosh, S., and Klass, D. L. "Conversion of Urban Refuse to Substitute Natural Gas by the Biogas™ Process." Paper presented at the Fourth Mineral Waste Utilization Symposium, Chicago, 1974.

Golueke, C. G., McGauhey, P. H., and Klein, S. A. "Comprehensive Studies of Solid Waste Management." 3rd Annual Report, SERL Report No. 70-2, Sanitary Engineering Research Laboratory, University of California, Berkeley, 1970.

Goodman, B. L. *Design Handbook of Wastewater Systems: Domestic, Industrial, Commercial.* Lenexa, Kansas: Smith and Loveless Division, Ecodyne Corporation.

Goss, W. P., and McGowan, J. G. "Transportation and Energy—A Future Confrontation." *Transportation* 1 (1972): 265–289.

Gramms, L. C., Polkowski, L. B., and Witzel, S. A. "Anaerobic Digestion of Farm Animal Wastes (Dairy Bull, Swine, and Poultry)." *Trans. American Society of Agricultural Engineers* 14 (1971).

"Guide to Reduction of Smoke and Odor from Diesel-Powered Vehicles." North Carolina: Southwest Research Institute and Office of Air Programs, EPA, Research Triangle Park, September 1971.

Hammond, A. L., et al. *Energy and the Future.* Washington, D.C.: American Association for the Advancement of Science, 1973.

Hannon, Bruce. "Bottles, Conservation, Energy." *Environment* 14 (March 1972): 11–21.

Harner and Shiften, Inc. "Study of Refuse as Supplementary Fuel for Power Plants." St. Louis, Missouri, 1970.

Hart, S. A. "Digestion of Livestock Manures." *Journal of Water Pollution Control Federation* 44 (1972).

Hensler, R. R., et al. "Effect of Manure Handling Systems on Plant Nutrient Cycling." In *Livestock Waste Management and Pollution Abatement.* St. Joseph, Michigan: American Society of Agricultural Engineers, 1971.

Herendeen, R. *An Energy Input-Output Matrix for the United States, 1963.* Document No. 69. Urbana: Center for Advanced Computation, University of Illinois, March 1963.

Hirst, E. "Energy Implications of Several Environmental Quality Strategies." Oak Ridge National Laboratory, March 1973.

Hirst, E. "Energy Intensiveness of Passenger and Freight Transport Modes: 1950–1970." ORNL-NSF Environmental Program-44, Oak Ridge National Laboratory, March 1973.

Hirst, E. "Transportation Energy Use and Conservation Potential." *Bulletin of The Atomic Scientists* 29 (1973): 36–42.

Hirst, E. and Herendeen, R. "Total Energy Demand for Automobiles." Society of Automotive Engineers, New York. Paper presented at International Automotive Engineering Congress, Detroit, January 1973.

Hoover, S. R. "Prevention of Food Processing Wastes." *Science* 183 (1974): 824–828.

Hurter, Donald A. *A Study of Technological Improvements in Automobile Fuel Consumption.* Preliminary Evaluation prepared for Arthur D. Little, Inc., for the U.S. Environmental Protection Agency, October 1973.

Hydrocarbon Processing 51 (September 1972): 111–222.

International Research and Technology Corporation. *Economic Impact of Mass Production of Alternative Low Emissions Automotive Power Systems.* Amended report prepared for the Department of Transportation, DOT-OS-20003, March 1973.

International Research and Technology Corporation. *Problems and Opportunities in Management of Combustible Solid Wastes.* Report prepared for the U.S. Environmental Protection Agency, Contract No. 68-03-0060, 1972.

Jenkins, K. H. "Statistical Summary of 1968 Inventory of Municipal Waste Facilities in the U.S." Washington, D.C.: Federal Water Quality Administration, U.S. Department of the Interior, 1970.

Johnson, G. E. "Production of Methane by Bacterial Action on a Mixture of Coal and Sewage Solids." U.S. Patent 3,640,846, 1972.

Jones, Charles. "A Survey of Curtiss-Wright's 1958–1971 Rotating Combustion Engine Technological Developments." SAE report #720468.

Kekany, John P., and Austin, Thomas C. "Automobile Emissions and Energy Consumption." Washington, D.C.: U.S. Environmental Protection Agency, Office of Air and Water Programs, May 1974.

Kenahan, C. B., et al. *Bureau of Mines Research Programs on Recycling and Disposal of Mineral-, Metal-, and Energy-Based Wastes.* Bureau of Mines Information Circular 8595, 1973.

Klein, S. A. "Anaerobic Digestion of Solid Wastes." *Compost Digest* 12 (1971): 6–11.

Klein, S. A., and Golueke, C. G. "Comprehensive Studies of Solid Waste Management." Final Report, SERL Report No. 72-3. Sanitary Engineering Research Laboratory, University of California, Berkeley, 1972.

Kornhauser, A. L., and Dais, J. L. "Assessing Area-Wide Personal Rapid Transit." Paper presented at the International Conference on Transportation Research, Bruges, Belgium, June 1973.

LaPointe, Clayton. "Factors Effecting Vehicle Fuel Economy." Society of Automotive Engineers Paper 730791, September 1973.

Leontieff, W. W. "Environmental Repercussions and Economic Structure: An Input-Output Approach." *Review of Economics and Statistics* 52 (1970): 262.

Leontieff, W. W. *Input-Output Economics.* Oxford, 1966.

Lingle, S. *Paper Recycling Through Source Separation.* Article available at Resource Recovery Division, Office of Solid Waste Management Programs, E.P.A., Washington, D.C., 1974.

Loehr, R. C. "Variation of Wastewater Parameters Public Works." May 1968.

Lowe, R. A. *Energy Recovery From Waste.* U.S. Environmental Protection Agency Report No. SW 36 d, 1973.

Lowe, R. A. *Energy Conservation Through Improved Solid Waste Management.* Washington, D.C.: Office of Solid Waste Management Programs, U.S. Environmental Protection Agency, 1974.

Lutin, Jerome M. "Personal Rapid Transit, Policy and Technology: A Case Study." Unpublished master's thesis, School of Architecture and Urban Planning, Princeton University, 1973.

Martin, L. R. "Agriculture as a Growth Sector–1985 and Beyond." Unpublished report to the Energy Policy Project, 1974.

McCarty, P. L. "Anaerobic Waste Treatment Fundamentals." *Public Works* 95 and 96 (1969).

Merchandising Week, New York, 1972 statistical issue.

Michel, Robert. "Costs and Manpower in Municipal Wastewater Treatment Plant Operation and Maintenance 1964–1968." *Journal of the Water Pollution Control Federation* (November 1970, update 1972).

Michel, R. L. and Johnson, W. J. "Cost and Manpower Hours for Operation and Maintenance of Municipal Wastewater Treatment Plants: 1957–1970." Unpublished report, Division of State and Local Water Programs, U.S. Environmental Protection Agency, 1970.

Michaels, R. M., and Maltz, A. B. "Energy Requirements in Urban Transportation." Paper presented at First Annual Illinois Energy Conference, sponsored by the University of Illinois and the State of
Illinois, 15 June 1973.

Midwest Research Institute. *Resource and Environmental Profile Analysis of
Nine Beverage Container Alternatives.* U.S. Environmental Protection Agency, Office of Solid Waste Management Programs, 1974.

Midwest Research Institute. *Resource Recovery Processes for Mixed Municipal
Solid Wastes, Catalogue of Processes.* Prepared for Council on
Environmental Quality, February 1973.

Midwest Research Institute. *Resource Recovery—The State of Technology.*
Prepared for the Council on Environmental Quality, NTIS PB 214
149, February 1973.

Midwest Research Institute. "The Disposal of Cattle Feedlot Wastes by
Pyrolysis." EPA Project 13040-EGH, 1971.

Miner, J. R. (ed.) *Farm Animal Waste Management.* North Central Regional
Publication 206, Agriculture and Home Economics Experiment
Station, Iowa State University, May 1971.

Ministry of Agriculture Fisheries and Food. *Modern Farming and the Soil.*
London: H. M. Stationary Office, 1970.

Mooz, W. I. "The Effect of Fuel Price Increases on Energy Intensiveness of
Freight Transport." Report R-804-NSF. Santa Monica, California:
Rand Corporation, 1971.

Morris. W. H. M. "Economics of Waste Disposal from Confined Livestock." In
Livestock Waste Management and Pollution Abatement St. Joseph,
Michigan: American Society of Agricultural Engineers, 1971.

Motor Vehicles Manufacturers Association of the U.S. *1972 Automobile Facts
and Figures.* Detroit, Michigan: MVMAUS, 1972.

Muhich, A. J., Klee, A. J., and Britton, P. W. *Preliminary Data Analysis: 1968
National Survey of Community Solid Waste Practices.* Public Health
Service Publication No. 1867. Washington, D.C.: U.S. Government
Printing Office, 1968.

Munson, Michael J., and Dean, Joenathan. "Trenton in the 1970's: Profile of a
Region in Flux," Working paper of the School of Architecture and
Urban Planning, Princeton University, 1974.

National Academy of Sciences. *Composition of Cereal Grains and Forages.* NAS
Publication 585, 1958.

National Academy of Sciences. "Report on Motor Vehicles Emissions."
Congressional Record—Senate, 28 February 1973.

National Center for Resource Recovery, Inc., *Materials Recovery System,
Engineering Feasibilities Study.* Washington, D.C.: CRR, December
1972.

National Center for Resource Recovery, Inc. "Resource Recovery: A Status
Report." *NCRR Bulletin 4* (1974): 2–10.

National Personal Transportation Study. "Annual Miles of Automobile Travel."
Report #2. Washington, D.C.: Department of Transportation,
Federal Highway Administration, April 1972.

National Petroleum Council. *U.S. Energy Outlook.* (December 1972): 52–55.

Nemerow, Nelson L. *Liquid Waste of Industry—Theories, Practices and Treatment.* Reading, Massachusetts: Addison-Wesley, 1971.

1970 Clean Air Act, U.S. Environmental Protection Agency, December 1970.

Office of Air and Water Programs. *Processes, Procedures, and Methods to Control Pollution Resulting from Silvivultural Activities.* Report No. EPA 430/9-73-010. Washington, D.C.: U.S. Environmental Protection Agency, 1973.

Office of Science and Technology, Executive Office of the President. *Patterns of Energy Consumption in the United States.* Palo Alto, California: Stanford Research Institute, 1972.

Office of Systems Analysis and Information, Department of Transportation. *Summary of National Transportation Statistics.* November 1972.

Oglesby, S., and Nichols, G. B. *A Manual of Electrostatic Precipitator Technology,* Part II: *Application Areas.* Southern Research Institute, August 1970.

O'Laughlin, Ann. *Organic Gardening and Farming* (November 1973): 37–40.

Perelman, M. J. "Farming with Petroleum." *Environment* 14·(1972): 8–13.

Pfeffer, J. T. *Reclamation of Energy From Organic Waste.* EPA 670/2-74-016. Cincinnati, Ohio: National Environmental Research Center Office of Research and Development, U.S. Environmental Protection Agency, 1974.

Pfeffer, J. T., and Liebman, J. C. *Biological Conversion of Organic Refuse to Methane.* Semi-Annual Progress Report (July 1, 1973 to December 31, 1973) to National Science Foundation. Washington, D.C., Report No. NSF/RANN/SE/GI-39191/PR/73/4, 1973.

Pimental, D., et al. "Food Production and the Energy Crisis." *Science* 182 (1973): 443–449.

"Pittsburgh Area Transportation Study." Vol. I. City of Pittsburgh in cooperation with U.S. Department of Commerce, Bureau of Public Roads, November 1961.

"Progress and Problems Concerning Standards and Approval of 1975 Heavy-Duty Engines and Vehicles." State of California, Air Resources Board, 19 September 1973.

"Pool It." Washington, D.C.: Highway Users Federation, 1973.

Rall, D. P. *A Review of the Health Effects of Sulfur Oxides.* Report prepared by the National Institute of Environmental Health Sciences, submitted to the Office of Management and Budget, October 1973.

Ramseier, R. O. "How to Melt the Artic and Warm the World." *Environment* 16 (1974): 7–14.

Ragone, D. V. "Review of Battery Systems for Electrically Powered Vehicles." SAE Report #680453.

"Research and Development Opportunities for Improved Transportation Energy Usage." Summary Technical Report of the Transportation Energy R & D Goals Panel. U.S. Department of Transportation, September 1973.

Resource Recovery Act of 1970. Public Law 91-512, 26 October 1970.

Rice, R. A. "System Energy as a Factor in Considering Future Transportation." Paper presented at the American Society of Mechanical Engineers Annual Meeting, December 1970.

Robinson, Peter C., and Coughlin, Francis A. "Municipal Industrial Waste Treatment Costs." *TAPPI* 54 (1971): 2005–2010.

Sawyer, George A. "New Trends in Wastewater Treatment and Recycle." *Chemical Engineering* 79 (29 July 1972).

Schwegler, R. E. "Energy Recovery at the Landfill." Paper presented at the 11th Annual Seminar and Equipment Show of the Governmental Refuse Collection and Disposal Association, 7–9 November 1973.

Searl, M. "Economics of the Production of High-Btu Gas from Coal." Appendix in Resources for the Future. *Supply Reports,* 1974.

Seidman, H., and Retzloff, D. "Evolution of a Rapid Transit System in a Low Density Metropolitan Area." In *Proceedings, Ground Transportation Symposium.* Santa Clara, California, June 1973.

Shultz, H. "Resource Recovery from Municipal Solid Waste." In *Proceedings Bioconversion Energy Research Conference.* University of Massachusetts, Amherst, 1973.

Smith, F. A. "The Quantity and Composition of Community Solid Waste." Unpublished report, Office of Solid Waste Management Programs U.S. Environmental Protection Agency, Washington, D.C., 1974.

Smith, F. L. Unpublished draft of a report by Fred Smith, Resource Recovery Division, Office of Solid Waste Management Programs, U.S. Environmental Protection Agency, Washington, D.C., 1974.

Smith, G. E. "Economics of Water Collection and Recycling." Working paper 6, Autonomous Housing Study, University of Cambridge, Department of Architecture, 1 Scroope Terrace, Cambridge, England, 1973.

Smith, R. "Electrical Power Consumption for Municipal Wastewater Treatment." Cincinnati, Ohio: U.S. Environmental Protection Agency Advanced Waste Treatment Research Laboratory, 1972.

Solid Waste Disposal Act. Public Law 89-272, 20 October 1965.

Stanford Research Institute. "Effective Utilization of Solar Energy to Produce Clean Fuel." Report submitted to the National Science Foundation by the Stanford Research Institute. Report No. NSF/RANN/SE/GI 38723/FR/74/2, 1974.

Starkman, E. "Statement on Conservation and Efficient Use of Energy, General Motors Corporation." Report submitted to the House Select Committee on Small Business, 10 July 1973.

Starkman, Ernest. "General Motors and Energy Conservation." In *1973 Report on Progress in Areas of Public Concern.* Warren, Michigan: General Motors Corporation, GM Technical Center, 1973.

Stearns, R. P., and Hansen, P. *A New Look at the Economics of Separate Refuse Collection.* Article available at Resource Recovery Division Office of Solid Waste Management Programs, EPA, Washington, D.C., 1974.

Sulfur Oxide Control Technology Assessment Panel. *A Projected Utilization of*

Stack Gas Cleaning Systems by Steam-Electric Plants, November 1972. Reprinted by the Committee on Interior and Insular Affairs, U.S. Senate No. 93-12, Pt. I, June 1973.

Sullivan, R. M. and Stanszyk, M. H. *Economics of Recycling Metals and Minerals from Urban Refuse.* Bureau of Mines Technical Progress Report, April 1971.

Taylor, J. C. "Regulatory Aspects of Recycled Livestock and Poultry Wastes." In *Livestock Waste Management and Pollution Abatement.* St. Joseph, Michigan: American Society of Agricultural Engineers, 1971.

Teller, Aaron. "Air Pollution Control." *Chemical Engineering Deskbook Issue* (9 May 1972).

Tietjen, C., and Hart, S. A. (1969) "Compost for Agricultural Land." *Proceedings of the American Society of Civil Engineers—Journal of the Sanitary Engineering Division* 95 (April, 1969): 269–287.

"Transportation Facts and Trends." Washington, D.C.: Transportation Association of America, July 1972.

"Trends of Affairs." *Technology Review* 75 (May 1973): 47.

"Trenton: Department of Planning and Development Takes an Activist Approach to Solve Transportation Problems." A City of Trenton Report.

U.S. Bureau of Census. *Statistical Abstract of the United States, 1972.* 1973.

U.S. Civil Aeronautics Board. "Report of Air Carrier Traffic Statistics." December 1963 and December 1972.

U.S. Council on Environmental Quality. *Environmental Quality.* 1973.

U.S. Department of Agriculture. *Wastes in Relation to Agriculture and Forestry.* Washington, D.C.: USDA, Miscellaneous Publication 1065, 1968.

U.S. Department of Agriculture—Hamilton Standard. *Proposal for Thermophilic Fermentation of Feedlot Wastes—Pilot Plant Evaluation.* 1974.

U.S. Department of Health, Education and Welfare. "Preliminary Data Analysis, 1968 National Survey of Community Solid Waste Practices." Cincinnati, 1968.

U.S. Department of the Interior. "Bicycling for Recreation and Commuting." Washington, D.C.: U.S. Government Printing Office, No. 461-880, 1972.

U.S. Department of Transportation, Federal Highway Administration. *Automobile Occupancy.* Report No. 1. April 1972.

U.S. Department of Transportation, Federal Highway Administration. *Highway Statistics 1970.* Washington, D.C.: U.S. Government Printing Office, 1970.

U.S. Department of Transportation, Federal Highway Administration. "Nationwide Personal Transportation Study." Report No. 1, Auto Occupancy. April 1972.

U.S. Environmental Protection Agency. *Compilation of Air Pollution Emission Factors.* (2nd ed.) Washington, D.C.: EPA, 1973.

U.S. Environmental Protection Agency. *Economics of Clean Water.* Vols. I and III, 1972.

U.S. Environmental Protection Agency, *Environmental News*. Washington, D.C.: January 1974.

U.S. Environmental Protection Agency. *Marblehead Materials Operations, Marblehead, Massachusetts*. Preliminary data, 18 June 1973.

U.S. Environmental Protection Agency. *Projected Wastewater Treatment Cost in the Organic Chemical Industry, Datagraphics, Inc.* Pittsburgh, Pennsylvania: Program Number 12070 GND, July 1971 (update of an original study by Cyrus M. Rice and Company).

U.S. Environmental Protection Agency. *Second Report to Congress, Resource Recovery and Source Reduction*. OSWMP, 1974.

U.S. Federal Power Commission. *Typical Electric Bills*. December 1971.

"Use of Gas by Residential Appliances." Arlington, Virginia: American Gas Association, November 1972.

Waller, Patricia F., Barry, Patricia Z., and Rouse, William S., "Motorcycles: 1. Estimated Mileage and Its Parameters." Chapel Hill, North Carolina: University of North Carolina Highway Safety Research Center.

Water Pollution Research Laboratory. *Agricultural Use of Sewage Sludge*. Notes on Water Pollution, No. 57. June 1972. (Available from the Director, Water Pollution Research Laboratory, Elder Way, Stevenage, Herts., England.)

"Why Net Weight Spells Nonsense on Canned Food Labels." *Consumer Reports* (October 1972).

Wise, D. L., Sadek, S. E., and Kispert, R. G. *Fuel Gas Production From Solid Waste*. Semi-Annual Progress Report fron Dynatech R/D Company to the National Science Foundation. Report No. NSF/RANN/SE/C-827/PR/73/4, 1974.

Wisely, F. E., et al. "Use of Refuse as Fuel in Existing Utility Boilers." In *Proceedings*, National Incinerator Conference, 4–7 June 1972.

Wrist, Peter E. American Paper Institute. Testimony, Hearings before the Committee on Public Works, House of Representatives. Ninety-second Congress First Session on H.R. 11896. H.R. 11895 to Amend the Federal Water Pollution Control Act, 7, 8, 9, and 10 December 1971.

Yeck, R. "Agricultural Biomass Byproducts and Their Effects on the Environment." Paper presented at the International Biomass Energy Conference, Winnepeg, Canada, 15 May 1973.

Zobrak, M. J., and Medville, D. "The Haddonfield Dial-A-Ride Experiment: Interim Results." Paper presented at the International Conference on Transportation Research, Bruges, Belgium, June 1973.

Index

List of Contributors

Robert H. Williams, Energy Policy Project

Margaret Fulton Fels, Center for Environmental Studies and Transportation Program, Princeton University

Michael J. Munson, Princeton University

Bruce Hannon, Center for Advanced Computation, University of Illinois, Urbana

Robert Herendeen, Center for Advanced Computation, University of Illinois, Urbana

F. Puleo, Center for Advanced Computation, University of Illinois, Urbana

Anthony Sebald, Center for Advanced Computation, University of Illinois, Urbana

William E. Franklin, Franklin Associates

David Bendersky, Midwest Research Institute

William R. Park, Midwest Research Institute

Robert G. Hunt, Franklin Associates

Alan Poole, Institute for Public Policy Alternatives, State University of New York, Albany

John Davidson, University of Michigan

Marc Ross, University of Michigan

David Chynoweth, University of Michigan

Ann Crampton Michaels, University of Michigan

David Dunnette, University of Michigan

Carl Griffis, University of Michigan

J. Andrew Stirling, University of Michigan

Don Wang, University of Michigan